About Island Press

Island Press is the only nonprofit organization in the United States whose principal purpose is the publication of books on environmental issues and natural resource management. We provide solutions-oriented information to professionals, public officials, business and community leaders, and concerned citizens who are shaping responses to environmental problems.

In 2000, Island Press celebrates its sixteenth anniversary as the leading provider of timely and practical books that take a multidisciplinary approach to critical environmental concerns. Our growing list of titles reflects our commitment to bringing the best of an expanding body of literature to the environmental community throughout North America and the world.

Support for Island Press is provided by The Jenifer Altman Foundation, The Bullitt Foundation, The Mary Flagler Cary Charitable Trust, The Nathan Cummings Foundation, The Geraldine R. Dodge Foundation, The Charles Engelhard Foundation, The Ford Foundation, The Vira I. Heinz Endowment, The W. Alton Jones Foundation, The John D. and Catherine T. MacArthur Foundation, The Andrew W. Mellon Foundation, The Charles Stewart Mott Foundation, The Curtis and Edith Munson Foundation, The National Fish and Wildlife Foundation, The National Science Foundation, The New-Land Foundation, The David and Lucile Packard Foundation, The Pew Charitable Trusts, The Surdna Foundation, The Winslow Foundation, and individual donors.

About the MIT-Harvard Public Disputes Program

The MIT-Harvard Public Disputes Program (PDP) is one of the largest and busiest components of the internationally renowned Program on Negotiation at Harvard Law School, an interuniversity consortium aimed at improving the theory and practice of conflict resolution. The PDP, which supports action research, mediation, and training activities, is committed to forwarding a new way of thinking about resolving disputes in the public sector. It exists to replace "win-lose" outcomes with "all gain" solutions to the highly controversial and complex problems of public policymaking. The PDP is currently directed by Professor Lawrence Susskind (MIT) and Professor William Moomaw (Tufts).

Negotiating Environmental Agreements

Negotiating

Environmental

Agreements

How to Avoid
Escalating Confrontation, Needless Costs, and
Unnecessary Litigation

Lawrence Susskind, Paul F. Levy,
and Jennifer Thomas-Larmer

ISLAND PRESS
Washington, D.C. • Covelo, California

Library of Congress Cataloging-in-Publication Data
Susskind, Lawrence.
    Negotiating environmental agreements : how to avoid escalating
  confrontation, needless costs, and unnecessary litigation / by
  Lawrence Susskind, Paul F. Levy, and Jennifer Thomas-Larmer.
      p.   cm.
    Includes bibliographical references and index.
    ISBN 1-55963-633-5 (paper)
    1. Environmental mediation—United States.   I. Levy, Paul F.
  (Paul Fidanque)   II. Thomas-Larmer, Jennifer. III. Title.
  KF3775.S87   2000
  344.73'046—dc21   99-37187
                                                                            CIP

Printed on recycled, acid-free paper

Manufactured in the United States of America
10 9 8 7 6 5 4 3 2 1

Contents

Acknowledgments   ix

Introduction   1

Part 1. The Mutual Gains Approach   17

Part 2. Putting Your Skills to the Test   41

Simulation 1. Gadgets, Inc.   53

Simulation 2. ChemCo, Inc.   86

Simulation 3. Bog Berries versus Federal Environmental Agency   89

Simulation 4. MC Metals   92

Simulation 5. Carson Extension   99

Debriefing Questions for Simulations 1–5   102

Part 3. Case Examples of Negotiated Agreements   105

Case 1. Mercury Discharge Permits   109
Jennifer Thomas-Larmer

Case 2. Shoreline Restoration on Martha's Vineyard   128
Gregory Sobel

Case 3. Coastal Zone Regulations in Delaware   143
Gregory Sobel

Case 4. Superfund Cleanup at the Massachusetts Military Reservation   167
Patrick Field, with Edward Scher

Part 4. Selected Readings   201

Reading 1.   *"They Treated Me Like a Criminal": Sanctions,*
             Enforcement Characteristics, and Compliance   203
             Joseph F. DiMento

Reading 2.   *The Negotiator's Dilemma: Creating and Claiming*
             Value   227
             David A. Lax and James K. Sebenius

Reading 3.   *Squaring Off at the Table, Not in the Courts*   240
             Lawrence Susskind and Laura van Dam

Reading 4.   *Mediation and Other Forms of Assisted*
             Negotiation   249
             Lawrence Susskind and Jeffrey Cruikshank

Reading 5.   *The Risks and the Advantages of Agency Discretion:*
             Evidence from EPA's Project XL   277
             Lawrence E. Susskind and Joshua Secunda

Bibliography   315

Mediation/Facilitation Resources   319

About the Authors   325

Index   327

Acknowledgments

Twice a year since 1993, Jack Connolly, Ira Alterman, John Connolly, Jr., and the rest of the staff at the Center for Management Research in Wellesley, Massachusetts, have organized and marketed the Negotiating Environmental Agreements workshop on which this book is based. They have been a most effective and supportive partner, and we thank them for the efforts they have made on our behalf.

The Program on Negotiation (PON) at Harvard Law School and the Consensus Building Institute (CBI) in Cambridge, Massachusetts, have also been important partners. PON has provided a home for the theory-building work of the MIT-Harvard Public Disputes Program (PDP), which produced the simulations contained in this book. CBI has served as the nonprofit "action arm" of PDP, allowing us to link up with a wide range of public- and private-sector agencies and organizations that need help negotiating environmental agreements, including several mentioned in this volume.

CBI Senior Associate Patrick Field and Senior Consultant Gregory Sobel were invaluable contributors to this volume. They helped us by reflecting on their experiences mediating environmental disputes and by writing up those experiences for inclusion in Part 3. Senior Consultant Joshua Secunda and Associate Jeffrey McDonough-Dumler provided much-needed help in gathering materials for the book. In addition, CBI staff members Polly O'Brien and John Mitchell provided unwavering assistance in preparing the final manuscript. Our many thanks to all of them.

We would also like to thank the following individuals for providing us with information on successful environmental negotiations: Kevin McManus, Eugene Benson, and Karen Rondeau from the Massachusetts Water Resources Authority; David Eppstein from the Medical Academic and Scientific Community Organization; Nancy Wheatley of the Orange County Sanitation District; Frank Sullivan at Beth Israel Deaconess Medical Center; Mark Spinale of the U.S. Environmental Protection Agency; and Mary Simmons Motte of TPI Composites, Inc.

Finally, we want to thank the more than 1500 people who have participated in the Negotiating Environmental Agreements workshops thus far. Their feedback has helped us to strengthen these teaching materials.

Introduction

Hundreds of environmental agreements are negotiated every week in the United States. Many involve the settlement of pending litigation. According to most estimates, 90 percent of these cases are settled before they ever reach a judge or jury, although many require extensive negotiation before they are resolved.

Other environmental negotiations are stimulated by permitting and licensing requirements. The U.S. Environmental Protection Agency (EPA) and the 50 state environmental agencies process hundreds of permit requests under the Clean Air Act, the Clean Water Act, and related statutes. During all these permitting activities, site reviews conducted by regulators are often contested by the companies involved, or by community groups or environmental organizations, leading to complex negotiations involving multiple parties. In literally thousands of jurisdictions—and before hundreds of administrative law judges—proponents, opponents, and regulators, or their hired guns, engage in permit negotiations all the time. These negotiations can take place before, during, or after formal permit requests are filed.

In these legal and regulatory settings, agreements are typically reached only after costly and bitter struggles. These battles—in addition to being the byproducts of regulation and litigation—are signs of our inability as a society to handle policy and political differences in an efficient and cost-effective way. The agreements reached often fall short (from the standpoint of any impartial observer) of addressing the underlying concerns that brought the parties together in the first place. Most represent little more than one side or the other "giving up," at least temporarily. Thus, even when regulatory, legal, and policy disputes are settled, it is possible that better agreements could have been crafted—that more could have been done to protect public health, ensure the careful management of scarce resources, or guarantee that the public's long-term interests are not sacrificed for short-term economic gain. The effectiveness of settlement agreements depends on how well the parties involved are able to deal with their differences through negotiation. Unfortunately, they are not often able to do it very well.

There are at least three reasons why regulatory and policy disagreements concerning environmental protection and public health are not resolved as creatively or cost-effectively as they could be. First, the parties involved often do not realize they are taking part in negotiations. Individuals involved in litigation, administrative appeals, permit discussions, or political action typically view these activities as battles to be won or lost. They are unprepared for and often unwilling to participate in the give-and-take required to produce agreements that meet the interests of all sides. Often, parties are represented by lawyers who are in no rush to settle because they bill by the hour. Second, many regulators claim they are not allowed to negotiate. The government's job, they assert, is to make decisions and enforce the law. Consistency ensures fairness, they believe, and no one deserves "special treatment." The fact that they have enormous discretion is not something they like to admit. Indeed, many elected and appointed officials believe that they do not have the legislative mandate they need to treat these issues as negotiable, even if they could achieve a better result. Finally, the parties to many environmental negotiations are utterly unprepared to pursue their own interests through negotiation. They simply do not have the skills needed to negotiate effectively.

For almost six years, the Environmental Policy Group at the Massachusetts Institute of Technology (MIT) has offered a workshop entitled Negotiating Environmental Agreements. The premise of the workshop is that *there is, indeed, something to negotiate when government regulators, the regulated community, and concerned interest groups square off across a table to debate environmental issues.* More than 1500 senior executives, government regulators, and interest group leaders have participated in these training sessions. Many report that they are now better able to deal with the problems that arise in legal and regulatory settings. In this book, we have summarized the key ideas and techniques presented at the MIT workshop. In fact, we have packaged the actual overheads, lecture notes, "game" materials, and background readings that are used in the workshop.

In teaching the workshop, we look at environmental negotiation from three perspectives. From the government's perspective, the question we ask is, "How can we use the discretion available to us to induce the regulated community to exceed minimum environmental protection requirements and voluntarily strive for superior performance?" To date, government regulators have rarely looked for opportunities to use their discretion in ways that might encourage the regulated community to go beyond minimum requirements. From the corporate perspective, the question we ask is, "How can we get the government to exercise its discretion in ways that allow us to meet legal requirements and community concerns at the lowest possible cost while maximizing our market share and our reputation?" Corporate officials have approached most regulatory negotiations as a confrontation. They have rarely tried to put themselves in the shoes of the regulators or help them meet their obligations. From the community's perspective, the question we ask is, "How can we get government and the regulated community to take our concerns seriously?" Interested outside parties are typically not just interested in everyone meeting minimally acceptable requirements—they want environmental impacts and public health risks reduced as much as possible. Yet they have rarely sought to encourage joint problem solving between regulators and regulatees or determine how they might contribute to that process.

Understanding the Status Quo

Imagine a typical set of events leading to a request for a permit to expand an existing industrial production facility. Assume the facility provides hundreds of jobs and is located in an industrial area. The company involved, we will call it Big Corp., has all the permits it needs to operate at present levels, but it wants to expand. To do that, it needs a new air-quality permit from the state environmental agency. The county government wants the facility to grow, because that will guarantee additional tax revenue. Government officials in the town of Niceville, where the facility is located, have reservations about the expansion plans because of public health concerns expressed by nearby residents.

The plant produces computers and computer parts, and its normal operation creates several kinds of emissions. The plant owners insist that they have always done everything necessary to meet all environmental legal requirements. Credible experts, however, claim that there is (a) some risk that the plant does not always run as cleanly as the owners claim—for example, during short-term malfunctions; and (b) some risk that even if the plant runs as promised, the health of plant workers and those living in the area could be adversely affected over time. People who suffer from certain respiratory illnesses are thought to be at particularly high risk. Some of the scientists are also concerned that existing air-quality standards are inappropriately low, but those standards are embodied in law and regulation and cannot easily be changed.

Based on these scientists' assertions, a local environmental advocacy group (we will call them Save the Earth) has filed suit against the company for alleged violation of environmental laws. Their hope is that the suit will, at the least, thwart Big Corp.'s expansion plans. The labor union at the plant, while concerned about adequate protection for its members, does not want to jeopardize the new jobs that would be created if the expansion goes ahead. The mayor of Niceville has asked the state public health agency to review the operation of the plant and provide a guarantee that area residents will not be harmed if the plant expands. Concerned residents have formed a group, called STOP IT!, that wants the plant shut down permanently. They claim they have been penalized long enough, and that because many of them are poor and are racial minorities, the plant owners are guilty of environmental racism. The plant manager is being pressed by senior corporate officials (in another state) to move forward with the expansion. Indeed, the plant manager has gotten strong hints that if the expansion does not move forward quickly, the plant will be shut down, although that is not generally known. The plant operates in a state where the EPA has agreed to let the state take responsibility for issuing air-quality permits because they have adopted higher standards than those prevailing at the federal level. The state regulators are besieged from all sides. They have no choice but to grant a permit if the proposed facility meets all legal requirements, but they fear some of the residents' concerns are valid.

In the negotiation world, we look at situations like this and ask how each side views its BATNA—its "best alternative to a negotiated agreement" (Fisher, Ury, and Patton, 1991). That is, what is most likely to happen to each group if no agreement can be worked out among them? If a group's members are optimistic about getting what they want by pursuing litigation or appealing to their elected representatives, they will not be inclined to negotiate. If, however, those same group members are pessimistic (or unsure) about the outcome of legal or political action, they have good reason to explore the possibility of a negotiated settlement.

We can only wonder how carefully Big Corp., Save the Earth, STOP IT!, and the state environmental agency have calculated the likelihood of winning in court (or in the "court" of public opinion), and whether they have considered the costs associated with achieving victory. Have they really stepped back and made a hard-headed estimate of their BATNA? In our experience, the senior officials at Big Corp. are inclined to view the situation through a legal lens, knowing that if they meet the letter of the law they cannot be turned down. They will likely be following the advice of their lawyers, some of whom stand to benefit financially if the case drags on. Members of STOP IT! will feel relatively powerless and will probably turn to their elected representatives for help in shutting down the facility if something is not done to reduce the risks. They are unlikely to realize that they can negotiate an agreement with Big Corp. that would leave the neighborhood substantially better off. Save the Earth's leaders are not concerned about the economic or social impacts of shutting down the plant, they are just interested in satisfying their members' desire to take immediate action to protect the environment. The group is therefore likely to pursue the lawsuit no matter what the chances are of losing; they view negotiations as "selling out." State and federal regulators are likely to assume that their job is limited to interpreting the relevant statutes and deciding whether or not the applicant has met the necessary requirements. The idea that these same regulators might take part in a face-to-face conversation (perhaps facilitated by a professional mediator) aimed at meeting everyone's interests (and certainly exceeding everyone's BATNA), is not in the forefront of anyone's mind.

A Better Way of Handling Environmental Disputes

Let's consider what a negotiated settlement in this case might include, and think about the steps involved in achieving it. We can imagine at least one deal that would allow everyone to come close to meeting their interests at an acceptable cost. Under such an arrangement, Big Corp. would be allowed to expand, but it would have to invest in pollution-prevention technology and change its operations sufficiently to minimize current waste streams and *reduce the risks associated with a plant malfunction to a level below that currently mandated by law.* In other words, the expanded plant would have to run "cleaner" than the existing facility (which already meets federal and state requirements).

Extra governmental monitoring arrangements, perhaps involving a nearby university and residents (who would be trained in the technical issues at the company's expense), would exceed anything the federal or state government is empowered to require. Big Corp. might also offer to underwrite a community-managed fund, perhaps in conjunction with a local hospital or public health agency, to track changes in the health of employees and community members.

Save the Earth would receive a promise of superior environmental performance from Big Corp.—performance exceeding what government regulators have the power to mandate. This promise could take the form of a legally enforceable contract spelling out penalties for noncompliance. Save the Earth would also get credit in a joint press release for having helped Big Corp. find new ways of preventing (rather than just cleaning up) pollution and ensuring that plant workers and residents of Niceville are protected. They might also get Big Corp. to contribute to a local land trust, which would then purchase an ecologically sensitive area near the plant that neither the county nor the state is willing to buy. In return for these gains, Save the Earth would drop its lawsuit.

STOP IT! would receive a promise from Big Corp. that any demonstrable environmental damage that the plant has already caused or might cause in the future (as determined by a scientific committee jointly appointed by Big Corp., the state, Save the Earth, and STOP IT!) would be mitigated or compensated. Also, Big Corp. and the county would promise to "insure" property values in the area so that homeowners who sold their homes after the expanded plant was in operation would be "held harmless" if the expansion had an adverse impact on the value of their property (i.e., they would be compensated for any loss in value at the time of subsequent sale).

State, county, and local officials would all be able to claim a share of the credit for bringing the conflict to a successful conclusion in a way that saved the cost of litigation, ensured that legal standards of environmental protection were exceeded (voluntarily), and restored some measure of confidence in government.

Obviously, when all the financial implications of this agreement are tallied, Big Corp. must come out ahead or it should not agree to such a settlement. If the long-term benefit of plant expansion is not greater than the short-term costs implied by the various payments and commitments enumerated above, it might be possible for the county, state, and federal government to provide subsidies or grants to Big Corp. (thereby reducing the company's cost) on the grounds that new jobs will be created, additional tax revenue will flow from the expansion, the cost of enforcing environmental standards will be reduced in the future (because the company will invest in new pollution-prevention equipment), and a terrific precedent will be set. The lesson of this story is that, by trading across issues that the parties value differently, a "package" can be constructed that leaves everyone better off than they had a right to expect, given a realistic appraisal of the probable outcome of going to court or continuing to fight it out politically.

Hundreds of agreements of this sort have been worked out around the country. Several are described in detail later in this volume. Every element of this hypothetical agreement has appeared in a real settlement somewhere in the United States. Settlements like this do not emerge full blown from the minds of individual corporate managers or elected officials, however. It takes intensive, face-to-face conversation among all affected parties, usually over several months, in which many options and constraints are considered. Also, it is often necessary for the parties involved to have the help of a professional mediator or facilitator. At the outset, no one trusts anyone else, and everyone works hard to maintain their other options. Over time, though, with the help of the mediator, the various stakeholders work with their "constituents" and each other to produce a package that exceeds their best estimate of what would happen if they walk away from the table. They do what they can to invent ways of meeting everyone's interests at the lowest possible cost. They apportion costs and responsibilities in a written agreement, and formulate a detailed implementation plan.

If all goes well, it should be possible to measure the success of such negotiations in three ways. First, the parties themselves should be *satisfied* that their interests have been met. All stakeholders should feel that they have achieved a better result at a lower cost than what they would have achieved if they had been forced to fight on. Only the parties themselves can make this assessment. Unfortunately, parties are often tempted to compare what they get via a settlement with what they wish would have happened. This is inappropriate, of course. They should, rather, compare the negotiated result with a realistic assessment of their BATNA or "walk-away" option.

Second, the outcome should be *efficient*. There are two ways to interpret efficiency. Efficiency might mean that the parties spent less time and money to achieve a specific result than what it would have taken to get that result using any other method. This can only be judged after the fact, and even then it involves a great deal of subjectivity. Measuring efficiency might also involve examining the agreement to see whether it can be embellished in a way that would produce additional gains to one side without leaving anyone else worse off. If not, we can presume that the result is truly efficient (i.e., optimal). It is important to have both an efficient process and an optimal outcome.

The third measure of success is the state of the *relationships* among the parties after the situation is settled. The parties should be in a better position to deal with their differences in the future as a result of having worked together. (Using more traditional, confrontational approaches, the opposite is usually the case!) The level of trust should have increased. If implementation becomes difficult later on, the parties should be able to reconvene easily, without having to resort to legal challenges or other escalatory moves. Not only the participants, but their organizations and their individual successors, tend to benefit when relationships are enhanced.

The Mutual Gains Approach to Negotiation

In the most general sense, all multiparty, multi-issue negotiations move through four stages: *preparation, value creation, value distribution,* and *follow through* (see Figure I.1). Unfortunately, many participants in environmental negotiations begin without doing the proper preparation. Then, they skip over value creation (the steps they can take to "make the pie larger") because they are afraid that appearing too cooperative at the outset will be viewed as a sign of weakness. Unfortunately, once a negotiation moves to the third phase—value distribution—it is too late to go back, and the parties are stuck "dividing a small pie." Although the third phase is predominantly competitive (gains to one side almost always require losses to others), value distribution can be handled so that relationships are left intact. Usually, though, participants in environmental negotiations seem so intent on getting a big piece of the pie for themselves that they fail to proceed in a way that maintains or builds relationships. Finally, most negotiators spend far too little time clarifying the details of implementation—what might go wrong and how to handle it—before signing an agreement. Once agreements begin to fall apart, it is almost always too late to address these difficulties in a collaborative and productive way.

According to the theory of mutual gains negotiation, a number of things must be done at each of these four stages to ensure the best possible results.

- *Preparation.* The preparation stage begins with an effort by each set of stakeholders to clarify their negotiator's mandate. Each group or organization needs to estimate its BATNA in the most realistic way possible. Each should also think about its interests, by asking "What are our real, underlying concerns, and why?" and "What are the

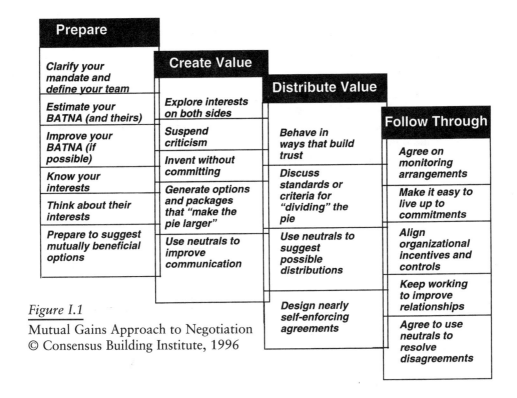

Figure I.1

Mutual Gains Approach to Negotiation
© Consensus Building Institute, 1996

things we need to accomplish, and in what order of importance do we rank them?" This should be followed by an effort to think through the other sides' likely estimate of their BATNAs and interests. Before the negotiation begins, each party should try to improve its BATNA and clarify its interests. For example, doing some background research, finding technical help, and figuring out a way to generate still another "walk away" option are all self-help strategies that can be used to improve one's BATNA. Polling members of the organization, role playing various trade-offs, and imagining the consequences of different outcomes can force a more clear-headed assessment of interests. The preparation stage is not complete until each stakeholder group has tried to formulate a mutually beneficial proposal—one that will meet its own interests well and the likely interests of others tolerably.

- *Value Creation.* Making the proverbial pie larger is not as difficult as many people think. The key, as our colleagues Roger Fisher, Bill Ury, and Bruce Patton have spelled out in their best-selling book, *Getting to Yes* (1991), is to "separate inventing from committing." Even people who are suspicious of each other need to put aside their animosities long enough to brainstorm packages of options that will help everyone do better than walking away. This is in every stakeholder's interest. Inventing options in this way requires listening carefully to what others have to say, agreeing to suspend criticism, and investing heavily in option generation without worrying until later about making any commitments. Sometimes a neutral facilitator can help, if the parties cannot do this on their own. The parties may need to adopt a ground rule that says no one has made an implicit commitment when they think out loud about possible options; commitments come later.

- *Value Distribution.* There are all kinds of ideas about how to get the most for yourself when a fixed pie is about to be divided. Some people think the key is to "bid high" and then trade concessions for concessions. This approach depends on being able to bluff or mislead, however, which undermines trust and works against the goal of building long-term relationships. Instead, as Fisher, Ury, and Patton (1991) suggest, the parties should use objective criteria, or reasons, to explain why they think a particular distribution of value is fair or appropriate. Often, the parties may need the help of a neutral to suggest possible plans for distributing value. Presumably, once all the value is distributed, the parties have reached agreement.

- *Follow Through.* Once a tentative agreement is reached, the parties should think carefully about all the things that might make it difficult to achieve what they have promised. Monitoring arrangements should be discussed, along with penalties for noncompliance. Organizational changes aimed at ensuring that everyone has their internal incentives and control properly aligned should also be reviewed. Dispute handling mechanisms and ways of ensuring ongoing communication should be specified before problems arise.

These are just some of the elements of the mutual gains approach to negotiation that can help parties involved in environmental disputes achieve better agreements. These elements are reviewed in more detail in Part 1 of this volume.

Obstacles to Using the Mutual Gains Approach

Although the theory and methods of mutual gains negotiation have been readily available for more than a decade, most participants in environmental conflicts in the United States continue to seek all-out victory through litigation or political maneuvering. Or, they approach negotiation as a win-lose proposition. This suggests that either the theory of mutual gain is flawed or the obstacles to using it are substantial. Because we have seen so many examples of this approach applied successfully, we reject the former explanation. The latter—the existence of formidable obstacles—is more convincing.

The first obstacle worth noting is the presumption of powerlessness that many parties, particularly community groups, sometimes feel. They assume that large corporations will get their way, so there is no point opposing them, or that regulators do not have the power nor the will to oppose economic growth. So, they hesitate to enter into negotiations of the sort undertaken by Save the Earth and STOP IT!

Linked to the feeling of powerlessness is the sense some groups have that they do not have the skills required to advance their interests. This presumes that groups must represent themselves rather than hire agents to negotiate on their behalf. This is not true. Groups are often well-advised to secure legal assistance. Similarly, some would do well to hire negotiators to represent them (Mnookin and Susskind, in press). Also, organizations sometimes fail to realize that they have skilled negotiators within their ranks, even though these may not be the elected or appointed officers in those organizations.

Another obstacle is the failure of leadership. Some heads of organizations, particularly elected or appointed officials in the public sector, presume that any willingness to negotiate will be read as a sign of weakness. The concept of "facilitative leadership"—in which leaders achieve success by unleashing the full capacity of an organization rather than doing all the work themselves—has not yet permeated all quarters of society (Schwarz, 1994). The notion that a leader can help a group meet its interests by negotiating effectively on its behalf (as opposed to "hanging tough" and risking everything on a court case) is still not widely understood. Furthermore, competition within an organization can work against the search for negotiated solutions. A person who wants to unseat a current leader is likely to claim that the leader's willingness to negotiate is an indication of weakness and a sign that change at the top is needed. Thus, the pressure to play to an internal audience sometimes gets in the way of an effective settlement negotiation.

Still another obstacle to the use of mutual gains techniques is the way the press covers public conflicts. Typical newspaper, television, and radio coverage almost always suggests that there are "good guys" and "bad guys." That is, one side is portrayed as doing the right thing, and their opponents, by implication, are doing the wrong thing. Rarely do the media provide sufficient background information for the public to make up its own mind about the claims on all sides. Furthermore, the media refuse to play the educative role many of us would like them to accept, settling instead for "reporting the news" as their only responsibility. Settlement negotiations are sometimes covered by the press at the outset, as part of a portrayal of the conflict. But reporters and editors rarely consider ongoing negotiations to be "news" (Kunde, 1999). Thus, it is not surprising when groups in conflict see little or no reason to sit down together to work out their differences; even if they succeed, it will not be news, and no one will get credit for having done the right thing.

In the absence of any formal "rules of the game," a great many parties are uneasy about the prospect of entering negotiations. To some, the time spent trying to find agreement seems wasted. They are particularly annoyed when others want to spend time on process issues, or negotiations over how the negotiations will proceed. If mutual gains-style negotiations were more common, parties could move more quickly to deal directly with the substance of their disagreements. As it is now, a great deal of time must be spent working out ground rules and clarifying how informally negotiated agreements will relate to other decision-making processes. Until the rules of the "new game" are fully understood, it will be necessary to make up-front investments of time to clarify how negotiations will proceed.

Another key obstacle is opposition from the legal field. Some attorneys graduated from law school before negotiation (or alternative dispute resolution, as it is now commonly called) was the popular elective it is today. So, they are uninformed. If this were the primary obstacle, however, it would soon be remedied, given the requirement of continuing legal education. In our experience, the problem is more pernicious. Some members of the bar apparently believe it is in their best interest to encourage litigation, even when the interests of their clients would be better served by a settlement. When we encounter parties to environmental disputes who are hesitant to come to the negotiation table, they have usually been told by counsel that if they participate in a negotiation they might compromise their chances of winning in court. The presumption is that if they reveal their true interests (what they would be willing to accept) in an informal context, this will put them at a disadvantage if the case goes forward. Putting aside the fact that the rules of evidence do not allow settlement offers to be cited in subsequent trials, it is not clear how clarifying one's interests can ever lead to an inferior outcome. Each party always retains the right to say no to any settlement it does not like, for whatever reasons. How can anyone expect to achieve their goals if they will not reveal to their negotiating partners what they want to accomplish?

The confusion, we believe, grows out of a failure to distinguish "interests" (underlying needs and concerns) from "positions" (stated demands), as Fisher, Ury, and Patton have so elegantly shown (1991). If we presumed that negotiation involved primarily an exchange of positions, then yes, it would be a mistake to reveal the minimal "amount" we would accept. The negotiation would move quickly to that level. However, we believe that the goal of negotiation is to help all sides exceed their BATNA by the greatest amount possible. The way to do this is to trade across interests that the parties value differently. Thus, it is crucial for each side to have a clear picture of the other's rank-ordered interests. Then, if one side can give something to its opponents (at low cost) and get something it values highly in return (at low cost to the other), value can be created and agreement will be much easier to reach.

If one is going to court, it should be because all other strategies have failed, or because there is a larger objective, like setting a legal precedent. It is not possible to know whether a settlement can be achieved if a party refuses to enter into good-faith negotiations. We can only assume that some lawyers put their own interests ahead of the interests of their clients when they advise them not to participate in settlement negotiations.

Ways to Overcome These Obstacles

Despite these obstacles, the mutual gains approach has been used countless times to achieve better environmental agreements. This section describes the keys to overcoming the most difficult obstacles.

The Help of Professional Neutrals

The number of professional mediators and facilitators with the background and skills needed to help parties settle environmental disputes continues to grow. Indeed, the roster of individuals providing this service on a full-time basis is expanding at a rate of more than 50 per year (Martindale-Hubbell, 1997). The EPA and more than a dozen state offices of dispute resolution maintain rosters of experienced environmental mediators. The quarterly newspaper *CONSENSUS*, published by the MIT-Harvard Public Disputes Program, carries a regional listing of more than 60 organizations in North America that provide environmental mediation services on a full-time basis (see the Mediation/Facilitation Resources list at the back of this volume). The availability of qualified individuals does not mean that it is easy to match up the right facilitator with the needs of a particular conflict situation, of course. This requires careful thought and consideration, particularly on the part of the "convenor" (the stakeholding agency or organization willing to raise the possibility of using a mediator and able to host a consensus building process).

Professional neutrals can offer specialized assistance at each stage of a negotiation or

Table I.1. Tasks of the Mediator: Breaking the Impasse

Phases	*Tasks*
PRE-NEGOTIATION	
Getting started	Meeting with potential stakeholders to assess their interests and describe the consensus building process; handling logistics and convening initial meetings; assisting groups in initial calculation of BATNAs
Representation	Caucusing with stakeholders to help choose spokespeople or team leaders; working with initial stakeholders to identify missing groups or strategies for representing diffuse interests
Drafting protocols and agenda setting	Preparing draft protocols based on past experience and the concerns of the parties; managing the process of agenda setting
Joint fact-finding	Helping to draft fact-finding protocols; identifying technical consultants or advisors to the group; raising and administering the funds in a resource pool; serving as a repository for confidential or proprietary information
NEGOTIATION	
Inventing options	Managing the brainstorming process; suggesting potential options for the group to consider; coordinating subcommittees to draft options
Packaging	Caucusing privately with each group to identify and test possible trades; suggesting possible packages for the group to consider
Written agreement	Working with a subcommittee to produce a draft agreement; managing a single-text procedure; preparing a preliminary draft of a single text
Binding the parties	Serving as the holder of the bond; approaching outsiders on behalf of the group; helping to invent new ways to bind the parties to their commitments
Ratification	Helping the participants "sell" the agreement to their constituents; ensuring that all representatives have been in touch with their constituents
IMPLEMENTATION OR POST-NEGOTIATION	
Linking informal agreements and decision making	Working with the parties to invent linkages; approaching elected or appointed officials on formal behalf of the group; identifying the legal constraints on implementation
Monitoring	Serving as the monitor of implementation; convening a monitoring group
Renegotiation	Reassembling the participants if subsequent disagreements emerge; helping to remind the group of its earlier intentions

Source: In *Breaking the Impasse: Consensual Approaches to Revolving Public Disputes.* New York: Basic Books.

dispute resolution process. Table I.1 enumerates the range of tasks that facilitators and mediators can be called upon to play.

Training

The participants in environmental disputes have many opportunities to acquire additional skills and understanding about the mutual gains approach to negotiation and its application to their situation. Dozens of university-based groups and independent training organizations offer general courses as well as specially tailored on-site programs. Most of the important concepts and methods can be explained in a two-day period; longer courses offer opportunities to practice what has been learned in a variety of simulated settings.

One of the most effective forms of training is a tailored program designed for *all* the participants in an actual negotiation situation (joint training). By learning the vocabulary and techniques of mutual gains negotiation in the same place at the same time, stakeholders can move a negotiation process forward much more quickly. When negotiators know that the others at the table are operating on the same assumptions they are, they are better able to understand what is happening and to proceed effectively.

Agreement About Ground Rules

Ground rules are mutually agreed-upon guidelines that help parties work together efficiently. Ground rules usually include behavioral guidelines (such as "Disagree without being disagreeable"), process rules (such as "No agreement will be sought on any item in a package until all the items have been discussed by the group"), and a detailed description of roles and responsibilities (such as "Alternates may be recognized to speak even when the primary participants are present"). Several examples of such ground rules can be viewed on the Web page of the nonprofit Consensus Building Institute (www.cbi-web.org). The sooner ground rules can be agreed upon, the more quickly a negotiation can be launched.

To help parties develop ground rules appropriate to their situation, a mediator or facilitator can prepare a pre-negotiation conflict assessment. Such an assessment is based on confidential interviews with the key stakeholders and usually produces a written summary spelling out suggested ground rules, an agenda, work plan, budget, and a recommendation on whether or not to proceed (Susskind and Thomas-Larmer, 1999).

Redefinition of the Functions of Leadership

As mentioned previously, the likelihood of reaching a negotiated settlement in many environmental disputes is often a function of the attitudes of various elected and appointed leaders—in the public sector, the corporate arena, and in the world of nonprofit action groups. Too many leaders have not yet learned that looking strong is not nearly as important as producing results for their constituents. Once they learn of the many benefits of facilitative leadership, they are more likely to adopt a mutual gains approach to negotiation (and, more important, be able to sell it to their members) (Schwarz, 1994).

Tapping New Sources of Power

There are many sources of power in a negotiation. Community groups, who often feel powerless, can form coalitions that have a combined leverage that exceeds the political strength that any one group would have on its own. They can also justify their claims with reference to a principle (such as "fairness requires that risk be distributed equally, regardless of income or class"), thereby increasing their bargaining power. When they appeal to principle, their strength is not merely a function of their political clout. Community groups can also create power by proposing "an elegant solution" (of the sort we describe in the Big Corp. case). By finding and suggesting an ingenious way of meeting the interests of all stakeholders, a community group can gain disproportionate leverage in an environmental settlement negotiation.

Adoption of New Norms

The federal government has enacted legislation calling on every federal agency to take a variety of steps to ensure that disputes in which they are involved are settled as quickly and effectively as possible. The Administrative Dispute Resolution Act of 1990 spells out the reasons for using a negotiated approach to settling a range of public disputes. Because of this legislation, a number of federal agencies have made substantial changes in the ways in which they deal with administrative and legal challenges to their activities (Susskind, Babbitt, and Segal, 1993). Similarly, quite a few states have or are considering enacting parallel legislation. All of this suggests that new norms are beginning to take hold.

Hundreds of community dispute resolution centers have also begun operating in the United States over the past two decades. These centers help and encourage community groups and individual citizens to settle their disputes through negotiation. Local officials are also being asked by their constituents to use alternative dispute resolution methods (like mediation) to work out disagreements without resorting automatically to litigation.

The theory of mutual gains negotiation can be applied successfully in a wide range of contexts—including pre-permit compliance negotiations, compliance negotiations, local health and safety permit negotiations, compliance penalty negotiations, and policy debates—at the local, state, national, and even international levels. The approach is equally relevant whether a few parties or a great many stakeholders are involved.

Organization of This Volume

Part 1 of this book includes a systematic exposition of the theory of mutual gains negotiation and its application to environmental disputes. This is presented using the overheads adapted from our Negotiating Environmental Agreements workshop. The overheads are annotated to anticipate and answer the questions we are typically asked when we present these materials in person.

Part 2 provides five simulations—or structured role-playing exercises—that participants in the Negotiating Environmental Agreements workshop use to test their understanding of the theory of mutual gains and practice their newly learned skills. The first simulation is called Gadgets, Inc. It involves negotiations among a metal plating firm, state and federal regulators, a trade union, and two environmental groups regarding how to bring the firm back into compliance with air and water pollution regulations. The second simulation is ChemCo, Inc. It deals with a negotiation between a company and a state agency regarding a protocol for monitoring air-quality emissions from a manufacturing facility. The third is called Bog Berries. It deals with the efforts of a federal agency and a company to negotiate permit-application parameters in the aftermath of a bitter intentional-dumping lawsuit. The fourth is MC Metals. In this simulation, the Occupational Safety and Health Administration is trying to decide what fines and penalties to impose on a company after an accidental fire has caused loss of life. The final simulation is called Carson Extension. In this game, a company illegally filled a wetland site years ago, but removing the fill now might cause more environmental harm than good. Community and environmental group representatives are at the table along with company spokespeople and senior staff of the U.S. Army Corps of Engineers.

Simulations are particularly instructive because they provide a setting in which negotiators can practice their skills with no concerns about "real world" consequences. Each simulation begins with a story highlighting a conflict among a set of hypothetical stakeholders. Their representatives have been asked to come together (in a very limited amount of time) to address their differences. At the end of the simulation section of the book, we provide a series of debriefing questions that will help the reader assess how well he or she has been able to grasp the mutual gains framework within each set of simulated negotiations. It is also possible to review some of the agreements that have been generated by workshop participants over the past few years by connecting to the Web site of the Environmental Policy Group at MIT (http://web.mit.edu/dusp/epg).

Part 3 offers four real-life examples in which the participants in high-stakes disputes worked out their disagreements through negotiation. For each example, we provide a short case history describing the negotiation process used to resolve the conflict, as well as copies of the resultant written agreement(s). The first example is a fairly straightforward permit negotiation case in which a group of Boston-area hospitals negotiated with the Massachusetts Water Resources Authority (MWRA) regarding permits for the discharge of mercury into the sewer system. All of the hospitals found they were exceeding the very-stringent discharge limit for mercury, yet they had no idea where the substance was coming from or why it was making its way into the waste stream. The hospitals and MWRA negotiated two creative agreements through which, among other elements, the hospitals were not fined for the violations while they worked to determine the causes of the problem. After extensive investigation and subsequent changes in their operations, two-thirds of the hospitals have come into compliance with the discharge standards.

The other three examples are more complex. The second involves a negotiated agreement among multiple federal, state, and local agencies and other interested parties regarding the restoration of a key roadway and barrier beach on Martha's Vineyard. The road was badly damaged by storms and erosion, but fixing it was no easy matter. It ran through an area of fragile wetland and coastal ecosystems that was protected under a variety of federal, state, and local statutes. Any restoration process would require up to 10 different permits, including a Section 404 permit from the U.S. Army Corps of Engineers. The parties entered these negotiations with a history of interagency conflict over the preferred solution to the problem. With the help of a professional mediator, however, the parties were able to reach an agreement concerning interim restoration.

The third example is a negotiated agreement developed by the Delaware Coastal Zone Regulatory Advisory Committee and submitted to the Delaware Department of Natural Resources and Environmental Control (DNREC). The committee, representing a cross-section of industrial, governmental, and environmental interests, was asked to formulate regulations for the management of industrial development in the coastal zone of Delaware. After many months of difficult negotiations, the participants reached consensus, and DNREC used the detailed agreement as the basis for draft regulations.

The fourth and final example focuses on a Superfund cleanup at the Massachusetts

Military Reservation (MMR) on Cape Cod, one of the most difficult groundwater contamination cases ever faced by the U.S. Department of Defense. By 1996, 11 "plumes" of contaminated groundwater and soil had been identified at the MMR. After a number of false starts, federal, state, and local officials, as well as a range of citizen activists and technical experts, reached agreement on how best to remediate the adverse impacts of the plumes. The case in this section describes one major stage of the negotiations. These four examples of negotiated agreements provide further evidence that the ideas we are presenting about negotiation can, indeed, produce results in practice.

Part 4 of this volume offers a series of readings that provide additional guidance and insight into effective environmental negotiation. At the end of the book we have included a selected bibliography of books and articles, and a list of mediators and facilitators, arrayed geographically.

Part 1

The Mutual Gains Approach

The mutual gains approach to negotiating environmental agreements is described in detail in this part. We begin by looking at the philosophy behind the approach and talk about what regulators, regulatees, and the community at large can learn from its concepts. We then compare traditional negotiation strategies and techniques with the mutual gains approach. We explain the concept of BATNA—"best alternative to a negotiated agreement"—and describe the strategic power of this concept in our negotiation framework. We then present and discuss the essential stages of the mutual gains approach: preparation, value creation, value distribution, and follow through. We place a heavy emphasis on the creation and maintenance of relationships throughout these stages. Finally, we discuss the applications of these concepts to common permitting and other regulatory situations. The part includes adaptations of the overheads we use in our workshop, accompanied by detailed annotations.

Philosophy of the Approach

Regulators and regulatees often have a high degree of skepticism concerning the efficacy of negotiation in the highly structured and legalistic environmental arena. Regulated companies often assume that regulators have little or no discretion when it comes to permitting, compliance, and enforcement. They fear that attempts to engage in negotiation will be perceived by regulators as attempts to "get around the rules" and will therefore backfire by generating even more stringent enforcement activities. Likewise, regulators are often convinced that they, in fact, have little discretion in their permitting and enforcement activities and that attempts to negotiate agreements will serve mainly to weaken environmental laws and regulations.

Our philosophy is that well-structured and thoughtful negotiations can result in gains for both regulators and regulatees, and for the community at large (see Figure 1.1). For the regulator, an effective agreement can produce voluntary compliance that goes beyond minimum standards required or mandated by law. For the regulated company, an effective agreement can offer flexibility in when and how requirements must be met and the opportunity to explain, face to face, the financial and commercial constraints on the regulated industry. For the community at large, agreements can result in better environmental performance and stronger commercial enterprises, yielding numerous benefits to the community.

What is there to negotiate?

For the Regulator
Enhanced environmental performance, beyond what is mandated or required.

For the Regulatee
Flexibility in when and how requirements must be met; attentiveness to the interests (needs) of the regulated community.

For the Community at Large
Voluntary efforts to improve environmental performance (beyond minimally acceptable levels) at the lowest possible cost and with the least disruption to the economy.

Figure 1.1
Philosophy of the Approach

The Essential Ingredient

The exercise of agency discretion is the key to negotiating optimal agreements (see Figure 1.2). We know that such discretion exists in most regulatory settings. Indeed, state legislators and Congress typically anticipate that enforcement agencies will interpret the law based on technological advances, precedent, financial factors, willingness of companies to cooperate, and a variety of other factors. It is not possible to write an environmental or public health law that can precisely fit the circumstances surrounding each factory, mill, or other production facility. Legislators intend for agencies to use their best judgment to reach the broadly stated goals set forth in a given statute. Courts, too, will generally defer to the expertise of an administrative agency in interpreting the law and carrying out its provisions.

Notwithstanding these facts, regulatory agency officials often feel obliged to assert that they have little flexibility, because they fear that flexibility will lead to being "used" by industries or will prompt complaints from advocacy groups and the press that a company is being given preferential treatment. We believe strongly, however, that regulatory discretion is a tool that can be used to produce results that are better for society. We would not expect a regulator to do less than carry out the law, as he or she understands that law. Likewise, however, we would not expect a regulator to forsake a chance to produce a more beneficial result than that anticipated in the law. We believe that negotiation is a means to accomplishing the latter end.

Regulatees must understand that flexibility also means a lack of uniformity. When a regulator and regulatee enter into negotiations, the chosen solution to a permitting or compliance problem might be different from that required of others in the industry. It is this variability that enables an environmental agreement to be tailored to the particular economic and financial concerns of a given regulatee.

The community, also, must accept that negotiations will likely produce different results in similar cases. The community has a right to expect that the deals and deal mak-

---

The key to negotiating optimal environmental agreements is the exercise of <u>agency</u> <u>discretion</u>.

Regulators:
Must acknowledge that they have a great deal of discretion—regardless of the explicitness of rules and regulations.

Regulatees :
Must confront the fact that the exercise of agency discretion will usually lead to "tailored solutions" in each case. Everyone will not be treated the same.

The Community:
Must accept the fact that the exercise of agency discretion (producing different agreements in similar cases) needs to be supported as long as deals and deal making are transparent and open to public review.

Figure 1.2
The Essential Ingredient

---

ing that lead to such disparate results will be transparent and open to public review. Environmental regulation, after all, is a process carried out for the public good, and the public officials associated with that process must remain accountable to the body politic.

The Goal for Regulatees

Regulatees should learn how to initiate and carry out a process of negotiation that does not in any way threaten the integrity of the regulatory process or individual regulators (see Figure 1.3). Indeed, the establishment of a respectful and trusting relationship is essential to reaching environmental agreements. The mutual gains approach is based on understanding the interests of the other parties. In this approach, both the substance and the process of the negotiations are critical. Action taken by both parties "away from the table" before face-to-face negotiations occur are important, too, in that they help provide people with a better sense of the context and substance of the other party's interests.

The mutual gains approach is both a strategy and a set of tactics. As a strategy, it provides a broad framework within which an environmental negotiation can take place. But it also provides the context for tactical steps that all parties might seek to employ. The approach is tied to specific behaviors exhibited and choices made before, during, and after face-to-face sessions. How can regulatees do a better job of finding out what regulators really need to know to do their job effectively? We explore ways they can improve communications with the many levels of agency personnel. We offer advice on how they can get interpretations of regulations before making major financial commitments. Finally, we provide insights into how regulatees can get readings from the agency about their "bottom line"—what they really would be willing to live with.

> **To learn:**
>
> - How to do a better job of finding out what regulators <u>really</u> need to know—without making them feel you are trying to compromise their integrity.
> - When, and under what conditions, to talk to agency personnel.
> - How to speed up communications, yet act in ways that <u>avoid</u> adversarial relationships.
> - How to interact with multiple levels of regulatory staff.
> - How to get interpretations of regulations before, rather than after, you've committed to a design or an investment strategy.
> - How to get agencies to let you know what they would really be willing to live with.

Figure 1.3
The Goal for Regulatees

The Goal for Regulators

Likewise, regulators need help understanding the interests and problems of regulated companies (see Figure 1.4). After all, regulators' goal should not be to achieve minimal compliance. Their goal should be to achieve results that are better than the minimum required by the law. Regulators need to understand how to improve communications with all levels of corporate personnel. We provide regulators with advice on how and when to offer interpretations of regulations before regulatees have made major financial commitments that might not satisfy the environmental objectives of the jurisdictions involved. We also offer our thoughts on how and when regulators should let regulatees know what the agency is really willing to accept in a given situation.

> **To learn:**
>
> - How to do a better job of finding out what regulatees really need to accomplish.
> - When, and under what conditions, to talk to regulatees.
> - How to minimize the time and effort involved in communications, yet act in ways that <u>avoid</u> adversarial relationships.
> - How to interact with multiple levels of corporate and interest group staff.
> - When to offer interpretations of regulations.
> - Whether to let regulatees (and concerned interest groups) know what you would really be willing to accept.

Figure 1.4
The Goal for Regulators

The Conventional Wisdom

We do not have to look far to see examples of the conventional wisdom regarding negotiation. Frequent travelers have likely read about the conventional approach in advertisements in airline magazines. Parents all too frequently find examples in their relationships with their teenage children—either as practiced by the teenagers, the parents, or both. Unfortunately, we also often see it employed in the context of environmental negotiations.

The traditional approach typically goes something like this (see Figure 1.5): First, come to the table with a clear set of demands, and make sure those demands are inflated beyond even your expectations. You know you are going to have to give up something, so start high. Only back off from your initial demands if concessions are made by the other side, and then do it grudgingly. When your opponents offer data and arguments, do your best to discredit those data and arguments and undermine their use in the discussion.

Do not forget to wear a mask. Never let your underlying feelings, concerns, or interests be seen by your adversary. Any indications of openness are a clear sign of weakness. Likewise, never show empathy for the other side, lest you give them leverage against you.

Finally, use pressure tactics to show that you are powerful. For example, intimidate people by raising your voice and banging your fist on the table periodically. Use outside pressure also. Threaten to get your opponent fired, perhaps. However you do it, be sure to engage in the kind of psychological warfare that breaks down your opponent's willpower so that you can win. After you win, gloat about it with your colleagues.

Does this sound familiar? We know it does, and we trust it makes you vaguely uncomfortable, whether you work for the government, a private firm, or a nonprofit organization. It probably makes you uncomfortable because, to do it, you know you will have to act—to pretend to be someone you are not. You may even have to lie. After all, if you start out by saying "We absolutely cannot pay any fine above $20,000," and then, after

---

1. **Determine what you want, then present inflated opening "demands."**

2. **Only offer concessions if concessions are offered to you.**

3. **Show no empathy for the legitimate concerns of the other "side."**

4. **Try to undermine their data and arguments.**

5. **Wear a mask.**

6. **Use pressure tactics to "put them off their game" or get them "to cave in."**

Figures 1.5
The Conventional Wisdom

hearing some valid arguments from the other side, you concede, "OK, we could go to $25,000," you have instantly revealed yourself as a liar. From that point on, the other negotiators will not trust anything you say; your power and influence have been greatly diminished, and both your short- and long-term relationships with the other parties have been damaged. The following illustrations will show how you can steer clear of these problems—and come up with better outcomes for all parties—using the mutual gains approach.

Challenging the Conventional Wisdom

Figure 1.6 outlines the major steps involved in the mutual gains approach to negotiation, which is markedly different than the conventional approach.

BATNA—A Key Concept

The mutual gains approach is founded on a key concept—the BATNA. BATNA is defined as the "best alternative to a negotiated agreement." It is each party's best estimate of what he or she will do if no agreement is reached. Think strategically for a moment. If you view negotiation as a means to an end, rather than an end in itself, you must consider other means to that same end, including other approaches that do not rely on negotiation. Only by considering the alternatives to negotiation can you assess the value of a potential negotiated settlement. Simply put, if, through negotiation, you cannot do as well for yourself as your BATNA, you should walk away from the negotiation and live with your BATNA.

This is just common sense, but many people enter negotiations without a clear understanding of their BATNA. Let's take a simple example. Say a firm's executives have received a notice of permit violation from the state Department of Environmental Protection (DEP). The executives' BATNA is to fight this notice through the administrative procedures established by the state agency, and then, if they lose, to

---

The Mutual Gains Approach

1. **Analyze and try to improve your BATNA. Raise doubts about their BATNA.**

2. **Probe to clarify your interests and theirs.**

3. **Invent options that meet your interests and theirs.**

4. **Use objective criteria to argue for the "package" you favor.**

5. **Negotiate as if relationships mattered.**

Figure 1.6

Challenging the Conventional Wisdom

appeal to the state court system. How do they value that BATNA? Their lawyers may tell them that they have a strong and convincing case if they ever get to court. But before taking this path, the executives need to consider its costs and benefits. If they pursue this option, they will incur direct costs relating to the salaries and fees of their staff, consultants, and attorneys. They will also incur indirect costs. The staff that is involved in fighting the legal battle will not be available to do their regular jobs—to improve the productivity and efficiency of their manufacturing processes. There is the potential for ongoing, unfavorable media attention while the case is proceeding. If the case goes to court, it will probably be at least three years (from now) before a decision is reached, during which time the company and the products it produces will be branded with the "corporate polluter" label, potentially hurting their market share, profitability, and the cost of capital in financial markets. Finally, the legal process may do serious damage to the firm's relationship with the DEP enforcement staff, who monitor this and every other permit every day of the year for the rest of this company's life.

On the regulator's side, too, a BATNA analysis might offer strategic direction. Officials at the DEP have issued a notice of permit violation. Instead of reaching a negotiated resolution with the firm, they can proceed with the administrative and judicial review process, using staff time and other resources that might be applied to more significant violations. What if, at the end of that process, the agency's decision is overturned by the state court? That would set a terrible precedent and would seriously diminish the deterrent effect that the agency had hoped to accomplish through this enforcement action.

If you are involved in a situation like this and think you might want to pursue negotiations, you must recognize that the first stage of any negotiation occurs "away from the table." Analyze your BATNA. That is, conduct a systematic and thoughtful assessment. Consider ways in which your BATNA might be improved. In the example above, if you are the firm in question, prepare an accurate and thorough summary of your exemplary compliance record over the previous 10 years, a document you can present to an administrative law judge or trial court judge should litigation become necessary. If you are the DEP, prepare a detailed summary of the warnings you have given to the firm before the notice of violation was issued, a summary of the technical-assistance documents you offered the firm to help it deal with the problems it faces, and scientific studies proving the detrimental human health effects of this kind of violation.

Before entering the negotiation room, you also need to analyze the other party's BATNA. At what point will the other side be likely to walk away? Once the negotiation begins, you should raise doubts about the other side's BATNA. Perhaps the firm has not reviewed the record of litigation for this category of permits, and perhaps it does not know that, say, 3 percent of all cases are successfully appealed through the courts. Perhaps the DEP staff person is not aware of a recent case, identical to yours, in which the courts established a precedent that supports your actions. These kinds of discussions should not be put in the form of threats. Ideas and concepts should be presented as facts that can have an influence on the other party's calculation of its BATNA.

Clarifying Interests

The conventional wisdom relies on asserting "positions"—stated demands. The mutual gains approach relies on clarifying "interests"—underlying needs and concerns. Clarifying interests means explicitly discussing them. Traditional negotiators might view this as handing over valuable information. We view it as providing information essential to reaching an agreement. As long as you know your BATNA, you have not weakened your negotiating power by telling the other sides your interests. You have made it possible for them to help you meet your interests. If the other sides cannot or will not respond, your BATNA tells you when it is time to walk away.

In discussing negotiations, professor Roger Fisher of Harvard Law School often gives the example of two sisters cooking together, working on two separate recipes, each of which calls for an orange. There is, however, only one orange left in the house. Each sister states her position: "I need that orange." After further discussion, they learn of their underlying interests. One sister needs the juice of the orange for her recipe. The other needs the peel. A successful conclusion results because they have gone beyond their stated positions and have tried to understand each other's interests. If these archetypal siblings can do it, so can you!

Inventing Options

Our goal is to use people's natural problem-solving instincts to help them satisfy their interests. We want to create an environment in which parties feel free to invent creative solutions to their problems. This can be done through brainstorming, a process of discussion designed to defer criticism and to hold each person harmless for any suggestions he or she might make. During brainstorming, ownership of an idea should be separated from the idea itself—that is, ideas should be depersonalized by transferring them to flip charts without attribution. The brainstorming process should not involve any commitment beyond the commitment to be creative. No party should be obligated to endorse any idea that has been put up on the board, even its own!

The purpose of inventing options is to "expand the pie." Figure 1.7 is a graphical representation of such a process. If our negotiators have prepared carefully, Party A should not accept any agreement that is "west" of his BATNA, and Party B should not accept any agreement that is "south" of her BATNA. Thus, point 1 represents the minimally acceptable agreement for both Party A and Party B.

Objective Criteria

Now, let us assume that our brainstorming sessions have been productive. We have come up with ideas represented by points 2, 3, 4, and 5 on Figure 1.7. All of these options—to the "northeast" of point 1—represent packages that are better for both parties than their BATNAs. Indeed, points 3, 4, and 5 are special in that they provide a graphical "frontier" indicating how far to the northeast our two parties are able to go. Theoretically, either party should be content with an agreement that memorializes either point 3, point 4, or point 5; but in fact each party will not be equally content among these three

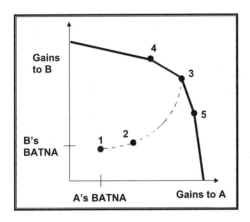

Figure 1.7
Creating and Claiming Value

points. Thus arises the issue of how to "claim" the value that the negotiation process has created.

It is important to find a way to engage in value claiming that maintains good working relationships. After all, the negotiators have invested significant time and resources and have made good progress. Why should they now backtrack? Moreover, they are going to have to work together—to live up to their commitments—in order to implement the agreement. Their relationship will be important to successful implementation. We offer the advice that the use of objective criteria in distributing value can help to maintain relationships. We give examples of this later.

Relationships

We have already foreshadowed the importance of relationships. It is possible to conduct a successful negotiation between two hostile parties, but it is much more productive when the parties have gained a measure of mutual trust. Such trust permits the parties to fully engage in the value creating process, and to calmly and clearly engage in a process of claiming the value that has been created. It also permits them to carefully design measures for monitoring the effectiveness of their agreement over time and modifying it in the future. We will give examples that support this premise later in this book, and we will shortly offer advice on how to build and maintain relationships.

Mutual Gains Approach to Negotiation

Figure 1.8 is a graphical display of the components of the mutual gains negotiation process. It provides a helpful "crib sheet" that is worth reviewing before entering each negotiation. We have already talked about the first three steps: preparation, creating value, and distributing value. The fourth step is equally important. This "follow through" step addresses the implementation of agreements and ensures that the desired results are obtained. Follow through involves five key substeps.

The first is to agree, as part of the negotiation, on procedures and approaches to be used in monitoring the implementation of a negotiated agreement. In a negotiation over

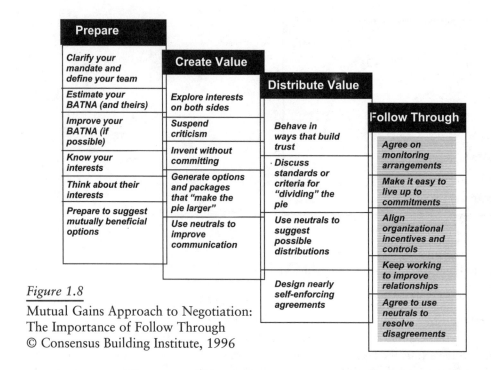

Figure 1.8

Mutual Gains Approach to Negotiation:
The Importance of Follow Through
© Consensus Building Institute, 1996

air emissions, for example, the parties should decide whether the corporation will conduct self-monitoring and report the results to the DEP, or perhaps contract with an independent laboratory to take samples. Alternatively, the DEP itself could conduct the monitoring. The parties will also have to determine how the information collected will be stored and distributed. We have been surprised by how many agreements fail to address these particulars. They are crucial to the successful implementation of an agreement, as well as to the ability of parties to reach other agreements in the future.

The second substep suggests that the parties should agree to measures that are achievable and that make it likely everyone will be able to live up to their commitments. "Stretching" is admirable in some cases, but here we are trying to reach sustainable agreements, so it is important to be realistic about mutual expectations. Success will breed future success. Unnecessary failure tends to breed distrust and future difficulties.

The third point, aligning organizational incentives and controls, means that the parties should assign monitoring responsibilities for a negotiated settlement to the organization(s) that have the most interest in ensuring that those obligations are met.

The fourth point is to keep working to improve relationships. The obvious reason for this is that the negotiators may well be facing each other once again at some time in the future. Now that they have built a foundation of trust, they should look for opportunities to reinforce that trust.

Finally, if there are future disagreements, parties should consider the use of professional neutrals (mediators and facilitators) to help resolve them. Even the best-intentioned parties often have difficulty going through the steps we have prescribed without outside help. It is now common practice in commercial contracts to provide for mediation as part of a contractual dispute resolution procedure. The same approach can be applied to environmental agreements.

Negotiating as if Relationships Mattered

In simulated negotiations, people "take on" their roles within minutes of reading their instructions. Within a short time, the individual playing "the regulator" or "the CEO" or "the environmental activist" becomes that person and tends to act in the stereotypical manner often assigned to such positions in society. The old adage, "where you stand depends on where you sit," has stunning applicability in these simulations.

What is striking, too, is that, within seconds of taking on their roles, workshop participants adopt the classic signs of distrust toward the other parties in the negotiation. The late Jeffrey Rubin discussed this dynamic at length in his book *Social Conflict: Escalation, Stalemate, and Settlement* (1994). He noted that a person's preconceptions about someone else strongly influence how that person views the statements and actions of the other. For example, if Party A enters a negotiation believing that Party B has a tendency to use imprecise language to avoid making explicit commitments, Party A will tend to interpret every statement Party B makes as supporting that preconception. If Party A sees Party B making a decision that Party A views as distasteful, Party A will attribute that action to disingenuousness, malevolence, or worse. In contrast, Party A knows that when he has to make a decision like that, he will be doing it for the best possible reasons, within a context of the highest personal integrity and honesty.

In light of these tendencies, it is especially important to the success of a negotiation for the parties to establish, build, and maintain trusting relationships (see Figure 1.9). We do not say that you should "negotiate as if relationships mattered" for altruistic rea-

---

- **Don't jeopardize long-term relationships by pushing too hard for short-term gain.**

- **Effective "cross-cultural" negotiation depends upon making sure you are being understood.**

- **The rewards of modest risk-taking are substantial.**

- **There will always be tension between the advantages of cooperation and the need to "compete."**

- **Good negotiators develop a repertoire of negotiating styles.**

- **You have to talk about a relationship to improve it.**

Figure 1.9

Negotiating as if Relationships Mattered

sons. We say it because the relationship creates the foundation upon which parties to a negotiation will be able to create value, distribute value, and follow through on their agreements.

We also know that it can be difficult to establish, build, and maintain trusting relationships. We offer suggestions here, but we remind our readers that negotiation is a means to an end and that your BATNA analysis is the linchpin of the whole strategy. If a failure to create productive relationships—notwithstanding your best efforts—means that you cannot achieve a result that is better than your BATNA, it is time to walk away from the negotiations, either permanently or until you can change the atmosphere or the context.

The techniques we offer in Figure 1.9 are, by nature, somewhat imprecise because they attempt to describe interpersonal relationships; but we have found them useful in our own negotiations. Most of the items are self-explanatory, but the last one is probably the most important: "You have to talk about a relationship to improve it." We are suggesting that a portion of your time at or near the negotiating table be devoted to an explicit discussion of the relationship among the parties. We are not urging a touchy-feely therapeutic analysis, but we are suggesting that you use a series of questions to give the other party a chance to comment on the quality of the negotiation process. For example: "Do you feel that we are giving each other a chance to fully explain our interests to one another?" "Am I being clear in how I explain things?" "Do you feel that I am getting a good understanding of your concerns?" "Are we giving proper consideration to how each of us will deal with our constituencies on returning to the office?"

In brainstorming, we usually advise against asking "yes/no" questions; in that context, a "no" can often close off potentially useful ideas. Here, though, a "yes" or a "no" is desired. We are jointly evaluating the process and our relationship, and we need to be extremely forthcoming to do that effectively. Some people find it helpful to set aside time during a negotiation to deal with relationship issues. Others look for natural opportunities to do so—just before or after coffee breaks or lunch breaks, or just before or after a session formally adjourns for the day.

Negotiating Permits

We now seek to challenge the conventional wisdom about permit negotiations—cases in which regulatory agencies often assume they have little discretion in writing permits and in which firms often assume that they have to create unbreachable walls of corporate resistance to protect their bottom lines. Our premise is that the mutual gains approach offers regulators an opportunity to accomplish a greater level of environmental protection than is dictated by the language of their enabling statutes (see Figure 1.10). Likewise, we assert that corporations can employ the mutual gains approach to derive permitting agreements that benefit from the regulators' discretionary authority to be more sensitive to the commercial interests of the firm.

In the following pages, we contrast the conventional approach a firm might use in seeking a permit with the approach it might use by following the mutual gains approach. The key characteristic of the conventional approach to note is that the firm's offerings are presented in a way that will inevitably be viewed by the regulators

> **Objectives of this exercise**
>
> **To challenge the conventional wisdom about regulatory negotiation.**
>
> **To introduce the " mutual gains approach " to regulatory negotiation.**

Figure 1.10

Negotiating Permits

as inelastic positions. Is there any reason to doubt what the regulator's response will be? The conventional wisdom offers no opportunity for joint problem solving. It creates a tennis court environment: One party hits the ball to the other party's side of the court as hard as possible, and then he or she hits it back with equal force. Eventually, one of them will tire or miss a shot. The mutual gains approach envisions the two parties as players on the same team in a doubles match, with the problem of defining a mutually beneficial outcome as the opponent. The two parties stand side by side, unsure of how they will handle what comes over the net, but cooperating to win the point together.

The mutual gains approach is designed, first, to secure an understanding of the other party's interests. This can only occur if conversations take place before a final permit application is submitted to a regulatory agency. Mid-level staff can meet, talk, and exchange information in a manner that does not bind either organization. The regulatory staff can discuss their statutory mandates and the precedents provided by previously issued permits. The firm can offer background on its industrial processes and earlier efforts to control pollution. Both can explain the decision-making structure of their respective organizations and the time and resource pressures under which they must operate.

We suggest that a firm openly present regulators with a range of options it could pursue to meet all relevant environmental laws. Under the conventional wisdom, this would be viewed as "giving away" too much information. We do not in any sense view this as a give-away. The firm still controls the decision about the options it chooses to present. Presumably, it will only present options that are financially and technically plausible. By presenting alternatives, though, it is offering the regulators a chance to analyze and comment in a way that provides the firm with a clearer sense of the agency's underlying interests. Instead of submitting one plan and waiting to see what the agency wants, the agency is invited to engage in a joint problem-solving exercise. Instead of raising suspicion and enmity among the regulatory staff by putting outside pressure on the agency to accept the single, final package submitted by the firm, a setting has been created that can lead to long-lasting, working relationships.

We understand that bureaucratic forces can result in delays. Here, too, we see a striking opportunity to resolve the problem. The conventional wisdom suggests increasing the pressure on the agency, threatening to use political ties or public relations to force agency action. Our advice is to call, once again, on the relationships that can be established and, in a nonthreatening way, discuss and reach a consensus on likely timetables. We know that agency personnel might feel reluctant to make commitments. After all, they have limited resources and never know when a higher-priority case might come through the door. Our approach relies on the use of shared knowledge, on the standards that have been established by previous agency action on similar permits, and on asking for ways in which to facilitate a more timely review. Because this approach is grounded in a respectful understanding of the forces and constraints operating on the agency, it requires the firm to make an effort to understand what those forces and constraints are.

It is ironic that corporations must be trained to behave in this manner with regulators. Every day of the year, in its interactions with suppliers and customers, a firm engages in an extensive pattern of consultation that enhances its own profitability as well as the needs of its business partners. We are advocating here that a business operate with a similar corporate imperative in its dealings with regulatory staff. Whether one views the regulator as a supplier of an essential production input—a permit—or as a customer with a strong interest in corporate environmental responsibility, there is good reason to treat that regulator as a business partner, as important as any other key supplier or customer. In fact, given the overwhelming influence that a regulatory agency has over corporate operations and profitability, it is hard to believe that a company would treat the regulator in any other fashion. But we know from experience that the kind of relationship we have been discussing is often foreclosed by the conventional wisdom. For the sake of its own well-being, a firm should devote the managerial, personnel, and financial resources necessary to pursue and carry out the mutual gains approach.

Key Issues in Permit Negotiations

Figure 1.11 illustrates the three key issues involved in most permit negotiations: the information that must be provided to regulators before the permit is approved and after it is issued; deadlines and timetables for meeting certain physical process standards and/or data requirements; and the process by which the permitting rules will be applied. Compared with the conventional wisdom regarding how to deal with these issues, the mutual gains approach offers no disadvantages—in time, money, or results—while providing the opportunity for superior outcomes.

- **Can you negotiate information requirements?**

- **Can you negotiate deadlines or time lines?**

- **Can you negotiate how rules will be applied in your case?**

Figure 1.11

Key Issues in Permit Negotiations

Permit Negotiation Example 1

The first scenario, described in Figure 1.12, concerns a company that knows it must receive a permit from the state before it can proceed with construction of a new facility. The conventional approach involves little or no interaction between the company and the regulatory agency during the design process. The company hires professionals to prepare a set of construction plans that will meet the manufacturing or other objectives of the corporation. When complete, these plans are delivered by a top corporate official to a senior regulatory official, usually with a statement akin to the following: "We are really in a hurry to begin construction of this plant and ask you to expedite your review and approval of our plans."

When put in this position, there is very little the regulatory official can say, beyond, "Thank you. We have a big backlog of permit requests, but we will get to it as soon as we can. Who in your company can my staff call if they have questions?" The corporate executive leaves with a sense of frustration, knowing that the application is now sitting in a stack on someone's desk.

What if the executive were to try the mutual gains approach instead? Using this approach, the corporation would seek to learn the underlying interests of the regulatory agency before showing up with a formal proposal. It would send mid-level staff to meet with the agency's mid-level staff—the ones who will ultimately perform the permit review—to ask questions about the relevant regulations and permit requirements. For example, what precedents exist in this area? What design suggestions have found favor in the past? What kinds of information would be helpful to the regulators when the application is finally submitted? Would the agency be amenable to conducting a preliminary review or simply offering comments on a number of options under consideration

A company knows it must receive a permit from a particular state regulatory agency before it can construct a new facility. How and when should it interact with the agency staff?

The Conventional Wisdom

The company should hire professional staff to prepare its construction plans. When they are complete, the company should prepare its permit application. With the completed application in hand, the company should send a top official to meet with the most senior person in the regulatory agency who will meet with them.

The Mutual Gains Approach

The company should send middle-level staff to meet with middle-level staff of the regulatory agency to learn more about the relevant regulations and permit requirements. The company should describe its interests and try to understand the agency's interests. The company should then develop multiple options for review by senior agency staff <u>before it finalizes its plans or permit applications</u> .

Figure 1.12
Permit Negotiation Example 1

by the company? Given the workload facing the agency, what is a realistic timetable for action?

Corporate officials will immediately recognize that this is precisely the kind of analysis that is done within a company when decisions are being made about expanding production capacity. Teams are created to evaluate likely customer demand, and contacts are made with potential customers who can provide useful feedback and ideas. Teams are created, too, to share ideas among the design staff, the construction staff, and the operating staff to ensure that whatever plant is designed meets everyone's needs. Companies do this because they know that flexibility decreases over time: The closer they get to construction, the fewer are opportunities for design changes that can improve a facility's cost-effectiveness.

When we look at it this way, it is almost inconceivable that a similar approach would not be employed in dealing with environmental regulatory agencies. After all, agencies can have as large an impact on the success of a new facility as any other party, internal or external to the company. Why wouldn't a company try to bring the professional staff of the agency into the process as early as possible, while there is still flexibility in the design process?

Permit Negotiation Example 2

Figure 1.13 describes a scenario in which a company has already completed what it considers to be its final plans and permit requests. How should they submit these plans to the agency?

The conventional wisdom suggests that the company first bring in lawyers to review the permit application to ensure it meets all legal requirements. Then, the company should file the package with the agency and contact political figures in the legislative and executive branch to put pressure on the agency to act quickly.

Assume that a company has developed what it considers to be final plans and permit requests. How should these be submitted to the agency?

The Conventional Wisdom

General counsel or outside legal staff should review the final application to be sure it meets the letter of the law. Examples or models of successful applications should be used as a basis for determining "what the agency wants." The final package should be submitted to the agency while endorsements are sought from appropriate members of the legislative and executive branches.

The Mutual Gains Approach

A "nearly final" version of the permit application should be reviewed with middle-level agency staff and then with top-level staff. Contingent modifications should be explored. A timetable for final review should be discussed. Relevant examples of previously approved permits should be requested. Information requirements should be examined. The advantages and disadvantages of "sponsorship" should be discussed.

Figure 1.13

Permit Negotiation Example 2

But imagine that you are a senior official in the agency. You have just received the application, as well as a phone message from a legislator saying how important this project is. Being responsive, you return the call to the legislator and thank her for her interest and explain that there is a large backlog of other applications because of funding cutbacks for the agency, but that you will do the best you can. If you feel true political pressure, you send the application to your civil service permit staff asking them to expedite it, and they respond that they will do the best they can. You will likely be rather resentful that the company is creating extra hassles for you and altering your normal work flow.

Under the mutual gains approach, the company would have first come to a more thorough understanding of the interests and concerns of the agency by talking to people involved in the permitting process. Mid-level company employees would have taken a "nearly final" version of the permit application to the agency to explore with mid-level staff whether and what types of modifications might be necessary to facilitate the issuance of the permit. The company would ask for recent relevant examples of permits and discuss how and if their particular case is covered by precedents. They would ask explicitly what types of information would be helpful to the agency in reaching a decision. If they feel comfortable bringing up the issue of political sponsorship, they should determine whether such sponsorship would in fact be helpful. The agency might be negative or neutral toward such involvement, or it might view such intervention as a way of strengthening its own support in the state legislature.

Permit Negotiation Example 3

Finally, we look at a scenario involving a company that has been waiting some time for a final decision on its completed permit application (see Figure 1.14). Telephone calls are not being returned. What should the company do?

The company has been waiting for some time for a final decision on its completed permit application. Telephone calls are not being returned. What should they do?

The Conventional Wisdom

The company should ask counsel to send a formal letter to the agency indicating what the company's legal options are if they are not given a favorable review quickly. The company should "step up the pressure" by exploiting political ties or favorable public relations.

The Mutual Gains Approach

Senior company personnel should seek a meeting with middle-level staff of the agency. The focus of the meeting should be on how the relevant rules and regulations are typically applied in a case "like this one." Deadlines and timetables should be discussed and put in writing if possible. Questions about how to facilitate a more timely review should certainly be asked. A summary of the meeting should be sent in writing to top agency staff.

Figure 1.14
Permit Negotiation Example 3

The conventional wisdom is to take a hard line, sending formal letters (threatening or not) to the head of the agency, asking political figures to intervene, or attempting to use the press or other public relations techniques to put pressure on the agency.

Most regulators would not respond well to this kind of pressure. In fact, they might become suspicious; they might think something is really wrong with the permit application and a longer and more extensive review is warranted. Even if they succumbed to the political pressure and forced their staff to issue the permit, they might be hostile toward that company in the future, perhaps ramping up compliance and enforcement activities to make sure the permit requirements are met.

The mutual gains approach provides an opportunity for the company to find out what is going on with the permit application in a helpful and trust-building fashion. It suggests that company officials meet with the mid-level staff of the agency and gain a better understanding of how the rules and regulations are usually applied in this kind of case. The company should ask about timetables and expectations, and what it can do to facilitate a more timely review. When the meeting is over, the company should send a summary of the meeting to all those in attendance—as well as senior agency staff—to memorialize the discussions.

The company's goal here, as above, is to develop a working relationship with the permitting staff and garner a sense of the agency's underlying interests. Having done this, there is the potential to introduce ideas, information, and approaches that can expedite the process in a manner consistent with the agency's view of its mandate. In contrast, the conventional wisdom causes relationships to suffer and stymies the transfer of useful information among the parties.

Key Elements of Negotiation Theory

Figure 1.15 restates the major concepts introduced in the previous pages. In our Negotiating Environmental Agreements workshop, it serves as an introduction to the Carson Extension simulation (see Part 2), which presents a multi-issue, multiparty negotiation, the successful resolution of which requires application of all the principles presented. We

- **Analyze and try to improve your BATNA. Raise doubts about their BATNA.**

- **Probe to clarify your interests and theirs.**

- **Invent options that meet your interests and theirs.**

- **Use objective criteria to argue for the "package" you favor.**

- **Negotiate as if relationships mattered.**

Figure 1.15

Key Elements of Negotiation Theory

thus go into more detail here in explaining some of the nuances of the five key elements of the mutual gains approach to negotiation.

"Analyze and try to improve your BATNA. Raise doubts about their BATNA."

Many people enter a negotiation without a true understanding of their own BATNA. This might be a result of wishful thinking, a lack of rigorous analysis of their own situation, or simply inadequate preparation. A BATNA analysis must be conducted before entering a room with other parties. If a party does not try to define and improve his or her BATNA "away from the table," the tactical decisions made at the table are likely to be less effective.

To enter discussions without knowing one's best alternative to a negotiated agreement is like bidding in an auction without knowing the balance in your bank account. Will you "win" the negotiation only to discover that you have insufficient funds? Or will you "lose" the negotiation only to find that you had more to offer?

Analyzing one's own BATNA requires an unsentimental analysis of what will happen if you cannot reach an agreement. If you represent a firm and you are taken to court by a regulatory agency or a public interest group, what are the direct and indirect costs of litigation? Beyond the legal fees and costs of expert witnesses, what will be the effect of the litigation on your corporate image? Do you produce a product or service that is sensitive to negative publicity, especially negative publicity relative to environmental issues? What are the likely fines and penalties if you lose in court? What actions might you be required to take if you lose, and what is their cost?

If you are a regulator, you too must carefully consider your BATNA before coming to the table. If the negotiation does not succeed, what are your agency's direct and indirect costs of taking a firm to court? What departmental resources will you use that might be better applied? What is the political effect of taking a major employer through the legal wringer? Does the case improve your ability to gain voluntary compliance with other industries, or might other firms view the case as an unnecessary diversion of your enforcement resources?

Evaluating the other party's BATNA is as important, and often more complex, than analyzing your own. It is the relationship between the two parties' BATNAs that creates what is called the "zone of possible agreement" (ZOPA). It is often possible to know more about the other party's BATNA than might seem obvious at first; but this, too, requires extensive pre-negotiation work. You must review the questions we have just asked above from the point of view of the other side. Put yourself in their shoes. Gather information from sources who face the same situation as the other negotiators.

Many of us have been in situations in which a strong-minded member of our negotiating team has said, "This will be our final offer, and they will just have to take it!" Such an approach might seem impressive, but if the offer is no better than the other party's BATNA, they will not take it. Our team can then find itself, by default, forced to accept our own BATNA, a result worse than we could have achieved if we had offered a pretty good alternative to the other side that would also have been acceptable to us (better than our BATNA).

BATNAs are not static. They can change before a negotiation begins, and they can change during the course of a negotiation. The multiparty Carson case exemplifies this. A firm (Carson Rug Company) has been found out of compliance in a past enforcement action and, absent a negotiated settlement, faces the possibility of a renewed court battle and penalties (its BATNA). One of the parties to the dispute is the local environmental group, Green Earth. At the outset of the negotiation, Green Earth seems to have a strong BATNA; they believe they have a good chance of winning the case in court if a settlement is not reached. The dynamics of the negotiation, however, typically raise doubts about Green Earth's perception of its BATNA and make it more likely to join an agreement. This can occur because the other parties to the settlement discussion (the town, the firm and its engineering consultant, and the environmental regulators) can decide to reach agreement among themselves, even if Green Earth will not sign on. They could then present this settlement to a judge if the case does go to court. A judge seeing such an agreement—supported by most of the key interest groups—might be more inclined to accept it than the uncompromising position offered by Green Earth.

The lesson here is fundamental to any negotiator's strategy. Work hard to estimate your own BATNA and understand the other party's BATNA. The range between the two creates a "zone of possible agreement." At the same time, recognize that BATNAs are dynamic, and you can take actions to improve your own BATNA or to cause the other party to reevaluate their BATNA.

"Probe to clarify your interests and theirs."

We discussed earlier the importance of distinguishing positions from interests, and here we emphasize the techniques that can be used to do so. In the now-classic story of the negotiation between Israel and Egypt after the Six-Day War, the main issue in dispute was the disposition of the Sinai Peninsula (see Fisher, Ury, and Patton, 1991, 41–42). Israel had taken possession of the Sinai during the war, and the positions after the war were clear: Egypt wanted it back, and Israel wanted to keep it. Then, President Carter helped the two sides clarify their interests. Egypt's interest was one of sovereignty. The Sinai had long been part of Egypt's history and heritage, and it was a matter of national pride that it should be owned by that country. Israel, however, had an interest in security. It feared that giving up control of the Sinai would permit the land to be used by Egypt or other Arab countries as a staging area for an invasion force. Once this distinction between interests and positions was made clear, an agreement was forthcoming: Sovereignty over the Sinai would return to Egypt (the Egyptian flag would fly), but the area would be demilitarized. With Egyptian troops nowhere near its borders, Israel's security interest was protected.

In the environmental arena, firms and regulators often do not understand one another's interests and thus tend to focus unprofitably on unhelpful positions. A firm's statement, "We cannot meet that emissions standard" often means, "We cannot profitably meet that emissions standard the way you regulators want us to. We are willing to make environmental improvements if we can do so in a way that is financially feasible and either improves or does not degrade our competitive position in the marketplace. We care about the quality of life in our community and want to present ourselves as good environmentalists." A regulator's statement, "You have to meet this emission standard" often means "We are trying to achieve certain environmental goals for our state. If you cannot do it the way we have said, show us an alternative that meets our standard and can be monitored to ensure that it does so over time. We care about jobs in our community and want to meet environmental standards in a way that maintains or improves your competitive position in the marketplace."

We are not so naive as to think that the process of clarifying interests is easy or that it will be accomplished in the first conversation between a regulator and a firm. We know from experience, though, that a willingness to begin the process is essential to reaching satisfactory agreements.

"Invent options that meet your interests and theirs."

Inventing options is the heart of a negotiation because it enables the parties to move "northeast" on the Creating and Claiming Value chart (Figure 1.7) and design an agreement that has the potential to offer both parties an improvement over their BATNA. Much has been written on this subject, but the key concept we seek to introduce here is that of "trading across differences," a process that offers an opportunity to create value.

Trading across differences is based on the assumption that two parties will value the same attribute in a different way. That difference becomes a commodity that can be offered in trade. The concept is analogous to international trading of goods or service, in that the act of trading improves the relative position of all parties.

In the Sinai example, President Carter was able to take the two countries' differing needs and values and use the Sinai peninsula itself in trade. This same object, a piece of land, was valued in different ways by the two parties, and the agreement between the two countries permitted each side to obtain the value it wanted from the land. Note that the peninsula itself did not move or change; the contractual relationship concerning the peninsula changed, to the satisfaction and betterment of both parties.

Let's explore other types of differences that can be traded to create value. There are many such examples in commercial relationships; indeed, they are what make such relationships possible. Here, we focus on a few examples that are particularly relevant to negotiating environmental agreements.

1. *The Time Value of Money.* Different parties may have differing discount rates, offering the possibility of trading across the timing of payments. For example, a firm that has the right to pay a penalty over a number of years is, from its point of view, paying less money than if the penalty were all to be paid immediately. This is because the company knows that it can use "the same" money differently during the intervening years, and those uses have a financial value. Thus, the firm has a high discount rate. An environmental regulator, however, may be indifferent to the time value of money. He or she is interested in announcing the total amount of the penalty, to demonstrate decisive action against a polluter. Whether a penalty is paid now or over time is not so important. Thus, the regulator has a low discount rate. The difference in the time value of money can become a tradeable commodity that produces value in the negotiation. Specifically, the same penalty paid over several

years (rather than immediately) imposes a different (lower) cost on the polluter. The regulator can announce the fine now and achieve the full "benefit."

2. *Services and Goods.* One party may view services and goods provided in terms of their retail value, but the other party may value those services at their wholesale value. An engineering firm involved in an environmental dispute might be willing to provide additional consulting services to help solve a problem, because it values those services at the firm's internal marginal cost. A regulator, however, knowing that another firm will charge its fully loaded retail price for such work, might be content to let the targeted company offer in-kind services as part of a compliance package. The difference in the perceived value of an hour of work becomes the tradeable difference that allows an agreement to be reached.

3. *Publicity.* One party may view publicity as important, while the other might view it as secondary. A regulator might allow a firm to announce an agreed-upon compliance action in a way that enhances the firm's reputation in financial or commercial markets. This announcement might be key to the company's long-term cost of financing or to maintaining market share. Meanwhile, the agency has achieved its deterrent goals with regard to other industries because the compliance action has gone ahead with no fear of appeal. The difference in the value of publicity is the tradeable commodity that helps produce agreement.

4. *Expectations About the Future.* Commercial enterprises often deal with different expectations of the future by designing contingent contracts. So, too, can regulators and regulated firms use their disparate expectation of future events to construct environmental agreements that include contingent responsibilities. A Rhode Island paint finishing company that had grown rapidly in the prior three years, for example, was unsure of its future level of growth. It reached an agreement with the state DEP that would permit certain levels of emissions up to a given limit, becoming more stringent if the company grew and reached higher levels of output. Company officials did not think that the business would continue to grow very quickly, but it knew that, if it did, it would have the revenues to dedicate to enhanced emission controls. The DEP knew that if the company remained small, it would not be a significant contributor to regional emissions, and so it would not need enhanced emission controls. But the agency expected that the company might grow dramatically, in which case a higher level of controls would be required. The difference in the parties' expectations about the future was incorporated into the agreement as a contingent obligation, permitting a trade that helped close the negotiation amicably.

These examples provide insight into how trading across differences can be used to create value for the parties in a negotiation. The process of inventing these options is a key part of any negotiation, and certain tactical approaches can facilitate the process. The use of brainstorming is very helpful, for example. In such sessions, the parties toss ideas out for later consideration, reserving criticism for the period following the brainstorming session. Another technique is to ask "What if?" questions, which prompt both sides to respond creatively.

"Use objective criteria to argue for a 'package' you favor."

Once value is created, it must be shared, and it is fair to say that many potential settlements founder on the issue of distributing the value that has been created during the earlier stage of a negotiation. If we return to our Creating and Claiming Value chart (Figure 1.7) we see that both parties are better off at points 3, 4, and 5 than they would be at point 1. You can bet, though, that the choice among those three points is as ripe for controversy as has been the movement from point 1 to the northeast "frontier." How can the parties share the value that has been created?

Tomes have been written about this subject, and we do not present here an exhaustive review of the literature. Rather, we simply advocate the use of objective criteria to help make this decision. By objective, we do not mean "technically correct." Objective in this instance refers to "ready and replicable measurability." Objective criteria for dividing value might include the following: "From each according to his ability and to each according to his need" or "Whatever is most likely to generate additional value in the future" or "However we divided the value the last time." A reference to precedents, as in this last statement, is an appeal to an objective criterion. Negotiators should ask: Are there measurable criteria that can help justify one solution versus another? And, when all else fails, in the absence of any objective criteria, can we split the difference equally between two attractive alternatives?

The difficulty that arises in jointly deciding how to share value is that each side in a negotiation will appeal to the objective criterion that is likely to give them the largest share of the value created. We offer no simple solution to this problem, but we do suggest that the ability of the parties to resolve this issue depends in great measure on the relationship that has been established between them. One side will feel more comfortable agreeing to the other's proposed criterion if the first believes he or she might be able to get more back later in future dealings. Note that we are not proposing that you adopt an altruistic viewpoint in reaching this conclusion: You are agreeing to a division of the pie in this instance because you believe that it is in your interest to do so over the long run. As Roger Fisher often points out, it is inappropriate to trade results for the relationship.

"Negotiate as if relationships mattered."

Relationships do matter, so it is important to act as though they do. No firm is going to work with a regulatory agency only once, and no agency is going to have only one interaction with a firm. If you represent a firm, view each conversation with your regulator as one in a series of business relationships, just as you would with a customer or supplier. If you are a regulator, view each conversation with a firm as one that will be reported throughout the body politic to legislators, your executive branch supervisors, and industry groups. The past spreads a long shadow. Trust is something that takes a long time to build up, but that is easily lost. We offer two simple rules. During a negotiation, "Say what you mean, and mean what you say." And when it comes time to act on the results of a negotiation, "Say what you are going to do. Then do it."

Beyond these rules, it is prudent to remember that it is easier to maintain relationships if you avoid a test of will. We have found that is helpful to focus on aspects of the relationship that build trust over time. In international negotiations among long-warring parties, diplomats often create scenarios that invoke "confidence-building measures." Knowing that a complete solution to hostilities may not be possible as the product of the first round of talks, ambassadors will agree to small steps that are easily achievable by both sides. They might, for example, agree to a two-week cease-fire to permit medical and food supplies to reach civilian casualties. The cease-fire, if successful, creates some confidence that the other party is to be trusted, and a basis has been established that allows the parties to move on to more complicated issues. Over time, a comprehensive settlement becomes possible.

A process that builds relationships enables parties to deal productively with one or the other's inadvertent failure to carry out some portion of a negotiated agreement, or with a future request by either party to modify the agreement based on new circumstances. One side is more likely to give the other the benefit of the doubt if the first feels that the second negotiated in good faith and did his or her best to carry out the terms of the agreement. This is an important consideration because many agreements need to be updated, modified, or completely reconsidered in light of unexpected changes or events.

Part 2

Putting Your Skills to the Test

The best way to practice and hone mutual gains negotiation skills is to test them in real-life environmental disputes. This can be risky, of course. When the stakes are high, no one wants to experiment with tools and techniques they have not yet mastered. It takes time to develop the confidence and dexterity needed to use these techniques effectively. Yet, without some kind of field test, there is no way to sharpen these skills.

The next best option is a highly structured simulation—a "game" that involves a hypothetical set of circumstances similar to those a negotiator is likely to confront in the real world. A good simulation puts a person in a realistic but manageable negotiation situation that is guaranteed to test newly acquired skills in a short period of time. Simulations provide a protected setting in which people can try new ways of doing things with few, if any, risks to their professional standing or ego.

Simulations are not the same as two other teaching tools with which they are often confused: case studies and role plays. Case studies are stories, usually written in a chronological fashion, that summarize real situations. They often include snippets of after-the-fact interviews with the people involved and some independent analysis of what occurred. When case studies are used in a classroom or workshop, the instructor can ask what the participants might have done (differently) at a key moment in the story. Participants are thereby encouraged to put themselves "in another person's shoes" and think about how they might have handled a particular situation.

Role plays are similar. They seek to capture a moment in a real or a hypothetical case at which decisions or actions were required. Typically, an instructor asks participants to take on the role of a character in the story and "play act" that part, sometimes in concert with others who have been assigned other parts. The participants then decide how they want to proceed. That is, they are free to play their assigned roles in any way they feel is consistent with the story, as they understand it. Role playing works best when participants have first-hand knowledge of similar situations on which to draw.

Simulations are similar to case studies and role plays, but they are more elaborately scripted. They put more constraints on the participants. Simulations are typically written for two to eight players, each of whom is assigned a different role. Each player receives an identical set of "general instructions," and a unique set of "confidential instructions" specific to his or her character. The general instructions typically include a short account of a situation (not unlike a condensed case study) that provides a clear picture of an upcoming negotiation (i.e., who will be at the table and what has transpired prior to the parties arriving). Stories of this sort are usually based on a mixture of real and imagined situations. The general instructions are designed to set up the negotiations and cause a very specific set of conflicts to arise. The confidential instructions spell out what each character is expected to achieve in the negotiations. Thus, players are not free to interpret their character's desires as they see fit. On the contrary, they are given a minimum acceptable outcome that they must accomplish, a clear set of priorities and trade-offs among issues or options, and enough information to understand why they hold the views they do.

Some simulations are scorable; that is, outcomes are presented in numerical terms. So, a person playing the corporate CEO in a negotiation with an environmental agency head might need to achieve a minimum score of 45 points in order to be able to reach agreement, and a score of 55 points if they want to be sure to get that next bonus. The confidential instructions for the CEO would then spell out the point value of each of a half-dozen possible outcomes on each of three or four issues (such as whether they get a permit, when it will take effect, and what restrictions will be imposed on their production facility). Under each issue there may be four or five specific options, each assigned a different point value. So, for example, the CEO might get 25 points for securing a commitment from the agency to issue a permit within a month, 20 points for within 3 months, or 15 points for within 6 months. The player can then pursue the negotiation with a clear sense of a minimum acceptable result as well as a detailed understanding of his or her aspirations.

Scorable simulations enable people playing the same role in different rooms or at different tables to compare their results. If there are 48 people in a seminar, for example, 6 at each of 8 tables, and one person plays the CEO at each table, it is interesting to compare the outcomes achieved by the CEOs at each table. Results almost always vary significantly among groups, even though all the players have the same instructions. Players' interpretations of the instructions, as well as their reactions to the negotiating strategies and personal styles of the other negotiators, make a big difference. By discussing each table's results in the full-group setting, participants learn about the relative effectiveness of their negotiating strategies and techniques.

Players should follow two basic rules to get the most out of a simulation. First, each person must act in a manner consistent with his or her assigned role. If players ignore their confidential instructions, the simulation loses its validity. Second, participants must not show their confidential instructions to the other players at their table before or during simulation. That is, they must not use the written instructions to prove to their fellow negotiators that they "have to get" a certain result in order to agree to a settlement. They must rely on their negotiation skills to achieve the outcome they want.

In the pages that follow, we present the general instructions for five simulations: Gadgets, Inc.; ChemCo, Inc.; Bog Berries; MC Metals; and Carson Extension. At the beginning of each simulation, we highlight the objectives and key issues raised and conclude each simulation with a summary of the key lessons participants should take from it. At the end of Part 2 we provide a series of debriefing questions to help participants think about what they have learned. We have included the confidential instructions for only one of the games (Gadgets, Inc.), because we want to maintain the confidentiality of the simulations for those who intend to use them as a learning tool. The confidential instructions are, however, available on-line (at http://web.mit.edu/dusp/epg) for those who want to download them either for training or for further analysis. Each of the five simulations is described in more detail below.

Gadgets, Inc.: A Sample Case

Gadgets, Inc. is a six-party negotiation focusing on (1) the terms under which a company must get back into compliance with certain state environmental regulations, (2) the prospect of using new pollution prevention technology to meet existing pollution control guidelines, and (3) the difficulties of involving a range of environmental advocacy groups in a negotiation. Because these same issues are covered to greater or lesser degrees in the four games that follow, we review Gadgets, Inc. in some detail here.

Gadgets, Inc. is a midsized metal plating firm that has been out of compliance with state regulations for eight months. Specifically, it has been discharging unacceptable concentrations of heavy metals into the sewage system and the air. As required by state regulations, the company has submitted monthly reports that record the discharges of 15 contaminants. Although these reports clearly revealed the violations, the agency overlooked those violations for five months. The agency has recently undergone personnel changes, however, and is now pursuing enforcement actions.

Citing financial difficulties, past good-faith efforts, and its importance as a large employer in the area, Gadgets has asked for an extension in paying the fines while it explores options for getting back into compliance. The state Department of Environmental Protection (DEP) is under increasing pressure from two environmental groups (one moderate and one tending toward extreme views) to force Gadgets to comply or shut down.

In the middle of this debate, the DEP announced that a new pollution prevention technology (the CLEEN system) was successfully tested in an experimental setting and might be helpful to Gadgets. The negotiation that follows focuses on how to handle the uncertainty surrounding the use of a new, controversial technology as part of Gadget's compliance plan.

Specifically, four issues must be resolved by the six parties.

1. What technology should Gadgets use—the tried-and-true SCRUB system or the new CLEEN system?
2. If the CLEEN system is selected, will Gadgets be given a subsidy to cover part of the costs of the system and its installation?
3. What fines will Gadgets be required to pay, and must the company shut down until it is back in compliance?
4. What monitoring arrangements will be put in place, and who will pay for them?

Each of the six players is given a great deal of technical information in the general instructions, as well as a confidential briefing paper that reviews his or her personal and organizational concerns in detail. The organizations represented include the U.S. Environmental Protection Agency (EPA) regional office, the state DEP, Gadgets, the Gadgets Workers' Union, the Newberg Bay Society (a scientifically oriented environmental group), and Deep Green (a well-known, more "radical" environmental group). The group's goal is to reach consensus, or at least an agreement that at least five out of the six parties can support. Caucusing is allowed. They have one and a half hours to negotiate.

On the first issue—the choice of technology—four options have emerged as possibilities:

1. Repair the current SCRUB system.
2. Replace the current system with a new SCRUB system.
3. Install the new CLEEN system in an open-loop fashion.
4. Install the new CLEEN system in a closed-loop fashion, exempt from the Resources Conservation and Recovery Act (RCRA).

The second issue involves a possible subsidy for installing the CLEEN system, if that system is approved by the group. Three options are on the table:

1. Gadgets covers the entire expense.
2. Gadgets gets a subsidy for half the value of the initial cost: 35 percent from the DEP and 15 percent from the State Manufacturing Development Fund (SMDF).
3. A contingent offer: The state will pay 25 percent of the initial cost, and if CLEEN fails, the state will reimburse an additional 65 percent of the initial cost.

The third issue involves fines and whether or not Gadgets should temporarily close until it comes into compliance. Seven options have been suggested:

1. Gadgets remains open and all fines are forgiven.
2. Gadgets remains open and pays three months of fines.
3. Gadgets remains open and pays eight months of fines.
4. Gadgets remains open and pays fines until in compliance.
5. Gadgets is closed until in compliance and all fines are forgiven.
6. Gadgets is closed until in compliance and pays three months of fines.
7. Gadgets is closed until in compliance and pays eight months of fines.

On the fourth and final issue—monitoring—five options have been identified:

1. The state monitors monthly.
2. EPA monitors monthly.
3. The state monitors quarterly.
4. EPA monitors quarterly.
5. No additional monitoring.

Given all the interests and BATNAs (best alternative to a negotiated agreement) described in the confidential instructions of the parties, at least six possible five-way agreements can be reached. It is not possible to reach a six-way agreement. We can represent the "zone of possible agreement" (ZOPA) as shown in Table 2.1. (The numbers in the second and third columns refer to the option numbers above.)

We can display the terms of the conflict embedded in the negotiation in greater detail as well. The interests of the various parties are outlined in Table 2.2. The number before the period indicates the ranked importance of that issue to that player. The numbers after the period indicate, in order, that party's priority choices for that issue.

Table 2.1. Zone of Possible Agreement (ZOPA)

Issue	Possible 6-Way Options	Possible 5-Way Options
1. Choice of technology	2	2, 3
2. Potential subsidy	None, thus no 6-way agreement can happen	2
3. Fines	4	3, 4, 5
4. Monitoring	1, 2	1, 2

The following are two sample agreements, or packages. Note that the average scores represent a rough estimate of the overall rank of the package agreement. This does not have any meaning for comparing between players. It is only useful for comparing how one player does in two different packages.

Package 1 consists of the following set of options:

- CLEEN system is installed in an open-loop configuration.
- Gadgets gets a subsidy from the DEP/SMDF.
- Gadgets stays open and pays eight months of fines.
- The state monitors Gadgets' performance monthly.

Table 2.3 shows how the participants would rank each of the elements of Package 1 and derives an overall score for it.

Package 2 consists of the following four options:

- The CLEEN system is installed in an open-loop configuration.
- Gadgets gets a subsidy from the DEP/SMDF.
- Gadgets is closed until in compliance and all fines are forgiven.
- The EPA monitors Gadgets' performance monthly.

Table 2.4 shows how the participants would rank each of the elements of Package 2 and derives an overall score for it.

If you look closely at these two possible agreements, you will note that Gadgets and the Union are better off with Package 1, while the DEP, the EPA, and the Newberg Bay Society are better off with Package 2. These "better" scores are a function of two things: the specific option selected on an issue and the relative importance of the issue to each party. These are the key ingredients for creating value. It is possible to get very creative, to add new issues and conjure up evidence that none of the other players has in front of them. That is perfectly acceptable, and it underscores our point that it is almost always possible to create value.

In the end, no matter how much value is created, the distribution of that value will be contentious. Note that there are no agreements that can meet Deep Green's interests. Why are they at the table then, and why do they stay? In part because participating in these negotiations gives them access to information. Also, they may be able to form a blocking coalition by making a firm alliance with the Newberg Bay Society. Note also that no package is "best" for everyone. That's what makes the negotiation interesting!

Table 2.2. Conflict Assessment Matrix for Gadget Simulation

Party	Major Concern	Attitude Toward Technology	Choice of Technology	Subsidy (if CLEEN approved)	Fines and Temporary Closing	Monitoring	Political Issues
State DEP	Promote use of experimental technology, bring Gadgets into compliance	Want to use Gadgets as a test for CLEEN	1. 4,3,2,1	2. 1,2,3	4. 4,3,2,1,6,7,1	3. 2,4,3,1,5	Governor and mayor have pressed DEP to find a way to keep Gadgets in state
EPA	Ensure that state abides by standards of the Clean Water Act and Clean Air Act	Distrust new technology, suspicious of state's motives	1. 2,1,3,4	4. 1,2,3	2. 6,7,5,4,3,1,2	3. 1,2,3,4,5	State should not use permitting process to create lab for local prof, then reap profit
Gadgets, Inc.	Bottom line, expediency, public perception, market share	Don't care, want problem resolved quickly as possible	3. 4,3,1,2	2. 2,3,1	1. 1,2,3,4,5,6,7	4. 5,3,4,1,2	Has received offer from southern city to relocate
Gadgets Workers Union	Keep jobs and improve occupational safety	Concerned about asbestos, which would be released if closed-loop system installed	2. 3,2,1,4	3. 2,3,1	1. 1,2,3,4,5,6,7	4. 5,3,4,1,2	Offended by lack of concern over employment issues by Deep Green and Gadgets' VP
Deep Green	Avoid any risk to environment	Conflicting study indicates risk, offended by state's economic motives	3. 2,1,3,4	4. 3,1,2	2. 7,6,5,4,3,2,1	1. 2,1,4,3,5	Longstanding distrust of state environmental staff
Newberg Bay Society	Maintain high standard of bay water and air quality for habitat and recreational uses	Trust state, willing to take chance for immediate improvement	2. 4,3,2,1	4. 2,3,1	3. 5,6,7,4,32,1	1. 1,2,3,4,5	Has worked closely with DEP on citizen monitoring programs

Table 2.3. Participants' Scores for Package 1

Issue	#1	#2	#3	#4	Average Score (lower is better)
DEP	1.2	2.2	4.2	3.4	6
EPA	1.3	4.2	2.5	3.1	7.75
Gadgets	3.2	2.2	1.3	4.4	6.5
Union	2.1	3.1	1.3	4.4	5.25
Deep Green	3.3	NA	NA	1.2	—
NBS	2.2	4.1	3.5	1.1	5.25
					Total: 30.75

Table 2.4. Participants' Scores for Package 2

Issue	#1	#2	#3	#4	Average Score
DEP	1.2	2.2	4.4	3.1	5
EPA	1.3	4.2	2.3	3.2	6.75
Gadgets	3.2	2.2	1.5	4.5	8.75
Union	2.1	3.1	1.5	4.5	7.5
Deep Green	3.3	NA	2.3	1.1	—
NBS	2.2	4.1	3.1	1.2	4.25
					Total: 32.25

There are better and worse ways of dividing up the value created, however. Not only must all groups find something in the deal that exceeds their BATNA, they must believe that the overall allocation of value is fair.

In our workshop, following a careful debriefing of the results of this game, we would typically highlight the following points.

1. Interest groups may strongly oppose innovations in environmental technology for reasons that are unrelated to the quality of the improved technology.
2. While environmental organizations generally share the goal of protecting the environment, their values and strategies may vary profoundly.
3. Sometimes all the important issues are not on the table openly. "Hidden issues" can affect the negotiation in many ways. In the Gadgets simulation, a hidden issue (soil degradation from a chrome plater vent) can be used strategically by two key groups.
4. The promotion of innovative pollution prevention technology by regulatory agencies is shaped by:
   - Personal incentives for regulators involved in the decision-making process, and
   - The conflicting mandates of environmental agencies to both promote innovation and regulate effectively.
5. The quantitative analysis of acceptable outcomes shows how different parties fare better with different agreements. In some cases, a certain agreement is better for most players. These types of contrasting scores raise important public policy ques-

tions (such as who deserves a better agreement, which party can live with a worse agreement for the sake of others, and so forth).

We now provide short introductions to the four remaining simulations, all of which touch on similar issues and teach related lessons.

ChemCo, Inc.: Negotiating Compliance Review Before the Fact

ChemCo, Inc. maintains a coal-fired generating plant on its grounds to provide electricity for its manufacturing processes. The company is negotiating with the state Department of Environmental Protection (DEP) to devise an acceptable strategy for monitoring air emissions from the generating plant. The DEP and ChemCo have met several times to discuss this matter. In a final meeting, ChemCo's CEO, environmental engineer, and public relations officer will seek agreement with the DEP's air-quality branch chief, environmental engineer, and public affairs officer on five issues.

1. Which of three types of emissions monitoring systems will be used to ensure that ChemCo is complying with air emissions standards?
2. How often must ChemCo report to the DEP on its emissions monitoring results?
3. How often will ChemCo's pollution-abatement equipment be tested, and who will pay for the testing?
4. How much will ChemCo contribute to the construction of ambient air-quality monitoring stations in the community?
5. How will a "violation" of emissions standards be defined?

The objective of this exercise is to show how the mutual gains approach can be used to negotiate the terms by which compliance will be judged. Specifically, the parties are being asked to negotiate the monitoring methods to be used, the assignment of responsibility for data collection and interpretation, and how the validity of monitoring results will be assessed. To accomplish these objectives, the parties must find a mutually acceptable way to deal with uncertainty, cope with concerns about setting a precedent, deal with differences in interpretation of technical information, understand the sources of bargaining power, and come to grips with the importance of public perceptions.

Bog Berries and MC Metals: Negotiating Your Way Back into Compliance

Bog Berries, a Fortune 500 cranberry processing company, was recently charged by the Federal Environmental Agency (FEA) with six counts of intentionally dumping chemicals into municipal sewers near its plant—the first time felony charges were ever filed by the FEA under the revisions of the Clean Water Act. Bog Berries was also charged with 72 misdemeanor counts of discharging acidic cranberry peelings and other allegedly harmful chemicals into municipal sewers and the Nemasket River over a 50-year period. During this time, Bog Berries officials repeatedly ignored pleas from town officials to stop.

After 11 months of legal wrangling, Bog Berries and the FEA worked out a plea bargain. Bog Berries pleaded guilty to 20 misdemeanor charges and one count of releasing wastewater into the river. They also agreed to pay a $400,000 fine, plus $100,000 that would go toward a new water treatment facility.

Although the court case has ended, several issues must still be resolved. Bog Berries must buy new equipment to better handle its waste, and also must acquire a new discharge permit. In the aftermath of this bitter lawsuit, then, Bog Berries and FEA officials are set to meet to discuss the permit application protocol. The negotiators must wrestle with five key questions.

1. May Bog Berries continue operating while its permit application is being processed?
2. Which technology should Bog Berries use to comply with the federal regulations?
3. What kind of testing will the agency require to ensure that the chosen method meets the regulations?
4. How often will the testing be done?
5. When will the permit application be due? And how quickly will the agency process the application?

A similar set of issues is embedded in the third simulation, MC Metals, which deals with negotiations concerning worker safety and health. Two MC Metals employees were killed, and five other people, including three firefighters, were critically injured as the result of a chemical fire and explosion caused by the burning of waste sodium. Investigators from the State Fire Marshal's Office and the federal Occupational Safety and Health Administration (OSHA) blamed the company for the fire, charging that "MC Metals knowingly violated workplace safety standards. . . ."

OSHA has proposed a series of fines and corrective actions and is not inclined to let the company return to full-scale operations until OSHA's demands are met. The negative publicity has been extremely damaging to the company. MC Metals' parent company also faces several multimillion dollar lawsuits filed by the families of the dead and injured firefighters and workers. Under OSHA regulations, MC Metals can contest and negotiate the charges and fines it is facing. Four issues are on the agenda for the upcoming settlement conference.

1. The future of the company's hazard communication program, including its system for labeling hazardous chemicals and training its employees
2. The design and implementation of the company's first-aid program
3. A possible change in the "category of violation" with which the company is being charged, from the more severe "willful" category to the less-severe "serious" category
4. A possible reduction in the proposed fine

The OSHA team participating in the negotiations has some disagreement among its members about the most appropriate penalties and corrective actions. The company team includes participants with very different personal agendas.

Like the Gadgets game, the Bog Berries and MC Metals simulations both show how company officials and regulators can use the mutual gains approach to negotiate remedies and timetables for getting a firm back into compliance. These negotiations are more difficult than the before-the-fact negotiations covered in the ChemCo case; the talks are complicated by the self-righteousness of the regulators (who are convinced they are dealing with "bad guys"), a serious loss of trust on all sides, and the impact of public perceptions on the demands imposed by the regulators. In addition, both the Bog Berries and the MC Metals simulations point to the importance of clarifying interests on all sides before searching for possible solutions.

Carson Extension: Negotiating Settlement

Stuart Carson owns Carson Rug Company, a medium-sized firm situated on the banks of the Melrose River. In an effort to expand his commercial space, Carson applied for a Section 404 permit from the Army Corps of Engineers to install a fill and riprap seawall that would extend into the river. The application was denied, due to potentially harmful effects on the river's fish habitat. Carson's second application, which proposed a smaller extension, was deemed environmentally sound and was approved. Carson hired a reputable engineering firm to do the fill work. A year later, however, a Corps inspector discovered that the new seawall extended beyond the authorized boundaries set by the 404 permit. When the Corps of Engineers finally went to court, some years later, to order the removal of the unauthorized extension, the court ruled in the Corps' favor.

Now 15 years later, the illegally placed fill has still not been removed. The town finally issued an enforcement order to Carson to carry out the removal, but three new sets of questions have arisen.

1. At this point, will the removal of the fill cause more environmental harm than good?
2. How quickly does the solution need to be implemented?
3. Carson has already been ordered to pay two-thirds of the cost of environmental remediation. Should he pay other civil penalties as well? Or are other supplementary environmental projects a legitimate alternative?

In this case, representatives from the town, the Corps, local environmental groups, and the engineering firm are all at the table with Carson. The game can be played with a mediator or without; we have included the general instructions for the mediated version. This is an excellent opportunity to explore the circumstances under which a mediator can be of help.

The simulation is intended to show that the mutual gains approach can be applied in settlement negotiations even after legal action has been taken. It is designed to raise three key questions: (1) What causes regulatees to comply or not? (2) When and under what circumstances are enforcement threats effective? and (3) When and under what circumstances are trades (or incentives) more appropriate?

Reaching Agreement

A great many negotiated agreements are possible in each simulation. They all fit within the "rules of the game"—the mandates contained in the confidential instructions given to all the parties—although not every solution produces equally satisfying results for all players.

Unfortunately, some groups fail to reach any agreement at all, even though a great many solutions exist to each simulated conflict. Group debriefings typically reveal three reasons why negotiators reach impasse. First, the parties do not use their time wisely. They do not prepare well during the time allotted for individual preparation and do not use their time together constructively. Too much time is spent repeating demands (that have no chance of being accepted by others) and too little time is spent generating mutually acceptable proposals. Second, posturing and bluffing get in the way of real problem solving. People often start their negotiations in a way that offends or irritates others around the table. At that point, demands escalate and the behavior of the negotiators becomes the key obstacle to working out a solution. Third, some of the parties hold out for complete and total victory (no matter how unrealistic) and let reasonably good outcomes slip away.

These five simulations drive home the key message of this book: The way to get what you want in an environmental negotiation, whether you are a regulator, a regulatee, or a member of an affected community, is to search for a low-cost way of meeting the other sides' interests in exchange for reciprocity. The simulations provide a "safe" setting in which to try out this new approach.

Simulation 1

*Gadgets, Inc.**

General Instructions

Gadgets, Inc., a multipurpose metal plating firm, has been out of compliance with state regulations for discharge concentrations of heavy metals in wastewater and air emissions for eight months. As required by state environmental regulations, the firm has submitted reports each month to the state Department of Environmental Protection (DEP). The reports accurately recorded concentrations of 15 contaminants. The violations were overlooked by the DEP for the first five months. Following a change in the DEP personnel three months ago, the violations were noticed.

When the DEP took note of Gadgets' violations, it contacted the firm to say that Gadgets must come into compliance immediately and that the firm owed the state five months' worth of fines. Gadgets officials expressed surprise. They had always faithfully and accurately reported information on discharges and had never before heard anything from enforcement officials.

Gadgets is a midsized firm, and completing environmental compliance forms is a very small part of the overworked plant manager's job. The manager did notice when the firm first failed to comply. The plant's pollution prevention system, subject to repeated failure, had broken down and was once again in need of expensive repairs. The manager notified Gadgets' owners, who instructed him to continue reporting contaminant concentrations accurately. Hearing nothing from the DEP after a few months, Gadgets officials decided the violation must not be too severe. Gadgets has been experiencing a tight cash flow and decided for the time being to take a Band-Aid approach to repairing its pollution prevention system. The system is currently operating, but it does not bring contaminant concentrations down to standards required by the state.

On notification by the state of fines owed, Gadgets officials immediately requested a meeting with the DEP. Citing economic hardship, past good faith efforts, and its role as one of the last manufacturing firms in the area, Gadgets asked to be granted an extension in paying fines owed while it explored options for coming into compliance. The DEP agreed, but said that fines would continue to accrue until the firm complied.

With little progress made, the DEP has recently come under increasing pressure from two local environmental groups, Deep Green and the Newberg Bay Society (NBS), to force Gadgets into compliance. Both organizations have demanded that the DEP close Gadgets until the firm is able to meet state regulations. Failing an order by the DEP, Deep Green and the NBS have threatened to request an emergency injunction. Deep Green organized pickets in front of Gadgets' administrative offices three times in the last month.

In the midst of this situation, the Innovative Technology Program (ITP) of the DEP announced that a new pollution prevention technology, the CLEEN system, had been successfully tested in the laboratory and in three small firms. ITP stated that it was seeking an appropriate midsized firm in which a full-scale CLEEN system could be tested. In response, the State Secretary for the Environment ordered Gadgets to work with ITP and develop a strategy to bring the firm into compliance.

ITP promotes the use of environmental technologies with the potential for improved environmental protection and/or cost savings. The technologies have not been adequately demonstrated to allow normal DEP permitting. ITP and Pine Tree State University operate a joint research program to develop more efficient environmental technologies. The CLEEN system was developed at Pine Tree State University under the auspices of this program.

ITP requires that permits for innovative technologies be approved on a case-by-case basis through negotiations involving the principal parties affected. ITP may also provide a partial subsidy through the State Manufacturing Development Fund for the installation of innovative technologies that are above market cost for current technology. In a few cases, the DEP has forgiven, in part or in whole, fines owed by firms in exchange for the firm's participation in ITP.

Within the DEP, the secretary's order elicited an enthusiastic response from ITP and a cry of protest from the Environmental Regulation Department (ERD). ITP staff felt that Gadgets fit the criteria for a CLEEN test case well. The ERD, responsible for monitoring firms and collecting fines, felt that the DEP would be letting Gadgets off the hook by allowing it to become a test case for an unproven technology. (See Tables 2.5 and 2.6, which describe the DEP's fine schedule and its implications for Gadgets.)

To manage the conflict within the DEP,

Table 2.5. State DEP Fine Schedule for Failure to Comply with Limits on Heavy Metals in Wastewater and Air Emissions

Continuous Days Out of Compliance	Daily Fine per Contaminant
1–7	$20.00
8–30	40.00
31–90	57.50
91–150	75.00
151–240	100.00
over 240	120.00

Table 2.6. Implications for Gadgets, Inc.

Time Period	Months Out of Compliance	Total Fines	% of Annual Profit
Discovery of failed compliance by the DEP to present	3.0	$9,020.00	2.5%
Beginning of failed compliance to present	8.0	$36,020.00	10.0%
Beginning of failed compliance to repair of current SCRUB system	8.5	$36,240.00	10.1%
Beginning of failed compliance to replacement of current system with new SCRUB system or CLEEN with open-loop configuration	9.0	$39,620.00	11.0%
Beginning of failed compliance to installation of CLEEN with closed-loop configuration	10.0	$50,420.00	14.0%

the secretary appointed her special assistant, A. Dickens, to handle the Gadgets problem. Following the process used by ITP, Dickens called a meeting of the principal parties. Representatives from Gadgets, the Gadgets Workers Union, the U.S. Environmental Protection Agency (EPA), Deep Green, and the Newberg Bay Society will meet today to decide how to bring Gadgets into compliance.

Context

Gadgets is located in Newberg, a city of 150,000 in an old industrial valley between New York and Philadelphia. The Newberg Bay Area has suffered severe air and water pollution for decades. A crusade spearheaded by Deep Green resulted in a federal court order to the state 10 years ago to clean the air and water in the bay. Newberg is located within the EPA's Region 24; the court order gave the Region 24 office a monitoring role over the DEP for the cleanup process. A variety of measures were imposed to improve Newberg Bay air and water quality.

The DEP is required to submit monthly reports to the EPA Region 24, detailing the concentrations of 15 toxic contaminants. The problem is twofold, involving both air and water pollution. First, Newberg's wastewater receives primary and secondary treatment at a local sewage facility. It is then piped into Newberg Bay. The treatment process does not remove all toxic contaminants from wastewater; toxins that pass through the treatment plant are released into the bay or are incorporated in semi-solid sludge. If the treated water exceeds federally imposed standards for concentrations of the 15 toxic contaminants, the state treasury is fined $25,000 a day until the treatment plant comes into compliance.

The sewage treatment plant separates semi-solid sludge material in raw sewage from water. The sludge is then processed into fertilizer pellets. The fertilizer pellets must meet strict state and federal standards for concentrations of contaminants, including lead and copper, in order to be sold. This prevents the uptake of contaminants by plants, which may in turn be consumed by humans. The standards are two-tiered, the stricter standard for "unconditional use," and a more moderate standard for "conditional use." For the past two months, the fertilizer pellets have not met the "unconditional use" standards for either copper or lead. The pellets of the last two months were sold, but at a reduced price.

To control the concentration of toxic contaminants in sewage entering the treatment plant, the state has imposed wastewater standards on large manufacturing firms such as Gadgets. The facilities are required to test their wastewater going to the treatment plant and submit reports to the DEP detailing the concentrations of the 15 toxic contaminants on a monthly basis.

For many years, Newberg Bay failed to meet minimum Clean Water Act criteria for surface waters. Three years ago, the bay was upgraded to a Class C water body, suitable for secondary contact recreation, industrial cooling uses, and as habitat for fish, other aquatic life, and wildlife. Presumably this improvement came as a result of measures imposed in accordance with the federal court order. The federal court order requires that, within the next 10 years, large portions of the bay meet Class B criteria, making those areas suitable for primary and secondary contact recreation, limited shellfish harvesting, and as habitat for fish, other aquatic life, and wildlife.

Significant decreases have been achieved in the volume of toxic contaminants contained in raw sewage entering the treatment plant. Improvements in water quality cannot be definitively attributed to any particular pollution prevention or control measure. The DEP officials believe that limits placed on and enforced against metal platers account for a fair amount of the decrease in heavy metals.

For each of the past eight months, Gadgets' wastewater has contained between two and five times the allowed concentrations of copper and lead, which are 2 of the 15 elements or compounds monitored by the state and federal governments.

The second part of Newberg's environmental problem is the chronic air pollution. Most of the town, including industrial parks, is located in a valley. As recently as 25 years ago, a green fog settled over the town—the product of coal-fired power plants. While most of the coal-related air pollution has been mitigated, several of the remaining manufacturing firms have permits for emitting substantial amounts of air pollutants.

Gadgets has two main fume exhaust vents. One, on top of the factory, is a fume exhaust for several miscellaneous metal plating operations. The second, on the side of the factory, vents fumes from the chromium plating process. Hard chrome platers release a significant amount of hexavalent chromium—known to be highly toxic and carcinogenic. This, and other heavy metals released out the top vent, are regulated under the Clean Air Act.

Gadgets is also required to submit monthly reports of these air emissions. As with the water contaminants, the DEP is responsible for holding Gadgets in compliance. Unfortunately, Gadgets has been steadily failing to hold air emission concentrations within the allowable concentration. Both the national and the local economies are currently robust.

However, manufacturing firms have been in the process of leaving the Newberg area for about 40 years, headed to southern states and foreign countries with less expensive labor and fewer taxes and environmental regulations. By 1980, 70 percent of the manufacturing jobs available in 1955 had been eliminated. Since then, two large firms employing 200 people each have transferred, and three smaller firms with a combined employment of 150 have gone out of business. Rumors have flown periodically over the past 10 years, predicting Gadgets' move to a southern state.

Gadgets, Inc. and the Gadgets Workers Union

Gadgets is a privately held firm with gross revenues for the last fiscal year of $12 million and a profit margin of 3 percent ($360,000). Gadgets employs 100 people, primarily first-generation Guava Islanders with high school educations. Production workers are unionized in the Gadgets Workers Union. Comparable positions, in terms of salaries, benefits, and working conditions, would not be available locally if workers at Gadgets were laid off.

Guava Island is a small island nation in the Caribbean off the southern coast of Haiti. Wracked by poverty and political strife, Guava Islanders have become one of the largest immigrant groups in the United States in recent years. The Guava Island population in Newberg is 10,000. Gadgets Workers Union was considerably strengthened several years ago in the process of negotiating a difficult labor contract with Gadgets management. The Union achieved many of its goals in the negotiation and has become an important voice for the local Guava Island population.

SCRUB System

Gadgets currently utilizes SCRUB, a multipurpose pollution control system. An atmospheric evaporator using distillation technology removes contaminants from its wastewater stream. SCRUB applies a heat source to wastewater at atmospheric pressure, and evaporation occurs via humidification. SCRUB's air emission control method uses a fume suppressant inhibitor—a technology that ultimately produces sludge. The sludge from the fume suppressant is cleaned every few weeks. SCRUB provides an "end of pipe" treatment, resulting in a concentrated residual of contaminants and water vapor, which is condensed back into liquid and released to the sewer. The precipitate is temporarily stored at Gadgets, then disposed of by a contracted agency. SCRUB is subject to fouling, corrosion, and equipment deterioration. These problems are typical of atmospheric evaporators and fume suppressants, which are commonly used commercial equipment. Gadgets has replaced its system twice in the past five years due to equipment failures, at great expense to the company. The most recent system failed eight months ago and has not been adequately repaired.

Repairing the current system would cost $35,000. Replacing the system with a new, identical atmospheric evaporator and fume suppressant would cost $40,000.

CLEEN System

The CLEEN system was developed by Prof. Elaine Dawkins of the Environmental Extension Program at Pine Tree State University, a joint program between the DEP and the university. CLEEN was designed to improve on existing recovery systems and to benefit the environment. Pine Tree State University holds the patent to the technology and would earn profit from its sale.

CLEEN uses flash distillation and vacuum evaporation in conjunction with a liquid/vapor separation system and energy recovery unit to treat wastewater. Vacuum evaporation occurs by lowering the pressure of the wastewater system, causing the liquid to boil at a lower temperature. Vacuum distillation is more expensive, but also more efficient than atmospheric evaporators. Vacuum distillation systems also allow greater opportunities for chemical recovery and reuse. CLEEN was designed to minimize fouling potential, improve efficiency, and eliminate problems inherent in existing systems that result in equipment deterioration.

CLEEN also treats air emissions with a new type of composite mesh-pad system. In principle, this works similar to the water treatment process, in that chemical recovery and reuse potentials are higher. The new composite mesh-pad system is designed to experience less fouling and degradation, hopefully making it more reliable. In addition, Pine Tree State University scientists claim a significant reduction in final heavy metal emissions by the CLEEN system.

CLEEN can employ either an open- or a closed-loop configuration. With a closed loop, CLEEN allows the return/reuse of concentrated plating solution and the reuse of purified rinse waters. With an open loop, CLEEN acts as end-of-pipe treatment.

CLOSED LOOP VERSUS OPEN LOOP. CLEEN has been reliably demonstrated as an adequate end-of-pipe treatment. On the other hand, the advantages to installing a closed-loop system would be considerable. Hazardous materials and treated water would be recycled directly into the manufacturing process, eliminating the need to monitor wastewater and air emissions for toxin levels or store and dispose of hazardous material. The federal criteria for a "totally enclosed" system are:

1. Directly connected to an industrial pollution process
2. Constructed and operated in a manner that prevents the release of any hazardous waste or any constituent thereof into the environment during treatment

If the Region 24 EPA office agreed that these criteria were met, the CLEEN system would be exempt from federal Resource Conservation and Recovery Act (RCRA) permitting requirements. The RCRA is the federal law governing the handling and disposal of hazardous materials. The firm's current recovery system produces hazardous sludge that must be stored and disposed of in accordance with the RCRA requirements, at considerable expense to Gadgets.

Anecdotal evidence exists to support claims regarding the system's potential to achieve recovery and reuse. A paper published by Dawkins cites successful laboratory testing and three pilot studies in one metal finishing shop and two circuit board manufacturing firms. Each of the pilot studies involved small businesses with one-third to one-half the waste stream volume as Gadgets.

DEP has already agreed that CLEEN systems installed with a closed-loop configuration would be exempt from state hazardous waste permitting requirements. The con-

cern exists among environmental groups that, if Gadgets is declared exempt from the RCRA requirements and the CLEEN system fails, workers and the environment will be put at an even higher risk. Environmental organizations are further concerned about the frequency and responsibility for additional monitoring of CLEEN beyond Gadgets' monthly reports to the DEP.

An objection to a closed-loop system has been raised by the Gadgets Workers Union. Construction to reconfigure the pipes would involve demolishing a part of the building insulated with asbestos. No matter what precautions are taken during the demolition process, residual asbestos would pose some long-term health risk to workers.

Installing CLEEN as an open-loop system would cost $55,000. Installing CLEEN as a closed-loop system would cost $75,000, including the cost to reconfigure the firm's pipes.

Environmental Organizations

Deep Green and the Newberg Bay Society, two local organizations, have played active roles in monitoring Gadgets' environmental impact on the bay area.

Deep Green, the radical environmental organization, has worked in the area for 15 years. While operating with a very small staff and budget, the organization has been extremely active in local environmental affairs. Its creative, high-profile "actions" in earlier years targeted the DEP for allowing the ecological decline of the bay. Deep Green was the lead organization in the coalition that filed the "Swimmable and Breathable Newberg Bay" lawsuit. This suit resulted in the federal order to the state to clean the bay and a subsequent reorganization of the DEP. Deep Green has successfully used the judicial system in several other cases as well, requesting that injunctions be ordered against firms out of compliance with environmental regulations.

In spite of progress made toward the improved health of the bay, Deep Green has remained suspicious of the DEP. In the local press, Deep Green has played the role of the DEP watchdog, frequently criticizing it as a politically motivated agency that bends easily to the demands of polluting businesses. (See Box 2.1.)

The Newberg Bay Society (NBS) is a membership organization with a staff of professional scientists and lobbyists. The NBS' membership includes many recreational users of the bay and its shores, including sailors, rowers, runners, and bicyclists, who are concerned about issues of air and water quality. In cooperation with the DEP, NBS runs a citizen bay air and water quality monitoring program and is concerned that levels of heavy metals remain within safe ranges.

Today's Meeting

Following ITP procedures, the DEP Secretary's Special Assistant, A. Dickens, has called a meeting of the principal parties affected to negotiate a strategy to bring Gadgets into compliance with state regulations. Issues to be discussed will include (1) the choice of a pollution prevention technology, (2) a possible DEP subsidy from the installation of a

---

BOX 2.1. NEWBERG DAILY GAZETTE ARTICLE
Negotiating Environmental Health: Gadgets and DEP to Talk Today
DEP Proposes "Experimental Technology" to Solve Chronic Release of Pollutants

NEWBERG—The State Department of Environmental Protection (DEP) will meet today with representatives from Gadgets Inc. management; Gadgets Workers' Union; the U.S. Environmental Protection Agency (EPA); and local environmental groups to formulate a plan for ending Gadgets' continued pollution of Newberg Bay.

For the past eight months, Gadgets, Inc., a metal plating firm in Newberg, has consistently released pollutants in its wastewater and air emissions at concentrations of two to five times state limits. In response, the DEP has proposed that Gadgets adopt CLEEN, an "experimental multi-media pollution prevention technology" under development at the Environmental Extension Project, a joint program of DEP and Pine Tree State University. Environmental groups are vehemently opposed to this suggestion.

"Installing the CLEEN system at Gadgets would pose an immediate threat to human and environmental health," stated S. Cedar, Director of Deep Green, the group responsible for the federal court to clean Newberg Bay ten years ago.

GSO International, an independent lab, tested the CLEEN system's abilities to remove heavy metals from wastewater and air emission streams of a metal plating shop in Norbridge, Connecticut. The study showed that the CLEEN system operated with only a 60% removal efficiency of metals at maximum treatment flow.

This finding contradicts the DEP's claim that CLEEN has a 99% removal efficiency of metals at maximum treatment flow. SCRUB, the system currently in use by most metal platers, cleans wastewater and air emissions to state regulatory standards with a 90% efficiency rate at maximum treatment flow.

Said Cedar, "We are concerned that the DEP wants to use the City of Newberg as a laboratory to develop technology from which it will earn profit." The [Pine Tree State University] holds the patent to the CLEEN system. Any profit will accrue to the Environmental Extension Project.

"We challenge DEP to stand behind its claims of the CLEEN systems superiority by making a contingent offer to gadgets," said Cedar. As part of the DEP's Innovative Technology Program, DEP should cover 25% of the installation cost. 'Failure' would be defined by ten continuous days of Gadgets failing to meet state limits for heavy metals in its wastewater and air emissions. If DEP fails to take up our challenge, it betrays its own lack of faith in the CLEEN system."

Gadgets had been using the SCRUB system for four years, until its system failed eight months ago. Despite accurate monthly reporting to DEP by the firm, the DEP failed to catch the problem for five months.

Through an agreement with DEP, Gadgets has not yet paid fines for its failure to comply with environmental regulations. Fines due now total $36,020. A possible reduction in fines will be discussed at today's negotiation.

CLEEN system, (3) the payment of fines by Gadgets, and (4) the frequency of and responsibility for monitoring. Present at the meeting will be:

C. Chung, of EPA Region 24
N. Dietrich, vice president of Gadgets, Inc.
M. LaSalle, president of Gadgets Workers' Union
S. Cedar, director of Deep Green
C. Eisen, chief scientist for the Newberg Bay Society
A. Dickens, DEP secretary's special assistant

The goal of today's meeting is to reach consensus on a package addressing each of the four issues listed earlier. Consensus is defined as agreement by at least *five* of the six parties. The EPA representative must agree to the group's final decision. If no consensus is reached, the DEP will decide the matter internally in consultation with the EPA.

The EPA representative needs to leave in an hour and a half to attend an important meeting. The parties must try to reach agreement by that time.

Confidential Instructions for C. Chung, EPA Representative

As you see it, your primary goal, set by federal court order, is to ensure that progress in the cleanup of Newberg Bay proceeds on schedule. The federal court arranged the EPA's oversight role of the DEP because the DEP had been ineffective and careless with its obligation to maintain the cleanliness of the bay.

You are suspicious now of the DEP's motives in testing and promoting new technology. You tend to agree with critics, from both the right and the left, who contend that the Environmental Extension Program is an opportunity for academics to conduct expensive research, putting the Newberg area natural environment at risk as its laboratory. You are uncomfortable that the state will earn profit from the sale of the CLEEN technology, and that the profits will be earmarked for further research by the Environmental Extension Program.

The Washington office of the EPA has declared that supporting the development of pollution prevention technology is an institutional priority. In fact, numerous programs exist to encourage such development. The director for Region 24, however, which includes Newberg, has shown little enthusiasm for the innovative technology initiative. On the other hand, the regional director is intent on making steady progress toward a "fishable, swimmable, breathable" Newberg Bay.

You are uncomfortable with making ad hoc decisions about environmental regulation in a meeting such as today's. You have received no clear instructions from your director about how to handle the situation. Inventing impromptu solutions that carry regulatory weight may result in serious consequences for all of the EPA. Another firm could point to today's decision as precedent and claim a right to similar treatment for itself. *You do not want to bear the burden of having negotiated an inappropriate settlement on behalf of the EPA. The logical approach from your point of view is to follow precedent and the EPA policy as close to the letter as possible.*

In order of importance to the EPA, the issues to be discussed today are:

1. Fines and the possibility of Gadgets' temporarily closing
2. Choice of technology
3. Monitoring
4. Possible subsidy (if CLEEN is approved)

Fines and Temporary Closing

You are most concerned about the matter of fines and a temporary closing. Other metal plating firms are watching this case closely; you do not want to be sending signals that environmental standards can be negotiated away.

Gadgets is clearly a threat to the environment at present and should be closed until it is prepared to comply with state regulations—it is simply a matter of following the law. Gadgets should also be compelled to pay the fines it has accrued, although some relief may be provided in light of lost revenue from a temporary closing. Allowing the firm to remain open with partial forgiveness of fines would make a mockery of environmental legislation and is unacceptable.

Choice of Technology

As discussed earlier, you view your primary goal as keeping the cleanup of Newberg Bay on track. The SCRUB system has been proven to remove contaminants from wastewater to a level compliant with state and federal regulations. The SCRUB system has some disadvantages in that it requires a great deal of maintenance. When properly installed and maintained, however, the SCRUB system operates with an efficiency of 90 percent removal of heavy metals at maximum flow.

You should therefore advocate that Gadgets install a new SCRUB system. The current SCRUB system is obviously causing problems and should be replaced. Failing a new system, Gadgets should simply repair the current system.

The CLEEN system uses several different kinds of technology, all of which have been proven to work somewhat effectively in the past. CLEEN installed as an open-loop system would be acceptable if frequent monitoring were performed.

With an entirely closed-loop configuration, CLEEN seems most risky and suspect. Theoretically, an entirely closed-loop system would capture hazardous materials for reuse, eliminating the need to dispose of them. This, in turn, would eliminate the need for the firm to comply with the RCRA procedures for the disposal of hazardous waste.

No system is entirely enclosed, however; all systems have valves, vents, and so on. Considering the technology is still in an experimental phase, it is to be expected that the system will fail frequently. The firm should have a contingency plan ready in those cases, being fully prepared to handle the disposal of hazardous wastes. If CLEEN is entirely enclosed and exempt from the RCRA procedures, the firm may not be prepared to do so.

Monitoring

If a CLEEN system is installed, you are concerned that third-party monitoring of the system occurs frequently. Since this is primarily the DEP's initiative, it seems only right that the state should shoulder the burden of increased monitoring.

You would prefer not to spend the EPA's resources on additional monitoring of a relatively untested technology, although funding does exist for such a purpose. A federal EPA program provides grants of several thousand to several million dollars on a competitive basis to fund the development of environmental technology. Given the regional director's lack of interest in the subject, Region 24 has paid minimal attention to this program. No grants have been made in Region 24, which means that a strong candidate from the region would probably win a generous award easily.

If you could convince the regional director to support the CLEEN system, it is likely that the EPA could provide the personnel and resources to perform monthly monitoring of the CLEEN system as installed at Gadgets. The regional director is a rather crusty old fellow, adamantly opposed to what he calls "patchwork regulation." He likes you personally, though. Your son and his grandson played on the same Little League team last year; you spent quite a few Saturday mornings cheering on the sidelines together. It is up to you whether you want to lobby him on this issue.

As the CLEEN technology is still experimental, installing it without providing for extra monitoring is unacceptable.

Possible Subsidy (if CLEEN Is Approved)

This issue matters the least to you. The EPA is not being considered as one of the sources for funding the installation, so the source of funding means little to you. All other things being equal, you would prefer not to see any tax money spent on this project. You are suspicious of CLEEN's abilities and the DEP's incentives behind promoting it. As it seems likely that the CLEEN system will fail, you consider Deep Green's proposal of a contingent offer on the part of the DEP unacceptable.

Given the EPA's oversight role of the DEP, your approval is necessary for a negotiated package to be considered legitimate. You do not want to agree to a package that satisfies only the EPA's most basic interests, however. *Try to get the group to agree to your first or second choice for each issue, especially your first two priority issues.* You need to leave in an hour and a half to meet with the regional EPA director. The meeting is to discuss another matter, but he will surely ask you the outcome of this negotiation.

OPTION SHEET FOR C. CHUNG, EPA REPRESENTATIVE

Issue 1: Choice of Technology

Priority	Options
1st choice	Replace current system with like system.
2nd choice	Repair current system.
3rd choice	Install CLEEN, open loop.
4th choice	Install CLEEN, closed loop, RCRA exempt.

Issue 2: Fines and Temporary Closing

Priority	Options
1st choice	Gadgets closed until in compliance and pays three months of fines.
2nd choice	Gadgets closed until in compliance and pays eight months of fines.
3rd choice	Gadgets closed until in compliance and all fines forgiven.
4th choice	Gadgets remains open and pays fines until in compliance.
5th choice	Gadgets remains open and pays eight months of fines.
unacceptable	Gadgets remains open and all fines are forgiven.

Issue 3: Monitoring

Priority	Options
1st choice	State monitors monthly.
2nd choice	EPA monitors monthly.
3rd choice	State monitors quarterly.
4th choice	EPA monitors quarterly.
unacceptable	No additional monitoring.

Issue 4: Possible subsidy (if CLEEN Is Approved)

Priority	Options
1st choice	Gadgets covers entire expense.
2nd choice	Subsidy for half the value of the initial costs: 35% from state and 15% from the State Manufacturing Development Fund.
unacceptable	Contingent offer: State will pay 25% of initial costs. If CLEEN fails, state will reimburse additional 65% of initial cost.

Confidential Instructions for A. Dickens, DEP Secretary's Special Assistant

Frustrated by internal battles at the DEP, the DEP Secretary for the Environment has appointed you to lead a process that will result in Gadgets' coming into compliance. Things within the DEP are, quite frankly, a mess. The DEP performs many different functions, some of them conflicting. Conflicting functions are separated into different, independent departments. This organizational structure prevents individual staff members from encountering conflicts of interest. At the same time, the structure encourages territoriality and does little to promote creative solutions to complex problems.

Until the past few weeks, the matter of Gadgets was being handled entirely by the ERD within the DEP. The ERD is responsible for monitoring firms and collecting fines. It is also responsible for reporting to the EPA, ensuring that the state is complying with standards set by the federal court order to clean Newberg Bay. If the treated water from Newberg's sewage facility or ambient air quality standards fail to meet federally imposed levels, the state is fined $25,000 a day.

The ERD reviews monthly compliance forms, like those that Gadgets submits, from over 7000 firms across the state. The ERD computer system is sadly out-of-date, and the staff is barely able to keep up with basic data entry for each firm. In addition, its efficiency was hampered until three months ago by several rather uninspired staff members. Following a department review, the underachieving staff members were removed, replaced by bright, young college graduates. At that point Gadgets' failure to comply was discovered.

On being notified of fines owed, Gadgets officials met with senior members of the ERD staff. Prior to that meeting, the governor sent a memo to the ERD. He is eager to see Gadgets remain in the state and requested that the DEP accommodate the firm as much as possible. Gadgets is a good employer; the governor is concerned about the loss of manufacturing jobs in the state. The ERD responded by agreeing to temporarily postpone Gadgets' fines payment. Fines would continue to accrue until the firm came into compliance, providing ample incentive for Gadgets to act quickly.

Weeks passed, however, and Gadgets made little progress toward repairing or replacing its pollution prevention system. Deep Green noticed and promptly published a three-part op-ed series in the *Newberg Daily Gazette*, criticizing DEP as "pro-industry, pro-pollution." The director of the DEP's Innovative Technology Program (ITP), who discovered the Gadgets case by reading the op-ed series, approached the Environmental Secretary with the suggestion that Gadgets become a test case for the CLEEN system.

The Environmental Secretary greeted this suggestion with enthusiasm. The secretary was one of the principal architects of ITP, which has recently come under attack by conservatives in the state legislature. The conservative majority leader claims that ITP is simply a mechanism for Pine Tree State University professors to conduct expensive research of dubious value, putting the public and the environment at risk with untested technology. ITP is currently undergoing a review by a special Lean Governance committee to determine whether funding will be renewed for the next fiscal year.

ITP has invested considerable time and money in the development of CLEEN, with overwhelmingly successful results. One independent lab performed a series of tests on CLEEN in the early stages of its development and discovered several design weaknesses. Until this morning's paper (see Box 2.1), those results had not been widely circulated. The weaknesses were addressed over the past few months in design reviews, but the improvements have not been tested outside a laboratory setting.

If CLEEN is successfully installed and operated at Gadgets, with the consent of the principal parties involved, ITP will be in a strong position vis-à-vis its critics. If CLEEN is not installed at Gadgets, there is a good chance that ITP's funding will not be renewed. Measures to prove ITP's worth need to be taken quickly, and the installation of CLEEN at Gadgets is the only way to accomplish this.

The Environmental Secretary thus ordered Gadgets to work with ITP toward the goal of quickly installing a CLEEN system. This had the purpose of achieving several objectives: saving ITP and taking a strong stance with the unresponsive Gadgets, while still honoring the governor's desire to encourage the firm to remain in-state.

The secretary's order was greeted by howls of fury from the ERD. Firms that become partners of the ITP often receive full or partial relief from fines owed, as well as subsidies to install experimental technology. Contaminant levels in ambient air quality and treated water from the sewage treatment facility have been escalating, although they are still safely below federal limits. In addition, fertilizer pellets produced in the past two months have failed to meet the strictest standard to be sold as "unconditional use" fertilizer.

Gadgets is obviously not responsible for all of the increase in contaminants. However, the ERD believes that "going easy" on Gadgets by providing fine relief or subsidies will send the wrong signal to other firms that are out of compliance. Further, the ERD believes that, given the trend toward increasing concentrations of contaminants, Gadgets should be required to install a system that has been proven to work. The ERD is also insulted that the Gadgets case was unceremoniously taken from its jurisdiction.

Tempers in the DEP office escalated quickly, effectively paralyzing the agency on this issue. In response, the secretary has decided essentially to solve the problem outside the DEP. The ITP uses a consensus building process to provide permits to firms installing experimental technology. Based on this model, the secretary has assigned you to lead a consensus building process involving the key stakeholders in the Gadgets case. The negotiation will determine not simply the details of a permit, but a much broader course of action. You will be the sole representative for the DEP.

You met with the Environmental Secretary last week and developed the following summary of goals and priorities for the agency as a whole. In order of importance to the DEP, the issues to be discussed today are:

1. Choice of technology
2. Possible subsidy (if CLEEN is approved)
3. Monitoring
4. Fines and the possibility of Gadgets' temporarily closing

Choice of Technology

The Environmental Secretary wants to see Gadgets used as a test case for the CLEEN system. Today you should advocate a *long-term vision* for improved environmental health. The development of more efficient technology necessarily involves failures along the way. Benefits of improved pollution-prevention technology applied industrywide would more than offset short-term releases of contaminants as the technology is refined.

The closed-loop configuration of the CLEEN system holds the greatest potential for pollution prevention and resource conservation. A closed-loop system approved by the EPA would also relieve manufacturers of the costs associated with complying with the Resources Conservation and Recovery Act. The RCRA procedures can raise the price of handling waste materials by a factor of 10. The closed-loop configuration also avoids the increasingly burdensome cost of hazardous waste disposal. Installing a completely enclosed system exempt from the RCRA would lower the costs of doing business accordingly.

It is true that the construction involved in installing a closed-loop system would involve the removal of asbestos. Airborne asbestos has received a good deal of press recently, due to a number of poorly performed asbestos removal jobs. The contract with the removal company would need to be carefully worded, including performance guarantees. With proper precautions taken, a minimal risk to worker health might remain, but the effects should be negligible.

Failing a closed-loop configuration, the CLEEN system with an open-loop configuration would be preferable to repairing or reinstalling a SCRUB system. Even an open-loop configuration would provide opportunities for refining the CLEEN system for use in a larger market.

Installing a new SCRUB system at Gadgets is very undesirable, but possible. If installed and maintained properly, the SCRUB system will remove contaminants from

Table 2.7. Cost to Innovative Technology Program of Possible Subsidy Packages *(italicized packages acceptable)*

	EPA Monitors	*DEP/ITP Monitors Monthly*	*DEP/ITP Monitors Quarterly*
Open loop, ITP/SMDF grant:	*$27,500.00*	*$39,500.00*	*$31,500.00*
Open loop, contingent offer:	*$44,500.00*	$56,500.00	$48,500.00
Closed loop, ITP/SMDF grant:	*$37,500.00*	$49,500.00	*$41,500.00*
Closed loop, contingent offer:	$67,500.00	$79,500.00	$71,500.00

air emissions and wastewater to the levels required by state regulations. A new SCRUB system would likely perform well for up to a year and a half.

Simply repairing the current SCRUB system at Gadgets is unacceptable. Given the history of the system, in all likelihood it would fail again shortly after its repair. The firm would have wasted scarce resources, and nothing would have been gained in terms of increased knowledge of pollution prevention technology.

Possible Subsidy (if CLEEN Is Approved)

ITP has $33,750 left in its budget to spend on CLEEN. In addition, there remains $11,250 from a grant from the State Manufacturing Development Fund to develop CLEEN. ITP's share of the combined costs of a subsidy for installation and subsequent monitoring cannot exceed $45,000, the sum of these two figures.

Deep Green proposed in the press this morning that the DEP show its faith in the CLEEN system by making a contingent offer to pick up 90 percent of the tab for its installation if the system fails. Considering that the CLEEN system is still in the development stage, it is likely that the system will fail from time to time as problems in the system are discovered and solved. Given ITP's tight budget for the current year and uncertain future, the program must be risk averse in its spending. It is impossible for the DEP to accept Deep Green's challenge.

You are counting on the EPA to assist in funding the subsidy of the CLEEN system installation and/or monitoring. The EPA's Web page states that supporting innovative pollution prevention technology is an institutional priority. The DEP has taken the initiative to develop the CLEEN system without financial or technical assistance from the EPA. Here is an excellent opportunity for the EPA to act on its stated priorities. Table 2.7 lists the possible subsidy packages, with those acceptable to ITP in italics.

Monitoring

If CLEEN is chosen, each monitoring visit will cost $1,000. If the group today decides that ITP should conduct monitoring, funding for the first year must come from the $45,000 currently available for Gadgets through ITP.

Given ITP's tight funding situation and uncertain future, both the director of ITP and the Environmental Secretary strongly prefer that the EPA conduct regular monitoring. If problems arise, Elaine Dawkins' team from Pine Tree State University would come out for a site visit to troubleshoot. Use the financial information in Table 2.7 as a guide. If CLEEN is not chosen, then the DEP has no funding available to perform extra monitoring.

Both the ITP and the ERD would want to see the CLEEN system monitored as often as possible. Frequent monitoring is important for ITP to refine the technology. The ERD would want to ensure that CLEEN did not cause Gadgets to fall out of compliance again.

Fines and Temporary Closing

The secretary believes that Gadgets should be allowed to remain open until it is able to come into compliance, but that the firm should pay all fines accrued. Closing the firm would place an overwhelming financial burden on Gadgets' management and workers. More than lost production, a closing may cause the firm to shut down or move out of state. The secretary is intent on observing the governor's desire to keep Gadgets in Newberg.

The secretary is willing to allow the firm partial relief from fines in exchange for the financial risk it would take on by installing the CLEEN system. If the decision today is not to install the CLEEN system, then the secretary is much less willing to forgive any amount of the fines.

Under any circumstances, allowing Gadgets to remain open and forgiving all fines is unacceptable. This would set a bad precedent for dealing with other firms and would tarnish the DEP's public image.

Try to get the group to agree on the DEP's first or second-rank option for all issues, but especially the two most important to the secretary. While the other parties to the negotiation are aware of the conflict that exists at the DEP, the secretary wishes to maintain a facade of a unified front as much as possible. In the highly politicized atmosphere of state government, the appearance of internal discord could be grounds for the secretary's—and your—swift dismissal. If no consensus is reached today, the DEP will be forced to solve the matter internally. This would in all likelihood expose the organization's divisiveness to the outside world. The secretary is counting on you to produce a consensus, one that meets the DEP's delicately balanced interests.

OPTION SHEET FOR A. DICKENS, DEP SECRETARY'S SPECIAL ASSISTANT

Issue 1: Choice of Technology

Priority	Options
1st choice	Install CLEEN, closed loop, RCRA exempt.
2nd choice	Install CLEEN, open loop.
3rd choice	Replace current system with like system.
unacceptable	Repair current system.

Issue 2: Possible Subsidy (if CLEEN Is Approved)
(See Table 2.7 for acceptable options.)

Priority	Options
1st choice	Gadgets covers entire expense.
2nd choice	Subsidy for half the value of the initial costs: 35% from state and 15% from the State Manufacturing Development Fund.
unacceptable	Contingent offer: State will pay 25% of initial costs. If CLEEN fails, state will reimburse additional 65% of initial cost.

Issue 3: Monitoring
(See Table 2.7 for acceptable options.)

Priority	Options
1st choice	EPA monitors monthly.
2nd choice	EPA monitors quarterly.
3rd choice	State monitors quarterly.
4th choice	State monitors monthly.
unacceptable	No additional monitoring.

Issue 4: Fines and Temporary Closing

Priority	Options
1st choice	Gadgets remains open and pays fines until in compliance.
2nd choice	Gadgets remains open and pays eight months of fines.
3rd choice	Gadgets remains open and pays three months of fines.
4th choice	Gadgets closed until in compliance and all fines forgiven.
5th choice	Gadgets closed until in compliance and pays three months of fines.
6th choice	Gadgets closed until in compliance and pays eight months of fines.
unacceptable	Gadgets remains open and all fines are forgiven.

Confidential Instructions for N. Dietrich, Gadgets, Inc. Vice President

Your most important concern is the bottom line. Gadgets' position is a bit precarious. Rumors have circulated predicting the firm's move out of state. In truth, if the firm is required to pay more than it can afford, it will be forced out of business. Today's negotiation is thus very important to Gadgets' future.

You met with Gadgets' Chief Financial Officer (CFO) last week to discuss how to evaluate the potential cost of the CLEEN system versus repairing your current SCRUB system or buying a new SCRUB system. Given Gadgets' experience with SCRUB, you and the CFO feel confident in predicting the frequency and costs associated with the SCRUB system, as well as the length of time before a SCRUB system would need replacing.

The problem, given that the CLEEN system is an experimental technology, is that the frequency and costs of maintenance and repairs are unknown, as is the life span of the system. To compensate, the CFO has developed spreadsheets predicting costs to Gadgets for two different scenarios. (See Tables 2.8 and 2.9.) The first scenario is that the CLEEN system will be successful and efficient; the second is that the system will quickly fail. The costs on the spreadsheets are calculated as the net present value of CLEEN to the firm under all of the possible packages that could be negotiated today. The net present value calculation takes into account maintenance and repair, replacement costs, savings from the increased efficiency of a closed-loop system, possible fines, loss of revenue if the plant is closed, possible subsidies, and inflation.

The first spreadsheet assumes that CLEEN is successful. This is accounted for in the calculation by assuming that CLEEN's life span will be eight years. Given the reports you have read reviewing CLEEN and conversations with the DEP staff, you are confident that the CLEEN system will be successful. You are planning to use this spreadsheet in evaluating packages of options proposed at today's meeting.

Gadgets' CFO is risk averse, however, and has provided you with another spreadsheet, "just in case." This spreadsheet evaluates the costs to Gadgets of various packages given CLEEN fails completely. This is accounted for in the calculation by assuming a life span of only two years for CLEEN. If any information comes up, the CFO said, which makes you think that CLEEN might not work as well as you hoped, then you should use the second spreadsheet to evaluate your options.

The president of Gadgets has instructed you to negotiate a package of no more than a net present value of $70,000 if you think the CLEEN system will fail and $80,000 if you think the CLEEN system will be successful. Packages that are acceptable are italicized.

Another complicating factor concerns a recent observation your plant manager made—discolored soil around the chrome plater vent on the side of the factory. You have an environmental assessment planned into next years' budget, but not much can be done until then. You're not sure who else knows about this, but one thing is certain—this information could further damage Gadgets' reputation.

As a last resort, if the negotiations seem to point toward Gadgets' permanent closure, you might use this soil issue as a threat. If Gadgets' goes out of business, then the chances for soil remediation are very low. The cleanup costs would fall on the DEP or the EPA. It's a gamble on Gadgets' reputation, but things can't get much worse!

In order of importance to Gadgets, the issues to be discussed today are:

1. Fines and the possibility of Gadgets' temporarily closing
2. Possible subsidy (if CLEEN is approved)
3. Choice of technology
4. Monitoring

Table 2.8. Net Present Value of Cost to Gadgets of CLEEN System
Scenario: CLEEN system is a success with a life span of eight years*

ALLOWED TO REMAIN OPEN	Fines Forgiven	Fines from Discovery (Present)	Fines from Failure to Comply (Present)	Fines from Failure to Comply (Compliance)
Repair current SCRUB system	$101,733.44	$110,753.44	$137,753.44	$137,753.44
Install new SCRUB system	$115,788.48	$124,808.48	$151,808.48	$155,408.48
CLEEN, open loop, no subsidy	*$61,027.98*	*$70,047.98*	$97,047.98	$100,647.98
CLEEN, open loop, DEP/SMDF grant	*$33,527.98*	*$42,547.98*	*$69,547.98*	*$78,147.98*
CLEEN, open loop, DEP contingent offer	*$47,277.98*	*$56,297.98*	$83,297.98	$86,897.98
CLEEN, closed loop, no subsidy	*$5,678.21*	*$14,698.21*	*$41,698.21*	*$56,098.21*
CLEEN, closed loop, DEP/SMDF grant	*−$31,821.79*	*−$22,801.79*	*$4,198.21*	*$18,598.21*
CLEEN, closed loop, DEP contingent offer	*−$13,071.79*	*−$4,051.79*	*$22,948.21*	*$37,348.21*
CLOSED UNTIL IN COMPLIANCE				
Repair current SCRUB system	$119,733.44	$128,753.44	$155,753.44	
Install new SCRUB system	$151,788.48	$160,808.48	$187,808.48	
CLEEN, open loop, no subsidy	$97,027.98	$106,047.98	$133,047.98	
CLEEN, open loop, DEP/SMDF grant	*$69,527.98*	*$78,547.98*	$105,547.98	
CLEEN, open loop, DEP contingent offer	$83,277.98	$92,297.98	$119,297.98	
CLEEN, closed loop, no subsidy	*$77,678.21*	$86,698.21	$113,698.21	
CLEEN, closed loop, DEP/SMDF grant	*$40,178.21*	*$49,198.21*	*$76,198.21*	
CLEEN, closed loop, DEP contingent offer	*$58,928.21*	*$67,948.21*	$94,948.21	

*Acceptable packages appear in italics.

Table 2.9. Net Present Value of Cost to Gadgets of CLEEN System
Scenario: CLEEN system is a failure with a life span of two years*

ALLOWED TO REMAIN OPEN	Fines Forgiven	Fines from Discovery (Present)	Fines from Failure to Comply (Present)	Fines from Failure to Comply (Compliance)
Repair current SCRUB system	$24,813.08	$33,833.08	$60,833.08	$61,058.08
Install new SCRUB system	$39,813.08	$48,833.08	$75,833.08	$79,433.08
CLEEN, open loop, no subsidy	$55,962.62	$64,982.62	$91,982.62	$95,582.62
CLEEN, open loop, DEP/SMDF grant	$28,462.62	$37,482.62	$64,482.62	$68,082.62
CLEEN, open loop, DEP contingent offer	$42,212.62	$50,270.00	$77,270.00	$80,870.00
CLEEN, closed loop, no subsidy	$63,929.91	$72,949.91	$99,949.91	$114,349.91
CLEEN, closed loop, DEP/SMDF grant	$26,429.91	$35,449.91	$62,449.91	$76,849.91
CLEEN, closed loop, DEP contingent offer	−$7,449.44	$1,570.56	$28,570.56	$42,970.56
CLOSED UNTIL IN COMPLIANCE				
Repair current SCRUB system	$42,813.08	$51,833.08	$78,833.08	
Install new SCRUB system	$75,813.08	$84,833.08	$111,833.08	
CLEEN, open loop, no subsidy	$91,962.62	$100,982.62	$127,982.62	
CLEEN, open loop, DEP/SMDF grant	$64,462.62	$73,482.62	$100,482.62	
CLEEN, open loop, DEP contingent offer	$77,251.07	$86,270.00	$113,270.00	
CLEEN, closed loop, no subsidy	$135,929.91	$144,949.91	$171,949.91	
CLEEN, closed loop, DEP/SMDF grant	$98,429.91	$107,449.91	$134,449.91	
CLEEN, closed loop, DEP contingent offer	$64,550.56	$73,570.56	$100,570.56	

*Acceptable packages appear in italics.

Fines and Temporary Closing

It is imperative that Gadgets be allowed to remain in operation as it corrects its pollution prevention system. A forced closure would be tantamount to putting the firm out of business for good. Stress the fact that Gadgets faithfully and accurately reported data to the DEP each month. When the DEP did not respond for five months, it led the company to believe that the regulations were not strictly enforced. The DEP shares part of the burden in the prolonged period of time for which Gadgets has been out of compliance. If the DEP had notified the firm earlier that fines would be imposed, the firm would have taken earlier steps to address the problem.

Gadgets should further be relieved from paying fines because it is willingly entering into the DEP's ITP. By investing in experimental technology, Gadgets is performing a service for the DEP, the metal plating industry, and the environment. More efficient technology, once refined and adopted industrywide, will benefit everyone. Gadgets is further taking on financial risk by choosing to adopt an experimental, rather than a tested technology. The future costs of the CLEEN system to the company are unknown; Gadgets should be compensated for that risk. For the above reasons, argue that Gadgets' fines should be completely forgiven. At most, the company should only pay for three months of fines.

Possible Subsidy (if CLEEN Is Approved)

If you remain confident that the CLEEN system will be a success, you should advocate that the DEP, along with the State Manufacturing Development Fund cover 50 percent of the capital costs. If you think the system is likely to fail, you should advocate that the DEP take up the challenge proposed by Deep Green in this morning's paper. Deep Green proposed that the DEP stand behind the CLEEN technology by making a contingent offer. The DEP would cover 25 percent of capital costs; then, if the technology failed, the DEP would reimburse Gadgets for an additional 65 percent of capital costs. If the system failed, Gadgets would have paid only 10 percent of total capital costs. Either way, as is clear from the CFO's spreadsheets, obtaining a subsidy is essential.

Choice of Technology

The closed-loop configuration of the CLEEN system holds the greatest promise for future savings. If the closed loop were approved by the EPA and exempted from the RCRA, Gadgets could save time, money, and headaches in handling hazardous waste. Installing a closed-loop system would also potentially help improve Gadgets' public image. Various environmental groups have picketed the firm several times in the past month. An innovative, pollution prevention technology may help convince the community that Gadgets cares about the local environment.

The open-loop configuration of CLEEN would still be preferable to repairing or replacing the high-maintenance SCRUB system. From Pine Tree State's studies on the CLEEN system, it seems to be a more efficient, reliable pollution prevention technology. Gadgets is willing to take the risk that it will be.

You would strongly prefer not to repair or replace Gadgets' current SCRUB system. Both options are financially poor decisions except under very constrained circumstances.

Monitoring

You care least about monitoring; you would prefer as little third-party monitoring as possible. You would prefer monitoring to be conducted by the DEP, because you have developed a good relationship with the ITP staff. Further, since the DEP's Environmental Extension Program developed the CLEEN system, they would be better able to answer questions and offer advice than the EPA staff.

Try to negotiate for your first or second-ranked option on all issues, but especially on the two issues most important to you. The future of the firm depends on your performance today.

OPTION SHEET FOR N. DIETRICH, GADGETS, INC. VICE PRESIDENT

Issue 1: Fines and Temporary Closing
(See Tables 2.8 and 2.9 for acceptable options.)

Priority	Options
1st choice	Gadgets remains open and all fines are forgiven.
2nd choice	Gadgets remains open and pays three months of fines.
3rd choice	Gadgets remains open and pays eight months of fines.
4th choice	Gadgets remains open and pays fines until in compliance.
5th choice	Gadgets closed until in compliance and all fines forgiven.
6th choice	Gadgets closed until in compliance and pays three months of fines.
unacceptable	Gadgets closed until in compliance and pays eight months of fines.

Issue 2: Possible Subsidy (if CLEEN Is Approved)
(See Tables 2.8 and 2.9 for acceptable options.)

Priority	Options
1st choice	Subsidy for half the value of the initial costs: 35% from state and 15% from the State Manufacturing Development Fund.
2nd choice	Contingent offer: State will pay 25% of initial costs. If CLEEN fails, state will reimburse additional 65% of initial cost.
3rd choice	Gadgets covers entire expense.

Issue 3: Choice of Technology
(See Tables 2.8 and 2.9 for acceptable options.)

Priority	Options
1st choice	Install CLEEN, closed loop, RCRA exempt.
2nd choice	Install CLEEN, open loop.
3rd choice	Repair current system.
4th choice	Replace current system with like system.

Issue 4: Monitoring

Priority	Options
1st choice	No additional monitoring.
2nd choice	State monitors quarterly.
3rd choice	EPA monitors quarterly.
4th choice	State monitors monthly.
5th choice	EPA monitors monthly.

Confidential Instructions for M. LaSalle, Gadgets Workers' Union President

The Union is most concerned about two issues: (1) job security and (2) occupational health and safety. The Union does not want to see a "solution" to the problem of Gadgets' noncompliance that causes the company to close, even temporarily, or relocate.

At the same time, the Union is adamantly opposed to accepting a closed-loop configuration of the CLEEN system. Construction required to install the system would involve tearing out an old section of the plant insulated with asbestos. The Union is concerned that, once released, residual asbestos would remain in the plant, posing a threat to worker health.

You've had some recent success in promoting the Union's interests with Gadgets' management, but only after relatively contentious negotiations. You have heard the vice president voice some interest in a closed-loop CLEEN system. This kind of egregious lack of concern for worker safety has you on the defensive. You are not totally opposed to the idea of trying to convince Gadgets' VP that a closed-loop option is out of the question in a private caucus.

One way you might do this is to mention some problems workers have noticed with the side vent (for a hard chrome plater). A few workers mentioned the soil near the vent is discolored. Also, every time it rains, the foul-smelling runoff from this soil makes its way into the creek adjacent to the factory. You suspect the soil is polluted, but you're not sure if other people know this. This could spell big trouble for Gadgets' management if another violation is uncovered. This is sensitive information, but it could be used to your advantage.

In order of importance to the Union, the issues to be discussed today are:

1. Fines and the possibility of Gadgets' temporarily closing
2. Choice of technology
3. Possible subsidy (if CLEEN is approved)
4. Monitoring

Fines and Temporary Closing

The Union is firmly opposed to a closing of Gadgets until the plant is able to come into compliance. The Union would be able to provide some allowance for the workers during the closed period, but only roughly 50 percent of what the workers would otherwise earn.

Union members rely on their salaries to support their families both in the United States and on Guava Island. Nearly all Union members send money home to extended family on Guava Island, where wages from overseas workers are often the only cash resource available to meet food, educational, and medical expenses. Without this resource, Union family members on Guava Island would literally be without the funds to provide for basic, ongoing needs. If wages of Union members are cut, the members must choose whether to meet their own food and housing expenses in the United States or cut back on funds sent to their families on Guava Island.

The Union believes that it is unfair that they and their families bear the brunt of the DEP standards. From the Union's perspective, the immediate economic harm to Union members and their families that would be caused by a plant closing far outweighs the environmental damage that would be caused by allowing the plant to remain open.

The Union is also concerned that a loss of revenue for Gadgets during a closed period may force the firm to close permanently. For similar reasons, the Union also believes that the fines imposed by the DEP should be forgiven or reduced, particularly if the firm installs the CLEEN system. Gadgets would be taking on financial risk by installing an experimental technology. Gadgets would also be performing a service for the DEP and the metal plating industry in general by allowing itself to be used as a test case for a potentially more efficient technology. The firm should be compensated accordingly.

Choice of Technology

The Union is willing, even eager, to see the CLEEN system installed at Gadgets; the SCRUB system has failed repeatedly. The Union is willing to test a new system—hopefully one that promotes long-term stability. As explained earlier, however, the Union finds the closed-loop configuration unacceptable, given the demolition that would be necessary.

The section of the plant that would need to be removed is insulated with friable asbestos. Friable asbestos crumbles to powder easily and becomes airborne. It is the most difficult type of asbestos to remove. Exposure to airborne asbestos may result in numerous negative health effects, including asbestosis, lung cancer, mesothelioma (cancer of the thin lining of internal organs), and plural plaques. Some studies have shown that asbestos exposure is also linked to increased incidence of cancer of the esophagus, colon, pancreas, and stomach.

At present, the asbestos is intact and well contained within the structure of the walls. As a result, health risk to workers is currently very low. Removal of the asbestos would disturb the intact structure, and fibers would certainly become airborne. Numerous buildings in the state have recently undergone asbestos removal operations. Inspection afterwards found levels of airborne asbestos dangerously higher than before removal. Several such cases have been well publicized, and Union members are strongly opposed to having the same thing happen at Gadgets.

The Union became a strong force several years ago while organizing for contract negotiations with Gadgets management. One of the major issues in the negotiation was the provision of health care. Gadgets management resisted providing workers with adequate, affordable coverage, showing a disregard for worker health. The Union is concerned that a similar disregard will be shown in this negotiation.

The biggest proponent of closing Gadgets, the Deep Green director, has openly stated that a plant closure is the only option. You believe, however, that he might be a valuable ally in preventing a closed-loop system. If the negotiations seems to favor a closed-loop option, you are not totally opposed to striking a deal with Deep Green—forming a coalition on technology choice. In addition, if you convince Deep Green that any kind of closure will shut down Gadgets altogether, they might give way on the fines and closing issue. You can do this by using the soil pollution issue strategically. If the soil really is polluted (which you're still not 100 percent sure about), then a plant closure will significantly reduce the chances of cleanup. This is because most companies who go out of business are negligent in cleaning up the environmental mess they leave behind. Once again, it's a gamble—but so is working in an asbestos-filled factory!

Possible Subsidy (if CLEEN Is Approved)

Gadgets will need financial assistance to purchase the CLEEN system. Gadgets will serve as a test case for a technology that the state has developed and wishes to market. The state should financially enable Gadgets to perform this service. To receive no financial assistance would be unacceptable; the firm would not be able to afford the CLEEN system.

The Union prefers the package that would provide the greatest contribution toward capital costs. The best package would be the joint ITP/State Manufacturing Development Fund grant covering 50 percent of installation costs. A contingent offer from the state would be attractive only if it looked as though the CLEEN system were likely to fail. From the reports provided by the DEP, it seems that the CLEEN system has been well researched and tested.

Monitoring

The Union cares least about monitoring. Generally speaking, the less often outsiders come looking around the plant, the better. With regard to the agency that conducts monitoring, the Union would prefer the DEP. If the CLEEN system is installed, the DEP would be in a better position to provide advice as a partner in the technology's development. Also, while Gadgets' experience with the DEP has been rocky at times, the DEP seems more flexible and understanding than the more remote, by-the-book EPA.

Try to get the group to agree to your first or second choice for each issue, especially the Union's top two priority issues. The Union is counting on you to negotiate a package that will keep Gadgets in operation and with a safe working environment.

OPTION SHEET FOR M. LASALLE, GADGETS WORKERS' UNION PRESIDENT

Issue 1: Fines and Temporary Closing

Priority	Options
1st choice	Gadgets remains open and all fines are forgiven.
2nd choice	Gadgets remains open and pays three months of fines.
3rd choice	Gadgets remains open and pays eight months of fines.
4th choice	Gadgets remains open and pays fines until in compliance.
5th choice	Gadgets closed until in compliance and all fines forgiven.
unacceptable	Gadgets closed until in compliance and pays three months of fines.
unacceptable	Gadgets closed until in compliance and pays eight months of fines.

Issue 2: Choice of Technology

Priority	Options
1st choice	Install CLEEN, open loop.
2nd choice	Replace current system with like system.
3rd choice	Repair current system.
unacceptable	Install CLEEN, closed loop, RCRA exempt.

Issue 3: Possible Subsidy (if CLEEN Is Approved)

Priority	Options
1st choice	Subsidy for half the value of the initial costs: 35% from state and 15% from the State Manufacturing Development Fund.
2nd choice	Contingent offer: State will pay 25% of initial costs. If CLEEN fails, state will reimburse additional 65% of initial cost.
unacceptable	Gadgets covers entire expense.

Issue 4: Monitoring

Priority	Options
1st choice	No additional monitoring.
2nd choice	State monitors quarterly.
3rd choice	EPA monitors quarterly.
4th choice	State monitors monthly.
5th choice	EPA monitors monthly.

Confidential Instructions for C. Eisen, Newberg Bay Society Chief Scientist

Your organization's primary concern is the improved air and water quality of Newberg Bay. NBS members are avid users of Newberg Bay and its shores. They have been encouraged by the progress made toward a cleaner bay over the last 10 years and are concerned that progress continue in a positive direction. Whatever technology is chosen today, it is essential that the performance of Gadgets' pollution prevention system be closely monitored in the future.

NBS is excited about the ITP. Members generally believe that ITP holds great potential for bringing about sweeping improvements in environmental health through more efficient, cost-effective pollution prevention technology.

As a scientist, you understand that the case of Gadgets cannot be viewed in isolation. The firm has not adequately repaired its SCRUB system for eight months. In the past five years, however, Gadgets has completely replaced its SCRUB system twice.

Based on your review of similar cases in other metal plating firms, the parties at the table today are presented with both a problem and an opportunity. The SCRUB system, used industrywide, is a high-maintenance technology, subject to fouling and failure. The stricter compliance standards developed by the state over the past 10 years have resulted in improved air and water quality, but have also raised the cost of doing business in Newberg.

The CLEEN system is a more efficient technology, which would be less expensive than the SCRUB system in the long run. If CLEEN were developed and adopted industrywide, the environmental benefits would be greater than any that could now be achieved with the SCRUB system. In addition, the long-term lower cost of CLEEN would ease the burden placed on local manufacturers.

As part of the research process, mistakes will be made. With the CLEEN system, it is likely that Gadgets will initially release concentrations of heavy metals that far exceed state limits. However, this pollution will be far outweighed by the ultimate benefit of having a more efficient pollution prevention technology adopted industrywide.

Today's negotiation takes place at a critical time. The ITP is currently under review by a special Lean Governance Committee of the state legislature. A conservative majority swept the legislature during the last election, having campaigned on promises to "trim away the fat of state spending." Rumor has it that ITP is on their hit list. ITP needs to make a bold, effective move quickly to establish its credibility. Past successes mean little in the current atmosphere.

The installation of CLEEN at Gadgets as a result of today's meeting is ITP's only opportunity. If the parties today decide against installing CLEEN at Gadgets, the state legislature will in all likelihood cancel ITP's funding for next year. The Newberg Bay Society thinks highly of the work of ITP and considers it a crucial element of the DEP. NBS members would be extremely upset if the ITP is canceled. It is important that today's negotiation goes well.

As a side note, the Environmental Secretary and a few like-minded individuals, some of them NBS members, initiated ITP several years ago. The secretary's assistant will likely be working hard today to save the program.

In order of importance to the Newberg Bay Society, the issues to be discussed today are:

1. Monitoring
2. Choice of technology
3. Fines and the possibility of Gadgets temporarily closing
4. Possible subsidy (if CLEEN is approved)

Monitoring

NBS is most concerned about the health of the bay. This requires frequent monitoring of pollution prevention technologies, especially if experimental. With experimental systems, operations will inevitably not proceed as expected. Problems with the technology are to be expected, but harm to the environment must be minimized. If the CLEEN system is approved, monthly monitoring is essential. Anything less frequent is unacceptable.

The DEP is best qualified to monitor the CLEEN system. ITP already has a working relationship with Elaine Dawkins of Pine Tree State University, who invented the CLEEN system. It therefore makes sense that the DEP conduct monitoring of the CLEEN system installed at Gadgets. ITP and Gadgets can be in close communication with Dawkins to address whatever problems might arise.

Choice of Technology

NBS is most in favor of the closed-loop configuration for the CLEEN system, as it presents the greatest opportunities for improvements in pollution prevention technology. The improved technology installed industry-wide would in turn affect improvements in environmental quality.

The CLEEN system installed as an open-loop would still allow the Dawkins team to further refine CLEEN by studying it operating in a midsized plant. The CLEEN system with an open loop is NBS' second choice.

Fines and Temporary Closing

NBS believes that Gadgets should pay all fines it accrues. The firm is directly polluting Newberg Bay and degrading the quality of the fertilizer pellets. Environmental regulations must not be negotiated away.

NBS also wants to see Gadgets closed immediately and remain closed until it can comply with state regulations. It is absurd that the DEP has allowed the firm to remain open this long. If the DEP does not agree to close Gadgets during this negotiation, NBS is prepared to work with Deep Green to request an emergency injunction against the firm.

Possible Subsidy (if CLEEN Is Approved)

NBS believes that the taxpayers should support the development of improved environmental technology. Ultimately, the public will benefit from improved environmental quality as a result of more efficient pollution prevention technology. It is unreasonable to require an individual firm to shoulder the entire burden of capital costs and financial risk from which the public will benefit.

This morning, Deep Green challenged the DEP in the *Newberg Daily Gazette* to make a contingent offer to Gadgets for 25 percent of the initial capital costs, followed by an additional 65 percent if the CLEEN system "failed." Based on the reports by Dawkins that you have read, you doubt that the system will "fail," as defined by Deep Green. The greatest help would be for the state to provide a joint grant with the State Manufacturing Development Fund to Gadgets.

Try to get the group to agree to NBS' first or second choice for each issue, especially your first two priorities. It is essential that Gadgets' pollution prevention system be vigilantly monitored, given the firm's history. At the same time, this is a golden opportunity to facilitate the development of more efficient pollution prevention technology and to help ITP win funding for another year. NBS members, who pay your salary with their contributions, are eager to see continued progress toward a fishable, swimmable, and breathable bay.

OPTION SHEET FOR C. EISEN, NEWBERG BAY SOCIETY CHIEF SCIENTIST

Issue 1: Monitoring

Priority	Options
1st choice	State monitors monthly.
2nd choice	EPA monitors monthly.
unacceptable	State monitors quarterly.
unacceptable	EPA monitors quarterly.
unacceptable	No additional monitoring.

Issue 2: Choice of Technology

Priority	Options
1st choice	Install CLEEN, closed loop, RCRA exempt.
2nd choice	Install CLEEN, open loop.
3rd choice	Replace current system with like system.
unacceptable	Repair current system.

Issue 3: Fines and Temporary Closing

Priority	Options
1st choice	Gadgets closed until in compliance and all fines forgiven.
2nd choice	Gadgets closed until in compliance and pays three months of fines.
3rd choice	Gadgets closed until in compliance and pays eight months of fines.
4th choice	Gadgets remains open and pays fines until in compliance.
5th choice	Gadgets remains open and pays eight months of fines.

| 6th choice | Gadgets remains open and pays three months of fines. |
| unacceptable | Gadgets remains open and all fines are forgiven. |

Issue 4: Possible Subsidy (if CLEEN Is Approved)

Priority	*Options*
1st choice	Subsidy for half the value of the initial costs: 35% from state and 15% from the State Manufacturing Development Fund.
2nd choice	Contingent offer: State will pay 25% of initial costs. If CLEEN fails, state will reimburse additional 65% of initial cost.
unacceptable	Gadgets covers entire expense.

Confidential Instructions for S. Cedar, Deep Green Director

Your primary concern is the continued progress toward a healthy Newberg Bay. You have given much of the last 15 years of your life to bringing Newberg Bay from one of the most polluted surface water bodies in the country to its present state. In addition, Deep Green's efforts have resulted in more breathable, clean air—a vast improvement from the "foggy" days of the last 50 years. Much progress has been made, but more work is still to be done. Whatever technology is chosen today, it is essential that the performance of Gadgets' pollution prevention system be closely monitored in the future. The progress that has been achieved must not be reversed.

You do not believe that unnecessary environmental risks should be taken in the name of scientific research. If the CLEEN system is installed and fails to perform properly, progress accomplished over the past 10 years toward a "fishable, swimmable, breathable" Newberg Bay will be undone.

You have a long-standing distrust of the DEP. In your view, it has repeatedly sided with industry at the expense of the environment. The ITP is an excellent example of this. ITP provides large grants to scientists at Pine Tree State University to develop products from which the university profits. While the products are ostensibly to improve environmental performance, they are also designed to cut costs for firms. The region has seen a large exodus of polluting industries in recent years. The state government is working hard with industry friendly programs like ITP to keep remaining polluting industries in the area.

After failing to notice that Gadgets was out of compliance for five months, the DEP has yet to collect any fines from the firm. At this meeting, you are sure that the DEP Secretary's Special Assistant will bargain with Gadgets to reduce the firm's fines in exchange for installing the CLEEN system.

You are offended that the DEP would use the Newberg environment as a laboratory for costly experiments at the expense of Newberg's environmental health. If a marketable product results from the experiments, then the state through the university will profit from the sales of the technology.

Further, you find Gadgets' blatant disregard of environmental health both shocking and appalling. Firms like this have no place in the city of Newberg. You have organized pickets in front of Gadgets over the past few months, replete with placards to that effect. If Gadgets closes or moves elsewhere as a result of the current conflict, it will be a victory for the Newberg environment.

Your goal today is to prevent an agreement from occurring. If no agreement is reached, the DEP will have to decide the matter internally. Your sources tell you that the DEP is badly divided over the Gadgets issue. Staff members from the ERD and the ITP have quit speaking to each other. The Environmental Secretary decided to hold today's meeting in order to deflect attention from the agency's divisiveness.

Meanwhile, ITP is under review by a special cost-cutting committee of the state legislature. ITP is the brainchild of the Environmental Secretary. It is now under attack by conservatives in the state legislature as a frivolous way to fund academics. ITP needs to prove its worth quickly. At this point, having the CLEEN system installed at Gadgets is its only chance. If no agreement is reached today, the DEP staff is likely to remain deadlocked on the issue of CLEEN for some time. As a result, ITP's funding for next year would likely not be renewed.

Last week, you and the director of the Newberg Bay Society announced that the two organizations would jointly file for an emergency injunction against Gadgets if the firm did not come into compliance. You fully intend to make good on that threat. If Gadgets installs the CLEEN system and the CLEEN system fails to adequately protect Newberg Bay, you will still file. You are concerned that the Newberg Bay Society, being more mainstream, will be willing to live with the CLEEN system. Though it is unproven and may make conditions worse, some Newberg Bay Society staff may be attracted by the promise of technological advancement. It is important to keep the environmental coalition as united as possible. Try to convince the representative of Newberg Bay Society today of your position.

You have also heard the Gadgets Workers' Union doesn't want a closed-loop CLEEN system, due to concerns about asbestos. You are willing to form a coalition with the Union, but only if this guarantees a blocked agreement. While you recognize the future political repercussions of blocking an agreement, today's meeting represents the best opportunity to improve Newberg Bay's environment.

If it appears that the other five parties are going to reach a consensus today, then you should work to have as many of your high-ranking options included in the final agreement as possible. In order of importance to Deep Green, the issues to be discussed today are:

1. Monitoring
2. Fines and the possibility of Gadgets' temporarily closing
3. Choice of technology
4. Possible subsidy (if CLEEN is approved)

Monitoring

Your most important concern today is monitoring. If the CLEEN system is installed, it is essential that Gadgets is monitored on a frequent basis by a third party. Experimental technology is, by nature, apt to fail. The SCRUB system is known to fail on a regular basis. Failures in either system must be known immediately, so those problems can be rectified. The crucial goal is to maintain the health of Newberg Bay, which means identifying failed pollution prevention systems as quickly as possible.

The DEP has shown itself time and again to be inefficient. You would therefore prefer that the EPA conduct the monitoring. Omitting third-party monitoring systems is unacceptable, as this poses an enormous risk to the environment.

Fines and Temporary Closing

Together with the Newberg Bay Society, you have threatened in the press in the past weeks to file an injunction against Gadgets if the DEP did not close the plant until it came into compliance. If the group reaches a consensus today, it is important that they agree to shut the plant until a pollution prevention system is repaired or installed. If the group agrees to allow the plant to remain open, it is unlikely that a judge would then grant an injunction.

Gadgets is harming the air and water quality of Newberg Bay with its release of heavy metals. The firm has done so with impunity for eight months. It must be stopped, both for the health of the bay and to send a message to other polluting industries.

Gadgets should also pay the fines they have accrued, beginning with the first day the firm was out of compliance and up until the firm closes or comes into compliance. Environmental laws should not be weakened by negotiating away the fine system.

Choice of Technology

You contacted a reporter friend at the *Newberg Daily Gazette* to write an article for this morning's paper on the subject of today's negotiations. The friend naturally interviewed you as a source. In the interview you referred to a study done by an independent lab, which found that the CLEEN system is actually much less effective than the SCRUB system. This study had apparently been repressed by the DEP.

The SCRUB system is not perfect, but, when properly maintained, it cleans wastewater and air emissions to the standards prescribed by state regulations. A new SCRUB system would likely perform better than simply repairing the old one.

The closed-loop configuration of the CLEEN system, exempt from the RCRA, is unacceptable. The system is likely to fail, still being in the development stage. If the firm is allowed to forego all capacity to handle hazardous waste in accordance with the RCRA guidelines, human and environmental health would be put at risk in case of system failure.

Possible Subsidy (if CLEEN Is Approved)

In the newspaper article this morning, you challenged the DEP to show its faith in the CLEEN system by making a contingent offer to pay for 90 percent of the installation costs if the system fails. If the DEP agrees to do this, you will feel more comfortable with both the CLEEN system and the idea of its being publicly subsidized. If they do not, you believe that public funds should not be used for such a risky project.

OPTION SHEET FOR S. CEDAR, DEEP GREEN DIRECTOR

Issue 1: Monitoring

Priority	Options
1st choice	EPA monitors monthly.
2nd choice	State monitors monthly.
unacceptable	EPA monitors quarterly.
unacceptable	State monitors quarterly.
unacceptable	No additional monitoring.

Issue 2: Fines and Temporary Closing

Priority	Options
1st choice	Gadgets closed until in compliance and pays eight months of fines.
2nd choice	Gadgets closed until in compliance and pays three months of fines.
3rd choice	Gadgets closed until in compliance and all fines forgiven.
4th choice	Gadgets remains open and pays fines until in compliance.
unacceptable	Gadgets remains open and pays eight months of fines.
unacceptable	Gadgets remains open and pays three months of fines.
unacceptable	Gadgets remains open and all fines are forgiven.

Issue 3: Choice of Technology

Priority	Options
1st choice	Replace current system with like system.
2nd choice	Repair current system.
3rd choice	Install CLEEN, open loop.
unacceptable	Install CLEEN, closed loop, RCRA exempt.

Issue 4: Possible Subsidy (if CLEEN Is Approved)

Priority	Options
1st choice	Contingent offer: State will pay 25% of initial costs. If CLEEN fails, state will reimburse additional 65% of initial cost.
2nd choice	Gadgets covers entire expense.
Unacceptable	Subsidy for half the value of the initial costs: 35% from state and 15% from the State Manufacturing Development Fund.

Simulation 2

ChemCo, Inc. *

Negotiating Compliance Review Before the Fact

OBJECTIVES

- Show how the mutual gains approach can be used to negotiate the terms by which compliance will be judged
- Negotiate the monitoring methods to be used
- Negotiate the assignment of responsibility for data collection and interpretation
- Negotiate how the validity of monitoring results will be determined

ISSUES

- Dealing with uncertainty
- Coping with the issue of precedent
- Dealing with differences in interpretation
- Understanding the sources of bargaining power
- Understanding the importance of public perceptions

General Instructions

ChemCo, Inc., is a manufacturing firm located in urban Shelton. Shelton is a small, working-class community in the Northeast, with a population of 20,000. The unemployment rate in Shelton is 10 percent (well above the national average). ChemCo employs 3000 people, making it the largest employer in Shelton and thus very important to the community, both economically and politically. While there are other manufactur-

---

* This case was written by Wendy Pabich under the supervision of Professor Lawrence Susskind at MIT. Copies are available from the Clearinghouse, Program on Negotiation, Harvard Law School (617-495-1684). This case may not be reproduced, revised, or translated in whole or in part by any means without the written permission of the Director of the Clearinghouse. Copyright © 1993, 1995 by the President and Fellows of Harvard College and the Consensus Building Institute. All rights reserved.

ing companies located in Shelton, none is as influential and as important to the community as ChemCo.

ChemCo maintains a coal-fired generating plant on its grounds to provide electricity for its manufacturing process. The generator uses coal to drive turbines that produce about 250 million BTUs (British Thermal Units) of heat energy per hour. The company is currently negotiating with the state Department of Environmental Protection (DEP) to devise an acceptable strategy to monitor the air emissions of the generator. These negotiations are very important to the company, the community, and the DEP. The economic impact on the community will be devastating if ChemCo is forced to cut back jobs as a result of too-stringent environmental regulations. On the other hand, much rests on this case in the view of the DEP. ChemCo is thought to be the primary contributor to air pollution in the area, and thus needs to be monitored effectively. In addition, several communities within the region are experiencing similar air-quality difficulties and regulatory questions. The precedent put forth by the outcome of this case will clearly impact the resolution of similar cases in the region.

The DEP regulations designate all coal generating plants producing 250 million or greater BTUs/hour as Class I. Class I facilities are required to perform continuous emissions monitoring (CEM) of their air emissions. CEM essentially allows for real-time, continuous measurement of certain pollutants as they are released through the stack. Plants producing less than 250 million BTUs/hour are designated as Class II and are not required to use CEM. However, Class II plants are required to perform either compliance tests or parameter monitoring. Compliance tests are one-time measurements of certain pollutants as they are released through the stack, and may be required with varying frequency depending on the needs of the DEP and the company. Parameter monitoring is an indirect, but continuous, measure of emissions, which tests various parameters of the combustion process (such as emissions rate, flame temperature, and retention) and infers emissions levels from those measurements.

In addition to emissions monitoring, the DEP requires that the pollution-abatement equipment used to control emissions be tested to ensure that it is effectively removing pollutants. ChemCo is currently using both scrubbers to control sulfur emissions and electrostatic precipitators to control particulate emissions. It has not yet been decided how often this equipment will be tested nor who will pay for the testing.

The ambient air quality in the state has been a problem for several years. During the past two summers, statewide ambient air readings have shown the state to be in violation of federal limits five or six times over the course of three months. Residents of Shelton are concerned that the air in their community is of equally poor quality. There are currently no ambient air monitoring stations in the city of Shelton, and the citizens are demanding that the DEP begin ambient air monitoring in their city. They are convinced that ChemCo is the primary contributor to local pollution.

The DEP and representatives from ChemCo have met several times in the past to discuss air emissions monitoring. You will now attend the last meeting between the two groups. The CEO, the environmental engineer, and the public relations officer from ChemCo will be present at the meeting, as will the DEP's Air Quality branch chief, environmental engineer, and public affairs officer. It is your job to work out and finalize the details of the monitoring agreement in the allotted time. Five issues need to be resolved:

1. *The type of emissions monitoring that will be used to ensure that ChemCo is complying with air emissions standards.* The three possible types of monitoring are: continuous emissions monitoring, compliance testing, and parameter monitoring.
2. *The timing of reporting.* The company is required to furnish the results of emissions monitoring efforts in the form of reports. The content of the reports has already been decided. However, you must now decide how often the firm is required to submit these reports to the DEP.
3. *The timing and payment of pollution abatement equipment testing.* By law, ChemCo's pollution control equipment must undergo periodic testing. It is unclear how often this testing should take place, or who will pay for it. It is up to the two groups to decide.
4. *Construction of ambient monitoring stations.* As a result of citizen concern over ambient air quality, and the perception that ChemCo is contributing to poor air quality, the DEP has requested that ChemCo help pay the capital costs associated with the construction of ambient monitoring stations throughout the city. This point is up for debate.
5. *The definition of a "violation" of emissions standards.* The law states that the company is liable for a fine of $100,000 per day in violation of emissions standards. How this standard is defined is negotiable.

LESSONS
- Recognize internal agreement is an important element in external negotiations.
- Work to clarify interests—listen more than you talk; play back what you think you've heard.
- Explore possible trades—but separate inventing from committing.
- Present arguments on their merits—emphasize "because" statements.
- Maintain multiple options for as long as possible—stress contingent possibilities.
- Keep something you can give in reserve.

Simulation 3

Bog Berries versus the Federal Environmental Agency*

Negotiating Your Way Back into Compliance

Objectives

- To show how the mutual gains approach can be used to negotiate remedies and timetables for getting back into compliance
- How quickly must you get back into compliance?
- What technological solutions are acceptable?
- What will the penalties be for noncompliance?

Issues

- Dealing with anger and self-righteousness
- Blaming the victim
- Coping with a loss of trust
- Dealing with differences in perception
- Understanding the sources of bargaining power
- Understanding the importance of public perceptions

General Instructions

Last year Bog Berries, a Fortune 500 firm, was charged with six counts of intentionally dumping corrosive chemicals into sewers near its Bogtown, Massachusetts, plant—the

---

first time felony charges were filed by the Federal Environmental Agency (FEA) under the revisions of the U.S. Clean Water Act. Bog Berries was also charged with 72 misdemeanor counts of discharging acidic cranberry peelings, preservatives, and other allegedly harmful chemicals into municipal sewers and the Nemasket River over a 50-year period, despite repeated pleas from Bogtown to stop. These counts occurred either before the new amendments were enacted or involved negligent, but not intentional, violations.

Company executives responded by downplaying the significance of the incident, claiming that they were being cited for "releasing small amounts of cranberries and cranberry skins into the Nemasket River and releasing cranberry juice into the town's sewage treatment system." They claimed that "at no time did Bog Berries endanger the public's health or the environment." Also, Bog Berries claimed, "The government might conceive that one cranberry falling from a truck into a river could constitute a violation of this regulation." The board of directors voted to plead innocent on all counts. The facts were as follows:

1. Bog Berries daily discharged 200,000 gallons of waste water that included "harmful chemicals, corrosive materials and excessive acidity" that threatened sewage facilities and the river. On several occasions, the company discharged pollutants directly into the Nemasket River.
2. This activity has been occurring for approximately 12 years.
3. Bogtown repeatedly warned Bog Berries that they were damaging the sewer system and violating federal regulations. Bogtown says that it frequently fined the company $200/day for such action over the past several years. This had no effect on Bog Berries' activities. In fact, Bog Berries refers to these payments as "surcharges," not fines. Bogtown requested the involvement of the FEA.
4. The firm is Bogtown's largest employer (over 500 people, or approximately 3 percent of the town's residents, work full-time at the plant; that number frequently doubles during the harvest season) and has strong ties with the town. As an example of this, the letterhead on official municipal stationary describes Bogtown as the "cranberry capital of the world." Over the course of four years, Bog Berries purchased $12 million in goods and services from local vendors. It paid $238,000 in property taxes, $152,000 in sewer bills, and $160,000 in water bills last year.
5. About 15 years ago, Bog Berries contributed $915,000, a substantial percentage of the total cost, to help build the town sewer facility it is now charged with damaging.

Eleven months into litigation, Bog Berries and the FEA worked out a plea bargain. Bog Berries pleaded guilty to 20 misdemeanor charges and one count of releasing waste water into the river. They were fined $400,000 plus $100,000 toward a new water treatment facility for Bogtown.

Despite this settlement, feelings on both sides are still raw. Bog Berries suffered severe public relations damage as the media tore them apart as a kind of eco-villain. Headlines ran the gamut from, "Bog Berries says Pollution 'Not our problem'" to "Dangerous Polluters Declare Innocence." Bog Berries is furious that the FEA allowed these exaggerations and/or misperceptions to continue in the press. The FEA points out that they suffered their share of PR problems as well. Bog Berries representatives repeatedly referred to them as "Eco-freaks" and "job killers" in interviews, saying that this trial amounted to a kind of enviro-McCarthyism. None of these comments made the local offices very popular with the regional or federal commissioners. The local FEA has received several reminders from the federal offices that the agency is a political body that ought to carefully choose its battles. If this is one they are going to choose, the federal office will stand behind them—but the local group had better be right. The pressure is on for both sides and neither is very happy with the other.

Now that the court case is over, Bog Berries still faces a dilemma. To continue operations it must acquire new equipment to handle the waste appropriately and it must also acquire a permit to discharge it. You are coming into a meeting, representing either Bog Berries or the FEA, to draw up an agreement stipulating the terms of the permit application. This is not a negotiation as to whether or not Bog Berries will be granted the permit. It is only to establish the application protocol, what each party can expect from the other.

Five primary issues are to be resolved in the meeting between the two parties:

1. Will Bog Berries be allowed to continue its current operating practices while the application is being processed?
2. What sort of technology should Bog Berries use to comply with the regulations? Three options are to be considered: (1) Cleaning their paved areas to prevent acidic build-up (sidewalk washing). This would cut down on acids in the storm water runoff system, but have little effect on industrial runoff into the sewage system. (2) Begin collecting their water and paying Bogtown to process it. (3) Installing an industrial pretreatment plant so that water discharged into the sewer system is not corrosive.
3. What sort of evidence will the FEA require to show that the chosen method does in fact meet the regulations? Testing could be done in-house, by an outside consultant, or by an FEA agent (either entirely or as a spot-checker).
4. The frequency of the testing is also up for debate. The options are continuously, monthly, annually, or only after storm events.
5. The timing of the whole application process is an issue. Bog Berries can have a deadline of 4 months from now, 6 months from now, 8 months from now, or 12 months from now. The FEA, in turn, can commit to processing the application in 4 months, 6 months, 10 months, or 12 months. While the deadlines that are acceptable may be dependent on other factors, any deadlines mentioned in this exercise refer only to Bog Berries submitting the application or the FEA processing the application.

Simulation 4

MC Metals*
Negotiating Your Way Back into Compliance

General Instructions

MC Metals, Woodville's largest employer (employing almost 1000 people) has been operating at only 40 percent of capacity since a deadly chemical fire and two explosions ripped through Building A of the factory on Spring Street, just west of downtown, one month ago. Two MC Metals employees were killed and five other persons, including three Woodville firefighters, suffered serious injuries as the result of the blaze, which occurred when waste sodium was being burned at the plant. One of the injured, Jake Jensen, a young firefighter who was a football hero at Woodville High just a few years earlier, remains hospitalized with burns over 75 percent of his body. The other victims have been released following treatment at area hospitals, but all will have to undergo extensive skin grafting.

Founded 70 years ago by brothers Mark and Charles Adams, MC Metals is now a wholly owned subsidiary of ACL (Advanced Concepts Ltd.), a multinational firm whose main office is in London. Worldwide sales exceeded $400 million in 1998. A few work-related injuries have occurred over the years at MC Metals, but until the explosions and fire two months ago, no fatalities or permanent injuries.

For a week after the fatal fire, Town Mayor Elinor Weeks Dennison ordered Building A sealed off, pending a report on the building's structural safety.

Investigators from the state Fire Marshal's Office and the federal government's Occupational Safety and Health Administration (OSHA), working jointly, issued their report last week. They clearly put the blame for the fire on the company. According to their

---

* This case was written by Dan DeLisi, under the supervision of Professor Lawrence Susskind and Paul Levy of MIT. Copies are available from the Clearinghouse, Program on Negotiation, Harvard Law School. It may not be reproduced, revised, or translated in whole or in part by any means without the written permission of the authors or the Director of the Clearinghouse. Copyright © 1999 by the President and Fellows of Harvard College and the MIT Department of Urban Studies and Planning. All rights reserved.

report, "MC Metals knowingly violated workplace safety standards through the excess burning of sodium in an area where substantial moisture was present, leading to the endangerment of its employees and the immediate community."

In accordance with the Occupational Safety and Health Administration Act of 1970, they have proposed that MC Metals be fined a total of $49,000: $42,000 under section 5(a), failure to secure a safe working environment; $5,000 under section 1910.1200, inadequate Hazard Communication Program, including a failure to provide proper labels and train employees in the handling of hazardous chemicals, listed as a repeat offense; and $2,000 for failure to provide blood-borne pathogen certification for designated first-aid employees.

It is not the size of the fines as much as the terrible publicity that has both MC Metals executives and town officials worried.

Background

The entire MC Metals complex, a red-brick structure constructed at the turn of the century as a shoe factory, was honored last year with a commendation from the State Historical Landmarks Commission as an example of effective re-use of architecturally significant buildings. MC Metals spent several million dollars to redo the interior of the factory complex, which has been hailed in Metallurgy Monthly as " . . . an ingenious example of state-of-the-art technology located within a gorgeous historic building." In a separate building next door, MC Metals houses its national headquarters. The Woodville town green, bordered by Town Hall, the police and fire departments, three 19th century churches, and a collection of imposing Greek revival homes, is less than a block away at the intersection of Main and Spring Street. Just to the west of the MC Metals complex is Woodville Falls, where developer Angela Redstone is currently constructing 40 huge new homes, all of which are expected to have $600,000-plus asking prices. Most of Woodville's homes, however, are far more modest.

Building Inspector Tom Chasen ruled that there were no structural defects in Building A, and work has resumed at MC Metals, but well below the factory's full capacity. Repairs have been made to Building A, where waste sodium had been disposed of in the past. However, MC Metals CEO John Schneider, acting on the advice of ACL's corporate counsel, has ordered that production of products involving sodium be temporarily halted.

There are rumors in Woodville that ACL might shut down the MC Metals plant entirely, shifting nearly 1000 jobs to a brand-new facility in Georgia. In fact, in a statement released to the *Woodville Times* recently, John Schneider stated that, "If the Woodville plant becomes too expensive to operate we will have to look for other options." Most MC Metals employees live in Woodville and surrounding towns, and the plant's closure would be devastating to the local economy. Another rumor circulating around town is that Angela Redstone has her eye on the Spring Street property for possible condominium conversion, but in a price range that would be well above the means of the people who work at MC Metals.

MC Metals has production plants in the United States, Canada, and Taiwan. Its production program includes powders made from the refractory metals tungsten, rhenium, tantalum, and niobium, as well as from nonferrous metals like cobalt and nickel. Most of the activity is centered on tantalum and niobium, metals used in the production of anti-lock braking devices, cellular telephones, and personal computers. Both substances arrive at the plant in salt form. Sodium is also used in a reduction process to extract the metals. This leaves an unreacted sodium residual, which is later burned as a waste product (to save money on disposal costs).

There is no question that the fire started as a result of the sodium burning. An initial explosion, which caused the injuries to the MC Metals employees, was followed by a second blast that occurred as firefighters attempted to put down the blaze, sending a deadly shower of molten sodium down on them. During the fire, as a precautionary measure, over 100 persons were evacuated from their homes, as were the construction workers at "Woodville Falls." All in all, witnesses say that employees, workers, and residents were lucky that this was not an even worse disaster.

The weekly *Woodville Times* has covered the story relentlessly. The paper, one of a chain of weeklies owned by Angela Redstone, has printed stories headlined: "Report Finds MC Metals a Repeat Offender" and "MC Metals Endangers Workers and Community." In a series of editorials, the *Times* has assailed MC Metals "and its absentee owners" for being "criminally negligent" and having a "long-time record of poor safety performance."

The MC Metals public relations team has tried to counteract some of this damage and correct several errors in the news reports. In general, the PR campaign has stressed the following.

The company's concern for its employees and the community is well established. Last year MC Metals donated more than $1 million to various local causes. Substantial college trust funds have been established for the children of the two MC Metals workers who died in the explosion, and the company has contributed a total of $40,000 to the "Jake Jensen Relief Fund," to assist his wife and two young children. Company HR staff are working with the other injured employees to ensure that they are in no immediate financial need.

No federal or state regulations exist covering the burning of sodium, although there are suggested guidelines—which MC Metals has followed. The person who authorized the increased burning of sodium at MC Metals prior to the fire has already been transferred. Similar fires and explosions should never happen again.

MC Metals has a good safety record. Two years ago, MC Metals instituted a new safety program, above and beyond what OSHA regulations require.

After an intensive investigation, OSHA and the state Fire Marshal found only minor infractions, including two that have nothing to do with the fire—labeling of an acetone container and blood-borne pathogen certification. MC Metals intends to contest all of the alleged infractions.

In this week's *Times,* the president of the Woodville Firefighters Union is quoted as saying, "MC Metals is covering up. The company has already killed two people. How many more need to die?" On the other hand, in the same story, the head of the MC Metals Workers' Union points out that company employees "have worked closely with the Fire Department many, many times on safety training programs. What happened two months ago was an accident, a terrible, terrible tragedy. But it really was a fluke."

MC Metals and its parent company are facing several multimillion-dollar lawsuits filed by the families of the dead and injured firefighters and workers. The suit filed on Jake Jensen's behalf blames the company for "failure to secure a safe work area, reckless endangerment, and neglect in providing essential information on the scene of the explosion." The case is built around the fact that company management and workers did not inform firefighters on the scene that there was moisture near the reacting sodium. The lawsuit also charges that the company mishandled hazardous waste (including the excessive burning of sodium).

Present Situation

MC Metals executives are eager to get the Woodville plant up and running again. The company's noncompliance status in OSHA's eyes and the public outcry is keeping this from happening. Under OSHA's Employer Rights regulations, MC Metals, following an inspection, can contest and negotiate the charges and fines through an Informal Conference and Settlement.

Given the high-profile nature of this case, the public outcry, and MC Metal's reluctant approval, OSHA has asked a representative of the labor union, the Fire Chief of Woodville, and a local resident and chemical expert to participate in a settlement discussion.

The four issues on the agenda are:

1. *Hazard Communication Program.*
    a. *Failure to adequately label hazardous chemicals.* MC Metals currently uses a system involving designated colors and numbers for safety levels and shapes for types of hazard. For example, a red label with a square means that this is a very hazardous chemical that, if inhaled, will cause lung damage. This is meant to suit the needs of the large immigrant population and nonnative English speakers in the workforce.

       Section 1910.1200(f)(6) of the Occupational Safety and Health Act states that: "The employer must ensure that labels or other forms of warning are legible, in English, prominently displayed on the container, or readily available in the work area throughout each work shift. Employers who have employees who speak other languages may add the information in their language to the material presented, as long as the information is presented in English as well."

       However OSHA's Hazard Communication Guidelines for Compliance state: "One difference between this rule and many others adopted by OSHA is that this one is performance oriented. That means you have the flexibility to adapt the rule to the needs of your workplace, rather than having to follow specific rigid requirements. . . ."
    b. *A failure to label acetone containers.* MC Metals buys acetone (used as a cleaning agent) in bulk to save money. The acetone is then poured into small containers and placed on a shelf with a sign marked "acetone," using the company's color-coded system. MC Metals interpreted the regulation to mean

that, if the acetone was not supposed to be moved, this would be acceptable. It was noted that this violation was totally unrelated to the accident.

    c. *The need to institute an effective training program that will familiarize workers with the hazards to which they may be exposed.* It is also essential to understand emergency procedures. At the time of the fire, too much sodium was being burned, and the plant manager did not adequately inform the firefighters of the hazardous situation when they arrived. Some important questions regarding the Hazard Communication Program training, if it is needed, are: How should it be done, and who should be involved (all plant workers, temporary employees, and office staff)? Should first-aid training be continued? If so, how? Who needs to be trained? With both programs, what should the timeline be? What assistance, if any, will OSHA provide in these efforts?

2. *First-Aid Program.* Failure to provide training for designated first-aid personnel on blood-borne pathogen exposure. The issue is who needs to have this training.

3. *Category of Violation.* MC Metals was burning excessive amounts of sodium through an unsafe, untested process, in an area of the plant where excessive moisture was present, creating a hazardous environment. MC Metals wants to shift the violation from the more severe "criminal/willful" category to the less severe "serious" category. MC Metals wants the citation for the Hazard Communication Program (the labeling system and the acetone container) and First-Aid Program to shift from the more severe "serious" category to the less severe "other-than-serious" category.

4. *Reduction of Fines.* OSHA has the prerogative to use its discretion in adjusting fines and violation categories only if it is convinced that supplementary actions justify such reductions.

The Upcoming Informal Conference and Settlement

The upcoming Informal Conference is expected to last for about one hour. The company would like to convince OSHA to drop its proposed fines and reduce the severity of the category of violation. Residents and town officials would like certain promises regarding future safety practices at MC Metals, although they certainly wouldn't want the company to close down the plant. MC Metal employees are concerned about worker safety, but they are also worried about losing their jobs if the plant closes. OSHA must be concerned about setting the appropriate precedent and ensuring worker and community safety. Everyone would like to minimize the number of lawsuits growing out of the accident, although those initiated by the families of the people who died are inevitable. The Environmental Protection Agency (EPA) has up until now remained on the sidelines. However, the EPA has indicated that if no agreement is reached, they may intervene under separate statutory authority.

    General counsel for MC Metals and the town solicitor in Woodville have drafted an agreement that everyone has signed. It ensures that any settlement offers made at this meeting cannot be cited in any subsequent litigation.

    The OSHA Area Director, S. O'Connor, has issued a statement saying that OSHA will try to reach agreement on all matters. The group will be asked to issue a brief press statement summarizing the terms of its agreement.

Participants at the Informal Conference and Settlement will be:

- *E. Douglas, OSHA Compliance and Safety Officer.* Douglas has been a Compliance and Safety Officer at OSHA for four years. After earning a bachelor's degree in political science and a master's in public policy, Douglas began working at OSHA and has risen through the ranks by dint of hard work and an in-depth technical understanding of worker safety issues. Douglas is zealous about enforcing OSHA rules and regulations. He has been called a "company killer" by some critics.

- *S. O'Connor, OSHA Area Director.* O'Connor has had a long career in safety compliance, which began 20 years ago with service as an Army officer. Following discharge, O'Connor was hired by Green Globe, the country's largest solid waste corporation, to be a safety manager responsible for enhancing and developing their safety program. Eight years ago, O'Connor started to work for OSHA as a compliance and safety officer and was quickly promoted to Area Director. O'Connor has a reputation for being effective and fair, with a unique ability to see all sides of every issue.

- *R. Flynn, Union Representative, MC Metals.* Flynn has worked at MC Metals in Woodville for nearly 20 years. He is currently a team manager in the Tantalum Production Division. Three years ago, Flynn was elected president of the company's union with strong support from all factions. Flynn has managed to maintain a strong working relationship with management and has been closely involved with implementation of safety programs.

- *J. Ciccarelli, Town Fire Chief.* Ciccarelli has been a firefighter for over 25 years and was appointed chief five years ago. Ciccarelli has won numerous awards for leadership and bravery. Two Woodville mayors have honored Ciccarelli for contributions to Woodville, particularly preventive safety measures. Over the past two years, Ciccarelli initiated a training program with MC Metals and other local companies whose work creates potential fire hazards. Ciccarelli is a familiar figure at MC Metals, knows the company's situation well, and has been asked to attend the Settlement Conference by the mayor.

- *H. Berman, Health and Safety Manager, MC Metals.* Berman, after receiving an MBA degree, began working for MC Metals in the Human Resources Department, quickly becoming the rising star of the company. Two years later, when MC Metals started a Health and Safety Department, Berman was promoted to Manager. Since then, Berman has worked with company executives and the union to implement a safety program going above and beyond OSHA regulations.

- *P. Schumann, Woodville Resident.* Schumann resides in one of the imposing homes on the Woodville Common, just a short distance from the MC Metals plant. Schumann earned a Ph.D. in chemistry, specializing in metals production, and now works with companies as a highly paid consultant on hazardous chemical safety. Though active in community affairs, Schumann has no prior relationship with MC Metals.

LESSONS

- Work to clarify interests on both sides.
- Work to rebuild trust.
- Present arguments on their merits; emphasize objective criteria.
- Stress contingent agreements and possible triggers.
- Explore the possible use of neutral parties.

Simulation 5

*Carson Extension**

Negotiating Settlement

OBJECTIVE
- To show how the mutual gains approach can be applied in settlement negotiations even after legal action has been initiated

ISSUES
- What causes regulatees to comply?
- When and under what circumstances are threats effective?
- When and under what circumstances are trades (or incentives) appropriate?

General Instructions

Carson Rug Company is a midsized, family-owned business located in Garth. The business is ideally located along the Melrose River and a major interstate within commuting distance of a large metropolitan area. This business and property is owned by Stuart Carson.

Stuart Carson, thinking of expanding his property to accommodate larger shipments and more clientele, applied for an Army Corps of Engineers Section 404 permit to place and maintain a fill and riprap seawall to extend into the Melrose River. Since the river is a complex ecological habitat, his original application was denied due to the extension's potentially harmful effects on the fisheries nearby. However, his second application, with specifications for a smaller extension, was determined environmentally safe and was

* This case was written by Holly Goo under the supervision of Professor Lawrence Susskind at MIT. Copies are available from the Clearinghouse, Program on Negotiation, Harvard Law School (617-495-1684). This case may not be reproduced, revised, or translated in whole or in part by any means without the written permission of the Director of the Clearinghouse. Copyright © 1993, 1995, by the President and Fellows of Harvard College and the Consensus Building Institute. All rights reserved.

approved. The difference between the original and reduced specifications was over 3000 square feet, almost halving the size of the authorized fill.

Stuart Carson contracted with the Hills Engineering firm to do the fill work. A year later, a Corps inspector realized the fill was not within the authorized bounds set by the 404 permit. Stuart Carson claims the noncompliance was unintentional and not his fault. He blames the engineering firm for misinterpreting his instructions.

In past cases of noncompliance, the violating party returns within compliance standards in accordance with the Corps and the permit, and also pays civil penalties. The severity of the penalty is based on the company's past compliance record, as well as whether or not the violation was deliberate. The actual technological solution to the violation is determined by the Corps to be the most environmentally sound, as well as cost and time efficient. However, they do consider recommendations from both the violating and other involved parties.

In this case, however, the Corps determined Stuart Carson's actions to be a deliberate and willful violation. The Corps believes he was well informed about the boundaries specified by the permit and the environmental impacts caused by extending beyond the specifications. Since this was not a continuing environmental harm, the Corps and the U.S. Attorney's Office placed this as a low-priority case, passing it from one assistant to another over the years. Thus the case of *U.S. versus Stuart Carson* was slow to go to court.

When the Corps of Engineers finally went to court to order the removal of the unauthorized fill and riprap, the court ruled in the Corps' favor. Settlement was that the fill would be removed to the authorized bounds according to plans drawn up by the Corps at two-thirds the cost to Stuart Carson and one-third the cost to the Hills Engineering firm. The Corps would organize and process the permit for removal. Upon receiving the plans and choosing a contractor, the removal of the unauthorized fill and riprap should occur within the 60 days with accommodations for bad weather.

By the time the court case was settled, six years had passed since the unauthorized fill was entered. The Corps had taken two additional years to formulate an environmentally sound removal plan. These plans were sent to Stuart Carson and Hills Engineering firm. The town is anxious for the resolution and issued an enforcement order to Stuart Carson to carry out the court-ordered removal.

By now, over 15 years have passed since the fill was illegally placed. The permit for the removal of the fill is still valid. You must negotiate a solution that is agreeable for all involved parties. The following three issues must be resolved:

1. *Environmental Considerations.* Can the situation be rectified 15 years later? Will the removal of the fill cause more harm than good? If removal is determined harmful, what other solutions are possible? How should the best solution be chosen?

2. *Time Considerations.* With 15 years already past, how quickly does the solution need to be implemented? Should recent bad publicity affect the urgency and implementation of the solution?

3. *Penalty Considerations.* The court has already determined that Stuart Carson is to

pay two-thirds of the cost of the environmental solution. Should he pay other civil penalties? Should Hills Engineering be fined as well?

You are about to enter a negotiation in which you will participate as one of the following parties: the lawyer from the Army Corps of Engineers, the environmental engineer from the Army Corps of Engineers, the representative from the Garth Town Council, Stuart Carson (the business and property owner), the representative from Hills Engineering, or the environmentalist from Green Earth. The meeting is being held in a private conference room in the Garth Town Hall. It has been called by the lawyer from the Army Corps of Engineers.

LESSONS
- Threats are only significant relative to the other party's BATNA (best alternative to a negotiated agreement).
- BATNAs are often unclear. Help the other side think through its BATNA.
- Bluffing is usually counterproductive.
- It is often possible to find trades of equivalent value, but offers to pay can be counterproductive.
- Unreasonable aspirations can often be the key obstacle to settlement.
- It is important to choose the right team spokesperson.
- Look for allies on the other side.

Debriefing Questions for Simulations 1–5

It is a good idea to answer a series of questions after each simulation. The following questions are designed to make sure that participants take away all possible lessons from their experience:

1. Which tables/negotiating groups got agreement? Which did not?
2. For those tables that did not get agreement, please describe the things that gave you difficulty or got in the way.
3. How did you try to deal with each of these obstacles?
4. For those tables that got agreement, please describe the basic elements of your agreement. (We almost always get a range of agreements.)
5. What do you think accounted for your success? Was each person completely satisfied with the outcome? Why or why not? Did you exceed your BATNAs?
6. In retrospect, how well did you use your preparatory time? What might you have done differently?
7. Did you use caucusing to build a winning coalition? What did you learn about that?
8. Did you do everything possible to create value? Can you give some examples?
9. When it was time to distribute value, what did you do to maintain relationships? Please give some examples.
10. How did you try to anticipate the problems of implementation in pulling together your agreement? Can you give some examples?
11. Of all the agreements you have heard described, which impresses you most? Why?
12. Let's turn to one of the groups with an impressive agreement. Who played the key role in formulating your agreement? (Turn to the person who seemed to have the greatest impact on the outcome.) Can you describe what you were trying to do? Can the others give their reactions?
13. Now that you have heard about some of the agreements reached, how do you evaluate both the process your group followed and the outcome you achieved? How might the group have done better? How might you (personally) have done better?
14. How would you describe your negotiating style? Do the others in your group confirm that? Do you think your negotiating style helped or hindered in this case? Do you think you could change your style if you had to?
15. Did the women in your groups negotiate differently from the men? If there were differences, can you describe them? Do you know what recent research and theory on the subject of gender and negotiation have to say?
16. Were there any aspects of cross-cultural negotiation represented in your group? Did these create difficulties? If so, please describe them. Do the others in your group confirm your diagnosis? If there were difficulties, to what do you attribute them? Do you know what recent research and theory on the subject of culture and negotiation have to say?
17. What role did scientific arguments or evidence play in the negotiations? In retrospect, what additional information do you wish you had going into the negotia-

tions? Why? Explain what impact that information might have had and why. Do the others in your group agree?

18. How would you describe the relationships with which your group ended? Will it be easy or hard the next time you meet? Why? What might you have done to produce even better relationships?

19. Do you think your group handled the process of conversation efficiently? What makes you think this? What could you have done to increase the group's efficiency?

20. Do you think your group got a fair outcome? What makes you say that? Do the others in your group (or in the room) agree with your definition of fairness? Did fairness play a big part in your negotiations?

21. Do you think that the parties in your group really intended to (and would be able to) live up to the commitments they made? Why or why not?

22. How might a mediator have helped your group? Please explain.

23. Explain the role that time pressure played throughout your negotiations.

24. Did anyone in your group lie? Did you know it at the time? How do you know it now? What impact did the lie have on the group and on the group's ability to get a good agreement? Did anyone bluff? Did you know it at the time? How do you know it now? What impact did bluffing have on the group and the group's ability to reach a good agreement?

25. Can you describe the sources of negotiating power that you had (or wished you had) in this simulation? What is the greatest source of power in a multi-issue, multiparty negotiation like this? How could you have increased your bargaining power? How might you have dealt with relative powerlessness more effectively?

26. How did the legal context within which you were negotiating shape the negotiations, if at all? Does this seem realistic to you? Why?

27. What were the most important lessons you drew from this simulation? What advice would you give to others playing your role in this simulation in the future.

Part 3

Case Examples of Negotiated Agreements

If the mutual gains approach to negotiating environmental agreements works, then there should be examples of actual agreements produced using these techniques. And indeed there are. In the pages that follow, we provide four such illustrations. Each case example is introduced briefly below.

Mercury Discharge Permits

The first case describes a permit negotiation involving the discharge of mercury, a highly toxic metal, into Boston's sewer system. In the early 1990s, the Massachusetts Water Resources Authority (MWRA) began including mercury as a regulated substance in its discharge permits for hospitals. MWRA had a zero-discharge standard for mercury, enforced at a level of 1 part per billion. Soon thereafter, a number of hospitals received notice that they were out of compliance with this standard; one was fined more than $100,000. The hospitals had no idea where the mercury was coming from, however, or how to keep it out of their waste streams. Instead of fighting the fines in court, a coalition of Boston-area hospitals and the MWRA began face-to-face discussions. A two-phase negotiation ensued, during which the parties developed two written agreements that outlined plans for jointly addressing the problem. In implementing these agreements, the two sides have worked together to determine and then eliminate the sources of the mercury contamination. As a result, the hospitals' average mercury concentration has dropped 83 percent, and a majority of the hospitals are now meeting the discharge standard. We have included in this part of the book a case study describing the negotiation process and copies of the two agreements.

Shoreline Restoration on Martha's Vineyard

The second case describes a negotiation among several federal, state, and local government agencies and other parties regarding roadway restoration and the prevention of beach erosion on Martha's Vineyard in Massachusetts. The roadway, an important route for emergency vehicles between the towns of Oak Bluffs and Edgartown, was being slowly destroyed by erosion and storms. Efforts to restore it, however, threatened the surrounding coastal ecosystems and required numerous federal, state, and local permits, including a Section 404 wetlands permit from the U.S. Army Corps of Engineers. With the help of a mediator, the various agencies and other interested parties forged an agreement outlining an interim plan for road and shoreline restoration. Included in this part is a short case study written by the mediator, as well as a copy of the final agreement.

Coastal Zone Regulations in Delaware

The third case describes the efforts of the Delaware Coastal Zone Advisory Committee—a negotiating group composed of representatives from industry, environmental groups, government agencies, and others. These diverse parties came together at the request of the governor of Delaware to develop recommendations for regulations to implement Delaware's Coastal Zone Act, an environmental and zoning law that prohibits heavy industry from building new facilities in the state's coastal area. The mediated negotiations—which began in an atmosphere of severe distrust and ill will among the parties—took more than a year. Included in this part is a case study written by the lead mediator, as well as a copy of the Memorandum of Understanding developed by the advisory committee.

Superfund Cleanup at the Massachusetts Military Reservation

The final case describes key turning points in a complex, multiyear negotiation among federal, state, and local governments and nongovernmental actors involved in the cleanup of a massive Superfund site at the Massachusetts Military Reservation (MMR) on Cape Cod. The Department of Defense is responsible for remediating the MMR's extensive and highly toxic groundwater contamination, but many players were involved in helping to determine an appropriate cleanup plan. The negotiations have involved the Air Force, the U.S. Environmental Protection Agency, the Massachusetts Department of Environmental Protection, four municipalities whose drinking water supplies are threatened, and a range of homeowner and environmental groups on Cape Cod. Together, these parties developed a report outlining goals, criteria, a specific decision-making process, and an enforceable schedule for cleanup of the 11 "plumes" of contaminated groundwater. We offer a case history of the MMR cleanup negotiations, written by one of the mediators, as well as a copy of the report.

What These Cases Teach Us

These four cases reflect the diverse issues, settings, and stakeholders that may be involved in what we broadly have been calling environmental negotiations. They illustrate how such negotiations can take place at a site-specific level, for example, involving only a few key parties, or they may involve statewide issues and dozens of stakeholders.

Despite their diversity, however, the four agreements and many others like them also have a number of things in common. First, they illustrate the complexity of most environmental negotiations. Such negotiations typically address contentious, multifaceted, and technically complex issues. To forge meaningful agreements, parties must often deal with a tremendous amount of science-intensive material. Second, they show how such negotiations tend to be managed (and should be managed) in a very transparent way.

That is, the process by which such agreements are negotiated is, itself, subject to some negotiation in order to ensure that no "back room" deals are made. Accountability in this kind of ad hoc decision making can only be assured through complete transparency. Finally, these cases reveal that even if all the stakeholding groups are not represented at the table, these groups must still give their approval—if only by withholding opposition when draft agreements are presented in various public forums.

Three of the four agreements we present were generated with the help of professional facilitators (the mercury case being the exception). It is enormously difficult, as we have pointed out in Parts 1 and 2 of this volume, to bring multiple parties together in a highly contentious situation without the help of a nonpartisan referee.

The "success" of these agreements could be evaluated in any number of ways. The most typical is to ask whether the agreements were produced at a lower cost and in less time than the outcomes that might otherwise have been generated in court or through a more conventional, political give and take. Such evaluations, however, must take account of what happens over a long period of time in order to be meaningful. Negotiated agreements, after all, may require more "up-front" time for getting organized and building trust among the parties, but they typically save a significant amount of time in the implementation and follow-through phases. We thus prefer to emphasize three other evaluation criteria: (1) the relationships created (and in place) when it comes time to implement the agreements; (2) the extent to which all stakeholders are satisfied in retrospect that they were treated fairly; and (3) the extent to which independent analysts, looking back on the information the parties had available to them, feel that all possible joint gains were maximized. We believe that the four agreements presented here more than pass muster according to these criteria.

Case 1

Mercury Discharge Permits

Jennifer Thomas-Larmer

Introduction

In February 1994, Beth Israel Hospital—one of the most prestigious medical institutions in the Boston area—was fined a whopping $118,400 for violating the federal Clean Water Act (CWA). The fine was levied by the Massachusetts Water Resources Authority (MWRA), the state government entity that regulates Boston-area sewage discharges under the mandate of the CWA. MWRA had fined Beth Israel after noting 16 instances of unacceptable levels of mercury in the hospital's waste stream. The agency has a zero-discharge standard for mercury, enforced at a level of 1 part per billion (ppb).

MWRA had given Beth Israel several warnings about the mercury violations, including a formal "notice of noncompliance" (NON). But hospital officials did not know how the mercury was getting into the waste stream, or how to stop it. "They had no idea what to do," said David Eppstein, director of policy and special projects at the Medical Academic and Scientific Community Organization (MASCO), a coalition of Boston-area hospitals and academic institutions. "They had never been asked to test for mercury before. They had no idea where it was coming from. They were not aware of spills having occurred."[1]

Beth Israel officials raised their dilemma with MASCO's other member hospitals. They discovered that many of those hospitals were also having to test for mercury for the first time and were facing enforcement actions as the result of mercury violations.

Indeed, MWRA had been adding mercury to the list of substances covered by discharge permits as each of those permits came up for renewal. Although the CWA does not specifically require the regulation of mercury discharges, the law authorizes agencies like MWRA to use discretion to determine which substances should be regulated. Mercury is a substance of concern to MWRA because it is highly toxic to both humans and wildlife. It can damage human cells and collect in muscle tissue, causing neurological toxicity and harming the kidneys and lungs (Sessler, 1998). MWRA is responsible for, and at that time had begun making remarkable progress in, the cleanup of the notoriously polluted Boston Harbor (Save the Harbor/Save the Bay, undated). MWRA

109

wanted to keep mercury out of the harbor, and out of the sewage sludge the agency processes and sells in the form of fertilizer pellets.

In 1994, it looked as though Beth Israel's fine would be the opening volley in a long and acrimonious legal battle. MWRA was determined to reduce mercury discharges. Yet the hospitals did not know how to stop the discharges and were determined to go to court to fight the fines.

Fast forward to 1999. At this writing, 63 percent of the hospitals' sampling locations that were in violation of the mercury standard have come into compliance with the 1 ppb enforceable limit. Those hospitals that are still having problems are working closely with MWRA to fix those problems—conducting source reduction programs, testing pretreatment technologies, and so forth. Along the way, MWRA and the hospitals worked together to discover valuable information about mercury sources and discharge prevention. They even received a joint award for toxics reduction and control from the governor of Massachusetts. To top it off, officials from MASCO and MWRA have developed productive working relationships and speak very highly of each other.

What happened in the interim to produce this success? Essentially, MWRA and the hospitals applied (though perhaps without realizing it) many of the principles of mutual gains negotiation. Instead of squaring off in court, they worked together toward the common goal of reducing mercury discharges. They negotiated two agreements that set forth the parameters and goals of their partnership and the way in which MWRA would exercise its enforcement discretion with regard to mercury (embodied in memos from Kevin McManus dated December 2, 1994 and March 6, 1997, presented later). In those negotiations, they explored interests, invented options, traded on things they valued differently, and developed workable agreements. This case study describes how they did it.

Phase One

We begin by discussing the interests and BATNAs (best alternative to a negotiated agreement) of the parties, and then describe the first phase of the negotiation and the implementation of the first negotiated agreement.

Interests and BATNAs

At the outset, MWRA officials had several key interests. Perhaps most important, they were committed to making continued progress in cleaning up Boston Harbor. In the 1980s, Boston Harbor was infamous for being the dirtiest harbor in the United States. The MWRA was created in 1984 specifically to clean it up—to take over sewage treatment responsibility from the beleaguered Metropolitan District Commission (Save the Harbor/Save the Bay, undated). By 1994, the agency had made great progress in that endeavor, but the job was not yet finished. Also, MWRA needed to ensure that its sewage sludge, which it had recently begun processing rather than dumping into the harbor, was "clean" enough to sell in the form of fertilizer pellets.

MWRA also had to prove to the U.S. Environmental Protection Agency (EPA), the hospitals, other industries, and the public that they were serious about reducing mercury discharges. The EPA oversees MWRA's pollution discharge control efforts and could bring legal action against MWRA if the agency were not adequately enforcing federal law. The hospitals, MWRA officials believed, were a significant source of mercury discharges. MWRA also did not want environmental groups to believe that the agency was lax in its enforcement; its good public image had to be maintained. Thus, MWRA could not appear to bend under pressure from the hospitals by, for instance, simply making the discharge standard less stringent. Ultimately, MWRA needed the hospitals to reduce their mercury discharges.

"We did not have what I would call an acute mercury compliance problem ourselves," explained Kevin McManus, Director of MWRA's Toxic Reduction and Control Department (TRAC). "That is to say, [the mercury level in] our effluent and our sludge products . . . was high enough that we should keep an eye on it, but compared to other pollutants it was not as significant." But, he added, "the difference was that mercury has been and will continue to be a serious public health concern."

MWRA officials' BATNA was to continue with traditional enforcement mechanisms—notices of noncompliance, fines, and so forth. But they knew this would likely lead to a court battle, as hospital officials seemed eager to fight the fines and the stringent discharge standard. MWRA might have eventually "won" in court. Nancy Wheatley, then in MWRA's Sewerage Division (which includes TRAC), believed the hospitals "didn't have any legal legs to stand on." But a protracted lawsuit would not have helped MWRA meet its interest of reducing mercury discharges; if MWRA won, the hospitals still would not know how to meet the standard. At the same time, a legal battle against Boston's prestigious medical community might not be a wise political move. As Eppstein pointed out: "It's one thing [for MWRA] to go up against private industry, and quite another to go up against people who are finding cures for cancer."

Indeed, the 29 hospitals represented by MASCO in the negotiations hold a prominent position in Boston and beyond. Included are some of the most well-known medical institutions in the world, such as the Dana-Farber Cancer Institute, Brigham and Women's Hospital, and Harvard Medical School, among others. MASCO's member hospitals account for about 1.5 million outpatient visits annually (D. Eppstein, personal communication, March 1, 1999).

The hospitals' primary interest was to escape from the trap they found themselves in, which involved ever-escalating enforcement actions and no clear sense of how to fix the problem. The fines could not be tolerated; many of the hospitals were undergoing cost-cutting measures and even mergers. Hospital administrators needed to determine where the mercury was coming from and then eliminate it.

Hospital administrators also had an interest in keeping confidential any information they uncovered about products or processes that were causing mercury to enter the sewage system. They felt that MWRA might use this type of information against them, through more-stringent regulations or heightened enforcement.

The hospitals' BATNA was, in the words of Eppstein, "money to the lawyers." Eppstein said that the facilities people from the hospitals were coming to him saying, "We don't have any idea where this is coming from, and the lawyers are . . . saying 'We are going to fight this down to the very end!'" Contrary to Wheatley's contention, hospital officials felt that MWRA could not win a head-to-head legal battle against the entire Boston-area medical community.

Negotiation of the First Agreement

Before pursuing litigation, a few key leaders from the hospitals and MASCO decided to approach MWRA officials directly. In a smart political move, MASCO hired legal consultant Jim Segel to assist them. Segel was a former state legislator who had helped to write the 1984 law that created MWRA, and, perhaps more important, he was a friend of John Fitzgerald, Director of the Sewerage Division at MWRA.

Segel contacted Fitzgerald and requested a meeting, to which Fitzgerald readily agreed. Present at this first gathering, which took place in mid-August of 1994, were Segel and Eppstein, representing MASCO, and Fitzgerald and Wheatley, for MWRA. After some discussion, the participants agreed in principle that the two sides should solve the mercury problem jointly, rather than fighting it out in court. They also agreed to create a forum through which representatives of MWRA and the hospitals could work together—they dubbed it the Mercury Products Workgroup.

Soon after this meeting, McManus became director of TRAC at MWRA and so became closely involved in the formation of the work group. At the same time, Eppstein began working to convince his member hospitals that pursuing joint activities with MWRA would be more productive than litigation. He tapped Rudman Ham, then Vice President for Operations at Children's Hospital and a well-respected figure in the medical community, to send a personal letter to selected senior executives at each hospital, describing the situation and requesting their support and cooperation. That letter—which was followed up with phone calls and a bit of arm-twisting—achieved its purpose. All MASCO member hospitals, along with several other medical institutions, agreed to work with MWRA.

On September 23, 1994, the Mercury Products Workgroup met for the first time. The group included representatives from the hospitals, MWRA, and several area corporations with mercury issues, such as Polaroid. At that first meeting, MWRA officials described the informal enforcement policy they proposed to guide the efforts of the work group—in other words, how they intended to exercise their discretion in enforcing the mercury standard. The hospital representatives requested that MWRA put that proposal in writing. Thus began the negotiations over the first agreement.

The initial draft was written by an official in MWRA's enforcement branch, who then turned it over Eugene Benson, Associate Counsel for TRAC. During the ensuing six weeks, numerous phone conversations and in-person meetings took place between MWRA and MASCO representatives. Most active in the discussions were Benson and McManus on the MWRA side and Eppstein, Segel, and Bob Gingras (a technical consultant) on the MASCO side.

"A lot of [the negotiations took place] between me and Jim [Segel] on the phone," said Benson. "I'd talk to Kevin [McManus] and then he'd talk to David [Eppstein] and then Jim and I would talk some more on the phone. Then we'd fax them slightly different proposed language, and so forth."

Indeed, there seemed to be two primary flows of information between the negotiating teams. The first was between Benson and Segel, the attorneys for each side who kept abreast of the legal ramifications of the different options. The second was between McManus and Eppstein (assisted by Gingras), who were more focused on the political and operational side of the debate. Both pairs of negotiators worked to maintain a good rapport.

"Kevin [McManus] and I were talking [on the phone] every two or three days during this time," said Eppstein. "We'd have 'off-line' sorts of conversations about how I've got to drag a few of these [hospital] guys kicking and screaming and he's got to change the nature of enforcement people to get them to agree to this, and why don't we try this, or why don't we try that. Informally, we had lots of discussions that then got translated into the various iterations of the document."

Through the course of discussions, a workable package of options was created. The primary components were as follows.

Elements Important to the Hospitals

- Enforcement proceedings beyond NONs would be suspended while the hospitals and MWRA actively worked together to determine the sources of mercury and the best ways to keep it out of the waste stream. In other words, compliance dates would be extended and fines would not be levied.
- Information discovered in the course of the joint investigation (regarding, for example, housekeeping and maintenance challenges and product information) would not be used against the hospitals in "enforcement case development" and would not be referred to other agencies.

Elements Important to MWRA

- MWRA would not change its 1 ppb enforceable limit for mercury discharges, but would temporarily suspend formal enforcement proceedings for violations of that limit.
- The hospitals and MWRA would actively work to correct the mercury discharge problem.
- "Intentional or grossly negligent" actions relating to mercury discharge by the hospitals would still result in monetary penalties.
- The agreement only covered mercury; the enforcement relationship between the hospitals and MWRA would remain "as is" for all other MWRA-regulated substances.

It is easy to see how the two sides were able to "create and distribute value" in their negotiations by trading across differences—by each giving up something of little value to themselves in return for obtaining something of greater value from the other. For example:

- The hospitals had a strong interest in receiving relief from monetary penalties. They did not care whether they received notices of violation (NOVs) or NONs—those enforcement actions had no effect on their finances. MWRA, on the other hand, was not as interested in collecting fines as they were in maintaining a strong enforcement presence and solving the mercury problem. By keeping the standard at 1 ppb and issuing NOVs and NONs to the hospitals as necessary, while at the same time suspending the issuance of fines and working to solve the problem, the interests of both sides were met.

- MWRA wanted to collect information from the hospitals regarding mercury sources and possible remedies, for use in their dealings with other mercury-discharging industries in the future. The hospitals, however, did not want to release information to MWRA that could be used against them in future enforcement activities. The decision to prohibit MWRA from using such information against the hospitals created a safe atmosphere in which the interests of both parties could be met.

- MWRA officials needed assurance that they were not giving up all of their enforcement power and that they could still take action if an egregious violation occurred. Hospital administrators felt fairly certain, however, that their staff would not do anything "intentional or grossly negligent" while the work group process was going on. It therefore did not "cost" the hospitals anything to agree that MWRA could take action in the case of an intentional or grossly negligent mercury problem. Essentially, the two sides exploited their differing levels of concern about what might occur in the future.

The agreement between MWRA and the hospitals was codified in a December 2, 1994 memorandum from MWRA to Mercury Products Workgroup participants.

Implementation of the First Agreement

After negotiating the first memorandum, the Mercury Products Workgroup set out to address the mercury discharge problem. To do so, they organized three subcommittees, one each on operations, infrastructure, and "end-of-pipe" issues. The work group process was monitored by a steering committee, which included representatives from MWRA and the hospitals.

According to MASCO's Web site (www.masco.org/mercury), the work group sought to:

- Identify sources of mercury contamination and develop recommendations for their control.
- Develop guidelines for the removal of residual mercury from hospital wastewater systems.
- Identify and evaluate potential mercury pretreatment systems.

In the course of their work, the subcommittees collected information from public databases, tested products to assess their mercury content, sent letters to product manufacturers requesting information on the content of products, and reviewed Material Safety Data Sheets. They also looked closely at the hospitals' piping systems and laboratory processes that might be causing mercury discharges. The result of these efforts was, according to MASCO's Web site, "the most comprehensive compendium of information dealing with the mercury discharge problem that is currently available anywhere in the United States."

Indeed, the investigations turned up a wealth of important information. "We were . . .

able to figure out where mercury was coming from that nobody knew about before," said Eppstein. "We found trace amounts of mercury in reagents, stains, and dyes. Boraxo soap pads, which everybody cleans their lab desks with, have 126 ppb of mercury in them. Everybody thinks they're doing a terrific job—they scrub down their desks, wash it down the drain, and there goes the mercury."

"The documentation of mercury bioaccumulating in the piping systems was another key discovery," said Eppstein. He said that, just as mercury bioaccumulates in fish tissue, it bioaccumulates in the living tissue that is flushed down the drain from hospitals, such as liver samples and biopsies. This tissue then gets trapped in the nooks and crannies of the piping system. Eppstein explained: "When you had a thermometer spill in the lab 20 years ago, what did you do? Pour it down the drain. So it sits in the trap, nobody's aware of it, it bioaccumulates in the biomass in the piping system, and then when you build a new lab on top of an old lab and all of the sudden you've got a triple flow [of water through the piping system], and [the trapped tissue] begins to slough off, you suddenly have a mercury problem and you have no idea where it's coming from."

The work group produced several reports ("Phase I reports") and developed a comprehensive database of products and their mercury content. The reports, it should be noted, were not "consensus documents"; they were developed primarily by the hospitals and were not officially approved by MWRA. But they did represent a significant step forward in understanding the mercury discharge problem.

Essential to the work group's success was MWRA project engineer Karen Rondeau, who coordinated the work group process. She organized the meetings, disseminated information to the relevant parties, kept meeting minutes, and helped to develop the database, among many other tasks. Eppstein calls her the "unsung hero" of the whole effort.

As a result of the knowledge gained through the work group's investigations and the hospitals' resultant source reduction activities, the hospitals' average mercury concentration dropped more than 70 percent between 1994 and 1997. In 1996, the hospitals and MWRA received a special award from the governor of Massachusetts in recognition of their success.

In early 1997, however, MWRA officials felt that more needed to be done to reduce mercury discharges. Significant progress had been made, but most hospitals still were not meeting the 1 ppb standard. Enthusiasm for and participation in the work group was waning. Once the Phase I reports were issued, it wasn't clear what should be done next. MWRA's Benson summarized the dilemma: "[A] lot of hospitals had plateaued in the wrong place." Even Eppstein, although he was not eager for MWRA to reinstitute more-stringent enforcement measures, admitted he was having trouble keeping hospital representatives motivated.

MWRA decided, therefore, that it was time to change the game plan. "There was not necessarily an agreement with MASCO that there needed to be another enforcement document...," explained Benson, "It was TRAC's decision that there needed to be some impetus to get people to move further forward." Thus began negotiation over the second memorandum.

Phase Two

Interests and BATNAs

MWRA's primary interest in the second round of negotiation was to have the hospitals' mercury discharges reduced further—to motivate the "laggards" to work harder to meet the standard. The hospitals' key interest was to make sure MWRA did not revert back to a traditional enforcement mode. Many of the hospitals were still not meeting the 1 ppb standard, so traditional enforcement would mean monetary penalties. They felt that their hard work and considerable progress warranted better treatment. Both the hospitals and MWRA also had an interest in maintaining the productive dialogue and good relationships that had developed.

Both sides' "best alternative to a negotiated agreement" was, as in the first negotiation, a reversion to traditional enforcement procedures. Such enforcement might also trigger legal action, as at the outset of the work group process. MWRA's BATNA was, however, stronger now than in the first phase. They now knew that it *was* possible to reduce mercury discharges dramatically; many of the hospitals had proven that. Those who were still well out of compliance could no longer claim that "they had no idea how to fix the problem." This strengthened MWRA's hand going into the second round of negotiation.

Negotiation of the Second Agreement

Both MWRA and hospital representatives conceded that the second round of negotiation was more difficult than the first. "Because we had more knowledge, [the negotiations] became much more technical," explained Eppstein. "I think there's a real lesson there: Ignorance is bliss, and it's easy to negotiate if both parties are ignorant. Armed with more information it becomes much more difficult, and you begin arguing [over the] technical stuff." Eppstein also noted that the first memorandum suspended all major enforcement actions, while this one was to result in MWRA-issued "enforcement orders" describing exactly what each hospital should do to further reduce mercury discharges. "Now you're going to use the memorandum to generate rulings based on orders that are given," Eppstein said, "So it becomes a guide." Clearly, more was at stake.

The negotiation process itself was much the same as in the first round. MWRA developed the first draft of a new memorandum, and then discussions ensued among McManus, Benson, Eppstein, Segel, and Gingras to clarify its fine points. The negotiation process took about six weeks, according to Eppstein, and included numerous telephone calls, the trading of drafts, and several in-person meetings, including a final session in which an acceptable package of options was crafted.

The fundamental concept contained in the document—which MWRA proposed and the hospitals reluctantly accepted—was that the hospitals' "sample locations" (literally, the sites from which discharge samples were taken) would be separated into two categories, and those two categories would be treated differently from an enforcement perspective. Hospitals that had sample locations with mercury discharge levels above a certain "cutoff point" would have to test end-of-pipe pretreatment systems and, if proven effective, install them rather than relying only on source reduction. (Those in both groups would still be exempt from fines while they continued their work group efforts.) The key point of debate, then, was the determination of the cutoff point.

Because end-of-pipe treatment is very expensive and the hospitals had doubts about its effectiveness, they were eager to have as high a cutoff as possible. "We started out wanting to say that . . . if you could stay below 10 ppb, that seemed reasonable," said Eppstein. "From our standpoint, . . . if you are going above 10, you've got a problem and you've got to figure out how to address it." MWRA officials did not feel that 10 ppb was sufficient, however. They saw that most sites were already below 10 ppb, and they wanted to create a meaningful incentive for people to move closer to the actual standard, which was enforced at 1 ppb.

To come up with a mutually agreeable number, MWRA and hospital representatives first agreed on a method for determining that number. They decided to simply analyze the distribution of discharge rates among the sample locations and set the cutoff at a level most hospitals could meet. They arrived at 4 ppb. "[O]f the 29 facilities," McManus explained, "the vast majority of them had been under 4 [ppb], and these other outlyers were dealing with some problems. . . . So, we thought 4 made sense because it appeared to be achievable." Those sites that fell under 4 ppb were designated Group 1, and those above 4 ppb were designated Group 2.

Although the hospitals had agreed to the decision-making method, they were not happy with the result it produced. Four parts per billion seemed much more onerous than their original proposal of 10 ppb. Through the course of the negotiations, however, the two sides brainstormed a few creative ways to make the deal more palatable for the hospitals. They "created value" by adding in other considerations and then handling those considerations in ways that favored the hospitals somewhat more than MWRA. Eppstein explained: "We agreed reluctantly, that, if [4 ppb] was going to be the [cutoff point], which we felt was too stringent, then there had to be certain things that would sweeten the pie for us." The other factors they put on the table included the following.

- *The definition of a "rare excursion" of mercury.* The idea was that some small number of occasional discharges above 4 ppb would not move a Group 1 site into the Group 2 category. The question was, what number of excursions per six-month period was "rare?"
- *The length of the "grace period" during which Group 2 sites could try to move to Group 1.* There was some discussion about how much time Group 2 locations should be given to try to get into Group 1, and so avoid the requirements of Group 2 membership. The question was, how long should the grace period be?
- *The timing of testing.* The issue of how often testing should be done was also on the table.

MWRA originally proposed that a "rare excursion" be defined as one excursion above 4 ppb in a six-month period. The hospitals argued for a higher number. They ultimately agreed that, although one excursion every six months should be the technical definition, two excursions would only trigger a "review of the mercury discharger's results over a longer period." Three excursions during a six-month period would result in a move into the Group 2 category.

MWRA had originally proposed a three-month grace period during which Group 2 sites could show results of less than 4 ppb and so move into Group 1. MASCO convinced them to extend it to six months.

On the timing of testing, the hospitals argued for every-other-month testing. But MWRA convinced the hospitals that only monthly testing would generate enough data to conduct meaningful analyses. "We knew that was true," said Eppstein. "We basically agreed with that, although it's onerous on our members. But if you're really going to monitor this, you've got to do it on a monthly basis."

It is clear that this negotiation, like the first, involved both creating value (developing creative ways to meet interests on both sides) and then claiming that value (putting together a package that exceeded, at least minimally, everyone's BATNA). As with the first agreement, this one was codified in a memorandum, dated March 7, 1997, from MWRA to the work group participants.

Implementation of the Second Agreement

Implementation proceeded as prescribed by the memo. The hospitals' discharge sites were split into two groups. Those in Group 2 were given six months to show results of less than 4 ppb. Most of them did meet that standard and moved into Group 1 (E. Benson, personal communication, March 2, 1999). The work group's subcommittees were reconfigured, and they continued their investigations. In December 1997, the work group issued three new reports, one from the Facilities Loadings Subcommittee and two from the End-of-Pipe Subcommittee (one on technology identification and one on pretreatment guidance).

The Facilities Loadings Subcommittee report revealed some interesting information—information that might have altered the negotiations if it had been discovered earlier. As described in the report, the subcommittee found that the hospitals' flow of wastewater into MWRA's sewage system was much less than previously assumed. The hospitals' total facility discharge flows were previously estimated to be 1.18 million gallons per day (MGD) for the first half of fiscal year 1995. After calculating that flow more carefully, this subcommittee found that a more accurate estimated flow was .35 MGD, or 70 percent less than originally estimated. In addition, it had previously been thought that the mercury discharge loadings from the 29 participating hospitals contributed between 2.6 and 3.6 percent of the total estimated MWRA system loadings for fiscal year 1995. The subcommittee found that a more accurate contribution was somewhere between 0.65 and 0.91 percent (Mercury Products Workgroup, 1997, p. 25). The hospitals felt that this new information proved that they were not as big a contributor to the mercury problem as previously thought, and so should be given more slack.

This new information not withstanding, MWRA began to issue enforcement orders to formalize the agreement described in the memo. Although this was expected, hospital officials were soon annoyed. "The orders seemed to revert, from our members' perspectives, back to the old way of doing things," said Eppstein. "It was like . . . the enforcement people were suddenly free to do their thing again."

McManus commented, "This was a question that was raised oftentimes, 'Is this a return to the old way of doing things?' We worked very hard not to have that as the final impression. I think that . . . in large measure it will be determined by how we interpret the various appeals and the various discussions we've had."

In response to this perceived reversion to the "old ways," the hospitals conducted detailed cost estimates of carrying out the orders issued by MWRA. They found that each Group 1 sampling location would have to spend $33,000 to comply with the enforcement orders, while each Group 2 site would have to spend a minimum of $93,000.

Essentially, the hospitals discovered that the agreement they reached with MWRA left them just barely better off than their BATNA. If they had been armed with the loadings information and cost estimates at the beginning of the second negotiation, they might have reached an agreement that better met their needs and interests. Instead, they worked to rectify the situation during implementation.

For example, most of the hospitals filed formal appeals of the enforcement orders. At the same time, Eppstein took action: "I went back to Kevin [McManus] and said, 'We can't live with this.'"

Another round of discussions ensued, in which MWRA and MASCO agreed that the requirements for Group 1 participation, in particular, were perhaps too onerous. MWRA had wanted all Group 1 members to conduct a comprehensive wastewater characterization study, which, according to MASCO's estimates, would have cost $18,000. MWRA agreed instead to review existing data (as a substitute) on a case-by-case basis and then determine whether such a study was needed. The requirements for Group 2 stayed the same, although MWRA gave a number of the hospitals more time to complete the tasks outlined in the orders.

Conclusion

Despite these ongoing challenges, both sides agree that the two rounds of negotiations were a success. To date, 63 percent of all hospital sampling locations that were not in compliance with the 1 ppb enforceable limit are now in compliance. Ninety-two percent of all sampling locations are showing discharges of 4 ppb or less. Only four sampling locations remain in Group 2 (E. Benson, personal communication, March 2, 1999). Overall, participating hospitals have reduced their mercury discharges by 83 percent since the project began in 1994 (D. Eppstein, personal communication, March 1, 1999).

It is clear that mutual gains-style negotiation resulted in numerous benefits for the hospitals, the MWRA, and the environment. By exploring interests, developing options, and creating and claiming value, the two sides were able to find creative ways to meet their interests. The result was an easing of the hospitals' financial burdens, a greatly improved understanding of mercury sources and remedies, and a significant reduction in the discharge of mercury into the environment.

MASCO's Web site sums up the benefits of the process this way: "The pooling of knowledge and the allocation of staff . . . have helped to produce results much more quickly and thoroughly than would have otherwise been possible. In addition, this collective approach to addressing common concerns has thus far saved [the hospitals] more than $2 million through the elimination of duplicate efforts that would have been required as part of individual compliance programs."

Benson agrees that the process has been a success in many ways. But he cautioned that other MWRA officials may think differently. "I'd say that there's a wide variety of opinion in TRAC overall about whether compliance could have been achieved . . . sooner than it was," he said. "Add to that the fact that some facilities were very active participants and some . . . showed up but did very little. . . . Well, there's a large spectrum of opinion about that piece of it."

Nonetheless, the relationship between MWRA and the hospitals has improved markedly since the project began. "There's more open communication now," said MWRA's Karen Rondeau. "[T]hey've become willing to ask questions. . . . I think that they've learned that we're just people doing our jobs, and that we can actually have a professional conversation with them and that doesn't mean they're going to be fined—which is nice."

At present, MWRA is reassessing its mercury discharge limits, as part of a process of renewing its EPA sewage discharge permit. The local-limit review process will likely be completed in early 2001. The hospitals are hopeful that MWRA will recommend raising the mercury discharge limit, but Benson said he could not speculate on whether that might happen. In the meantime, the second memorandum continues to guide the enforcement relationship between MWRA and the hospitals.

NOTE

1. All of the quotes in this case were obtained via in-person or telephone interviews. The following interviews were conducted: Eugene Benson and Karen Rondeau, MWRA, May 1, 1998 (in person, joint interview); Eugene Benson, MWRA, March 2, 1999 (by phone); David Eppstein, MASCO, March 6, 1998 (in person) and March 1, 1999 (by phone); Kevin McManus, MWRA, March 17, 1998 (in person); Mark Spinale, Environmental Protection Agency, April 7, 1998 (by phone); Frank Sullivan, Beth Israel Deaconess Medical Center, May 12, 1998 (by phone); and Nancy Wheatley, Orange County Sanitation District (formerly MWRA), April 23, 1998 (by phone).

The following is the 1994 negotiated agreement, embodied in a memo from MWRA to the hospitals.

Massachusetts Water Resources Authority

Charlestown Navy Yard

100 First Avenue

Boston, MA 02129

MEMORANDUM

To: Mercury Products Workgroup Participants

From: Kevin McManus, Director, TRAC

Date: December 2, 1994

Re: MWRA Enforcement of Mercury Discharge Prohibition During Existence of
           Workgroup

This memorandum is designed to clarify MWRA enforcement issues regarding mercury
discharges, as discussed at the September 23, 1994, Mercury Products Workgroup meeting. Since then, some workgroup participants have asked the MWRA to clarify the policy in writing and discuss how cooperation between the MWRA and workgroup participants might impact ongoing enforcement cases.

- Mercury is a prohibited substance, with an enforceable limit of 0.001 mg/l.
- The MWRA will continue to issue Notices of Violations (NOVs) for first time mercury
  discharge results above 0.001 mg/l, and escalated enforcement documents, such as the
  Notice of Noncompliance (NON), for any sewer user with repeat mercury discharge
  violations.
- The MWRA will grant extensions of mercury compliance dates issued in NONs, Settlement Agreements, and other enforcement documents, as appropriate. At this time, it
  appears that these extensions may last well into 1995. Extensions will be granted to a
  workgroup participant if it has met the following criteria:

    1. The workgroup participant is actively attempting to correct the mercury dis-
       charge problem and is working under a written corrective action plan or similar
       agreement with the MWRA, or an enforcement order, that includes the work
       group participant's approach and a timetable, and that requires a consideration of
       source control, product substitution, treatment, and facility maintenance; and

    2. The workgroup participant is keeping MWRA compliance staff updated on all
       compliance actions on a regular basis as specified in its agreement or enforce-
       ment order.

- If a workgroup participant has compliance issues in addition to mercury, the MWRA
  will treat those issues separately and require the workgroup participant to resolve
  those issues as soon as possible, given the nature of the problems.
- Workgroup participants must sample and report according to their permits and any
  outstanding enforcement orders or agreements, subject to the workgroup participant's
  right to appeal a permit or order and the MWRA's right to amend the requirements. All
  results of samples taken at representative sample locations following EPA protocol are
  required to be sent to the MWRA, even if the sample results are in addition to those
  required by a permit or order (see attached letter from MWRA's Associate Counsel on
  this issue). Results of samples taken at non-representative sample locations need not
  be submitted to the MWRA.
- MWRA staff participate in the Mercury Products Workgroup and associated subcommittees to help resolve the mercury discharge problem by providing coordination,
  information, and, as resources allow, analytical testing services when the new MWRA
  Central lab begins operating. We think information sharing during this process is very
  important and wish to encourage an open discussion of issues. To further that end,
  information presented during the workgroup sessions (e.g., housekeeping practices,
  product information, staff not adhering to standard operating procedures, mainte-

nance challenges, etc.) shared with the MWRA staff will not be used in enforcement case development, and will not be referred to other agencies, unless there is a violation resulting from a flagrant and unacceptable practice such as intentional dumping, or if a violation will: a) harm or interfere with the sewer system; b) cause pass through or interference; c) cause the MWRA to violate a law or permit requirement; d) harm treatment plant receiving water or violate water quality; e) endanger or threaten to endanger the life, health, or welfare of persons, or the public health, safety, or welfare, or the environment, or public property; or f) constitute a nuisance. The typical mercury discharge violations we are seeing do not meet any of these criteria.

- The MWRA may take enforcement action for violations outside the scope of the workgroup. Examples of such violations include new process discharges not covered by an existing permit and intentional bypass of pretreatment systems. We think we should continue to view such intentional violations as serious problems because participation in the workgroup cannot excuse such serious intentional violations.

- The results of sampling for mercury at permit sampling locations, done during the duration of the workgroup process, will not be used to assess monetary penalties to workgroup participants, unless the violations resulted from intentional or grossly negligent actions outside the scope of the workgroup's goal of eliminating ongoing mercury discharges, or are in violation of an agreement or enforcement order. Examples of intentional or grossly negligent actions that may result in enforcement include intentional bypasses of pretreatment and mercury dumping. We want to encourage additional sampling, when appropriate, but participation in the workgroup cannot excuse serious intentional or grossly negligent violations not the result of accepted practices. In addition, as required by EPA, 40 C.F.R. 403.8(f)(2)(vii), we will use all sampling data from representative locations to determine compliance status and whether a discharger is in Significant Noncompliance.

The following is the 1997 negotiated agreement, embodied in a memo from MWRA to the hospitals. See Figure 3.1 for a graphical representation of the terms of the agreement.

Massachusetts Water Resources Authority
Charlestown Navy Yard
100 First Avenue
Boston, MA 02129

MEMORANDUM
To: Sewer Users with an MWRA Sewer Use Discharge Permit
From: Kevin McManus, Director, Toxic Reduction and Control Department

Date: March 6, 1997

Re: MWRA Enforcement of Mercury Discharge Prohibition (the safe harbor from escalated enforcement for mercury violations)

This memorandum sets forth how the Massachusetts Water Resources Authority (MWRA) will exercise its enforcement discretion regarding mercury discharges, effective July 1, 1997. The MWRA will create an enforcement "safe harbor" in which it will not take escalated enforcement action, such as the imposition of financial penalties, for sewer users with mercury discharge violations who take the steps required by this memorandum to reduce and eliminate their discharges of mercury.

The enforcement safe harbor will be as follows:

- Mercury prohibition. Mercury is prohibited from being discharged to the MWRA sewer system (360 C.M.R. § 10.024 1). To take into account the method detection limit for mercury and test method variability, the MWRA uses an enforceable limit of 0.001 mg/l for mercury. Discharges at or below 0.001 mg/l for mercury are not considered violations of the mercury prohibition.

- Enforcement for mercury violations. The MWRA may issue a Notice of Violation for a first time mercury discharge above 0.001 mg/l and an escalated enforcement document, such as a Notice of Noncompliance (NON), for repeat or serious mercury discharge violations.

- Escalated enforcement safe harbor. For sewer users who are actively attempting to correct their mercury discharge problems as required by this memorandum, the MWRA will not escalate enforcement beyond the NON and enforcement order level for mercury violations and will grant extensions of mercury compliance dates in NONs, other enforcement documents, and settlement agreements for sewer users in Groups 1 and 2, as follows:

- Group 1 defined. Group 1 consists of sewer users with mercury discharge results consistently at 0.004 mg/l or less at all their sample locations, except for a rare excursion above 0.004 mg/l.

- Group 2 defined. Group 2 consists of sewer users with mercury discharge results above 0.004 mg/l at a sample location, unless those results are a rare excursion.

- Initial placement in a group. In July 1997, the MWRA will inform each mercury discharger of which group it is in, based on sample data from July 1996 through July 1997, on a sample location by sample location basis.

A sewer user that has its first mercury violation after January 1, 1997, at a sample location will be placed in Group 1 for up to six months to give it an opportunity to reduce and eliminate its mercury discharge without pretreatment. If the first three months of data show that the sewer user is making progress in reducing its discharge of mercury but still has discharge results above 0.004 mg/l, the MWRA may elect to keep the discharger in Group 1 for an additional three months.

- More than one sample location. Group placement is on a sample location basis. A sewer user with more than one sample location may be in Group 1 for some of its sample locations and Group 2 for other sample locations, based on the discharge history of each sample location.

- Change in group placement. A sewer user placed in Group 1 that then discharges mercury above 0.004 mg/l at a sample location, except for a rare excursion, will be moved to Group 2 for that sample location.

- Rare excursion. For purposes of this memorandum, a rare excursion is one mercury result above 0.004 mg/l in a six month period. Three mercury results above 0.004 mg/l in a six month period is not a rare excursion. If two mercury results in a six month period are above 0.004 mg/l, the MWRA will review the discharger's mercury results over a longer period of time and the magnitude of the results above 0.004 mg/l. It is not a rare excursion if there is an emerging pattern of more than one mercury result above 0.004 mg/l in successive six month periods, or there are two results above 0.006 mg/l in a six month period.

- Mercury compliance. Each sewer user, regardless of group, will be required to work actively toward having no greater than 0.001 mg/l of mercury in its discharges.

- Specific requirements for Group 1 sewer users. Each Group 1 sewer user must have a written agreement with the MWRA or be under an MWRA enforcement order that includes: a description of the sewer user's approach to correct its mercury discharge problems; a timetable for actions to be taken; the requirement to implement and operate mercury source control and reduction strategies (including product substitution and wastestream segregation) and facility maintenance plans; and the requirement to evaluate the feasibility of mercury treatment options. A sewer user in Group 1 may install mercury pretreatment if it chooses.

- Specific requirements for Group 2 sewer users. Each Group 2 sewer user must have a written agreement with the MWRA or be under an MWRA enforcement order that, in addition to the requirements of Group 1, includes the requirement to evaluate, design, install, and operate a full-scale end-of-pipe pretreatment system for mercury within six months of notice from the MWRA that it is in Group 2 unless the MWRA and the sewer user agree upon a different schedule or a modification of the schedule. The MWRA will provide an extension of the six month time limit to evaluate and install pretreatment if the sewer user's initial evaluation of a promising pretreatment technology shows that the technology would have little mercury removal efficiency. If a sewer user has achieved a consistent mercury discharge of 0.004 mg/l or less, except for a rare excursion, when it has completed pilot testing, it will not be required to install pretreatment unless it again exceeds 0.004 mg/l for mercury, taking into account this allowance for a rare excursion as defined in this memorandum.

- Mercury pretreatment. To implement the pretreatment requirement, a sewer user shall, at a minimum, perform a wastestream characterization study, do side-stream and full-scale pilot testing, and modify and upgrade system components to achieve optimum performance. If the results of pilot testing show that the system can most likely reduce mercury concentrations to 0.001 mg/l or less, the sewer user shall install and run the system on a full-scale basis, unless it has achieved compliance without the use of the system. If the results of pilot testing show that the system can reduce mercury concentrations, but most likely not to 0.001 mg/l or less, the sewer user will be required to install the system, operate the system, and then refine the system to achieve 0.001 mg/l or less in its discharge, unless at the time of installation the sewer user demonstrates that it can achieve equal or more effective mercury removal results with another pretreatment system, which it then must implement and refine.

- Interim mercury limit. The MWRA cannot provide a system-wide or industry type interim limit for mercury as a part of an enforcement safe harbor. The mercury discharge prohibition is a regulation that may be changed only through the local limit review, MEPA, and regulations revision process. The MWRA anticipates undertaking a review of its local limits within the next eighteen months. A facility that enters into a settlement agreement with the MWRA in which it agrees to install an end-of-pipe pretreatment system will be given an interim mercury discharge limit for nine months at the sample location where pretreatment will be installed. The MWRA will base the interim limit on an average concentration of the sampling data at the location over the previous twelve months (or longer if there are fewer than twelve sample results), removing high results that appear to be atypical for the location from the calculation of the average. If the sewer user does not install pretreatment, the interim limit will be considered forfeited by the sewer user and never in effect.

- Sampling requirements. All mercury dischargers will be required to take at least one representative sample per month at each designated sample location where mercury may be present, have the sample analyzed for mercury, and report the result to the MWRA each month. The MWRA may require more frequent sampling as it deems appropriate. As required by EPA, 40 C.F.R. 403.8(f)(2)(vii), the MWRA will use all sampling data from representative sample locations to determine compliance status and whether a sewer user is in Significant Noncompliance.

  The results of sampling for mercury at permit sampling locations, done by a Group 1 or 2 sewer user or the MWRA during the duration of the safe harbor, will not be used by the MWRA to assess monetary penalties, unless the violations are not within the safe harbor because they resulted from intentional or grossly negligent actions or were in contravention of an MWRA agreement or enforcement order. See the section below on mercury violations not within the safe harbor.

- Compliance reports. Sewer users in Group 1 will be required to submit quarterly compliance reports to the MWRA, discussing the actions they took each quarter to reduce and eliminate the mercury in their discharges. Sewer users in Group 2 will be required to submit monthly compliance reports to the MWRA, showing their progress toward implementation of pretreatment and discussing the other actions they took to reduce and eliminate mercury in their discharges.

- <u>Removal from the safe harbor.</u> A sewer user who fails to do the required work, take the required samples, or submit the required reports, will be considered outside the safe harbor and will be subject to further enforcement, including the imposition of monetary penalties for noncompliance with the mercury prohibition.
- <u>Other violations.</u> If a sewer user has compliance issues in addition to mercury, the MWRA will treat those issues separately and require the sewer user to resolve those issues as soon as possible, given the nature of the problem.
- <u>Other sampling and reporting.</u> In addition to the sampling and reporting required under this mercury enforcement discretion memorandum, sewer users must sample and report according to their MWRA permits, orders, and agreements, subject to the sewer user's right to appeal a permit or order and the MWRA's right to amend the requirements. All results of samples taken at representative sample locations following EPA protocol are required to be sent to the MWRA, even if the sample results are in addition to those required by a permit order. Results of samples taken at non-representative sample locations need not be submitted to the MWRA.
- <u>Mercury violations not within the safe harbor.</u> The MWRA recognizes that time, resources, and strong commitment are necessary to attain mercury compliance and that an escalated enforcement safe harbor is appropriate for sewer users who are doing the necessary work with the necessary commitment to achieve mercury compliance. There are, however, mercury violations that are not within the safe harbor because they result from intentional or grossly negligent actions that could have been prevented or were done in contravention of an MWRA enforcement order, agreement, or regulations. Those violations include new processes or discharges not covered by an existing permit, intentional bypasses of pretreatment systems, mercury dumping, and dilution to meet the mercury line. Violations of 360 C.M.R. § 10.021 are also not covered by the safe harbor. The MWRA may take enforcement action, including the imposition of monetary penalties, for violations not within the safe harbor.

This memorandum is not intended to create any legal rights for any sewer user. The MWRA may change or end the safe harbor if it experiences an increase in the amount or concentration of mercury in the influent to, or effluent from, its treatment plants or in the fertilizer pellets it produces from its treatment plant residuals. The MWRA may change or end the mercury safe harbor as other circumstances require, in the sole discretion of the MWRA. The MWRA does not anticipate extending the safe harbor or any specific provisions of this memorandum beyond its next local limits study, when it will review whether it should change its mercury discharge prohibition.

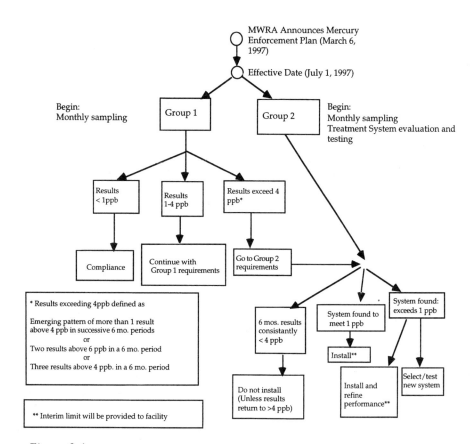

Figure 3.1

A Graphical Representation of the 1997 Agreement

Case 2

Shoreline Restoration on Martha's Vineyard

Gregory Sobel[1]

Ferocious Atlantic storms in 1991 and 1992 eroded much of Sylvia State Beach on the island of Martha's Vineyard in Massachusetts, undercutting a critical roadway connecting two island towns. The storm damage brought to a boil a long-simmering conflict among a dozen federal, state, and local agencies. The key issue in debate was how to control beach erosion and prevent further deterioration of the roadway (which was an essential route for emergency vehicles), while protecting the fragile barrier beach and wetland habitat adjacent to the road. Complicating the situation was the fact that road and shoreline restoration activities would require up to 10 different permits from the various federal, state, and local agencies.

During 1995 and 1996, I facilitated a series of consensus building meetings among the interested agencies, elected officials, and public interest groups. The three all-day sessions, which were held over the course of four months, resulted in a signed and enforceable agreement establishing measures to protect the beach and roadway for a 5- to 10-year period, until long-term solutions could be developed and implemented. This case study describes the history of the conflict, the various parties' interests, and the negotiation process. A copy of the written agreement is attached. This account is based on public documents and public statements made by the parties; no confidential communications are disclosed.

History of the Conflict

Sylvia State Beach connects the towns of Oak Bluffs and Edgartown on Martha's Vineyard. The 2.5-mile-long beach is owned by the Massachusetts Department of Environmental Management (DEM) and maintained by the Dukes County Commission (DCC). It is a barrier beach, as defined in the Massachusetts Wetlands Protection Act's regulations, and is bordered to the east by Nantucket Sound and to the west by Sengekontacket Pond. State Beach is a popular recreational area for island residents and visitors. It is also a nesting area for the piping plover, a protected endangered species.

Beach Road, a state highway under the jurisdiction of the Massachusetts Highway Department (MHD), runs the length of State Beach. It provides a critical link for emergency and other vehicles between the two towns.

Coastal engineering structures such as jetties, groins, and seawalls have been built along State Beach with debatable results. Some stakeholders believe that without past measures, such as the installation of groins (stone piles held in place by wire mesh) and periodic beach nourishment (the addition of sand trucked in from other locations), State Beach would not exist today. Others believe that the disruption of natural erosion patterns caused by "hard-engineered structures" has worsened the erosion and led to the road damage.

All the stakeholders agree that erosion of the beach, coupled with Beach Road's low elevation, has resulted in extensive damage to the roadway. The road was temporarily closed to traffic several times immediately following moderate to major coastal storms.

Following a severe storm in December 1992, the road was closed while MHD undertook repairs, believing that the repair work would be allowed under the state Wetlands Protection Act pursuant to an Emergency Certification pending before the Oak Bluffs Conservation Commission. The commission ultimately did not approve the work, however, and the Massachusetts Department of Environmental Protection (DEP) took enforcement action against MHD for altering the wetlands habitat without a permit. Later, the DEP allowed the road repairs to remain and began a long series of meetings with MHD and the other concerned agencies to try to develop near-term and long-range solutions for the erosion problems.

During 1993, state and local agencies met numerous times and advocated different and often mutually inconsistent measures to protect the beach and roadway. Even though they invested hundreds of hours, the agencies were not able to agree on short- or long-term measures to address the beach and road erosion problems. At times, the parties seemed to have reached agreement, only to have it unravel when the agencies differed in their recollections or one agency changed its position. The Army Corps of Engineers (the Corps) offered detailed plans and funding for an engineered solution to the erosion problems, but withdrew those plans when state regulators would not endorse them. As time went by, interagency communications on these issues grew more acrimonious.

Fortunately, MHD, the DEP, and other key parties did eventually agree on emergency actions that could be taken in the event of damage from coastal storms. They also agreed to undertake a joint investigation into long-term solutions for protecting the beach and road. (MHD began that study in late 1995.) As discussions proceeded on the scope of the long-term plan, however, MHD, the DEP, and other interested parties determined that interim short-term measures needed to be identified, permitted, and implemented until an approved long-term alternative was developed.

In October 1995, MHD contacted the Massachusetts Office of Dispute Resolution (MODR) for help in organizing and facilitating an interagency "partnering" effort to build agreement on interim measures. (Some of the participants in the process preferred the term "partnering" to "mediation," because the former implied an ongoing relationship among organizations with a shared interest. They believed that "mediation," by contrast, suggested that there was a legal conflict between competing organizations.) MODR recommended several private-sector practitioners from its Environmental Mediator Panel (a roster of mediators experienced in resolving environmental disputes). MHD, in consultation with the DEP, selected me to facilitate the project.

I began by conducting a conflict assessment, during which I interviewed representatives of the interested agencies, elected officials, and public interest groups. I found that the parties had sufficient overlapping interests, a willingness to reach agreement, and the capacity to negotiate such that the prospects for a successful consensus building effort were good. MHD invited several dozen people to participate in the partnering sessions, which were collectively dubbed the Interim Erosion Control Workshop. Sessions were held in November 1995, January 1996, and March 1996.

The Parties' Interests

The parties all appeared to agree that the beach and roadway needed to be stabilized in some way, and that the recreational and biological values of the area should be maintained. Otherwise, their interests and views differed considerably.

The Massachusetts Highway Department is mandated by statute to maintain all state highways, including Beach Road. MHD, along with the state DEM and others, had already spent tens of thousands of dollars and years of effort to stabilize State Beach and protect Beach Road. MHD convened the workshop to develop a consensus among the key parties on additional measures to maintain the roadway, at a reasonable cost to the public, until the long-range alternatives analysis could be completed. An agreement on short-term measures would allow the agency to do its job without interference from the other government entities.

The state DEP is the final decision-making agency for matters arising under the Wetlands Protection Act and Massachusetts Chapter 91, two of the state laws controlling activities regarding barrier beaches. The DEP officials believed that beach erosion and the subsequent damage to the road were natural phenomena, and that, in a pure sense, the roadway should not be there. Recognizing that the road was needed by the community and unlikely to be removed, however, the DEP's main interest in the negotiations was to minimize impacts on the tidelands. The DEP representatives expressed reservations about allowing any actions on the sensitive barrier beach for which the impacts were not completely known. The DEP and its sister agency, the Massachusetts Coastal Zone Management Office (CZM), cited state Executive Order 181 in their arguments; the order allows coastal engineering structures on barrier beaches only in very limited circumstances. CZM shared regulatory authority with the DEP and provided expertise on technical issues regarding barrier beach management. During the workshop, as in previous negotiations, CZM staff often pressed for more information about the possible negative impacts of the beach stabilization options considered.

As the owner of State Beach, the DEM would provide partial funding for any agreed-upon interim measures. They were prepared to invest several hundred thousand dollars in protecting the beach, but only in conjunction with a significant financial contribution from the two towns.

Edgartown and Oak Bluffs placed a high priority on both maintaining the beach for recreational purposes and keeping the road open for vehicular traffic. The town governments were represented in the negotiations by members and staff of their Boards of Selectmen and Conservation Commissions. Town government representatives worried about a repetition of past mistakes, such as when State Beach was stabilized with sandbags, which later broke apart and dispersed to other Vineyard beaches. Edgartown's shellfish officer also participated in the workshop. He advocated actions that would benefit shellfishing in island waters.

Dukes County, comprising all of Martha's Vineyard, was represented by a member and a staff member of the Dukes County Commission (DCC). The Martha's Vineyard Commission (MVC), a regional planning agency, also participated in the workshop. The MVC had convened meetings in the past to try to resolve State Beach and Beach Road protection disputes. Among their stated objectives in these negotiations was an end to turf wars among the other entities.

The Army Corps of Engineers had installed four groins in past years and believed that, except for immediately south of the groins, the devices had succeeded in stabilizing the area. The Corps' 1993 proposals, which included additional groins and beach nourishment, were shelved when the DEP would not support the plan by issuing a Clean Water Act consistency determination. As the workshop began, the Corps' plans were still on the books and could still be funded; however, the proposal was based on a project life of 25 years, and the Corps was not eager to complete the project if the groins might be removed in 5 to 10 years when a permanent plan was implemented.

Two members of the state legislature also sent staff to the workshop. They encouraged the other parties to find solutions to both the road and beach protection issues, and offered to support the consensus building effort with legislation as needed.

Friends of the Sengekontacket (FOS) was the leading nongovernmental organization involved in the workshop. FOS had advocated beach protection over the years, organized volunteers for planting beach grass and undertaking other beach stabilization activities, and conducted public education about environmental protection of Sengekontacket Pond, State Beach, and associated wetlands.

The Massachusetts Division of Fisheries and Wildlife (DFW) also participated, to ensure that no decisions were made that would violate the Massachusetts Endangered Species Act. DFW was not a major player in the negotiations, but did watch closely for activities that would have an adverse impact on the piping plover. In the past, the agency had vetoed a plan to move sand from the southern end of State Beach to the northern end, because it would have constituted "mining" the plover's habitat. The agency believed construction could be done on the beach, as long as it did not take place during the nesting season. DFW generally favored widening and stabilizing the beach as habitat improvements.

Because of their overlapping jurisdictions, all of the interested local, state, and federal agencies were compelled to reach a consensus on interim measures to protect State Beach. No single agency could solve the problem alone. Protection activities, after all, would likely require more than 10 distinct permits from nine different agencies. Therefore, no organization had a good alternative to a negotiated agreement.

The Negotiations

Participants in the Interim Erosion Control Workshop acted as a kind of negotiating committee. Most were technical or policy staff members, however, and were not the final decision makers in their respective organizations. Therefore, although they clearly represented their organizations and were able to develop terms of agreement, most did not have the authority to finalize any agreement during the sessions. Deliberations within each organization between workshop sessions were thus essential to developing consensus. Moreover, the final draft agreement needed to be formally ratified by all participating organizations, in some cases after those organizations consulted with constituents and the general public.

The overall goal of the workshop was full agreement among the various organizations on interim erosion control measures for Beach Road and Sylvia State Beach. During the morning of the first session, the group adopted three specific objectives for the process: (1) protect Beach Road, (2) maintain the recreational values of the beach area, and (3) do not degrade the beneficial function of the resources. It was agreed that each objective should be accomplished "to the extent possible." This early agreement on common objectives, which encompassed several key interests, helped set the right tone for effective collaboration.

Next, workshop participants discussed the period of time that any agreement they might reach would be in force. After taking into consideration the time frame for completion of the long-term alternatives study, subsequent consultations among stakeholders, the permitting process, and project design and construction, workshop participants decided that the interim measures would be in place for 5 to 10 years. This temporal scoping gave some assurance to those most concerned with the possible negative impacts of erosion-control activities that their decisions would be implemented for a relatively short period of time.

The afternoon of the first session began with a discussion of the interests and objectives of each participating organization. While most participants knew one another from working on these and other issues, the discussion of interests and the morning's agreement on workshop objectives helped focus the parties on desired outcomes rather than the acrimonious history of the dispute.

Next, workshop participants brainstormed a list of 14 potential options for interim erosion control along Beach Road. They operated under the ground rule that all suggestions would be considered and that no option would be ruled out at this stage. I recorded the options on flip charts. Participants then discussed the pros and cons of each option and made additional comments about them, all of which were listed on the flip chart and included in a written summary of the meeting. One of the options they discussed, for example, was "stabilization discs"—concrete slabs installed just below the sand's surface to break wave energy. Stabilization discs are inexpensive and easy to install and remove; they could be taken out during the summer when major storm events are less likely and more people are using the beach. On the other hand, the discs are aesthetically displeasing, may create a safety hazard, and are not a proven technology. Another option discussed was the use of plastic mats, which are secured underwater near the shore and designed to dissipate wave energy before it hits the beach. The mats are relatively inexpensive and easy to install, but there was concern that pieces of plastic would break away and wash ashore. Workshop participants also considered relocating Beach Road inland. The design and construction of this option would have been costly, however, and its impacts on coastal resources raised permitting problems.

The second session of the workshop was devoted to narrowing the options and refining those deemed worthy of more attention. Objective criteria were used to analyze all the options—criteria such as cost and funding sources, time frame for completion, design and construction considerations, and permitting requirements. After applying these criteria, the group placed each option in one of three categories: options to be advanced, options to be discarded, or options still pending. At the request of the group, two technical experts from the Woods Hole Oceanographic Institute made presentations at this session and addressed questions about options. These experts were active throughout the workshop, in fact, sharing the results of their research on the dynamics of the beach and their projections of the likely impacts of various erosion control options.

Also at this session, two work groups were formed. One was established to research key questions raised by the group. Another was charged with preparing a draft Memorandum of Agreement (MOA) to be used as a negotiating text for the final session of the workshop.

Many details of the MOA were hammered out during the final session. The agreement that was reached was seen as a reasonable set of measures to address the erosion problems at hand, as well as an opportunity to gain new information concerning sand transport at State Beach that may be valuable to long-term study and future management of the resource.

The final MOA contained several key provisions. First, it authorized construction of one to three temporary adjustable wooden groins made of nonleaching treated timber (rather than the stone and wire variety that had been installed in the past). The groins were to be constructed, monitored, and maintained in combination with the beach nourishment project outlined below. To address concerns about unexpected negative impact on sand deposition, the MOA stated that if the groins were determined to be causing accelerated erosion or other adverse impacts, additional beach nourishment, groin adjustment, groin removal, or other appropriate measures would be taken.

Beach nourishment was the other active measure adopted to stabilize the beach. The MOA specified nourishment engineering standards and the conditions under which renourishment would be allowed. The agreement also established two multiagency Technical Advisory Committees, one to work on project design and the other to oversee monitoring and remediation.

The parties also agreed to work together to dredge Sengekontacket Pond. If the dredge material proved to be appropriate for beach nourishment, it would be used for that element of the project. Pond dredging was expected to have a number of collateral benefits for the pond as well, including enhancement of water quality and circulation, improved navigability, improved public boat access to the coast, and enhancement of pond fisheries.

The MOA established an annual maintenance and monitoring program, in which the parties to the agreement will review the project annually for operations, functions, and maintenance. If any repairs become necessary, the parties agreed to meet to work out the appropriate measures to be taken to address the repairs or modifications.

The MOA also laid out a schedule for permitting and project construction. It specified the permits required and allocated the costs among MHD, the DEM, and the towns.

Finally, a dispute resolution provision was included in the MOA. It stated that parties shall first attempt to resolve informally any disagreements concerning implementation. If informal consultations do not resolve the disagreement, the MOA required MHD to reconvene the parties for discussion, fact-finding, mediation, and any other activities that would facilitate resolution.

The mutual gains approach employed in this negotiation was clearly successful. After exploring interests, brainstorming possible options while suspending criticism, and generating possible "packages" of options, the negotiating group settled on an agreement that met the interests of all the parties. The agreement met their shared objectives of protecting Beach Road and maintaining the recreational and biological values of State Beach. It met other interests as follows.

- MHD got an agreement that all parties believed would protect Beach Road and that would cost considerably less than other options. The MOA memorialized the assent of all the permitting authorities, including those who had denied permits to MHD in the past. After such a thorough exploration of all the options and the written concurrence of each organization, MHD felt confident for the first time that a multistakeholder agreement about Beach Road protection would not unravel.
- The Corps of Engineers also was assured by the concurrence of all permitting agencies that intergovernmental squabbling would be replaced with cooperation. As a result, the Corps agreed to renew its technical support for the project after three years on the sidelines.
- The DEP, CZM, and the other parties most concerned about unexpected negative impacts of erosion-control activities appreciated the fact that the two measures adopted could both be adjusted depending on how they worked in practice. The wooden groins could be lowered or even removed if they accelerated erosion. Indeed, of all the hard-engineered structures, the temporary wooden groins had the lowest projected risk of negative impacts. Beach nourishment would be done only to the extent necessary to replenish sand to agreed-upon levels. The monitoring provision provided a means by which these parties could formally assess the impacts of the work, discuss any concerns that might arise, and make adjustments as needed.
- The DEM was satisfied with the joint funding arrangement. The towns found it acceptable as well after it was modified to limit their funding responsibilities to three years.
- DFW concluded that implementation of the agreement would likely benefit, not damage, the habitat of the endangered piping plover.
- FOS and the Martha's Vineyard Commission, who had worked behind the scenes for years to build consensus on the protection of State Beach, finally had an agreement among all the stakeholders on an environmentally sound solution. The MOA laid out a special role for FOS as a leader of public education for the project and the broker of improved communications, particularly among community residents, town government, state environmental agencies, and MHD. FOS and town government representatives were also pleased with the provisions regarding the dredging of the Sen-

gekontacket Pond, which they felt would create important side benefits for the environmental health of the pond and the shellfishery.

The decision to dredge the pond is perhaps the best example of how the parties "expanded the pie" during these negotiations. The dredging helped to fill the primary need for beach nourishment materials, but provided secondary benefits as well. It was a solution that created value not anticipated by most parties when the negotiation began.

The MOA is now being implemented. The temporary adjustable groins have been installed, Sengekontacket Pond has been dredged, and the dredge material is being used as nourishment for State Beach. As a result, erosion has abated at the beach and Beach Road is no longer in immediate danger of being undercut. The maintenance and monitoring program of the MOA is collecting information about sand transport that has been supplied to the consultant conducting the long-term alternatives study, improving the database on which that study is being built. The parties have not needed to use the formal dispute resolution provisions of the MOA, as they have worked through implementation issues directly and informally.

NOTE

1. Gregory Sobel is a nationally known environmental mediator and attorney who has mediated more than 60 environmental and other public policy disputes and facilitated numerous consensus-based processes. Issues have included brownfields redevelopment, PCB cleanup and natural resource damages, wetlands protection and development, land use, beach access, endangered species protection, aquifer contamination, and ski area expansion, among others. From 1989 to 1995, Mr. Sobel was with the Massachusetts Office of Dispute Resolution (MODR), and from 1993 to 1995 he served as MODR's Environmental Program Director and Senior Mediator. Since then, he has operated his own practice, Environmental Mediation Services. Mr. Sobel was the sole mediator on the Martha's Vineyard project.

Memorandum of Agreement
Regarding Beach Road in Oak Bluffs
November 21, 1996

Section I—Statement of Purpose

This agreement is made this ____ day of _____, among the Massachusetts Department of Environmental Protection ("DEP"), the Massachusetts Highway Department ("MHD"), the Massachusetts Department of Environmental Management ("DEM"), the towns of Oak Bluffs and Edgartown (the "Towns") and the Dukes County Commissioners ("DCC"), because they have mutually agreed that it is in the public interest to proceed promptly with the actions called for herein.

The below Agreement sets forth an Interim, short-term alternative to attempt to reduce storm damage to Beach Road agreed to by all parties named herein at the second of two "Interim Erosion Control Workshops" held on January 10, 1996. Although all parties have conceptually agreed to try this Interim measure, the proposed alternative represents the preferred choice of MHD. These workshops were developed and held by MHD and facilitated by Greg Sobel, consultant to MHD. This interim temporary alternative is an attempt to protect the roadway until a long-term erosion control measure and storm damage reduction is implemented, pursuant to applying for and obtaining all applicable permits. This alternative is also seen as an opportunity to gain new information concerning sand transport at Sylvia State Beach that may be valuable to future management of this resource as well as the ongoing long-term study.

In the spirit of cooperation and partnering the representatives of the following private organizations and public agencies participated in the Interim Erosion Control Workshops in support of the process utilized to determine the alternative outlined in this document: Representative Eric T. Turkington; State Senator Henri Rauschenbach; Friends of Sengekontacket ("the Friends"); Martha's Vineyard Commission ("MVC"); Oak Bluffs Conservation Commission; Edgartown Selectmen; Edgartown Conservation Commission; Edgartown Shellfish Warden and Edgartown Harbormaster, Arthur Gaines and Graham Giese of Woods Hole Oceanographic Institute/Sea Grant Program and Marine Policy Center; MHD; DEM; DEP; MCZM; U.S. ACOE; MDFW and NHESP.

In entering into this agreement, it is the Parties' objective to facilitate resolution of interim storm damage minimization to Beach Road and Sylvia State Beach, while providing an opportunity for completion of MHD's analysis of long-range alternatives to protecting Beach Road and managing the barrier beach complex, while at the same time, adhering to the Wetlands Protection Act and other applicable regulations.

Section II—Background

Sylvia State Beach is located on the island of Martha's Vineyard in the Towns of Oak Bluffs and Edgartown. Sylvia State Beach, owned by "DEM" and maintained by the "DCC" is a barrier beach as defined in the Mass. Wetlands Protection Act regulations at, 310 CMR 10.29 and identified in the Mass. Coastal Zone Management Barrier Beach Maps as BB ≠ Ob-1. Sylvia State Beach (SSB) is bordered to the East by Nantucket Sound and Sengekontacket Pond to the West. There are two fixed inlets into the pond, one at the northern end of the barrier beach and the other centrally located on the barrier beach.

The barrier beach is approximately 2.5 miles in length. This agreement is intended to address erosion in the area beginning at the northern inlet in the vicinity of the existing Stone Groin Field and extending approximately 500 feet past the southern inlet or 7000 +/- feet.

Beach Road, a State Highway under the jurisdiction and maintenance of the MHD, runs the length of Sylvia State Beach. It provides an important link for emergency and other vehicles between Oak Bluffs and Edgartown. It is a paved two-lane roadway with a paved shoulder for parking adjacent to the beach as well as a paved bike path offset from the road. Longshore sediment volume and transport to SSB may have been reduced and interrupted over the years through construction of a variety of coastal engineering structures (jetties, groins, seawalls, etc.) northeast of the pond and through channel construction and maintenance. Erosion of the beach, particularly that area immediately downdrift of the last two stone groins, coupled with Beach Road's low elevation relative to storm surge and waves, has resulted in storm damage to Beach Road. The road has in the past been temporarily closed to traffic during and immediately following moderate to major coastal storm events due to storm overwash and the need for maintenance and repair of the storm damaged roadway. Beach Road along Sylvia State Beach has not sustained significant damage since the December 1992 Northeaster due, in part, to the dune building, plantings, beach nourishment and management efforts coordinated by the Friends through the Friends of Sengekontacket Barrier Beach Task Force.

In 1993, a portion of the pond was dredged by the DEM and the towns to improve navigation, water circulation and water quality apparently reduced by the formation of sand shoals within the pond. This project included beach nourishment of SSB with the dredged material providing temporary shore and road protection. On several different occasions MHD has placed several thousand cubic yards of beach nourishment material to provide additional temporary protection of Beach Road from storm damage.

The Long Term Alternative Study requirement is embodied in a Memorandum of Understanding entered into between the MHD and DEP on December 2, 1993 and amended on November 15, 1994 and again on June 21, 1995. Condition number 7 required MHD to develop a long-term plan to address the issues of road maintenance and wetlands protection along Beach Road. As discussions between the agencies proceeded on the scope of the long-term study it was determined that interim short-term measures would need to be identified, permitted and implemented until an approved long-term alternative was found.

Section III—Interim Short-Term Alternative

The interim short-term alternative, selected by MHD and agreed to by all participating parties herein is as follows:

1. Temporary Adjustable Wooden Groin Construction

MHD, DEM and the Towns will construct one to three temporary adjustable wooden groins (TAG).

The temporary adjustable groins shall be strategically placed on Sylvia State Beach downdrift of the existing groins at approximately the same 400 foot intervals as the existing groins. This interim alternative shall have a life expectancy not to exceed 10 years. The groins shall be comprised of nonleaching treated timber or other such temporary materials. The groins shall be constructed, monitored, and maintained in combination with the beach nourishment outlined below. If the groins are determined to be causing accelerated erosion or other adverse impacts, additional beach nourishment, groin adjustment, groin removal or other immediate appropriate measures may be required of the applicant.

MHD and DEM will be responsible for filing and obtaining all necessary federal, state and local permits and for complying with other applicable requirements relative to the groin construction, including final design plans and specification.

2. Beach Nourishment/Groin Cell Renourishment

DEM, MHD and the Towns will conduct a beach nourishment project. The beach nourishment shall be engineered so as to provide an adequate volume of sediment to fill the above-referenced groins to entrapment design. A series of permanent control points shall be installed along the groins. The control points shall be installed at points where 25% and 50% of the groin cell volume would be eroded. Once the nourished beach within a cell or cells has eroded to the 50% mark, renourishment, adjustment of the TAGs or other appropriate remediation measures, as determined by the Technical Advisory Group established herein and approved by the permitting Agencies, will be required and performed by the Towns and DCC with cooperation and assistance from DEM and MHD. Any renourishment or other approved remediation measure shall be initiated within sixty (60) days, completed as soon as possible, but no later than six (6) months from approval. Groin adjustment shall be completed within sixty (60) days. The sediment necessary for the beach nourishment/renourishment shall be obtained primarily from the dredging project described below or any other compatible island source (e.g., other permitted dredge projects, borrow pits, etc.).

3. Dredging of Sengekontacket Pond

The Towns, DEM, and MHD will work cooperatively to dredge Sengekontacket Pond. The dredge materials, if of a compatible nature, shall be used for the beach nourishment and groin filling project(s) described above. Dredging of Sengekontacket Pond shall provide the primary means of obtaining sand to be used for beach nourishment as described in Section III.2 above. An advantage of obtaining sand by this means is that pond dredging is expected to have a number of collateral benefits to the pond, including: enhancement of water quality and circulation; improved navigability; improved public access, via boats, to the coast; and enhancement of pond fisheries. It is anticipated that an added benefit is that the dredge materials that will be utilized for the beach nourishment/groin construction project, including periodic renourishment, may also provide a level of protection to Beach Road until such a time as the long-term study has been completed, and a preferred alternative chosen, permitted and implemented.

Because the dredge materials shall be used as materials for the beach nourishment project, the Towns shall coordinate with the MHD and DEM relative to the beach nourishment project described above.

The dredging plan design, review and permit filing shall follow the same outline and timeline procedures as established for the groin construction and beach nourishment above.

It is understood that MHD and DEM will be responsible for filing and obtaining all necessary federal, state and local permits and for complying with other applicable requirements relative to the dredging.

4. Annual Maintenance and Monitoring Program

Upon the completion of the construction of the groins, dredging of the pond and the beach nourishment project, the parties to this agreement shall review the total project annually for operations, functions and maintenance. Beach profiles and quarterly reports shall be prepared by MHD with the cooperation and assistance of the Towns, DCC, MHD and the Friends. Beach Profiles and quarterly reports shall be submitted to the Technical Advisory Committee, DEP, MCZM and the Conservation Commissions for review, comment and approval. Maintenance of the groins with regard to repair, adjustments, etc. shall be the responsibility of the DCC with assistance and advice from DEP, MHD, DEM, CZM and the Conservation Commissions. Beach nourishment maintenance as well as maintenance dredging will be the responsibility of the Towns in cooperation with the DCC and financial assistance from MHD and DEM. The Friends will assume a role in the planning, facilitation, and implementation of the monitoring and research activities to evaluate the effectiveness of this interim alternative.

If any repairs or modifications become necessary, the parties to this agreement shall meet to discuss the appropriate measures to be taken to address the repairs or modifications. The mechanism and responsibility for adjustments of the groins shall be outlined in the design plan for the groins. The maintenance and monitoring shall be performed as described in the Final Monitoring and Maintenance Program (M.M.P.) dated September 6, 1996 and attached as Appendix #1. [Eds. note: This appendix is not included here.]

The Towns, MHD, DEM, and DCC shall be responsible for initiating the annual review meetings and undertaking any necessary repairs or modifications relevant to the project. The Towns shall be responsible for implementing any repairs or modifications that the parties agree to.

If Beach Road is damaged or lost because of the non-permanent nature of the above described measures, MHD will, in compliance with the Wetlands Protection Act, take minimal steps necessary to reopen the roadway, and will inform and work with DEP and the Town Conservation Commissions to establish the necessary actions to reopen the roadway. At the request of MHD, DEP and the Conservation Commissions shall reopen the issue of alternative short-term measures which may be taken to protect Beach Road, until a long-term solution is agreed upon, permitted and implemented and will include all parties to this agreement.

5. Education and Facilitation

See Appendix #2.

SCHEDULING:

Notwithstanding this document, MHD, DEM and the Towns shall proceed with the design, monitoring and maintenance plan, permitting and construction pursuant to the following schedule:

- **April–June 1996**—a Section 404 permit application shall be filed with the U.S. Army Corps of Engineers for the temporary wooden groins, dredging of Sengekontacket Pond and Beach Nourishment as well as other applicable Federal, State and Local permit applications, including a Notice For Project Change with MEPA.

- **August–October 1996**—The issuance of the U.S. ACOE, Section 404 permit, Orders of Conditions, Chapter 91 permit/license, 401 Water Quality Certificate, CZM Federal Consistency, other applicable permits.
- **October 1996**—for Advertisement of Project.
- **November 1996**—for contract initiation and groin construction.
- **November 1996**—to commence dredging.
- **March 15, 1997**—for completion of project.

Section IV—Permits Required

Natural Heritage Sign-Off

Order of Conditions - Oak Bluffs and Edgartown

Local Wetlands By-Law - (Dependent upon applicant)

Chapter 91 Permit and License

401 WQC - Dredging and Groins

MEPA - Project Change or new Certification

CZM Federal Consistency

USACOE - 404 Permit

Martha's Vineyard Commission - D.R.I.

DEM Authorization

Section V—Estimated Costs and Contributions

As stated in Section III, Item 1 the interim alternative shall have a life expectancy not to exceed 10 years. However, as outlined below, the financial commitment of the participating parties dedicates funding for a three-year period. The provisions set forth under Section III, Item 4, "Annual Maintenance and Monitoring Program" require the parties of this agreement to reconvene if repairs or modifications become necessary. If said repairs or modifications occur subsequent to the three-year funded maintenance program then MHD, DEM and the Towns will need to address the financial aspect of such repairs or modifications.

1. Total Construction

a. Estimated Cost:	$666,667
b. Contribution MHD/DEM (75%):	$500,000
Towns (25%):	$166,667

TOWN OF OAK BLUFFS

The town of Oak Bluffs will contribute, subject to Town Meeting approval, the sum of $83,000 or 12 1/2% of the total cost of the project, whichever is the lesser amount. Further the town of Oak Bluffs will, at the earliest possible time, bring before a Town Meeting the request for the above mentioned funds.

TOWN OF EDGARTOWN

The town of Edgartown will contribute, subject to Town Meeting approval, the sum of $83,000 or 12 1/2% of the total cost of the project, whichever is the lesser amount. Further the town of Edgartown will, at the earliest possible time, bring before a Town Meeting the request for the above mentioned funds.

2. Annual Maintenance Program (Three Years)

a. Estimated Costs: $100,000
b. Contribution MHD/DEM (75%): $ 75,000
   Dukes County (25%): $ 25,000

Dukes County will contribute the sum of $25,000 per annum or 25% of the total cost of the maintenance of the project, whichever is the lesser amount.

3. Education and Facilitation

See Appendix #2.

Section VI—Dispute Resolution

1. The Parties shall attempt to resolve informally any disagreements concerning implementation of this Agreement or any work required hereunder.
2. If a Party objects to this agreement, to any written approval, disapproval, claim, demand or determination of one or more of the other Parties made in accordance with this Agreement, said Party shall notify DEP and MHD in writing of its specific objections within seven (7) days of receipt of said written approval, disapproval, claim, demand or determination.
3. The MHD will then reconvene the workgroup for discussions, meetings, fact-finding, mediation, and any other activities which will facilitate resolution of the objection. At any time, the objecting Party may be required to submit a more complete written statement of its objections and the factual and legal basis for such objections.
4. After the dispute has been resolved or the date for completion of dispute resolution has passed, the Facilitator, or his/her designee, shall issue a written statement setting forth the agreement or his or her findings and the final determination in the matter. Such agreement or determination will be incorporated as a modification, if applicable, pursuant to Section VII below.
5. Entering objections pursuant to this section shall not be cause for delay of the implementation of any work not specifically the subject of the written notice of objections unless it is functionally dependent to the work objected to. Deadlines for other work which is specifically the subject of the written notice of objections shall be extended an amount of days equal to the number of days by which the project has been delayed during "dispute resolution."

Section VII—Modifications

1. This agreement may be modified or amended by written agreement of the Parties.
2. In the event that unanticipated circumstances beyond control of any party to this

agreement, prevents that party from complying with deadlines proved herein, including but not limited to delays in obtaining federal, state, and local permits, any party responsible for undertaking work described above may request in writing, that this agreement be modified pursuant to this section so that the activities outlined in this agreement can be performed.

Section VIII—Reservation of Rights

1. Notwithstanding the parties' performance pursuant to this agreement, nothing in this agreement shall be construed as or shall operate as barring, delaying, diminishing, or adjudicating or in any way affecting any legal or equitable right of the DEP or Conservation Commissions, to take any action at any time, including actions under c. 131, § 40 and regulations promulgated thereunder, with respect to the subject matter covered by this agreement, or in any way affecting any other claim, action, or demand which any Party may have with respect thereto.

Appendix #2

Although the Friends bear no responsibility, financial or otherwise for the work outlined in this agreement the group has offered to extend its proactive involvement. The Friends will coordinate communication between the Barrier Beach Task Force members and the island based media. Leadership for planning public forums and special presentations for the general public and to disseminate information, will be the responsibility of the Friends in cooperation with the Towns and agencies.

The Friends will be accessible to the community for their views on the beach and this Interim proposal and build support for volunteer effort, such as vegetative plantings, as needed. The Friends will facilitate communication between the community, Towns, island based agencies, Executive Office of Environmental Affairs Agencies and MHD.

The Friends has long recognized the importance of environmental education to enhance the public understanding of these natural assets. Fortunately, several organizations have existing programs within the barrier beach complex. The Friends will continue to support these programs and promote the development of new initiatives utilizing applicable information published in the "Guidelines for Barrier Beach Management in Massachusetts."

Case 3

Coastal Zone
Regulations in Delaware

Gregory Sobel

Delaware's Coastal Zone Act (CZA) is a powerful land use law prohibiting new heavy industry from being built in Delaware's coastal region while allowing existing heavy industry to continue operating. As of late 1996, regulations to implement the CZA had not been adopted, even though the law had been on the books for 25 years. The undefined and informal regulation system used by the state's Department of Natural Resources and Environmental Control (DNREC) frustrated environmentalists and industry alike. In addition, environmental and industry groups were often at odds over implementation of the law.

Prior to 1996, DNREC had made several unsuccessful attempts to adopt formal regulations for the CZA. In 1991, for example, DNREC convened a diverse group of stakeholders to try to develop regulations collaboratively. That effort failed, however, for several reasons. The decision rules of the ad hoc committee were unclear, with the chairperson declaring "agreement" when provisions were supported by just two-thirds of committee members. Also, it was never clear how DNREC and the Coastal Zone Industrial Control Board (CZICB) would translate the recommendations of the committee into regulations. As a result, several very different versions of regulations, all based on the committee's work, were released in the years that followed. Each version was opposed by at least one key stakeholder group. The last set of regulations DNREC proposed prior to 1996 was struck down on procedural grounds by the Delaware Court of Chancery. The ad hoc committee process was not assisted by a mediator.

In late 1995, DNREC decided once again that regulations had to be drafted and that another multistakeholder negotiation group should be convened. But given the long history of conflict among the parties, DNREC officials were not sure that consensus building would be feasible. So, they hired a team of mediators from the Consensus Building Institute to conduct a conflict assessment.

This case study describes that conflict assessment process, the key stakeholders' views and interests, and the "regulatory negotiation" that ensued among the diverse parties.[1] It describes how the parties were able to create and claim value on their way to reaching agreement. A copy of the Memorandum of Understanding (MOU), to which the parties ultimately agreed, follows the case history.

The Conflict Assessment

A "conflict assessment" is a tool mediators use to determine who has a stake in a dispute, what their interests are, and whether the situation is appropriate for consensus building.[2] The conflict assessment we conducted in this case involved interviewing 57 stakeholders representing the full range of interests and perspectives. The assessment helped DNREC and the other stakeholders to better understand the issues, interests, and opportunities involved in promulgating regulations using a consensus-based approach. I was the senior mediator on the conflict assessment team, which included Patrick Field, Willa Kuh, and James Gascoigne.

After reviewing the findings from the interviews, the conflict assessment team concluded that the situation was not then ripe for a successful assisted negotiation. Among the important negative factors was the fact that the perceived BATNA of the industry stakeholders was so strong that we felt they would not bring sufficient flexibility to the negotiating table. Specifically, they were relatively content with the status quo; the implementation of the case-by-case permitting process, although involving some uncertainty, generally resulted in decisions favorable to their interests. Because industry representatives were concerned that negotiations would lead to regulations less favorable than the status quo, they therefore had an incentive to block agreement. Although industry members indicated a willingness to come to the table if invited by Delaware Governor Thomas Carper and DNREC Secretary Christophe Tolou, the conflict assessment team had doubts about the potential for success.

Nonetheless, we could envision a set of changed conditions that would make consensus building more likely to succeed. The conflict assessment report thus recommended that Governor Carper and DNREC, led by Secretary Tolou, convene a negotiating committee only if these conditions could be created. The report emphasized, first, that all key parties must recognize that they can achieve the best results for their interests through good-faith negotiations. This was most likely to occur if stakeholders recognized that (1) the existing informal permit system would be replaced by formal regulations even if negotiations were not successful, and (2) the regulations proposed in lieu of a consensus agreement would likely not meet the interests of all parties. DNREC had to communicate these points to stakeholders before a group could be convened.

Another critical precondition for success was a commitment from DNREC to follow the negotiating committee's guidance if consensus was reached.[3] The other conditions involved building on the work of the 1991/1992 unassisted negotiations; an endorsement of the process from leaders of the state's executive and legislative branches; ground rules that, among other things, specified the protocols for reaching agreement; and participation in the negotiating committee by all key stakeholder groups. The report also included detailed advice about the structure of the process, budget, and timelines.

These recommendations were agreed to by Governor Carper and Secretary Tolou. Tolou announced that DNREC was committed to establishing new regulations, either through negotiation or through the traditional promulgation process. He further stated that these regulations would meet the dual goals of providing industry in Delaware's coastal zone the flexibility to stay competitive and prosper while requiring those same industries to assist in the overall improvement of the coastal zone's natural environment. These pronouncements created the incentives parties needed to negotiate in good faith, setting the stage for a successful negotiated rulemaking. Put another way, Tolou's statements weakened the BATNAs of all the parties, such that all would prefer negotiating an acceptable agreement to living with their "walk-away" options.

In the fall of 1996, the first meeting of the Delaware Coastal Zone Regulatory Advisory Committee was convened. I co-mediated the negotiated rulemaking with Sarah McKearnan and Willa Kuh.

The Negotiators' Views and Interests

The advisory committee's 20 members represented a diversity of interests. They included individuals from the Sierra Club, the Delaware Nature Society, Dupont Corporation, CIBA Specialty Chemicals, the Chemical Industry Council, trade unions, the farming community, Diamond State Port Corporation, the state planning office, DNREC, and other organizations. For this case analysis, we lump these representatives into three categories: industry, environmentalists, and government.

The stakeholders' interests and perspectives are summarized in this section. The views described here are drawn from the published conflict assessment and statements made in public. No confidential communications have been disclosed.

Views on the History of the Conflict

Notwithstanding the absence of regulations, most stakeholders believed that the Coastal Zone Act was largely a success. It had protected Delaware's coastline from new industrial development for 25 years while allowing existing industry to prosper. No new heavy industry was allowed south of the Chesapeake and Delaware Canal, in effect reserving the southern Delaware coast for recreation, fishing, and residential development.

Stakeholders disagreed, however, about whether DNREC's efforts to interpret and apply the law to individual permit applications were effective. Industry representatives felt DNREC's case-by-case method of administration was working, citing the fact that only a handful of the 200 permits issued were appealed. Environmentalists were not as pleased with DNREC's implementation of the law. They believed the agency should have denied certain of the permit requests to better protect the coastal zone, and they were not confident about the agency's ability to make the "hard decisions." Environmentalists also explained that they did not have the resources to challenge all inappropriate permits; otherwise they would have filed more appeals.

Most stakeholders viewed the 1991/1992 unassisted negotiations as productive in some respects, but ultimately disappointing and frustrating. They noted that the ad hoc committees' "agreement" on several important issues often did not represent anything close to unanimous approval, and that several highly contentious issues were not in any sense resolved.

Key Interests

The environmental and industry representatives involved in the negotiations had very different interests and concerns. Industry representatives were interested in maintaining the economic viability of their firms. They needed to be able to compete effectively in a rapidly changing and intensely competitive global marketplace. They needed the flexibility to change their processes and products as business conditions required, without undue regulatory restrictions or bureaucracy. Industry representatives also wanted more certainty about the permitting process. Environmentalists, on the other hand, were interested in the long-term environmental health of the coastal zone. They felt that improving the region's environmental health should be the primary goal of new regulations, and that excessive deference to business flexibility would undermine that goal. Environmentalists also wanted to ensure that the permitting process created by the regulations allowed ample opportunity for public involvement and input. The main interest of the government representatives was simply to reconcile these different viewpoints so that effective and clear regulations could be promulgated once and for all.

The differing interests of environmentalists and industry led to differing perspectives on some of the central issues in debate. For example, the two sides held diverging views about "offsets"—a topic around which much of the negotiation ultimately revolved. Specifically, they disagreed over the rules regarding how permit applicants (seeking approval for changes in industrial processes) could "offset" projected environmental degradation with measures to improve environmental quality. The two sides struggled with how to measure the proposed impacts and offsets so valid comparisons could be made. Many environmentalists believed that mitigatory projects should take place in the same vicinity as the proposed environmental impact—or at least within the coastal zone. They also felt that offset activities should involve the same environmental medium as the potential impact. So, for example, environmentalists believed a proposed increase in nitrogen dioxide emissions should be offset by reduced nitrogen dioxide emissions nearby in the coastal zone (by shutting down another production line, for instance), and not, for example, by a land preservation project 30 miles inland. Industry representatives wanted the flexibility to be creative, however, and argued that such strict rules would both limit their ability to change in response to business conditions and cause them to forego cost-effective opportunities for significant environmental benefits. Industry also worried about establishing a system that would be so complicated that they would not be able to craft permit proposals with any certainty about how the agency would rule.

Another issue on which the two sides differed was credit for past good works. Industry wanted credit for past actions that yielded environmental improvements, noting that huge investments had been made by "good corporate actors" in the coastal zone, leaving relatively few cost-effective environmental projects remaining. Environmentalists countered that most of the environmental improvements made by industry were done to fulfill the requirements of existing law, and so were not deserving of extra credit.

The Negotiations

We first describe the process used to reach agreement and then analyze how the group created and claimed value in their development of that agreement.

The Process

The advisory committee held three negotiating sessions of two days each between the fall of 1996 and December 1997. First, the representatives discussed each others' interests. Then they brainstormed options for meeting those interests. They "invented options without committing," meaning that all agreements reached were considered tentative until a complete package of recommendations was agreed to by the full committee. This allowed the negotiators to more freely agree on individual provisions knowing that they would have the opportunity to consider the entire package of tentative agreements before finalizing their consent. This ground rule also gave negotiators incentives to consider trade-offs—to accept some provisions they did not prefer as long as other provisions were included, such that the full set of agreements met their overall interests.

After the second negotiating session, the mediators prepared a draft of the proposed MOU, addressing offsets and many other issues, which thereafter served as the focal point for negotiations. Over the many months that followed, negotiators offered successive improvements on this "single negotiating text" until a final MOU was adopted.

In the course of their discussions, DNREC and other parties answered factual questions posed by committee members and collected and presented requested information. For example, the agency prepared documents reviewing the history of permit issuances and various pollution trends. Also, an advisor to one of the negotiators prepared extensive materials describing how other jurisdictions had measured changes in environmental health.

Between plenary sessions, several work groups developed proposals for consideration by the entire committee. One work group negotiated language to address offset issues, for example. While not accepted outright by the full committee, this language served as the basis for the agreement on offset provisions that was ultimately reached by the committee. The mediators facilitated work group sessions on request and, at times, shuttled among negotiators to test proposals under consideration by interest group caucuses. We also served as confidential advisors when parties wanted our help developing new approaches or needed a "reality check" on ideas under consideration.

In December 1997, a draft MOU was tentatively approved by the negotiators, pending a public forum scheduled for January 1998 and consultations with constituents. At the forum and for the following two-week period, the public commented on the draft MOU and related concerns. DNREC then worked with the committee to revise the MOU. The final MOU was signed by all but one member of the committee at the closing negotiating session on March 12, 1998. The final member signed the agreement the following week, after further consultations with her organization's leadership.

Trading across Differences to Reach Agreement

In the end, the advisory committee was able to craft an agreement that successfully met the primary interests of all stakeholders. The key to the agreement was this: The new CZA regulations should ensure continuous environmental improvement in the coastal zone while providing industry with the flexibility to remain competitive in the global marketplace. Toward this end, the committee developed and recommended a regulatory scheme (detailed in the attached MOU) involving regulatory exemptions, permitting requirements, and offset provisions. The scheme allows industry in the coastal zone to add new products, change existing products, increase production capacity, add new processes, and modify existing processes, as long as these activities (1) assure environmental improvement in the coastal zone and (2) meet the other criteria outlined in the Coastal Zone Act. (The other criteria—such as "aesthetic effect" and "effect on neighboring land uses"—were not in dispute and so were not discussed during the negotiations.)

Much of the work of the advisory committee involved determining how this conceptual scheme would operate in practice—in particular, how the issue of offsets would be handled. First, the group had to determine how environmental impacts and their proposed offsets would be measured. To resolve this issue, the group adopted the innovative notion of environmental indicators. The negotiating group proposed, and DNREC agreed, that within 12 months of the ratification of the MOU, DNREC would develop a prioritized set of coastal zone environmental goals and indicators. The indicators would serve multiple purposes. They would assist DNREC in developing an accurate picture of the environmental quality of the coastal zone and help create a baseline from which to measure trends. The indicators would also provide permit applicants a means for assessing the potential impacts of proposed changes in facility operations and proposed offsets on the coastal environment. The committee agreed that the goals and indicators will be reviewed periodically and revised as conditions in the coastal zone change and scientific methods for tracking and analyzing those changes evolve.

To address concerns about stakeholder involvement in setting the goals and indicators, and to ensure scientific soundness, the committee recommended that DNREC establish an Environmental Indicator Technical Advisory Committee (EITAC). This group would include technical experts and representatives from various stakeholder groups, including heavy industry and manufacturing in the coastal zone, industry outside the coastal zone, agricultural interests, environmental advocacy groups, and organized labor. The advisory committee agreed that EITAC meetings should be open to the public and any reports generated by the EITAC be made public. The committee also agreed that DNREC's process for developing and prioritizing the indicators should include other opportunities for public review and comment.

On the issue of proposed offsets in permit applications, the committee agreed that, as DNREC considers those applications, offsets within the coastal zone in the same environmental medium and at the same site should be preferred. Offsets proposed outside the coastal zone, in other media, or at another site within the zone, but resulting in greater environmental benefit, should also be considered.

Concerning credit for past actions, the negotiating committee agreed that DNREC could consider past *voluntary* environmental improvements when determining the magnitude of required offsets. However, any proposed new project with new offsets must, in and of itself, assure improvement in future environmental quality in the coastal zone. It was also agreed that a company's history of compliance with environmental standards should be used by DNREC in gauging the applicant's ability to carry out an offset proposal. Thus, a company with a poor enforcement record would have a greater burden in convincing the agency it can implement an offset proposal with minimal supervision. The compromises reached on how to consider past corporate actions thus allowed both positive and negative industrial activities to be taken into account, while ensuring that future improvement to the coastal environment would be the key to getting a permit approved.

It is clear that advisory committee members were able to create and claim value by "trading" on their differing interests—each giving up something of lesser value while getting something of greater value. The environmentalists, for instance, did not mind if companies had increased flexibility, as long as the coastal zone was protected. And industry did not mind helping to protect and improve the environment as long as they were allowed to change their industrial practices without undue interference. So while it may have first appeared that the two sides' interests were directly in conflict, the negotiators were able to discover ways to meet both interests simultaneously.

The offset provisions were the key to making the trade work. Industry felt that, if they were to accept the "continuous environmental improvement" requirement, they needed the freedom to propose a wide range of offsets. Environmentalists would only agree to the flexible offsets language if it was tempered with a few key limitations. Those limits included the agreement that credit for past good deeds would be limited to those undertaken voluntarily and not otherwise mandated, and the fact that companies with poor environmental records would be subject to greater oversight as they implemented offset projects. The other element of the bargain important to environmentalists was the preference afforded to offset proposals in the coastal zone and in the same environmental medium as the negative environmental impacts of the permitted activity. With these caveats, and industry's agreement to promote continuous environmental improvement, the environmentalists could accept the flexible offsets provisions.

Another trade-off was structured around the different views of the parties about the timing of the permitted activity compared with the implementation of any offset. Industry negotiators wanted to be allowed to proceed with their proposed industrial activities as soon as a permit was issued. Environmental representatives felt this was risky, because offsets would not be implemented and their results evaluated until the permitted industrial change was already completed. The compromise reached by the group was that the permit must include well-defined and measurable offset commitments that are independently auditable by DNREC and available for review by the public. The offsets would be enforceable and the permit would have to include inspection, reporting, and notification obligations. Moreover, DNREC would give preference to offsets that occur simultaneously with the implementation of the proposed industrial activity. The applicant would also be required to submit any available scientific evidence about the efficacy of the proposed offset in producing its intended results.

Ensuring Proper Implementation

Advisory committee members wanted to make sure that their agreement was implemented in its totality. That is, they did not want the courts to be able to strike down certain elements of the package but allow the implementation of others. So, the negotiators specified which provisions would stand if others were invalidated. For example, the committee decided that their agreements on the precise "footprints" beyond which existing heavy industry in the coastal zone could not expand would be valid even if other provisions of the agreement were struck.[4] On the other hand, should the provisions dealing with environmental improvements and offsets be invalidated, the entire regulation, other than the footprint provisions, would be null and void. This understanding was necessary to preserve the central trade around which the entire agreement was built—continuous environmental improvement for industry flexibility to change industrial processes. This is a good example of how a negotiating group can anticipate, and take steps to rectify, possible implementation problems.

The Outcome

After the committee heard public comment on its draft MOU, made revisions, and approved the final product, they signed the MOU and presented it to Governor Carper. Carper also signed the agreement. DNREC then prepared draft regulations based on the MOU and circulated the draft. The advisory committee concurred that the draft regulations were consistent with the MOU, and DNREC forwarded the regulations to the Coastal Zone Industrial Control Board for promulgation. In recent months, the CZICB held public hearings. Some members of the negotiating committee have testified in support of the draft regulations, while, consistent with the ground rules for this process, no members testified against the draft. The regulations have recently been adopted.

NOTES

1. "Regulatory negotiation" is a mediation process in which interested stakeholders develop regulations by consensus that, if successful, are then promulgated by the agency responsible. The term is used interchangeably with "negotiated rulemaking."
2. My view is that before addressing the design of any consensus building process, a thorough conflict assessment must first consider the threshold question of whether an assisted negotiation is likely to succeed at all. The time and financial costs of consensus-based negotiations are considerable and should only be undertaken when the prospects for success are strong. An ill-advised or poorly prepared negotiation of any kind can exhaust and frustrate the participants, leaving them worse off than before. Sometimes, a conflict assessment reveals that a consensus building process would be counterproductive even when the sponsoring agency is eager to proceed.
3. As is standard for negotiated rulemakings, DNREC, the sponsoring agency, was a member of the negotiating committee and had the same power to block consensus as any other com-

mittee member. Thus, an agreement would be reached only if DNREC concurred with all other members of the committee.

4. The footprints were the most important agreement reached in the 1991/1992 ad hoc committee process.

Memorandum of Understanding

From the Delaware Coastal Zone Regulatory Advisory Committee to the Delaware Department of Natural Resources and Environmental Control

March 19, 1998

Introduction

This Memorandum of Understanding contains recommendations from the Delaware Coastal Zone Regulatory Advisory Committee to the Delaware Department of Natural Resources and Environmental Control (DNREC). The recommendations advise DNREC on the content of the regulations that DNREC will promulgate to implement the Coastal Zone Act.

The Advisory Committee held a Public Forum on January 13 whereupon members of the public were provided an explanation of the December 30, 1997 draft of this MOU and were encouraged to offer comments and suggestions for its improvement. For two weeks following the Forum, DNREC received additional written comments from interested citizens, worked with the Advisory Committee on revisions to the document and subsequently prepared this March 12, 1998 final MOU for the Advisory Committee's formal ratification and transmittal to DNREC.

Once DNREC has received the final version, the agency will prepare draft regulations consistent with the MOU's recommendations. The Advisory Committee will then be provided an opportunity to review the regulations to be sure they are consistent with the recommendations contained in the MOU. DNREC will then transmit the draft regulations to the Coastal Zone Industrial Control Board for its review and adoption.

The Advisory Committee has been and continues to be facilitated by a team from the Consensus Building Institute (CBI) of Cambridge, Massachusetts. The facilitation team can be reached at _____, ext. 17.

I. Environmental Improvement and Industry Flexibility

These recommendations are built around two linked goals. First, the regulations shall ensure environmental improvement in the Coastal Zone. Second, the regulations shall allow industry flexibility.

In order to meet these goals, the regulatory process should be designed so that each heavy industry facility can obtain permits to add new products, change existing products, increase production capacity, add new processes and modify existing processes so long as these activities are: 1) undertaken in a way that assures environmental improvement in the Coastal Zone; and 2) undertaken in such a way that they meet the six criteria outlined in the Coastal Zone Act.

In addition, the regulatory process should be designed so that each manufacturing facility, public sewage treatment facility, and public recycling facility can obtain a permit either to initiate operations in the Coastal Zone or to modify its existing operations so long as these activities are: 1) undertaken in a way that assures environmental improvement in the Coastal Zone; and 2) undertaken in such a way that they meet the six criteria outlined in the Coastal Zone Act.

Regulatory mechanisms developed by DNREC to meet the dual goals of environmental improvement and industry flexibility must be implemented simultaneously. In practice, this means that each grandfathered heavy industrial facility, manufacturing facility, public sewage treatment plant, and public recycling facility should be allowed increased flexibility in permitting and operations only after DNREC has developed a carefully defined procedure for assessing applications to ensure that proposed activities meet the environmental improvement standard, as well as the six criteria cited in the Act.

In particular, DNREC will need to develop several tools to better assess whether activities proposed for Coastal Zone permits will ensure environmental improvement. First, DNREC will develop a set of environmental goals specifically for the Delaware Coastal Zone. Second, DNREC will develop a set of prioritized environmental indicators to assess and track progress towards these environmental goals.

It is important to note that the development of these Coastal Zone environmental indicators is likely to take longer then the development of the regulations themselves. During the period after the regulations have been promulgated, but before the indicators are developed, DNREC will issue permits as otherwise prescribed in the new regulations. Applicants will still be required to describe the likely impacts of their proposed activities on each of the six criteria cited in the Act. The Secretary will use this information to make a determination about whether a permit should be granted.

Provisions of the regulations relating to increased flexibility of industrial operations and environmental improvements in the health of the Coastal Zone need to be clearly identified. If subsequent to the issuance of regulations, any of the environmental improvement or industry flexibility provisions in the regulations are invalidated (for example, by court action) then the entire set of Coastal Zone Act regulations will be void, except for the footprint definitions and designated boundaries developed by the 1992 Ad Hoc Committee, and the provisions relating to public notice.

Furthermore, if any other provisions (other than the provisions relating to increased flexibility of industrial operations and environmental improvements in the health of the Coastal Zone) are invalidated, then only those particular provisions will be void. All other provisions will remain operational.

As DNREC proceeds with implementation of the regulations, no materials or any supporting reports, previous draft MOUs, prior drafts of regulations or any materials whatsoever that have been used throughout this consensus building effort, shall be used to interpret the regulations.

II. Tiered Permitting

The Advisory Committee recommends that DNREC establish a tiered system of Coastal Zone Act permitting. Such a system adds efficiency to the permitting process, by tailoring the extent of regulatory review to the expected impacts of the proposed project. Under the tiered approach, an industry will be required to obtain a Coastal Zone Act permit only in those instances when a proposed new manufacturing facility, or a change in the operations of a heavy industrial or manufacturing facility, may have a negative impact on one or more of the six criteria cited in the Act [7 Del. C. Section 7004. (b)]. In those instances when an industry is proposing an activity which will not cause a negative impact to any of these criteria, it can propose moving through a streamlined regulatory process.

The Advisory Committee recognizes that negative impacts do not include facility shut downs, personnel layoffs, negative impacts on state tax revenues and other business-related issues which in and of themselves have no direct negative environmental impacts.

DNREC should establish three tiers of regulatory review:

Tier I   Activities under Tier I will be exempt from the permitting process. A company which wishes to initiate a Tier I activity does not have to apply for a Coastal Zone permit or notify DNREC of its plans.

Following is a list of examples of Tier I activities. This list is intended by the Advisory Committee to be illustrative, rather than exhaustive.

- maintenance and repair of existing equipment and structures;
- replacement in-kind of existing equipment or installation of in-line spares for existing equipment;
- installation and modification of process equipment which does not include routine emissions, nor increase emissions from existing support equipment beyond existing permit limits;
- installation and operation of pollution control and safety devices mandated by federal or state law;
- research and development activities, as long as they do not involve the construction of a new facility;
- repair and maintenance of existing electrical generating facilities, so long as such operations do not require a new or revised air pollution, water pollution, hazardous waste permit, wetland or subaqueous lands permit;
- back-up emergency and stand-by sources of electrical power to adequately accommodate industry needs when outside supply fails or is not available;
- any project which is exempt from existing Delaware Air, Water, Hazardous Waste and Solid Waste regulations, or a de minimis situation where no regulations exist; and
- any project which is initially reviewed by DNREC under Tier II, and then determined by DNREC to be a Tier I activity.

Tier II

Activities under Tier II will require a notification process. If an industry wants to propose a change in its products or processes that is not among those exempted from the permitting process by definition (Tier I), and the company believes that the activity will have no negative impact on the environmental health of the zone or on any of the six criteria named in the Act, then the company may choose to initiate a Tier II notification process.

At a minimum, any project which requires a new or re-negotiated air or water permit should be included in this tier. Proposed new manufacturing facilities which will operate in the Coastal Zone also fall under Tier II. In addition, new research and development facilities proposed for operation in the Coastal Zone will be included in this Tier. This applies both to new R & D facilities associated with an existing manufacturing or heavy industrial facility in the Coastal Zone, and new R & D facilities which are not associated with an existing use.

In effect, this notification process will be a revised version of the status determination process in use by the agency currently (and is essentially the same procedurally). The notification process will involve an exchange of letters between the company and DNREC prior to the initiation of the proposed activity. The company's letter should detail the proposed activity and indicate its expected impacts on all of the criteria included in the Act (the exact required content of this letter will need to be defined by DNREC in the regulations). Once correspondence from the applicant has been received, DNREC will review it and decide whether the proposed activity is Tier I or Tier III. This determination will be communicated to the company via written correspondence. DNREC should designate a time frame for the completion of its determination. The Advisory Committee recommends that this time frame be set at twenty-one business days.

If DNREC determines that the proposed activity will not produce any negative impacts on the six criteria, then the company will be given an approval to proceed without a permit. If DNREC determines that there will be negative impacts on any of the six criteria, then the company will be required to either refile under Tier III by submitting an application for a Coastal Zone permit, or drop the proposed project.

In those instances where DNREC determines that a project is a Tier I activity (after a Tier II notification), DNREC shall publish said determination as a legal notice similar to that required for permit approvals. As such, this determination will be subject to appeal as any permit approval would.

If a facility applies for a Tier II notification and DNREC determines that a project is a Tier I activity, that facility will be allowed to implement the approved Tier I activities. If after a public notice, a member of the public appeals the Tier I determination, the approved Tier I activity will not be delayed or terminated. If an appeal to the Tier I activity is upheld by the CZICB then the applicant will, if they choose to proceed with the project, apply for a Tier III permit.

DNREC will give public notice of all Tier II applications and provide for a ten-day period for comments to assist the Secretary before a decision is reached.

Tier III
Activities under Tier III will require a Coastal Zone permit. Included in this tier will be any activities proposed by either manufacturing facilities or heavy industrial facilities currently operating in the Coastal Zone, which have the potential to create negative impacts on any of the six criteria described in the Coastal Zone Act. In addition, any proposed activity which includes an "offset proposal" will automatically be included in this Tier.

The public shall be notified of any proposed activities which DNREC designates as Tier III after reviewing a company's written description of what is being proposed. In addition, all correspondence between DNREC and applicants for Coastal Zone permits will be part of the public record. DNREC will include in the draft regulations a clear description of how this public notification and participation process will take place. In developing this description, DNREC should review, and where appropriate borrow from, the Freedom of Information Act, the provisions on public notice and public participation in the 1992 Ad Hoc Committee's draft regulations, and other DNREC policies on public participation.

III. The Environmental Impact Statement

The applicant will place all information about the environmental impacts of the proposed project in the Environmental Impact Statement portion of the application. There will be a description of the required content of the Environmental Impact Statement (EIS) in the regulations themselves. It will be the responsibility of each applicant seeking a Coastal Zone permit to include in the Coastal Zone Permit application any and all information necessary for the Secretary to make an informed decision on the application.

At a minimum, the applicant shall be required to incorporate into the EIS a description of how the proposed activity will measurably increase air emissions, water discharges or otherwise cause negative environmental impacts on the Coastal Zone environment. An applicant shall also include in the Environmental Impact Statement a description of how any negative impacts from the proposed project will be offset, either as part of the proposed activity itself or through an enforceable offset proposal. If the applicant proposes an enforceable offset, the description shall include all information needed to clearly establish:

A. how the offset proposal will be carried out;

B. what the likely environmental benefits will be and when they will be achieved;

C. what if any negative impacts will result, and when;

D. what scientific evidence there is about the efficacy of this strategy in producing its intended results; and

E. how the projected results—both beneficial and negative—can be tracked in the future.

The applicant may also provide evidence of past voluntary environmental improvements[1] and/or investments made prior to the time of application.

IV. Principles for Assessing an Application

In assessing an application, the Secretary will consider how the proposed project will affect the six criteria cited in the Act, including environmental impacts, economic effects, aesthetic effects, number and type of supporting facilities and their anticipated impacts on these criteria, effect on neighboring land uses, and compatibility with county and municipal comprehensive plans.

Any negative environmental impact associated with a proposed project will have to be more than offset, thus assuring continuing improvement in the Coastal Zone environment. The Secretary will only grant Coastal Zone permits in those cases where the overall environmental impacts of the total application, both positive and negative, assure improvement in the quality of the environment in the Coastal Zone.

Therefore, activities proposed for a Coastal Zone permit which would measurably increase air emissions, water discharges, or would cause negative impacts on the Coastal Zone environment, shall include provisions for net environmental improvement of the Coastal Zone environment. These environmental improvements may be part of the permitted activity itself or realized through an enforceable offset proposal that will be implemented by a date agreed to by the company and DNREC.

DNREC will develop within 12 months of the promulgation of Coastal Zone Act regulations a set of Coastal Zone environmental goals and appropriate environmental indicators which will highlight the most significant environmental challenges to the Coastal Zone (see Section VI for more detail.) These indicators will be " prioritized" in accordance with their significance to achieving the Coastal Zone environmental goals. These prioritized indicators will provide Coastal Zone permit applicants a good idea of which types of future offset investments will yield the greatest environmental benefit and will allow a determination of which investments are most cost-effective. These indicators should also provide the rational basis for permit decisions that involve offset proposals.

Offset proposals will be evaluated by the Secretary using the following criteria:

• The Secretary will place a higher priority on offset projects within the Coastal Zone, in the same environmental medium as the source of degradation of the environment, that occur at the same site as the proposed activity requiring a permit, and that occur simultaneously with the implementation of the proposed activity needing an offset.

• Although offsets in the same environmental medium are preferred, there will be circumstances when offsets in other media provide greater environmental benefit or otherwise make sense, and will be considered by the Secretary.

- In addition, the Secretary will give more weight to offset proposals that: 1) have established track records and are likely to succeed from a technical standpoint; and 2) will produce beneficial effects that are verifiable.
- If an applicant includes in its permit application evidence of past voluntary environmental improvements and/or investments made prior to the time of application, DNREC will consider this history of environmental performance in determining the magnitude of the required offsets for the proposed project (with the understanding that the total project must assure improvement in the quality of the environment in the Coastal Zone).
- The Secretary will also consider the applicant's ability to carry out such improvements as evidenced by its compliance history. Compliance with environmental standards and enforcement histories of facilities is not in itself a factor in determining the required magnitude of the potential offset project, but will be used by DNREC in gauging the applicant's ability to carry out the offset project with a minimum of supervision.

V. DNREC Permitting Responsibilities

DNREC will meet the following responsibilities during the permitting process:

A. The Secretary shall make permitting determinations and environmental impact assessments, in writing, based on all of the expected environmental impacts of the total project on the health of the Coastal Zone, including both positive and negative impacts. Impacts may be related to air and water emissions, or they may be related to other factors such as the viability of wildlife habitat, the protection of wetlands, or the creation or preservation of open space. The Secretary will develop and use a set of prioritized environmental indicators as a tool for assisting these determinations. (See VI, below).

B. The Secretary shall also include in the written determination an assessment of the degree to which the project is consistent with the other criteria in the Coastal Zone Act: economic effects, aesthetic effects, number and type of facilities required, effect on neighboring land uses, and compatibility with county and municipal comprehensive plans for development and/or conservation.

C. The Secretary shall consider likely cumulative impacts of proposed activities on the environment and the relevant environmental indicators.

D. DNREC will only approve an application which includes an offset proposal if the proposal describes well-defined and measurable commitments or accomplishments which are independently auditable by the Department, and available to the public via the Freedom of Information Act (FOIA). Each offset proposal must also include a projected timeline for the implementation of the proposal.

E. While it is the applicant's responsibility to fully describe an offset proposal in the Environmental Impact Statement, it is the Secretary's responsibility to carefully assess whether the applicant's offset proposal will offset negative impacts of the project, and thus ensure environmental improvement in the Coastal Zone.

F. All offset projects must be incorporated into the Coastal Zone permit as an enforce-able condition of the permit. Since some of the benefits of "flexibility" are achieved immediately upon issuance of a permit (i.e., permission to proceed), and most ben-efits of "environmental improvement" are achieved over time, the permit itself must include well-defined and measurable commitments or accomplishments which are independently auditable by the Department, and available to the public via the Freedom of Information Act (FOIA). DNREC will also include inspection, reporting and/or notification obligations in the permit depending on the company's compliance record and the nature of the offset project.

G. The continuing validity of permits shall depend upon achieving all commitments, including those contained in the offset proposal. If the applicant fails to implement the proposal fully and in accordance with the agreed-upon schedule, then DNREC will have the authority to void the permit and to impose appropriate penalties on the applicant.

H. With the exception of information which is determined by the Secretary to be pro-prietary or trade secret within the bounds of the FOIA, it is essential that all par-ties, including the public, continue to have adequate opportunities to review and comment on all aspects of the permitting process.

I. Where an offset project in itself requires a permit be issued by one or more regula-tory programs within DNREC, the Secretary shall issue the Coastal Zone permit only after all applicable permit applications for offsetting projects have been received and deemed administratively complete by DNREC. Such Coastal Zone per-mits shall be approved contingent upon the applicant carrying out the proposed off-set in accordance with an agreed-upon schedule for completion of the offset project. Said schedule will be included in the Coastal Zone permit as an enforceable condi-tion of the permit.

J. Should a Coastal Zone permit applicant fail to receive, within 180 days of issuance of the Coastal Zone permit, any and all permits required to undertake an offset pro-ject, the applicant, except for good cause shown by the applicant for additional time, will be required to submit an entirely new application for the Tier III activity, including impact assessments, permit fees and a new proposed offset project

VI. Relevance/Use of Environmental Indicators

In evaluating an application for a Coastal Zone permit, DNREC should consider a set of "environmental goals"[2] and prioritized "environmental indicators"[3] designed as a tool to measure and monitor the health of the Coastal Zone.

The environmental indicators should be: 1) developed and maintained by DNREC; 2) developed within twelve months of the completion of this MOU and open for public review and comment; 3) used as a basis for assessing environmental impacts associated with proposed changes in facility operations and proposed offsets; and 4) reissued peri-odically.

These indicators will serve several important purposes. First, they will assist DNREC in developing a more accurate picture of the health of the Coastal Zone, and measuring trends in this health over time. Second, they will assist DNREC and project applicants in the permitting process, by providing a means for evaluating the potential impacts of proposed changes in facility operations and proposed offsets on Coastal Zone health. Finally, the indicators will provide a basis for explaining decisions made during the permitting process to applicants and to the public.

Following are several more specific recommendations for how the set of environmental indicators for the Coastal Zone should be developed and maintained. These recommendations should not be included in the regulations themselves. Instead, they should be included in a separate guidance document prepared by DNREC (see Section XI below).

1) DNREC will be responsible for defining, prioritizing, and making a matter of public record the set of goals and indicators for Coastal Zone health. Once goals for Coastal Zone environmental health have been established, DNREC will select a detailed set of indicators to determine the status of Coastal Zone health as measured against those goals, and to monitor progress over time.

2) DNREC will periodically review and reissue the Coastal Zone environmental indicators (perhaps bi-annually). As conditions in the Coastal Zone change, and scientific methods for tracking and analyzing these changes evolve, it may be necessary to add or change some indicators, or drop others. It may also be necessary to reprioritize them as some parameters of environmental health improve and others decline. DNREC's periodic review of the indicators will allow for these kinds of adjustments to be made.

3) DNREC's process for developing and prioritizing the indicators will include opportunities for formal public review and comment. To ensure that the public has opportunities to provide input into the development and any subsequent revision of the environmental indicators, the Advisory Committee recommends that DNREC establish an Environmental Indicator Technical Advisory Committee (EITAC). A substantial proportion of the members of the EITAC should be technical experts. The Committee should also include representatives of various stakeholder groups, for example, heavy industry and manufacturing in the Coastal Zone, industry outside the Coastal Zone, agricultural interests, environmental advocacy groups and labor. EITAC meetings should be public and any reports generated by the Committee should be made available to the public.

VII. Definitions of the Port of Wilmington, Research and Development, Docking Facility, Bulk Product Transfer and Public Sewage Treatment Facilities and Recycling Facilities

In addition to the broad guidance described above, the Advisory Committee has reached agreement on recommendations for several specific provisions in the regulations under the Coastal Zone Act. These are described below:

Port Boundaries

DNREC will incorporate the following definition of the Port of Wilmington into the definitions section of the regulations (please see attached map for a visual illustration of the boundaries described below) [Eds. note: This map has not been included.]:

> The current boundary of the Port of Wilmington is the area beginning
> at the intersection of the right of way of US Route I-495 and the south-
> ern shore of the Christina River; thence southward along said I-495
> right of way until the said I-495 right of way intersects the Reading
> Railroad Delaware River Extension; thence southeast along the said
> Reading Railroad Delaware River Extension to its point of intersection
> with the Conrail Railroad New Castle cutoff; thence southward along
> the Conrail Railroad New Castle cutoff until it intersects the right of
> way of U.S. Route I-295; thence eastward along said I-295 right of
> way until the said I-295 right of way intersects the western shore of
> the Delaware River; thence northward along the western shore of the
> Delaware River as it exists now to the confluence of the Christina
> and Delaware Rivers; thence westward along the southern shore of the
> Christina River to the beginning point of the intersection of the said I-
> 495 right of way and the Southern shore of the Christina River.

This definition should delineate the docking facilities which will be entitled to an exemption under Section 7002(f) of the Coastal Zone Act, provided, however, that the docking facilities which are exempted include:

a. those located on lands owned by the Diamond State Port Corporation (DSPC) and which are located within the Port of Wilmington as defined herein as of the effective date of this MOU;

b. any docking facilities located on lands or facilities acquired by DSPC at any time in the future and which are located within the Port of Wilmington as defined herein;

c. docking facilities located on privately owned lands within the Port of Wilmington as defined herein which:
   i. have been granted a Status Decision extending the bulk products transfer exemption prior to the effective date of these regulations; or
   ii. receive a Status Decision (or Tier II determination) demonstrating that:
      1) the docking facilities at the proposed use location bear a reasonable geographical relationship to the DSPC taking into account both the commercial and technological requirements; and
      2) the docking facilities at the proposed use location demonstrate interdependence and integration of the proposed facilities and operations within the DSPC operations.

Docking Facility

DNREC will incorporate the following definition of docking facilities into the definitions section of the regulations:

> Docking facility means any structures and/or equipment used to tem-
> porarily secure a vessel to a shoreline or another vessel so that materials,
> cargo, and/or people may be transferred between the vessel and the shore,
> or between two vessels, together with associated land, equipment, and

structures so as to allow the receiving, accumulating, safekeeping, storage, and preparation of cargoes for further shipment, and administrative maintenance purposes directly related to such receiving, accumulating, safekeeping, storage, and preparation of cargoes for further shipment.

Research and Development

DNREC will incorporate the following definition for Research and Development (R & D) into the definitions section of the regulations:

R & D activities are those in which R & D substances are used in quantities that are not greater than reasonably necessary for the purposes of scientific experimentation or product and process development. The R & D substances must either be the focus of R & D itself, or be used in the R & D activity focusing on another chemical or product. R & D includes synthesis, analysis, experimentation or research on new or existing chemicals or products. R & D encompasses a wide range of activities which may occur in a laboratory, pilot plants or commercial plant, for testing the physical, chemical, production, or performance characteristics of a substance, conducted under the supervision of a technically qualified individual. R & D is distinct from ongoing commercial activities which focus on building a market for a product rather than just testing its market potential. General distribution of chemical substances or products to consumers does not constitute R & D.

The regulations should treat proposed R & D activities (as described in the definition above) as distinct from proposed new R & D facilities. Whereas R & D activities will be included in Tier I of the tiered permitting process, new R & D facilities will be included in Tier II. This applies both to new R & D facilities associated with an existing manufacturing or heavy industrial facility in the Coastal Zone, and new R & D facilities which are not associated with an existing use.

Bulk Product Transfer

The definition of "bulk product" in the regulations will use the definition of "bulk" in Webster's Unabridged Dictionary: "in a mass; loose; not enclosed in separate packages or divided into separate parts." The definition should include examples of bulk products, such as grain, oil, gas, and minerals. It should also make clear that individually packaged items (such as autos, machinery, bags of salt, palletized items, etc.) are not considered bulk products.

Public Sewage Treatment Facilities and Public Recycling Plants

DNREC will incorporate a definition for public sewage treatment and public recycling plants into the regulations.

The definition for recycling plants could be taken from Federal Register, Vol. 56. No.

191. 10/2/91: "Recycling plants are industrial facilities whose primary products are recycled materials. The term recycle means the series of activities, including collection, separation, and processing, by which products or other materials are recovered from or otherwise diverted from the solid waste stream for use in the form of raw materials other than fuel for producing heat or power combustion."

DNREC will also clarify the exemption for public recycling facilities. The Advisory Committee recommends that DNREC define "public facilities" to mean facilities that are both publicly owned and also publicly operated.

VIII. Recommendations Based on the Ad Hoc Committee's Work

Sections of the recommendations developed by the Ad Hoc Committee to DNREC in July 1992 should be incorporated by DNREC into the new draft regulations. The specific language recommended for adoption is included in Attachment I. [Eds. note: This attachment is not included here.] This is not a complete version of the 1992 draft submitted to DNREC; instead, it is a compilation of all those sections for which there is a consensus agreement among members of this Advisory Committee. In addition, there are a number of areas in this draft regulatory language where the Advisory Committee is recommending that DNREC add provisions or language on particular topics. These recommendations to DNREC are included as footnotes in the regulatory text in Attachment I. They are also listed below (please note that citations refer to sections of Attachment I).

It is important to note that a few of the provisions contained in Attachment I may not be consistent with the recommendations in this MOU. An example might be the provisions on status determination. While the MOU suggests that the "status determination" process should become a "Tier II notification process," the term status decision appears often in Attachment I. DNREC will iron out these inconsistencies as draft regulations are developed. However, the Advisory Committee wishes to state clearly that the recommendations in the MOU should take precedence over the draft regulatory language when conflicts arise.

1. General Recommendations

- DNREC should ensure that the uses of the terms "non-conforming" and "manufacturing" are consistent throughout the regulations.
- DNREC should ensure that the different tiers comprising the tiered permitting system are clearly defined in the regulations. These definitions could be placed in Section II with the other definitions.

2. Definitions

- Under the definition for "Administratively Complete," DNREC should indicate the time-frame for determining that an application is administratively complete. The Advisory Committee recommends a time-frame of twenty-one business days.
- Between the definition "Bulk Product Transfer Facility" and "Department," DNREC should add a definition of "certify" (the process that applicants will use to legally attest to the truth of their submittal). This standard for the Coastal Zone Act should be consistent with that used in other environmental regulatory programs.

- Between the definition of "Docking Facility" and "Heavy Industry Use," DNREC should add a definition of "Environmental Impact Statement" that includes a reference to the use of environmental indicators.
- Under the definition of "Potential to Pollute," DNREC should consider whether there is a need to add language indicating that the Secretary will consider risk management and offset controls in evaluating a proposed use's potential to pollute.
- Also between the definition of "Potential to Pollute" and "Research and "Development" DNREC should add a definition for "Public Sewage Treatment Plants and Public Recycling Plants." (see Section VII above.)
- In the definitions section, DNREC should add a definition for "trade secret" or "confidential information" (DNREC should choose which term to used based on the Attorney General's recommendation). This definition should be consistent with the definition included in other relevant laws and regulations. The definition should make clear that the Secretary makes the final decision on an applicant's claim of confidentiality—and that the applicant must clearly identify the claimed confidential sections.

3. Uses Regulated

- Between provisions a) 1) B) and a) 1) D), DNREC should add a provision on public sewage treatment plants and public recycling plants.
- DNREC should move provision a) 1) D) to the section of the regulations on abandonment.
- DNREC should ensure that the provision a) 1) F) appears in other appropriate locations in the regulations.
- Under provision b) 1) A), DNREC should add new text on the Port of Wilmington.
- Under the provision b) 2), either here or in the section of the regulations on "flexibility," DNREC may want to add other conditions under which the Secretary would permit the construction of pipelines on docking facilities serving as bulk product transfer facilities.
- Under the provision d) 1) D), DNREC should elaborate on this concept in the draft regulations.
- Also under d), DNREC should add a section on electric power delivery facilities that are not regulated and the treatment of certain auxiliary power generating facilities.

4. Administration of the Act

- At the end of the provision c) 2) A), DNREC should include a comprehensive list of the criteria cited in the Act.
- Under the provision c) 2) B), DNREC should add a time-frame for using this right.
- DNREC should modify the provision c) 4) B) to include a description of how environmental indicators will be used.
- DNREC should add a section d, on the public availability of information. The content of this section should be guided by DNREC's Guidance Document regarding the Freedom of Information Act. In addition, this section should be consistent with other state and federal laws.

- DNREC should ensure that this section is written in such a way that the administrative process protects trade secrets. A definition of trade secrets may be needed.

IX. Monitoring, Reporting, and Penalties

In their applications for Coastal Zone permits, applicants should be required to include a clear description of any projects designed to produce environmental improvements, as well as a timetable for their completion. This will ensure that DNREC can include a description of the proposed activities in the permit itself, and can carry out straightforward and objective reviews of progress towards fulfilling permit conditions.

All applications for Coastal Zone permits should be "certified" (in the sense that the applicant legally attests to the truth of the submittal). Permit holders whose permit is conditioned on projects designed to produce an environmental improvement will be required to regularly report to DNREC (and to the public) on the progress made relative to their commitments. DNREC will carefully review and analyze these reports.

If commitments agreed to by the applicant as a condition of a permit are not being fulfilled, the permit holder will be in violation. The regulations shall reference the specific authorities DNREC has to impose penalties in the event that a permit holder does not comply with the conditions of the permit.

To ensure that the public is kept fully informed about the regulatory process under the Coastal Zone Act and about the health of the Coastal Zone generally, the Secretary will issue a report twelve months after the regulations are promulgated, and every twenty four months thereafter. The report will include:

1) A description of progress towards environmental goals developed by DNREC for the Coastal Zone;
2) Information on the general trends in the environmental indicators, in the form of narrative text as well as charts and graphs that will be easily understandable to a lay reader;
3) A list of permits issued, a brief description of the status of activities under those permits, and a review of selected existing permits and actual versus projected environmental benefits; and
4) A description of the cumulative impacts of permitted activities on the environmental indicators.

In addition to preparing this report, DNREC will maintain Coastal Zone regulation public records including:

1) permit applications and decisions including all permit conditions;
2) DNREC's annual report on the health of the Coastal Zone;
3) Tier II letters and decisions; and
4) status decision applications and decisions.

X. Public Notice Procedures

With the exception of information which is determined by the Secretary to be proprietary or trade secret within the bounds of the FOIA, it is essential that all parties, including the public, continue to have adequate opportunities to review and comment on all aspects of the permitting process.

In addition to the standard channels for public comment which are already required (either by current laws or regulations, or under the federal or state FOIAs), the Secretary should provide an opportunity to citizens who are particularly interested in the Coastal Zone Act and the determinations and permits that might be granted under the Act, to subscribe to a direct notification process. Such a process would provide notification by mail and/or other means to interested persons of permit or other activities occurring under the Act or subsequent regulations.

The Coastal Zone Act regulations should summarize all requirements for public notice in one separate section on "Public Notice Procedures." This would be a gathering together of all the separate requirements under one heading. Placing all the requirements for public notice in one section of the regulations serves the interests of the public, DNREC and the applicants.

XI. Preparation of a Guidance Document

The Advisory Committee recommends that DNREC develop a guidance document to accompany the regulations, that should include:

1) An applicant's initial contact with DNREC about a proposed Tier I, Tier II, or Tier III activity through the conclusion of the appeals process. This should be accompanied by a flow chart clearly illustrating how the different steps are sequenced.

2) A checklist of materials that DNREC must receive before an application will be designated "administratively complete."

3) A clarification about the relationship between the prior "status determination" process and the new Tier II notification process.

4) A description of DNREC's proposed process for developing, prioritizing, and revising the environmental indicators. When DNREC forms an Environmental Indicators Technical Advisory Committee (EITAC) or other such committees to assist in developing the indicators, then the guidance document should include a mission statement for the Committee.

The guidance document need not be developed simultaneously with the regulations, but ideally will be issued by the time the regulations are promulgated. If possible, the Advisory Committee would like to have an opportunity to comment on the guidance document before it is issued.

NOTES

1. "Voluntary improvements" is defined here as improvements (related, for example, to emissions reductions, habitat creation, spill prevention—provided each is definite and measurable) which were made by a facility without any federal or state requirement to do so.

2. "Environmental goals" are a collection of broad and strategic environmental priorities and objectives for a region. Environmental goals for the State of Delaware are presented in DNREC's Environmental Partnership Agreement—an agreement co-signed by the U.S. Environmental Protection Agency and the Department.

3. An "environmental indicator" is a numerical parameter which provides scientifically based information on important environmental issues, conditions, trends, influencing factors and their significance regarding ecosystem health. Indicators inherently are measurable, quantifiable, meaningful and understandable. They are sensitive to meaningful differences and trends, collectible with reasonable cost and effort over longer time periods, and provide early warning of environmental change. They are selected and used to monitor progress towards Environmental Goals (see above.)

The following members of the Coastal Zone Regulatory Advisory Committee signed off on this Memorandum of Understanding relating to the development of regulations governing administration of Delaware's Coastal Zone Act:

David Baker
Council of Farm Organizations

David Healey
United Auto Workers

Donald Crossan
Citizen Representative

John Deming
CIBA Speciality Chemicals

Lorraine Fleming
Delaware Nature Society

Deborah Heaton
Sierra Club

Justice Henry R. Horsey (retired)
Citizen Representative

David Hugg III
State Planning Office

Julius Klimowicz
ZENECA Chemicals

James Lisa
Delaware Economic Development Office

Jim Lynn
Dupont Corporation

Adam McBride
Diamond State Port Corporation

Tom Molin
United Steel Workers of America

Robert Molzahn
Connectiv

Russell Peterson
Former Governor of Delaware

Grace Pierce-Beck
Delaware Audobon Society

Lewis Purnell
Citizen Representative

Dan Scholl
Office of the Governor

Christophe Tulou
Department of Natural Resources and Environmental Control

Bill Wood
Chemical Industries Council

Case 4

Superfund Cleanup at the Massachusetts Military Reservation[1]

Patrick Field, with Edward Scher[2]

The soils and groundwater that lie beneath the Massachusetts Military Reservation (MMR) are saturated with the toxic remnants of more than 50 years of active military use. The MMR has been used as an armed forces base since 1911 (*Plume Response Plan,* 1994, p. 2–1). The reservation comprises 34 square miles (approximately 22,000 acres) and borders the towns of Bourne, Falmouth, Mashpee, and Sandwich on Cape Cod in Massachusetts—approximately 70 miles south of Boston. The military, in the standard practice of the day, built and used unlined landfills, poured excess jet fuel off into the ground, and serviced large numbers of tanks, trucks, and other vehicles with their gas, oil, and hydraulic needs. Over time, petroleum products, aviation and motor fuels, solvents, laboratory chemicals, and wastes leached down through the sandy soil and into the Upper Cape's aquifer—the area's sole source of drinking water.

In 1978, prior to any detailed knowledge of the extent of contamination, the town of Falmouth discovered an alarming problem: A recently installed municipal well (the "Ashumet Valley well") was foaming like dishwater. Given that an old base wastewater treatment plant sat upgradient from the well, the assumption was quickly made that the plant was to blame. The municipal well was shut down, and the town lost 25 percent of its water supply.

Spurred by such a disconcerting discovery and its adverse consequences, the Department of Defense initiated an Installation Restoration Program (IRP) on the site of the Otis Air Force base (a part of the MMR) in 1982. The Air National Guard was put in charge of the IRP. By 1986, the IRP had expanded to an investigation of the entire reservation, including areas controlled by the Army and the U.S. Coast Guard. By 1987, 73 possibly contaminated "study areas" were identified on the base, 43 of which eventually required further evaluation.

As study progressed, citizens became increasingly alarmed about the quality of their water supply. In 1986, the National Guard Bureau agreed to provide replacement costs for the lost Ashumet Valley well and pay for residences with private wells to hook up to town water (which is safer because it is more closely monitored and regulated). In 1986 and 1987, the town of Mashpee had private wells in a neighborhood known as Briar-wood tested for contaminants. Sampling results found levels of trichloroethylene (TCE) and tetrachloroethylene (PCE) that exceeded state and federal drinking water standards in seven wells. In 1989, the U.S. Environmental Protection Agency (EPA) proposed that the MMR be placed on the National Priorities List of the Comprehensive Environ-mental Response Compensation and Liability Act (CERCLA), more widely known as Superfund.

As investigation continued and public concern increased, more and more attention became focused on cleaning up the base. No sooner would the military get a handle on one problem, establishing source areas of pollution and the possible related groundwater contamination, than another unpleasant surprise would arise elsewhere. For instance, in early 1990, after the MMR had been placed on the Superfund priority list, yet another major site of contamination was discovered. A summer camp adjacent to the MMR offered the town of Mashpee land to drill a new municipal water supply. Once again, the water was contaminated. Another test well 1000 feet away yielded the same problem. That well's water contained 3000 parts per billion (ppb) of benzene. The federal drink-ing water standard for this toxin is 5 ppb. To make matters worse, EDB, a potent car-cinogen, was also detected at levels significantly above federal and state standards. Rumor had it that you could light this water on fire.

The town of Mashpee had inadvertently drilled into a new "plume" of groundwater contamination. A plume, as defined at the MMR, is a body of groundwater containing contaminants that exceed safe drinking water standards established by the EPA. This plume came from leaks in a pipeline that was used to transport fuel from the Cape Cod Channel, across town land, onto the base.

By 1994, 10 plumes had been identified. (Yet another would be discovered in the fall of 1996 and even more in 1998.) One was caused by run-off from storm drains. One was caused by a base landfill. Others were caused by chemical spills of one kind or another. The Installation Restoration Program was charged with identifying, investigating, delin-eating, and ultimately cleaning up this entire extensive contamination.

This case study describes the multiagency consensus building process that is being used to make decisions regarding the cleanup of the MMR. It first discusses a crisis point in 1996—the crisis that led the various interested agencies to adopt a new and more productive way of working together. Then, after briefly describing the "strategic partnering" process that was implemented, it describes the negotiation of several key issues relating to cleanup: an enforceable schedule, goals and criteria, and a decision-making process. Finally, the analysis discusses the role of the facilitation team and the progress of the effort to date. The case provides a clear example of how mutual gains–style negotiation can be effectively utilized even in the most complex of environ-mental regulatory situations.

Project Crisis

On January 22, 1996, the prime engineering contractor for the Installation Restoration Program released a partially completed design for the containment of seven plumes of groundwater contamination at the MMR. This design included large-scale pump-and-treat systems that would pull water from wells installed into the plume, treat the plumes aboveground through carbon filtration, and then re-inject the treated water back into the aquifer. (These are also known as extraction, treatment, and re-injection systems, or ETRs.) Though the design was only 60 percent finished, it met with extraordinary opposition from regulatory agencies, the public, and even from within the military. If implemented, the design would require pumping 27 million gallons of groundwater per day—more than Cape residents collectively used each day to meet their water needs. Critics charged that the proposed water pumping rates would cause severe ecological damage and perhaps even salt water intrusion into the aquifer. Resistance to the "60 percent design," as it came to be known, came as a blow to the IRP's engineering contractor and the Air National Guard. The Guard and the regulators had made considerable effort to build and secure public acceptance of the cleanup goal of total and simultaneous containment of the plumes.

Formation of the TRET

In mid-March of 1996, responding to the 60 percent design crisis, high-level officials at the Department of Defense, the EPA, and the DEP created a Technical Review and Evaluation Team (TRET, for short). This team, composed of more than 20 experts from various agencies and scientific disciplines, would review the 60 percent design, investigate alternatives, and analyze impacts to the environment and surrounding communities. The aim of this initiative was to, as quickly as possible, identify what pieces of the 60 percent design could be implemented and seek out an alternative and viable remedial design approach that met both regulatory requirements and public acceptance. The TRET involved all the parties—the public, regulatory agencies, the military, and contractors—in its decision-making process.[3]

The TRET was very successful in its endeavors. In May 1996, just four months after the crisis had begun, the TRET released a final report. The report recommended that each of the plumes be addressed singly, as opposed to simultaneously as in the 60 percent design. It asked people to take a more measured response to the individual risks posed by each plume. The TRET recognized that "plumes cannot be managed individually without acknowledgment of the interconnectedness of the aquifer system" (*Toward a balanced strategy*, 1996, p. 13), but each plume had distinctive characteristics that should inform design and decision making. The report also highlighted the need to balance the desire to solve the problem quickly and comprehensively with the uncertainty that would attend the cleanup. Consistent with this exhortation, the final report called for an "incremental" approach. The report's recommendations on how to proceed with plume containment received support from most of the opponents to the 60 percent design.

Based on the findings presented in the TRET final report, the military and its contractors prepared a strategic plan for the cleanup of the MMR groundwater plumes, drafted in May and finalized in July of 1996. This strategic plan specified containment actions for two of the plumes; for the others, it identified data gaps and specified ways to close these before proceeding to action. This new plan embraced many of the "guid-ing principles" identified by the TRET, such as taking a balanced approach by weighing all the impacts of action (and no action) and using an "iterative" approach. The TRET had set all concerned parties on a new and more feasible trajectory for decontaminating the plumes.

Strategic Partnering Begins

The Technical Review and Evaluation Team had brought the program from deadlock to the formulation of an iterative, plume-by-plume approach incorporating ecological as well as hydrological concerns, but the painstaking work that would turn these ideas into specific designs for engineered cleanup systems had just begun. While the TRET had generated various options and laid out a set of broad objective criteria for how to pro-ceed, the agencies had a great deal of work to do together to get the systems designed, agreed to, constructed, and up and running. For instance, the Installation Restoration Program engineering team, along with the EPA and the DEP, would have to decide if an extraction, treatment, and re-injection system would be appropriate at each plume, and if so, what orientation, location, and pumping rates would best meet cleanup objec-tives. If an ETR system was not feasible, then what other technologies could be installed? Toward the end of the TRET's work, the IRP had identified a technology known as "recirculating wells," which appeared to have fewer adverse ecological impacts than the ETR systems. Thus, the IRP engineers and regulators needed to review how and where this technology might best be used.

The comments received on the Strategic Plan highlighted several issues that would need to be resolved by the parties. While the TRET's approach was generally supported, the agencies and many community members raised the concern that the TRET's rec-ommendations would give rise merely to more study and investigation. Some activists demanded that the Air Force avoid "paralysis by analysis" and move forward with con-crete actions. The environmental agencies expressed the need to significantly speed up the schedule for activities laid out in the strategic plan. The EPA remarked: " . . . the entire Comprehensive Plume Response Plan and Schedule should be reevaluated and revised to reflect a more expeditious design and implementation process for all plumes" (Final draft of the Massachusetts Military Reservation Installation Restoration Plan, 1995, p. 292, comment #581).

The issue of working relationships also needed to be addressed. The IRP, EPA, DEP, and the citizen groups had not worked effectively together during the development of the 60 percent design. The IRP had not foreseen the ecological impacts posed by their design, but neither had the environmental agencies forced the IRP to review such crite-ria. Lingering anger, mutual incrimination, and deep distrust were the fallout from the rejection of the 60 percent design. Even though the TRET had helped to break the impasse, it was clear that the key agencies—the IRP, the EPA, and the state's DEP—needed to develop more effective working relationships with one another and with the citizen teams, local elected officials, and interested residents, if the TRET's vision was to be realized. The parties would have to find ways to address problems earlier, resolve disputes as quickly as possible, and ensure ongoing progress. The Air Force proposed a "tiered partnering approach" to supplement the existing citizen teams and on-going regulatory-regulatee meetings.

Partnering, begun as a means to ensure smoother contractor-client relationships on major construction projects, had been used in Air Force and Navy environmental programs elsewhere. Broadly speaking, partnering seeks to overcome the more traditional, adversarial regulator-regulatee relationship by encouraging regulators, the military, and contractors to work more closely and in greater collaboration with one other. "Partners" typically participate in joint training prior to beginning the work of design and construction, discuss up front how they are going to work together, identify common goals, and develop clear means for how they will resolve the disputes that will inevitably arise. The cleanup program at Fort Ord in California, for instance, had employed partnering. As one staff member from that program said: "We're not always singing 'Kumbaya' with everybody. We agree to disagree, then just go forward to solve the problem" ("Broken trust," 1997). At other sites, the Navy estimates to have saved some $24 million as well as speeded cleanup on several base decontaminations in the EPA Region IV (the Southeast) using partnering (Paley, 1997).

The Air Force believed that partnering—as a means of working together to revise, hone, and transform the TRET's broad recommendations into detailed cleanup system designs—would help structure communication and decision making at the Massachusetts Military Reservation, both among multiple organizations and within organizations. They thus proposed the following: At the ground level, the Remedial Program Managers (RPMs) from the DEP, EPA, and IRP would meet on a weekly basis to discuss the cleanup. The RPMs would wade through the day-to-day technical decisions necessary for designing, constructing, and operating complex cleanup systems. When and if the RPMs could not resolve an issue or came across key policy differences, they would elevate these to their managers. The managers of the RPMs would be part of another, higher-level management group, known as the Management Review Group (MRG). And finally, on an occasional basis (perhaps once a year), the highest levels of each of the main organizations would meet. This Executive Review Group (ERG) would include the Regional Administrator for the EPA Region I, the Secretary of Massachusetts's Executive Office of Environmental Affairs (the cabinet-level secretariat encompassing the state's DEP as well as other state agencies), and the Undersecretary of the Air Force who was the head of its environmental programs.

The EPA and DEP were skeptical of this approach. Both agencies had an interest in being able to act unilaterally and independently, if needed; they did not want that power to be supplanted by the "partnering" concept. After all, these agencies might want to issue public condemnations and apply political pressure to keep the highest levels of the Air Force focused on the project. (During the controversy surrounding the 60 percent design, very high levels of Air Force management at the Pentagon became involved.) They might also need to pursue enforcement actions or even litigation to force the program back on track. Would any of these authorities be given up? Did partnering mean that they were somehow taking responsibility for the Air Force's contamination, or only for appropriate and effective oversight of the cleanup of that contamination?

Clearly, pressure was on the Air Force to take swift and effective action to begin cleanup. U.S. Senators John Kerry and Ted Kennedy were watching closely. Massachusetts Governor William Weld was working to keep the project in the limelight and the Pentagon focused on taking action. John DeVillars, head of the EPA's Region 1, was working to put the heat on the military too. The regional paper, the *Cape Cod Times,* followed the project closely and frequently printed highly critical articles on the cleanup program and its management.

Citizens groups also had an interest in how partnering proceeded. They wanted to make sure they were not excluded from decision making. How would they monitor decisions? Would these meetings be open to the public? And how would these new "management" groups fit into the citizen advisory committee structure?

Cautiously, and partly in response to assurances from the head of the Air Force's Defense Environmental Restoration Account (DERA), the environmental agencies agreed to try the partnering approach. The RPMs began meeting weekly, the MRG monthly. No party made any formal commitment to the approach, but agreed to test it meeting by meeting. The parties requested that the team of facilitators from the Consensus Building Institute, the team who had been assisting the Technical Review and Evaluation Team, facilitate the meetings of the RPMs and the MRG, record "unbiased and reliable" meeting summaries, and assist the parties between meetings in clarifying issues and reaching agreements.

In the first few meetings of the Management Review Group, the parties made adjustments to encourage openness and trust and to make sure citizens groups' interests were met. Generally, only the three Remedial Program Managers and their technical consultants would attend the weekly (and sometimes more frequent) meetings. However, the RPM meeting summaries would be posted on the MMR IRP Web page, initially maintained by the facilitation team to help ensure neutrality. In addition, selectmen from the four surrounding towns—who had been organized into a Senior Management Board (SMB)—would also be involved. The SMB had solicited the support of a technical consultant paid for by the Air Force, and this consultant would listen in to RPM meetings via conference call and report to the selectmen on a regular basis. The agencies agreed that it made sense to welcome the four SMB town selectman as official members of the Management Review Group. Thus, there would be a clear and strong link between the SMB and the new MRG. Like the RPM meeting summaries, the MRG agreed to have their meeting summaries posted on the Web page. Finally, to ensure consistency between the agency tiered partnering groups and the citizen teams, the RPMs attended and participated actively in the Joint Process Action Team (JPAT) meetings, held once or twice per month in the early evenings. The JPAT was formed when the Plume Containment Team (PCT) decided to meet with all other citizen teams (the PATs) during the 60 percent design. Finally, the TRET would also continue to meet, and would report to the SMB, the MRG, and the RPMs as needed.

With the parties now organized into a set of facilitator-assisted decision-making groups, substantive work needed to begin at once. The MRG members were anxious to begin the extensive negotiations needed to keep the program on track and move rapidly forward toward cleanup. Through the partnering approach, the various parties began negotiating three key issues: (1) an enforceable schedule for cleanup, (2) goals and criteria for cleanup, and (3) a process for making cleanup decisions.

Setting an Enforceable Schedule

The state DEP and the EPA expressed a strong interest in establishing a set of enforceable milestones leading up to the actual start-up of cleanup systems, even though the exact nature of the remedial system was not yet decided upon. The environmental agencies wanted commitments from the Air Force; and they wanted a way to leverage pressure and, if necessary, fine the Air Force to ensure program progress. In a project with ever-new discoveries of contamination, reconsidered decisions, budgetary restraints, and intensive politics, the regulators wanted to bring order, certainty, and progress. The agencies suspected that, unless there was a timetable attached to the program, the military might study the problem well into the new millennium, learning more, doing little, and avoiding extensive expenditures for as long as possible.

The EPA and DEP suspected that the Air Force would strongly resist developing an enforceable schedule. After all, Air Force engineers were not yet prepared to recommend appropriate cleanup technology. They could not recommend, for example, the exact orientation of a line of ETR wells for a particular plume, the number of wells needed, the kind or location of a treatment plant, the possible pumping rates, or where re-injection wells might best be installed. How could a schedule be built when no one knew what exactly was to be scheduled?

The Air Force did have some interest in setting milestones, however. Citing an influential recent report on Superfund cleanup at federal facilities (Federal Facilities Environmental Restoration Dialogue Committee, 1996), the Air Force agreed that they might be able to set "out-year" milestones. (Out-year milestones are those that fall in years beyond the standard two-year budgeting cycles utilized by the Air Force.) While the Air Force's reputation would be put at risk if the milestones negotiated were unrealistic and could not be met, such milestones would allow the Air Force to bring certainty to its budget cycle. This was particularly important, given that the Massachusetts Military Reservation program was draining a significant portion of the Air Force's national cleanup budget. The Air Force also hoped that the schedule would "fix" in place the technical program for each year, so that, once agreed upon, the regulators could not ask for more and new activities unless they adjusted the schedule accordingly. The Air Force also wanted to see the program move from investigation to cleanup: They wanted to get in, clean up, and get out.

So, the parties had identified common interests—certainty and progress—that, for quite different reasons from the perspective of each, they could use to build agreement. Over the next several months, the Remedial Program Managers and the Management Review Group began to build an enforceable schedule for the installation of remedial systems at six different groundwater plumes.

Trading Across Issues: A Schedule and Design Goals

As they began negotiating the schedule, the Air Force also recognized that they needed goals and criteria for cleanup, so that they and the environmental agencies could agree on what "success" would be. Air Force representatives realized they did not want to agree to a schedule unless they knew by what objective criteria their efforts would be judged. They did not want the regulatory agencies to be able to say: "We'll know a good design when we see it." So, even though the Air Force already had some incentives for agreeing to a set schedule, they wanted the agencies to work with them to set clear design parameters as well.

Thus, the Air Force requested that the parties agree to a clear set of goals that any proposed system should accomplish and a set of objective criteria by which various alternative designs could be weighed against one another. The environmental agencies were amenable to this demand, especially since ecological criteria were foremost among the missing elements that had brought about the demise of the 60 percent design. Essentially, the Air Force and the regulatory agencies "traded" across their differing interests: The agencies agreed to jointly develop design goals and criteria, which the Air Force wanted, in return for setting an enforceable schedule, which the agencies wanted.

To further protect itself, the Air Force also requested that the parties make explicit the assumptions used to construct the out-year enforceable schedule. The Air Force hoped that if the assumptions changed, they would be able to obtain adjustments from the environmental agencies. The Air Force was willing to make commitments, as long as they were contingent upon certain assumptions such as obtaining property access for drilling and construction and finding no significant new data that would alter their understanding of the plumes.

Negotiating Goals and Criteria

A project engineer from the Air Force's contractor wrote the first draft of the design criteria. One criterion was a maximum level of pond "drawdown" that a design might cause. Meeting this measurable criteria would ensure that any cleanup system would not lower the water levels of adjacent ponds or rivers to the point of causing significant ecological harm. Another criterion was that the designed system must capture a high percentage of the contaminants in the plume. A facilitator suggested placing these criteria in a matrix, which any stakeholder could review to judge design alternatives against one another.

As discussions proceeded, the original and relatively simple matrix grew in complexity. With the 60 percent design crisis looming large in their minds, players sought to identify all possible issues that might later derail a new design. The Air Force, EPA, and DEP wanted to identify every issue that might later influence, jeopardize, or kill a remedial design.

The design criteria, dubbed the Decision Criteria Matrix, were developed in broad form by the various members of the Management Review Group. Detail and complexity were added by the Remedial Program Managers, with the assistance of various consultants. Week after week, for several months, the RPMs reviewed drafts of the matrix and accompanying text prepared by the Air Force, negotiated sentence by sentence, criterion by criterion, and began to finalize a full document that would be made available for public comment. Every few months the matrix, whatever form it was in, would be brought before the Management Review Group, with the key outstanding disagreements highlighted by the Remedial Program Managers.

During this time, the members of the Management Review Group had to negotiate the thorny questions of cleanup standards and overall cleanup goals. It was one thing for the parties to agree that contaminants should be treated, and quite another to agree on what level of treatment was required. The EPA required that contaminants be treated to federal drinking water standards, or "maximum contaminant levels" (MCLs). However, state regulations called for treatment to "background" levels—the levels of contaminants occurring naturally in the Cape's environment. (For most volatile organic compounds, the background level would be zero.) At first, the Air Force felt inclined to meet only the EPA's interests, because the state had never signed on to the regulatory mechanism governing the cleanup (the Federal Facilities Agreement, or FFA).

State officials made clear that they would be very dissatisfied, however, and would raise strong concern publicly and involve the governor, if necessary, if the Air Force did not agree to the more stringent state standard. The EPA officials could not enforce the more stringent standard under their existing federal statutes, but they could agree to the more stringent standard if the Air Force agreed. The Air Force assessed its interests and BATNA and concluded that (1) it was technically feasible to treat contamination to background; (2) it was wise to meet the state's interests in order to avoid a media and public outcry against the Air Force; (3) it was wise to try to minimize any conflict between the EPA and the DEP, if possible, to avoid receiving conflicting regulatory direction from the two agencies; and (4) years down the road when the Air Force sought to turn the remedial systems off, it would need state approval. In short, if they did not meet state standards now, they might very well not be able to turn their systems off later.

Once the parties agreed to treat the extracted contamination to background, they had to agree how much of the overall contamination should be extracted in the first place (i.e., what the overall goal of cleanup ought to be). Should they extract every last drop of contaminated water? Or would 95 percent be enough? How about 90 percent? The Air Force wanted to be able to capture the maximum amount of contamination that was feasible, considering such other factors as engineering complexity, marginal costs of extraction, neighborhood construction impacts, and the increased environmental gain from that construction.

The state was insistent that the parties agree to a goal of 100 percent capture. After all, this was a state regulation. And, significantly, the local citizens and activists wanted the state to be tough—there were too many past mistakes and failures. Many members of the public wanted its state environmental enforcer to leave as little "wiggle" room as possible. The Air Force rebutted that by agreeing to this "so-called goal," they would be agreeing de facto to a new cleanup standard. The state held firm, stating that this was only a goal, not a requirement. The Air Force raised the concern that if they agreed to such a goal, it would set a nationwide precedent in the Air Force's environmental program. The state countered that they had to enforce state standards, whether or not they had implications for parties that also did business elsewhere.

The parties generated several options for language. One suggestion was: "The ... goal is selecting a remedy alternative that will achieve final cleanup solutions." Another suggestion was: "Maximize capture and treatment of contaminants." Finally, one of the Remedial Program Managers circulated the state's specific regulatory language, which had strict requirements but was tempered by the phrase "if technically and economically feasible." This existing language provided the parties an objective, outside standards on which to base their decisions. Air Force officials stated that if they were going to agree to this language, the EPA and DEP would have to agree to the explicit assumptions behind the enforceable milestones for the yet-to-be-designed remedial system that would meet this and other goals. The parties then negotiated back and forth over what assumptions would be included in the overall Decision Criteria Matrix and on what grounds an extension to the schedule might be granted.

Finally, after several months of development, the parties were approaching an agreement. The original few criteria and goals had evolved into a complex set of hydrogeological, ecological, and socioeconomic criteria. Ultimately, the matrix included 19 primary balancing criteria and some 30 subordinate ones. Some criteria were quantifiable (the percent capture of contaminant mass estimated by modeling) and some were qualitative (the socioeconomic impacts of construction on affected neighborhoods). The state, for instance, wanted to ensure that quality of life and impacts on the tourist season and the economy were included to protect local residents. The EPA wanted to ensure that the criteria were consistent with Superfund requirements. The TRET had already recommended that a quantifiable set of ecological criteria be included, such as the drawdown criteria on the water level of ponds and rivers.

To ensure that the matrix would be usable by the public, the parties agreed to a format somewhat like that used in *Consumer Reports*. The various features of the alternatives would be compared in a table using full, half, and empty circles, generally representing favorable, acceptable, and unfavorable ratings. In addition, the matrix would be accompanied by detailed text, including quantifiable criteria and explanations. (The resulting consensus report, "Plume Response Decision Criteria and Schedule," follows this case analysis.)

The Management Review Group and Remedial Program Managers decided not to weigh the criteria against one another. They thus avoided what would have likely proved to be a painful battle, pitting human versus ecological health and construction impacts on the environment versus those impacts on neighborhoods and human communities. The two groups (MRG and RPMs) recognized that balancing the various criteria would have to be part of the final negotiations over the plume remedial alternatives.

The parties had traded across a whole host of goals, criteria, assumptions, and caveats to reach agreement. Air Force had agreed to more stringent cleanup goals in return for the state's buy-in to the overall process and agreement on a set of shared, explicit assumptions. The state was able to appear strong and tough with the "100 percent capture" goal while the Air Force was left with a "way out" of 100 percent capture if this goal proved to be technically impossible or inordinately expensive and inefficient. The EPA was able to secure an agreement that met and even exceeded its regulatory requirements, while preserving and improving its working relationship not only with the Air Force, but with the state DEP too. Jointly, the parties had created a thorough, comprehensive set of objective criteria that would avoid the design mistakes and oversights of the past while providing a clear basis to frame negotiations and make decisions.

The negotiation of these objective criteria and goals was valuable for several reasons. The negotiating process helped the parties build trust and confidence in one another, two qualities lacking up to this point. The parties were building agreement step by step rather than attempting to sign, seal, and deliver a final plan as they had tried to do with the comprehensive plume management plan. In addition, as well as paying attention to the substance of the negotiations—this or that date, this or that criteria—the negotiators were paying close attention to the process—how to build agreement across a diverse range of stakeholders.

Building a Decision-Making Process

With the decision criteria matrix in place and the enforceable schedule negotiated, one important piece was missing—the linkage between the matrix, the schedule, decision making, and public involvement. The Remedial Program Managers and the Management Review Group, including the town selectmen from the four affected towns, along with community involvement staff and the facilitators, sought to develop a process for implementing this complex matrix and schedule. They negotiated a process that could be applied to decision making on four plumes.

The process the parties ultimately agreed to was as follows. First, the Air Force's engineering consultants, with the advice of the Technical Review and Evaluation Team, would hone and refine possible cleanup alternatives through computer modeling. In turn, a long list of alternatives would be brought before the Remedial Program Managers, who would evaluate them according to a few key criteria such as percentage of plume capture and the ecological thresholds established by the TRET. As the alternatives were whittled down from hundreds to tens through numerous modeling runs, the Joint Process Action Team would be brought up to speed and their advice solicited. The JPAT would have a chance to suggest other alternatives as well as express their preference for some alternatives over others. Periodic public and neighborhood meetings would keep residents informed all along the way.

With the alternatives narrowed down to five or eight, the detailed matrix would be filled out and brought before the towns and affected neighborhoods. Fact sheets, poster boards, informal community get-togethers, and facilitated public meetings would spread the word, educate citizens about the alternatives, and most important, ask them to voice an opinion on which alternative or alternatives they preferred during a 30-day public comment period. The process also allowed towns or others to bring forward different alternatives, even toward the end of the process, if they thought they would meet the objective criteria laid out.

Finally, with a detailed matrix filled out for the remaining alternatives, the input of the citizen teams and general public, the DEP, the EPA, and the Air Force would sit down to negotiate and select the preferred cleanup alternative. The Management Review Group and the Remedial Program Managers hoped that through this process, unlike the 60 percent design, a broad public, regulatory, and responsible party consensus would emerge. All the parties would be involved in every aspect of the negotiation: developing the negotiation process, generating options, analyzing these options according to the objective criteria established, narrowing the options to a few key choices, and influencing the final selection.

The process the players had laid out was far different than the standard CERCLA (Superfund) process, or, as the state liked to refer to it, "the CERCLA snake." Instead of presenting to the public a "preferred alternative" after an extensive and lengthy review done primarily among the environmental agencies and the Air Force, the public would have input into the development, refinement, and narrowing of the remedial alternatives. The public would build an understanding of the alternatives, their advantages and disadvantages, and the decision-making process along the way. Finally, well informed by public meetings, informal neighborhood meetings, poster sessions, and fact sheets, once the five or so best alternatives were developed, the public would have an opportunity to weigh in on their preferences, rather than simply react to the preferences of the cleanup program and the regulators.

The Role of the Facilitation Team

The CBI-based facilitation team was active throughout all of these discussions.[4] In addition to facilitating meetings, the team helped to coordinate the various groups and to bring more consistency, clarity, and coordination among issues and parties. In addition, when a major dispute arose over one issue or another, because the facilitators knew both the parties and the issues well, they were able to talk to parties privately, shuttle between them when necessary, and help mediate these disputes more effectively.

Specifically, the CBI team facilitated the weekly meetings of the Remedial Program Managers and monthly meetings of the Management Review Group. This entailed developing agendas agreeable to all, working on key issues individually with the parties between meetings over the phone, and writing meeting summaries. At the RPM level, it became clear that it was very important for the facilitator to track the agreements reached by the RPMs and the key action items, or to-do list, needed each week. Thus, the facilitators developed a detailed meeting summary format to help track key issues, agreements, and next steps.

The facilitators also continued to facilitate the Technical Review and Evaluation Team. This service not only provided for efficient and constructive meetings of the TRET—a group sometimes known for digressing on time-consuming technical points—it also provided an important link among the TRET and other groups. The facilitators could help the TRET key into issues being considered by the Remedial Program Managers and the Management Review Group, while apprising those groups of some of the issues considered important by the TRET. In addition, because the TRET, exercising its independence as it was designed to do, at times irritated one party or another, the facilitation team could step in to help resolve disagreements and overcome frustrations and criticisms.

In addition, the facilitators continued to assist the citizen team meetings and public meetings and assist the Senior Management Board selectmen and other members in developing their meeting agendas. Just as at the RPM level, the facilitators worked with the JPAT and its meeting recorders to ensure that to-do items and next steps were tracked carefully from meeting to meeting. In turn, these to-do items were kept on the agendas of the Remedial Program Managers so that all three key parties—the Air Force, the EPA, and the DEP—could remain accountable and responsive to citizen requests and concerns.

Finally, on occasion, the facilitators provided process reviews and evaluations. For instance, as the TRET completed its final report, and in the transition to a new Air Force contractor, the team evaluated the TRET's past efforts and made process suggestions for how the TRET might move forward. At the MRG level, the facilitation team offered annual progress reviews of the Management Review Group and the Remedial Program Managers; and helped the MRG and RPMs develop a clear set of roles and responsibilities. With the help of surveys, interviews, and joint team meetings, CBI also helped the citizen teams review their work and plan for the future.

Conclusion

The tiered partnering initiated in the late summer and early fall of 1996, viewed very skeptically at first, ultimately succeeded. The Remedial Program Managers and the Management Review Group, in conjunction with significant input from town selectmen, citizen team members, and the public, had developed a detailed, comprehensive, transparent, and highly structured process for decision making. The partnership had weathered the disagreements, disappointments, and conflicts along the way from the release of the TRET's Final Report to the completion of the decision criteria process. An enforceable schedule had been put in place. The objective criteria for decision making had been established. Trust was substantially, though perhaps not completely, rebuilt. The agencies had begun to develop not only working relationships, but personal relationships and mutual respect. Now, the program partners were ready to begin the difficult—but now well-organized and clear—task of deciding on remedial designs to actively clean up the contamination.

Epilogue

As of December 1998, the Air Force had met all enforceable deadlines except one. While the schedule was very tight and did cause the Installation Restoration Program engineers consternation as new information came to light suggesting modifications to designs or raising new uncertainties, the schedule moved the cleanup forward. The agreement on the schedule did not always provide the Air Force the leverage it had hoped when new contamination came to light. The regulatory agencies pushed hard to meet all the enforceable deadlines already set, as well as establish new ones for new activities. Nonetheless, a sure sign of the transition from investigation to cleanup came as the parties saw the investigation budget for federal fiscal years 1998 and 1999 fall significantly while the design and construction budget increased dramatically.

The Air Force, EPA, and state DEP reached a negotiated agreement on the remedial design for three of the four plumes as planned and on time, using the decision criteria matrix process. The fourth plume took more time. After an additional year of technical and public review focused on the possibility that natural attenuation without a mechanical system might clean up the plume naturally, the parties reached a decision on a focused, conceptual remedial design for this plume.

The plume cleanup designs reflected a careful balance of the numerous criteria, taking into account public concerns and, in particular, the affected neighborhoods' needs. The decision criteria matrix process helped the decision makers avoid fatal flaws like those of the 60 percent design. In each case, the three parties—the IRP, EPA, and DEP—announced their consensus jointly to the public. For the first time in the program's history, the logos of the three agencies appeared side-by-side at the top of press releases and public presentations announcing the decision. While not all members of the public were fully satisfied—for instance, some activists felt that the designs were not aggressive enough—the decisions found strong support from many citizen team members, local elected officials, and neighborhood residents. No public outcry, media attacks, or litigation ensued. In fact, the announcement of the agreements by the parties was covered only briefly in local and regional papers—a far cry from the extensive and highly critical coverage received during and shortly after the delivery of the 60 percent design.

From the TRET's report in May 1996 to the end of the decision criteria matrix process in December 1997, the numerous stakeholders had moved from impasse to progress, from distrust and mutual incrimination to trust and joint effort. The way forward, as one MRG member was fond of saying, had not been always easy or pain-free, but it had been found.

Notes

1. The introduction to this case is derived from a case published in *The Consensus Building Handbook* (Scher, 1999). "Negotiating Superfund Cleanup at Massachusetts Military Reservation," in L. Susskind, S. McKearnan, and J. Thomas-Larmer, eds. *The Consensus Building Handbook.* Thousand Oaks, Calif.: Sage Publications. The remainder of the case analysis was written specifically for this volume.

2. Patrick Field is a Senior Associate at the Consensus Building Institute and a mediator/facilitator with extensive experience mediating multistakeholder dialogues on environmental policy and management issues. He facilitates several ongoing negotiating groups at the MMR. Mr. Field is the co-author of *Dealing with an Angry Public* (1996) as well as numerous consulting reports, negotiation simulations, and journal articles. He also provides training in negotiation, facilitation, and consensus building to public-sector clients in the United States and Canada. Mr. Field received his Master's in City Planning from MIT. Edward Scher is an Associate at RESOLVE Center for Dispute Resolution in Washington, D.C. Previously, Mr. Scher was an Associate at the Consensus Building Institute. He also served as a Peace Corps volunteer in Uruguay, where he assisted local community groups in their efforts to promote natural resource conservation on the coast of the Rio de la Plata. Mr. Scher holds a Master's in City Planning from MIT.

3. The work of the TRET is detailed in *The Consensus Building Handbook* case.

4. The CBI-based facilitation team is composed of Gregory Sobel (lead mediator), Patrick Field (project manager and mediator), Kim Vogel (mediator), and, at various points in the process, mediators Jack Wofford, John McGlennon, Sarah McKearnan, David Fairman, and John Glyphis. CBI president Lawrence Susskind provided general guidance and oversight.

Plume Response Decision Criteria and Schedule

April 24, 1997

1.0 Introduction

A very important time in the clean-up phase for plumes at Massachusetts Military Reservation (MMR) is the decision point when the plume-response alternative is selected. This document presents a matrix to be used to summarize and compare response alternatives. This evaluation matrix builds upon the September 1995 Interim Record of Decision. The goal is to select a remedial alternative that achieves final cleanup solutions. There are numerous factors considered by many key participants in the screening, evaluation and selection of a response alternative. This rating system is in the form of a matrix chart called "Plume Response Alternatives Evaluation Matrix" and is contained in Appendix I.

The purpose of this Alternatives Evaluation Matrix is to provide a tool whereby the audience (principally members of the public and regulatory staff) can see at a glance how individual alternatives compare one to another. Specific evaluation criteria, such as "percent capture of plume" are listed on individual rows within the matrix chart. Each alternative is listed as a column heading in the body of the chart. The estimated performance of each alternative with respect to each of the evaluation criteria is rated in comparative terms such as "low impact," "moderate impact," or "high impact" and that rating is presented in the column corresponding to the alternative being considered. The individual criteria and the manner in which the Alternatives Evaluation Matrix is filled out are presented below.

Among other key goals, this matrix works toward defining cost-effective alternatives that maximize capture and treatment of contaminants and cleanup of plumes to background levels if technically and economically feasible while balancing impacts on human health and the environment.

The concept is similar to that used in the magazine *Consumer Reports,* where features of similar products are compared to each other in a table so that the reader can see each product's advantages and disadvantages in order to make an informed choice on which product holds the most value for them. Figure 1 is the Plume Response Alternative Process Flow Diagram which shows the process of making a selection and the incorporation of the matrix in this system. The diagram also shows public involvement throughout the process. The matrix is a table which condenses the screening process, the criteria considered and the preferred choices of stakeholder groups for each alternative considered. By nature of its design, it utilizes a qualitative approach in use and application, and must always be used in conjunction with professional judgment and sound management.

Future use and application of this tool may require necessary refinements to the decision criteria. Such changes will be finalized through consensus of the Management Review Group.

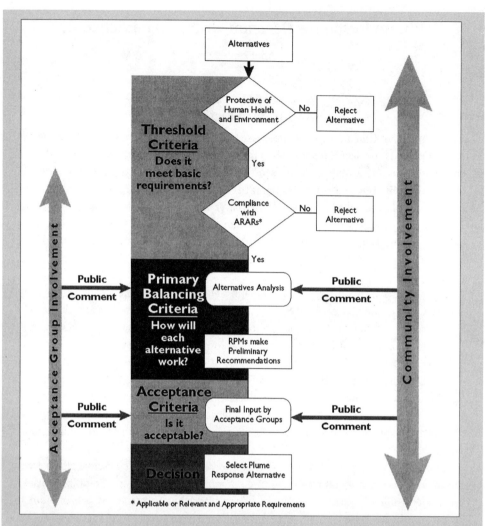

Figure 1
Plume Response Alternative Process Flow Diagram

1.1 Matrix Criteria

The matrix is divided into three components; (1) Threshold Criteria, (2) Primary Balancing Criteria and (3) Acceptance Criteria. These criteria are derived from the nine criteria presented in the "National Oil and Hazardous Substance Pollution Contingency Plan; Final Rule 40 CFR 300.430" and modified to create this site specific tool for evaluating potential response alternatives for Massachusetts Military Reservation plumes. The following summarizes the three criteria involved.

1.1.1 THRESHOLD CRITERIA

The threshold criteria are used to identify response alternatives which are protective of human health and the environment, and are expected to provide an acceptable balance between plume capture and hydrologic and ecological impacts. Threshold criteria provide "pass or fail" indication for further detailed evaluation in the Primary Balancing Criteria. Failure to pass threshold criteria results in the rejection of the alternative or requires modifications to enable it to meet threshold values.

1.1.2 PRIMARY BALANCING CRITERIA

The Primary Balancing Criteria are then used to evaluate alternatives which have passed the threshold criteria. The Primary Balancing Criteria are focused on four general factors or issues that relate to the overall completeness, practicality and cost of the alternative. The general factors are:
- Effectiveness and Permanence
- Effectiveness of Treatment System
- Implementability
- Cost

As can be seen in the matrix in Appendix I, evaluation with respect to each of the above factors entails consideration of a variety of sub factors. The alternatives are evaluated using both qualitative and quantitative information. The Primary Balancing Criteria present the strengths and weaknesses of each alternative for comparison to each other and will provide DoD, regulators and affected communities a tool to make a balanced and informed assessment in identifying the preferred alternative.

1.1.3 ACCEPTANCE CRITERIA

The respective organizations, agencies and community groups ("acceptance groups") must be continuously involved in the assessment of each alternative. These groups include Public at Large, Neighborhood, Process Action Teams, Senior Management Board Selectmen Representatives, Department of Public Health/ATSDR, Natural Resources Trustees, Environmental Protection Agency, Massachusetts Department of Environmental Protection, and Department of Defense. After the Threshold and Primary Balancing Criteria portions of the matrix have been assessed, each of the acceptance groups will indicate their preferred, acceptable and unacceptable alternatives.

2.0 Use of the Alternatives Evaluation Matrix

2.1 Process

The effectiveness or completeness of plume containment, capture, changes in water levels in nearby water bodies and changes in groundwater flow paths or flow rates will be estimated using one or more of the following tools:
- Application of groundwater simulation models
- Pilot test results
- Extrapolation of technology data from other sites
- Engineering calculations and/or estimates
- Experience at other remediation sites

Each potential alternative must go through a series of questions and answers to assess its potential to address clean-up at MMR. It is possible that some alternatives cannot meet the strict criteria required, or that certain characteristics are unacceptable to stakeholders and the alternative will be rejected or abandoned. Alternatives which meet criteria will be evaluated and compared in the matrix.

The process for filling out the matrix is guided by the *Explanation of Criteria* provided in Appendix II. Definitions are contained in Appendix III. Wherever possible, the rating will be based on quantitative results from the groundwater modeling or other techniques listed above. For example, the percentage of plume that is assumed to be captured can be estimated and expressed as a percentage. In other cases, the rating may reflect a subjective interpretation of a calculated value or estimated range. An example in that case would be rating the ecological impacts resulting from physiochemical changes to pond inflows. Finally, some ratings may be purely subjective in that they are extrapolated from past experience or from discussions with community members.

The first draft on filling out the matrix is performed by the design teams consisting of Air Force Center For Environmental Excellence technical staff and Jacobs Engineering. These groups will provide all the back-up and draft a narrative to explain the key features and characteristics of each alternative. The design team will also have access to and interaction with the expert panels of the Technical Review and Evaluation Team for each plume.

The process would flow as follows:

1. The technical groups and the Remedial Project Managers will fill out the matrix for all the alternatives.
2. The Remedial Project Managers will keep the Management Review Group and respective chains of command apprised of the progress and matrix development for each plume.
3. The matrix will be presented and reviewed by the groups listed (Public at Large, Neighborhood, Process Action Teams, Senior Management Board, Boards of Selectmen Representatives, Department of Public Health/Agency for Toxic Substances and Disease Registry, Natural Resources Trustees and Technical Review and Evaluation Team).
4. Neighborhood and community forums will reevaluate the alternatives. Posterboards and information sheets will be presented to the groups listed, showing how the alternatives are evaluated. Issues on the matrix will not be changed, but the rating may need to change as a result of the forums.
5. The RPMs recommend the preferred Plume Response Alternative.

By using the above process, all working groups and the public should be in a position to understand the 'preferred' alternative.

In keeping with the spirit and intent of the Community Involvement Plan, this decision-making process will be subject to review through a public comment period. This approach will ensure that community stakeholders have the opportunity to participate in the evaluation process through which remedies will be chosen to best address the Massachusetts Military Reservation contamination plumes. The public will be updated about ongoing developments through participation in public meetings, representation on the various citizen process action teams, news releases and environmental updates issued by the Installation Restoration Program office.

2.2 Preferred Alternatives Selection Process

Each plume is unique in its location, size, mobility and contaminant characteristics. Therefore, the selection process and eventual implementation of a remedy will be unique and specific for each plume.

In the best of cases, an alternative which is protective of human health and the environment and has widespread acceptance will be identified. This ideal situation would make identification and communication of the remedy selection easy.

In the event that consensus is not reached, the Remedial Project Managers will further investigate stakeholders' preferences and make every attempt to understand the nature of objections and preferences. They will ensure that all the acceptance group's concerns and comments are heard and understood. They will work among themselves to determine if an alternative can be modified or compromises can be incorporated to make an alternative more attractive to the majority of the groups. After this process, the Remedial Project Managers will recommend a course of action. Remedial Project Managers will ensure that the process is diligently implemented with incorporation of public involvement. The RPMs will also keep their respective upper management apprised of the activities and developments in the process.

3.0 How the Matrix is Incorporated into the Schedule

As plume response simulations are run, and potential response alternatives are identified, updated information will be shared at the public meetings of the stakeholders and other "Acceptance Criteria Groups," as listed in section VII of the matrix. The identification of response alternatives will be worked through the Technical Review and Evaluation Team, through Science Advisory Panel presentations, and formalized Process Action Team and Senior Management Board meetings. These meetings provide opportunity for input, concerns and requests for clarification from the public prior to finalizing the assessment of alternatives. The tentative timeline for these public meetings is shown in the schedules contained in Appendix IV. [Eds. note: Appendix IV is not included here.]

As the decision point approaches, specific and focused meetings for the community, Process Action Teams and Senior Management Board will be scheduled to present alternatives. There will be a series of joint neighborhood Joint Process Action Team meetings, Posterboard Sessions, and Fact Sheets specifically targeted to provide information and solicit public input in building consensus for the selected response alternatives. The forum, content and delivery of these specialized meetings will be coordinated with the Public Information Team and will be conducted under the auspices of the Community Involvement Plan objectives.

The intent is to hold two key public meetings for each plume. The first is simply to present the alternatives and initiate community dialogue on preferences. The second meeting is intended to show the public the pros and cons of each alternative using the matrix. The official public comment period will extend approximately 2 weeks beyond this second meeting, allowing an average of 8 weeks for comments on a specific plume.

By the time the decision point arrives, the pros and cons of each alternative considered should be well understood. The date on the schedule for the decision point is when the public affirmation of the selected response alternative is expected and implementation begins.

The schedule for the technical activities leading up to response alternative identification and selection, as well as the public meetings for plumes CS-10, Ashumet Valley, LF-1, and SD-5 South are contained in Appendix IV. Also included at Appendix IV is the Options Implementation Schedule showing estimated time frames between decision points and system start-up.

To keep the program on track, the Air Force has agreed with regulatory agencies that certain enforceable milestones must be met. Appendix V contains a summarized schedule reflecting these enforceable activities for all of the plumes referenced in the *Comprehensive Plume Response Plan*. These schedules are also presented for public comment. [Eds. note: Appendix V is not included here.]

4.0 Incorporation and Enforceability

This "Plume Response Decision Criteria and Schedule" (Criteria Document) is Appendix VI to the Federal Facilities Agreement (FFA) for the Massachusetts Military Reservation, and as such will be appended to and made part of the FFA, and shall be enforceable thereunder. The Department of the Air Force (USAF) and Environmental Protection Agency (EPA) agree that USAF's commitment to use the evaluation procedure in this Criteria Document shall constitute a "term" or "condition" of the FFA, including but not limited to Sections II, XVII, XX and XXI of the FFA.

APPENDIX I

EVALUATION CRITERIA	Proposed Alternatives						
	ETR		Recirc Wells		Hybrid		Natural Atten
(Alternative Solutions as applicable)	Alt A	Alt X	Alt B	Alt X	Alt C	Alt X	
THRESHOLD CRITERIA							
I. Overall Protection of Human Health and the Environment							
A. Human Health							
1. Are the exposure pathways eliminated, reduced or controlled?							
B. Environment							
1. Are the impacts of response alternative on threatened or endangered species and habitats acceptable?							
2. Are the impacts of response alternative within hydrological and ecological threshold(s)?							

II. Compliance with Applicable or Relevant and Appropriate Requirements (ARARs) as defined in the September 1995 IROD)						
PRIMARY BALANCING CRITERIA						
III. Effectiveness and Permanence of Response Alternatives						
A. Effectiveness						
1. Estimated % Capture of Plume by volume (100% is goal, if technically and economically feasible)						
2. Estimated % Contaminant Removal by mass						
a. Ethylene Dibromide (EDB)						
b. Volatile Organic Compounds						
c. Semi-volatiles						
d. Inorganics						
3. Impacts on other plume(s)						
B. Impacts associated with uncaptured portion of the plume						
1. Human Health Risk						
a. Carcinogenic						
b. Non-carcinogenic						
2. Ecological Risk						
3. Socio-Economic						
4. Water Supply						
C. Characteristics of uncaptured portion of plume						
1. Volume						
2. Mass						
3. Persistence (duration)						
4. Surface Water Impacts						
D. Institutional controls for plume area						
1. Property use restrictions required						
2. Connections to public water supplies						
3. Adequacy of Institutional Controls						

a. Human Health							
b. Ecological							
4. Other							
IV. Effectiveness of Treatment Systems							
A. Treatment System Efficiency : Does effluent achieve background levels? (Background levels are goal, if technically and economically feasible)							
1. Ethylene Dibromide							
2. Volatile Organic Compounds							
3. Semi-volatiles							
4. Inorganics							
B. Final Disposition of Treatment System Residuals							
C. Risks to workers associated with handling/treating/disposing of residuals							
D. Does response alternative satisfy statutory preference for treatment as principal element							
V. Implementability							
A. Time factors:							
1. Duration to partial system start-up							
2. Duration to full system start-up							
3. Estimated duration of system operation							
B. Reliability of technology							
C. Coordination requirements with regulators and other agencies							
D. Property Access Considerations							
E. Risks associated with construction							
1. Human Health							
a. Carcinogenic							
b. Non-carcinogenic							
2. Ecological							
F. Impacts associated with construction							
1. Socio-Economic							
2. Environmental							
G. Risks associated with operations							
1. Human Health							

a. Carcinogenic								
b. Non-carcinogenic								
2. Ecological								
H. Impacts associated with operations								
1. Socio-Economic								
2. Environmental								
VI. Cost								
A. Total Capital Cost								
B. Operating and Maintenance Cost - annual								
C. Life-cycle cost								
ACCEPTANCE CRITERIA								
VII. Acceptance of response alternative								
A. Public at Large								
B. Neighborhood								
C. Process Action Teams								
D. Senior Management Board Selectmen Representatives								
E. Department of Public Health/ATSDR								
F. Natural Resource Trustees								
G Environmental Protection Agency								
H. Massachusetts Department of Environmental Protection								
I. Department of Defense								

APPENDIX II: PLUME RESPONSE DECISION CRITERIA, APRIL 24, 1997

Threshold Criteria

I. Overall Protection of Human Health and the Environment

A. Human Health:

    1. Are exposure pathways eliminated, reduced, or controlled?

        ■ "Yes" if all exposure pathways are eliminated or significantly reduced and implementation and operation of the action or Response alternative does not create new exposure pathways. Significant reduction means that the health risk associated with any remaining or reduced pathways is expected to fall within acceptable CERCLA ranges.

        □ "No" otherwise.

B. Environment:

    1. Are the impacts of the response alternative on threatened or endangered species and habitats acceptable?

- ■ "Yes" if species are absent or impacts are within an acceptable range.
- ☐ "No" if impacts are unacceptable.
- ? "Unknown" if species are present and impacts occur but effects cannot be determined.
1. Are the impacts of the response alternative within hydrological and ecological thresholds?
    - ■ Yes
    - ☐ No

II. Compliance with Applicable or Relevant and Appropriate Requirements (ARARs), as established in 1995 Interim Record of Decision (IROD):
- ■ Yes
- ▨ "Yes," with Waiver as per CERCLA
- ☐ No

Primary Balancing Criteria
III. Effectiveness and Permanence of Response Alternatives
A. Effectiveness:
1. Estimated % Capture Plume, calculated by volume (100% is goal, if technically and economically feasible):
    - ■ 100% capture
    - ▨ 95%–100% capture
    - ☐ Less than 95% capture
    Note: For natural attenuation the capture efficiency is assumed to be 0%.
2. Estimated % Containment Removal by Mass: Mass removal percentages will be calculated for: (a) EDB, (b) VOCs, (c) semi-volatiles, and (d) inorganics. Clean up to background if technically and economically feasible is assumed to be 100% removal and is expressed as a range as follows:
    - ■ 100% removal to background levels if technically and economically feasible
    - ▨ 90%–100% removal
    - ☐ Less than 90% removal
3. Impacts on Other Plume(s):
    - ■ "Acceptable" if no other plumes are affected, or there are no unacceptable impacts on existing or planned capture and treatment systems.
    - ☐ "Unacceptable" if otherwise.
B. Impacts associated with uncaptured portion of plume:
1. Human Health Risk: Cumulative human health risks would be estimated using the Baseline Risk Assessment, and any new updated data.
    a. Carcinogenic:
        - ■ Less than 10^{-6}
        - ▨ Within 10^{-6} to 10^{-5}
        - ▨ Within 10^{-5} to 10^{-4}
        - ☐ Above 10^{-4}
    b. Non-Carcinogenic:

- ■ Below Hazard Index of 1.0
- ☐ Hazard Index of 1.0 or Higher

2. Ecological Risk: Would be estimated using the Baseline Risk Assessment and updated data.
   - ■ Below Hazard Index 1.0
   - ☐ Hazard Index of 1.0 or Higher

3. Socio-Economic: Qualitatively considers potential impacts on commercial and residential interests, recreational areas and historical and archeological sites.
   - ■ Low impact
   - ▨ Moderate impact
   - ☐ High impact

4. Water Supply: Qualitatively considers impact on usability of groundwater supply by residents, business, industry. Greater impact consideration given to existing wells or current groundwater usage (immediacy of use/need).
   - ■ Low impact
   - ▨ Moderate impact
   - ☐ High impact

C. Characteristics of uncaptured portion of plume:

1. Volume: The uncaptured portion of the plume would be identified and delineated. The volume will be expressed as a percentage of total plume volume. This value would be computed for the total uncaptured portion of the plume but not for specific contaminants.
   - ■ 0% uncaptured
   - ▨ 0%–5% uncaptured
   - ☐ More than 5% uncaptured

2. Mass: The uncaptured portion of the plume would be identified and delineated. Mass will be expressed as a percentage of total mass.
   - ■ 0% uncaptured
   - ▨ 0%–5% uncaptured
   - ☐ More than 5% uncaptured

3. Persistence (duration): This value, based on modeling predictions would be the time (expressed as a range of years) required for the entire uncaptured plume to travel to its discharge point or for concentrations within the plume to decrease to values that are no longer threats to human health or the ecology, whichever is longer.
   - ■ Less than 10 years
   - ▨ 10 to 20 years
   - ☐ Greater than 20 years

4. Surface Water Impacts:
   - ■ "No" if the uncaptured plume attenuates to concentration values that are no longer threats to human health or the ecology before reaching a fresh or marine surface water discharge point.
   - ☐ "Yes" otherwise.

D. Institutional controls of the plume area (captured and uncaptured):
    1. Property use restrictions required:
        - No property use restrictions are required to eliminate exposure pathways under any potential future land use.
        - Some restrictions are required.
        - Many restrictions are required.
    2. Connections to public water supplies: Refers to whether or not a connection will be necessary now or in the future.
        - "None" if the current of future path of the plume is currently served by public water supplies.
        - "Some" if 1–25 public water supply connections must be extended.
        - "Many" if more than 25 connections must be extended.
    3. Adequacy of Institutional Controls:
        a. Human Health:
            - "Adequate" if federal, state, or local regulations exist that provide the necessary control(s) and corresponding inspection and enforcement functions also exist and these controls are commonly implemented and historically effective.
            - "Questionable" if federal, state, or local regulations exist that provide the necessary control(s) and corresponding inspection and enforcement functions also exist but these controls are not commonly implemented or exercised or they have not been historically effective.
            - "Inadequate" if federal, state, or local regulations which provide the necessary control(s) do not exist or if corresponding inspection and enforcement functions do not exist.
        b. Ecological:
            - "Yes" if federal, state, or local regulations exist that provide the necessary control(s) and corresponding inspection and enforcement functions also exist.
            - "No" if otherwise.
    4. Other: To be determined as specific evaluation criteria are developed.

IV. Effectiveness of Treatment System

A. Treatment System Efficiency: Does effluent achieve background levels? (Background levels are goal, if technically and economically feasible.):
    1. Ethylene Dibromide
        - Yes
        - No
    2. Volatile Organic Compounds
        - Yes
        - No
    3. Semi-Volatiles
        - Yes
        - No

    4. Inorganic
- ■ Yes
- □ No

B. Final Disposition of treatment system residuals:
- ■ Destruction
- ▪ Mixed (combination of destruction and transfer)
- □ Transfer

C. Risks to workers associated with handling/treating/disposing of residuals:
- ■ "Low" if volume and/or nature of residual contaminants will not present operational uncertainties and risks.
- ▪ "Moderate" if volume and/or nature of residual contaminants will be a concern but manageable.
- □ "High" otherwise

D. Does response alternative satisfy statutory preference for treatment as principal element:
- ■ Yes
- □ No

V. Implementability

A. Time factors:
    1. Duration to partial system start-up: The estimated time frame from decision point until startup for a significant portion of the overall system. ("Significant" means that higher concentration portions of the plume are being addressed or that containment of at least a quarter of the plume volume is affected.)
- ■ Less than 12 months
- ▪ 12 to 24 months
- □ Greater than 24 months

    2. Duration from decision point to system start-up:
- ■ Less than 12 months
- ▪ 12 to 24 months
- □ Greater than 24 months

    3. Estimated duration of system operation: The estimated duration that the proposed plume response alternative will have to operate.
- ■ Less than 10 years
- ▪ 10–20 years
- □ Greater than 20 years

B. Reliability of Technology: Reliability will be re-evaluated after completion of pilot tests:
- ■ "High" when operating systems which use accepted, proven technologies. Activated carbon, air stripping, vacuum extraction and ETR, would be scored high.
- ▪ "Moderate" when operating systems which use developing or new technologies. Synthetic carbon filtration, cavitation/oxidation, recirculating well technology and in situ bioremediation would be scored moderate.

        □ "Low" when operating systems that use emerging technologies such as reactive walls that have greater uncertainty in effectiveness.

C. Coordination Requirements with Regulators and Other Agencies:

        ■ Response alternatives which require a minimal degree of regulatory and agency involvement to obtain approval will be scored high.

        □ Response alternatives requiring performance tests or elaborate treatability testing or extensive permitting will be scored low.

D. Property Access Considerations:

        ■ "High" if treatment systems are constructed entirely on MMR or available public lands.

        ▪ "Moderate" for lands with "likely" access.

        □ "Low" for private properties with "questionable" access.

E. Risks Associated with Construction:

   1. Human Health: Carcinogenic risks and hazard indexes are revised to reflect the impacts of construction activities on exposure pathways and construction workers are added as receptors. The exposure time is limited to the duration of the construction activity and only current land uses are considered. Cumulative human health risks would be estimated using the Baseline Risk Assessment, and any new updated data.

     a. Carcinogenic:

        ■ Less than 10^{-6}

        ▪ Within 10^{-6} to 10^{-5}

        ▪ Within 10^{-5} to 10^{-4}

        □ Above 10^{-4}

     b. Non-Carcinogenic:

        ■ Below Hazard Index of 1.0

        □ Hazard Index of 1.0 or Higher

   2. Ecological: Would be estimated using the Baseline Risk Assessment and updated data. Chemical-specific ecological hazard indexes would be re-calculated as needed to reflect construction impacts on exposure pathways or containment concentrations.

        ■ "Low" if there are no significant adverse impacts on ecological systems; minimal disturbance of endangered species, elimination of habitat, activities in wetlands or any protective setback from wetlands or water bodies, drawdowns of surface water bodies or change in chemical composition of surface water bodies, and deforestation of old growth trees.

        □ "High" if there are significant adverse impacts on ecological systems.

F. Impacts Associated with Construction:

   1. Socio-Economic: Qualitatively considers potential impacts on commercial and residential interests, recreational areas and historical and archeological sites.

        ■ Low impact

        ▪ Moderate impact

        □ High impact

   2. Environmental:

- ▪ "Low" if there are no significant adverse impacts on ecological systems; minimal disturbance of endangered species, elimination of habitat, activities in wetlands or any protective setback from wetlands or water bodies, drawdowns of surface water bodies or change in chemical composition of surface water bodies, and deforestation of old growth trees.
- ▫ "High" if there are significant adverse impacts on ecological systems.

G. Risks associated with operation:
1. Human Health: Carcinogenic risks and hazard indexes are revised to reflect the impacts of operation exposure pathways and workers and community are added as receptors. Cumulative human health risk would be estimated using the Baseline Risk Assessment, and any new updated.
   a. Carcinogenic:
      - ▪ Less than 10^{-6}
      - ▨ Within 10^{-6} to 10^{-5}
      - ▨ Within 10^{-5} to 10^{-4}
      - ▫ Above 10^{-4}
   b. Non-Carcinogenic:
      - ▪ Below Hazard Index of 1.0
      - ▫ Hazard Index of 1.0 or Higher
2. Ecological Risk: Would be estimated using the Baseline Risk Assessment and updated data. Chemical-specific ecological hazard indexes would be re-calculated as needed to reflect operation impacts on exposure pathways or containment concentrations.
   - ▪ Below Hazard Index of 1.0
   - ▫ Hazard Index of 1.0 or Higher

H. Impacts associated with operation:
1. Socio-Economic: Qualitatively considers potential impacts on commercial and residential interests, recreational areas, and historical and archeological sites.
   - ▪ Low impact
   - ▨ Moderate impact
   - ▫ High impact
2. Environmental
   - ▪ "Low" if there are no significant adverse impacts on ecological systems; minimal disturbance of endangered species, elimination of habitat, activities in wetlands or any protective setback from wetlands or water bodies, drawdowns of surface water bodies or change in chemical composition of surface water bodies, and deforestation of old growth trees.
   - ▫ "High" if there are significant adverse impacts on ecological systems.

VI. Cost (Present Value in thousands of dollars)

A. Total Capital Cost
B. Operating and Maintenance Cost - annual
C. Life-cycle cost (Capital cost and O&M cost)

Acceptance Criteria
VII. Acceptance of Response Alternative
- ■ Preferred
- ▨ Acceptable
- ☐ Unacceptable

A. Public at large
B. Neighborhood Groups. Public opinion will be qualitatively assessed by the Public Information Team (PIT) and the Remediation Program Managers (RPMs) by assessing the sentiment of public meetings as well as by analyzing the comments received on plans at public meetings.
C. Process Action Teams
D. SMB Selectman representatives from the four affected Towns (Mashpee, Bourne, Falmouth and Sandwich): "Yes" or "No" responses developed through a process established by the participants.
E. MA Department of Public Health and Agency for Toxic Substance and Disease Registry.
F. Natural Resources Trustees. These currently include: Air Force, National Oceanic and Atmospheric Administration, Commonwealth of Massachusetts, Army, Department of the Interior and Veterans Administration.
G. Environmental Protection Agency
H. Commonwealth of Massachusetts Department of Environmental Protection
I. Department of Defense

APPENDIX III: DEFINITIONS

ARAR (Applicable or Relevant and Appropriate Requirements). Federal or State laws and regulations that must be met during the implementation and at the completion of the remedy.

Background. Levels of chemicals which exist in the environment in the absence of contamination resulting from the disposal site of concern.

Capture. Actions taken to abate, contain or recover a contaminant by a remedy.

Carcinogenic Risk. For human health risk, carcinogenic risk is a measure of the health risks for contaminants of concerns which are known or suspected to cause cancer.

Cleanup. Actions for removing contaminants from the environment.

Containment. Actions taken to prevent further migration of a contaminant plume.

Decision Point. The time at which the plume response alternative is selected.

Decision Criteria. The factors evaluated and compared in the Plume Response Alternative Evaluation Matrix.

ETR (Extraction/Treatment/Reinjection). A system which extracts groundwater, treats it to reduce or eliminate contaminants and reinjects the treated water into the aquifer.

Feasibility of Achieving Background. Capability of a response alternative achieving background levels of contaminant.

A. TECHNOLOGICAL

Not feasible if:

- The existing technologies or modifications cannot remediate to a level of no significant risk, or to levels which approach or achieve background; or
- The reliability of the identified alternative has not been sufficiently proven and a substantial uncertainty exists as to whether it will effectively reduce risk; or
- Alternative does not or cannot be modified to meet other regulatory requirements.

B. ECONOMIC

The benefits of implementing an alternative and reducing the concentrations of contaminants in the environment to levels which approach or achieve background justifies related costs unless:

- Incremental cost for alternative is substantial and disproportional to the benefit of risk reduction, environmental restoration and monetary and nonmonetary values; or
- The risk of harm to health/safety/public welfare/environment by the alternative cannot be adequately controlled.

Feasibility of 100% Capture.

A. TECHNOLOGICAL

Not technically feasible if:

- The existing technologies or modifications cannot attain 100% capture;
- The reliability of the identified alternative has not been sufficiently proven and a substantial uncertainty exists as to whether it can attain 100% capture; or
- Alternative does not or cannot be modified to meet other regulatory requirements.

B. ECONOMIC

The benefits of implementing an alternative and attaining 100% capture justifies related costs unless:

- Incremental cost for alternative is substantial and disproportional to the benefits;
- The risk of harm to health/safety/public welfare/environment by the alternative cannot be adequately controlled.

Hazard Indices. For human health risk, hazard index is a measure of the health risks for contaminants of concerns which are not known or suspected to cause cancer. For ecological risks, hazard index is a measure of the risks for contaminants of concern.

Hybrid. A system made up of a combination of different technologies.

MCLs (Maximum Contaminant Levels). The maximum concentration of a given contaminant allowed in drinking water under State and Federal regulations.

MRG - Management Review Group. This group consisting of senior management representatives from Air Force Center For Environmental Excellence (AFCEE), Executive Office of Environmental Affairs (EOEA) the Massachusetts Department of Environmental Protection (DEP), and Environmental Protection Agency (EPA), the Air Staff (AF/ILEVR), The Secretariat (SAF/MIQ) and the four Senior Management Board selectmen make decisions on policy and management issues at MMR's clean-up program.

Natural Attenuation. The process by which a compound is reduced in concentration over time by natural processes.

No Significant Risk. A level of control of each identified substance of concern at a site or in the surrounding environment that no such substance of concern shall present a significant risk of harm to health, safety, public welfare or the environment during any foreseeable period of time.

Non-Carcinogenic Risk. see Hazard Index

PATs - Process Action Teams. This team consists of four sub-groups which provide input on policy, management and technical issues concerning the clean-up at MMR. The following teams make up the PATs.
- **ITT - Innovative Technologies Team.** Provides input on use and development of innovative environmental technologies at MMR.
- **LRWS - Long Range Water Supply Team.** Provide input on technical issues involving Regional water supply development and supply in the four adjacent towns water districts, as it relates to clean-up efforts at MMR.
- **PCT - Plume Containment Team.** Provides input on policy and management and technical issues involving numerous plume response activities.
- **PIT - Public Information Team.** Provides input on community outreach and public involvement efforts.

Pilot Test. Demonstrations of technologies/systems to evaluate performance under field conditions. The results are used to develop alternatives and design full-scale treatment systems.

Plume. A body of groundwater containing contaminants exceeding Maximum Contamination Levels (MCLs), as defined by multiple samples from multiple wells. In the absence of MCLs, a risk-based level will be established.

Recirculating Well. A process for capturing, treating and releasing groundwater within the same well. This process is not expected to adversely impact the water table.

Plume Response Alternative. A specific configuration of treatment system(s) to be compared and evaluated.

Residuals. The hazardous and/or non-hazardous byproducts of a treatment process which require disposal.

RPMs (Remedial Program Managers). The RPM team consists of the Program Managers appointed by Massachusetts Department of Environmental Protection (DEP), Environmental Protection Agency (EPA), and Air Force Center For Environmental Excellence (AFCEE). This team provides critical day-to-day input, direction and decisions on schedule, enforceable milestones and technical progress and overall operations of the project.

SMB (Senior Management Board). This group consists of the selectmen of the four adjacent towns (Bourne, Mashpee, Falmouth and Sandwich), Coast Guard, MA National Guard, Department of Environmental Protection (DEP), Environmental Protection Agency (EPA), and Department of Public Health (DPH). Their current tasking is to provide input on policy and management issues involving plume containment actions of public concern and review the work of all other citizen involvement teams, including the PATs.

Treatment. A method, technique or process designed to change the physical, chemical or biological character or composition of contaminated groundwater.

TRET (Technical Review and Evaluation Team). This group of hydrogeological and ecological experts contain scientists from Massachusetts Department of Environmental Protection (DEP), Environmental Protection Agency (EPA), HAZWRAP/Oakridge National Laboratories, Waste Policy Institute, AFCEE, Cape Cod Commission, United States Geological Survey (USGS), University of Utah, Kansas State University, the Science Advisory Panel, Woods Hole Oceanographic Institution and other local scientists. The TRETs task is to advise the RPMs, AFCEE and its contractors on technical and scientific issues of concern.

Part 4

Selected Readings

Introduction

Part 4 includes five supplementary readings. We chose these selections in light of the questions most often raised by participants in the Negotiating Environmental Agreements workshop. The first reading, by Joseph DiMento, looks at the problems of enforcement that often give rise to environmental negotiations. This selection reviews the various sanctions often applied in environmental regulatory situations in the United States and the kinds of negotiations such compliance-getting tactics engender. There are differing opinions about the extent to which criminal sanctions are likely to produce greater compliance with environmental laws and regulations. One side feels that criminal sanctions imposed on individuals will not do much to enhance the capacity of an understaffed organization to meet a variety of technically sophisticated requirements. The alternative view is that only a direct threat to individual corporate leaders will move them to invest what is required to ensure that they are in compliance. This article looks at corporate environmental liability under a range of statutes in the United States and shows how pressures to comply are likely to be viewed from the standpoint of the regulated community. We are particularly interested in the way that corporate attitudes shape environmental negotiations.

The next two readings, by Lax and Sebenius, and by Susskind and van Dam, look at the problems of trying to create joint gains in what are usually win-lose contexts. Lax and Sebenius look at the question theoretically, emphasizing the need to find a balance between the cooperative behaviors that create value and competitive behaviors that allocate gains and losses. Susskind and van Dam look at the problem in the context of trying to formulate national environmental regulations. Historically, federal agencies drafted what they thought were reasonable regulations and then hunkered down to defend themselves against the hostile reactions of corporate attorneys and advocacy groups. In recent years, negotiated rulemaking has emerged as an alternative. This is a context within which environmental regulations now take place and where the mutual gains approach has helped all "sides" come closer to achieving their objectives.

The Susskind and Cruikshank excerpt details the roles that mediators play in negotiations. The reading describes the invaluable service mediators and facilitators can provide to negotiators, particularly in multiparty, multi-issue situations and those in which relationships are strained.

The final selection, by Susskind and Secunda, reviews Project XL, the Environmental Protection Agency's recent effort to promote a more flexible approach to achieving environmental standards.

List of Readings

1. DiMento, J.F. (1986). "They treated me like a criminal: Sanctions, enforcement characteristics, and compliance" (Chapter 5). In *Environmental law and American business: Dilemmas of compliance* (pp. 77–102). New York: Plenum Press.

2. Lax, D.A., and Sebenius, J.K. (1986). "The negotiator's dilemma: Creating and claiming value" (Chapter 2). In *The manager as negotiator: Bargaining for cooperative and competitive gain* (pp. 29–45). New York: Free Press.

3. Susskind, L., and van Dam, L. (1986, July). "Squaring off at the table, not in the courts." *Technology Review* 36–44, 72.

4. Susskind, L.E., and Cruikshank, J. (1987). "Mediation and other forms of assisted negotiation" (Chapter 5). In *Breaking the impasse: Consensual approaches to resolving public disputes* (pp. 136–185). New York: Basic Books.

5. Susskind, L.E., and Secunda, J. (1997). The risks and the advantages of agency discretion: Evidence from EPA's Project XL. *UCLA Journal of Environmental Law and Policy* vol. 17, no. 1, pp. 67–116.

Reading 1

"They Treated Me Like a Criminal": Sanctions, Enforcement Characteristics, and Compliance*

Joseph F. DiMento

During our trial . . . our attorney asked to bring in a cross-section of the community which we were affiliated with, as character references.

We could have brought two busloads. We brought in approximately 50. They were . . . firemen, policemen, other growers and just personal friends. This impressed the judge in the case so much he reduced the fines and sentence considerably . . . just on this.[1]

I am writing to express my astonishment and indignation over the Board of Public Works' withdrawal of a $105,000 fine imposed on Culligan Deionized Water Service, Inc.

I cannot believe that such a fine would "put the company out of business." Indeed if the Times article (July 22) is accurate Culligan accepted between $5 million and $25 million from its clients before dumping the untreated waste into the city sewage system (with virtually no overhead but the cost of running a truck to the nearest sewer). If anything, the fine should have been much higher.

I also cannot believe the remaining penalty—jail for the Culligan president—will effectively deter such violations in the future. Serving 90 days in a minimum-security country club with other white-collar criminals seems a small price to pay for endangering the health of sanitation workers and the general public (especially when the profits of such crime continue to draw interest in the bank).

---

* Reprinted from DiMento, J.F. (1986). "They treated me like a criminal: Sanctions, enforcement characteristics, and compliance" (Chapter 5). In *Environmental law and American business: Dilemmas of compliance* (pp. 77–102). New York: Plenum Press. All citations and notes in this reading refer to the source book.

A punishment that better fits the crime might be to sentence [the executive] to spend 90 days personally cleaning up the sewers that his company contaminated.

—L.M. Dryden
San Gabriel[2]

Enforcement: Necessary But Not Sufficient

Efforts to achieve compliance with environmental law most often focus on a strong enforcement policy. As in many other areas of the criminal justice system, the almost unavoidable conclusion is that laws do not function smoothly because of a weak or nonexistent enforcement approach. Not enough violators are identified; when identified, not enough are sanctioned; and when they are sanctioned, penalties are insufficiently severe to communicate the fact that violations will not be tolerated.

This perception, as it relates to environmental law, is partially accurate. In the broadest understanding of the term, a sound enforcement policy is necessary to affect corporate and small-business behavior. But enforcement is to be understood to mean a system: A full enforcement system encompasses the sanction, the resources of the enforcing agent, the severity and certainty of the punishment's being imposed or an incentive's being awarded, the manner in which the regulated business perceives the enforcement policy, and the enforcement agency's relationship with other branches of government.

The Nature of the Sanction

Which sanction works best to promote compliance with environmental law? The question has no unambiguous answer. Chapter 3 introduced several perspectives on the efficacy of alternative sanctions. Here we delve deeper in order to survey the views of scholars, business people, and enforcers on the calculations undertaken in evaluating threats.

In a famous discussion of the criminal law, Packer (1968, p. 354) characterizes as "totally unexplored" the question of what makes the criminal sanction effective when "respectable" offenders are involved: conviction, jail sentences (imposed or actually served), publicity. "Our information about this kind of issue is mere impression and anecdote." Part of the reason for lack of knowledge has been that in criminal cases conviction rates for regulatory violations have been low and imprisonment quite rare.

Although some theorists hold that the deterrent effect (and ultimately the compliance rate) is greater for criminal law than for civil sanctions (Glen, 1973), others feel that in the areas of social and economic regulation, simply making an activity criminal is not sufficient to effect deterrence (Stone, 1978). Still others feel that, practically, there is little difference between criminal and civil law since the public does not equate moral turpitude with corporate environmental wrongdoing.

We can learn something about the efficacy of criminal sanctions in environmental law from empirical studies of deterrence. But the answers are limited. A body of deterrence research suggests that severity of punishment deters criminal behavior (Bean and Cushing, 1971; Erlich, 1973; Gibbs, 1968; Gray and Martin, 1969; Tittle, 1969; Tittle and

Logan, 1973); but some researchers reach opposite conclusions (Schwartz, 1968; Waldo and Chiricos, 1972). Not only are research results contradictory, but application to the organizational target is not direct. Only in a few cases have empirical results involved the corporate criminal (Braithwaite and Geis, 1982).

Nevertheless, some theory quite strongly posits a deterrent effect of punishment in the organizational setting (Braithwaite and Geis, 1982; Chambliss, 1966; Packer, 1968). Chambliss considers white-collar criminals as eminently deterrable because their actions are often based on calculated risks, not on passion, as is the case for many other criminal behaviors. Braithwaite and Geis (1982) conclude that the reorientations which deterrence based on punishment require are more easily made by organizations than by individuals: "A new internal compliance group can be put in place much more readily than can a new super ego" (p. 310). Braithwaite and Geis (1982) summarize:

> The evidence on the deterrent effects of sanctions against corporate crime is not . . . voluminous. But the consensus among scholars is overwhelmingly optimistic concerning general deterrence. This may in part reflect an uncritical acceptance of the empirically untested assumption that because corporate crime is notably rational economic activity, it must be more subject to general deterrence. (p. 304)

But the effects of punishment must be better understood before public policy concludes that criminal sanctions are the enforcement mode of preference, for the empirical work on punishment leaves open two important questions for regulatory compliance: Might effects related to punishment derive as well from noncriminal ways of influencing business? And even if criminal punishments are effective, might not other incentives be equally or more effective with fewer costs and negative or regressive outcomes? Before concluding that public policy should rely mainly on punishment to gain compliance, further analyses of decision making within the firm are necessary.

The Business Perspective

In general, business people consider criminal sanctions for environmental violations, although acceptable in the abstract, infrequently appropriate and rarely applicable to their situations. This finding from the executive interviews is no surprise, but the passion with which business people attack the use of criminal sanctions may be (see also Clay, 1983). Business contrasts occasional "inadvertent" or "negligent" noncompliant activity with serious health and safety problems.

Clay (1983) reports that although a majority (54 percent) of interviewed California business people concluded that jail terms should sometimes be imposed on violators of occupational health laws, most concluded that criminal sanctions were not appropriate in the cases in which they were charged with California OSHA violations. Respondents (90 percent) felt that the sanction should be reserved for serious violations committed by others in industry (Clay, 1983). Some enforcement officers concur. That criminal enforcement "tends to involve only fringe elements of the regulated community" was an attitude expressed by a small number of surveyed enforcers.[3] One respondent put the matter precisely: "Violations would have to be egregious, repeated, and intentional with total disregard for the environment and public health."[4]

A small farmer expressed outrage at the use of the criminal law in his case:

> I was just completely taken [aback] with the type of handling. They [government enforcers] treated me like a criminal. They told us to go to [City X] and get printed and mugged. It was damned infamy for this area because it was me . . . and I'd say a half dozen other industry involved people. I'd say 10 percent of this area were in federal court getting printed and mugged like a bunch of common thieves.[5]

Many businesses consider criminal sanctions inconsistent with the regulatory problems they confront. Criminal sanctions result in "overkill."[6] Business people use the term in two senses. Because criminal fines and imprisonment are excessive punishments, they should not be used. And, if used, these sanctions lead to attributions to the company of behaviors that are not involved in violations. Criminal remedies are thus unfair, since the public will make associations which devastate the firm's competitive profile.

Industry describes counterproductive outcomes of the criminal sanction. Industry will "overcompensate" or overcomply, negatively affecting the firm's attempts to innovate; industry will be chilled by potential criminal punishment from sharing ideas with others. "God knows what we've overlooked internationally because of fears of [criminally suspect] contacts across the industry," said one automotive executive. Reportedly chilled also are legitimate attempts to challenge regulations: "You can't ever test a regulation [under criminal sanction threat]. You can't go to the judge and say 'EPA was exceeding its bounds.' . . . It's hard to imagine a case where the criminal sanction works well."[7]

In evaluating the effects of sanctions on compliance, a long-range perspective is necessary. Government can bring a criminal charge against a company whose operatives, if convicted, serve a sentence or pay a fine and then close down the company and begin business under a new name. This mobility is a challenge to the deterrent effect of all sanctions in many areas of business crime; but violators of environmental law may be more apt to establish a new identity after imposition of a criminal sanction than those convicted of more commonly understood crimes. This resilience exists because many highly polluting businesses have low profiles within a community. Citizens may hardly know that the business—indeed the service itself—exists. What is more, executives of such businesses themselves may be "invisible" within the area.

Criminal sanctions may also interfere with cooperative government-business relationships. Business people overwhelmingly see themselves as law-abiding. Environmental law should promote information gathering on polluting activities and encourage compromises on societal goals. Criminalizing an act only gets in the way of business's social "contract" to behave in a reasonable manner. Threatening to use criminal law obstructs the system of values that has evolved between the two sectors.

Scholtz (1984), reasoning through game theory, advocates cooperative strategies because confrontation raises the costs of enforcement and compliance beyond a reasonable level, benefiting neither government nor industry. "At some level of stringency, compliance costs will become so high that firms preferring voluntary compliance at the previous level of stringency will now prefer taking their chances as evaders, imposing higher costs of confrontation on firm and agency alike" (p. 281). The argument that use of criminal strategies promotes business evasion of law is partially valid (Scholtz, 1984), yet can become a rationale to emasculate legal control of white collar crime.

Business also fears that criminal laws are misused once media descriptions of environmental damage touch public emotions. Present-day knowledge (e.g., about health effects) is applied to deeds performed years ago. A notorious recent manifestation of the problem is the *Johns-Manville* case; workers are bringing numerous suits against the company for health problems allegedly associated with exposure to asbestos. Practices considered standard and acceptable and indeed required by government during World War II are linked to asbestos-caused cancer and other diseases. A new group of environmental lawsuits also challenges common laboratory and construction uses of formaldehyde.[8] Businessmen feel that they are being held to an ever more stringent standard of care; criminal sanctions represent a new disincentive to entering the chemical manufacturing and use businesses.

Many business people associate criminal sanctions with deliberate life- or property-threatening activity and consider application to their actions as grossly unreasonable.[9] Only very marginal industries or marginal units within industries would behave so antisocially as to merit criminal punishment. And if subordinates do engage in illegal behavior to protect the company and/or their own jobs, management should not be criminally punished. Rather, the firm should have the flexibility to address the problem by firing these employees. Business executives are very concerned about criminal liability for employee behavior which they did not authorize.

Not surprising is the business preference for self-policing. But, in candor, some executives are realistic about public reactions to this notion:

> [Self-policing] . . . I think philosophically is a better system. . . . I think [a] society which operates through a combination of self-policing with appropriate performance standards and periodic audits . . . is the most cost-effective system. . . . Fundamentally it depends on the honesty of the population . . . (I realize though the) general belief that industrial sources are likely to be, if not generally dishonest, resisting all kinds of regulations.[10]

The suspicion is that businessmen consider those effective approaches which limit their ability to manipulate enforcement to be unacceptable. Industry opposition to the noncompliance penalty (NCP) suggests this conclusion. NCP is a provision of the Clean Air Act added in 1977 (section 120) to augment civil and criminal sanctions available under the act:

> Congress added section 120 to the Act because it anticipated that even the augmented civil and criminal penalty scheme would not create sufficient incentives for sources to comply with air quality standards. . . . Congress also hoped that the section 120 penalties would increase administrative flexibility in enforcement of the Act, by serving as a middle ground between stiff criminal sanctions or shutting down of noncomplying facilities. . . . Equally important, by removing the economic benefits of noncompliance, Congress

hoped to place polluters on the same economic footing as those who had limited their emissions through increased anti-pollution expenditures.[11]

Penalties reflect the value to a source of noncompliance. The amount charged includes capital and operating costs and maintenance expenses which the firm avoids by failure to comply. To determine penalties the EPA developed a "mathematical penalty calculation model" which addresses benefits derived by violators and costs which a firm has incurred. Thus, under the NCP, government collects the amount of money that a firm has "earned" because of its failure to comply. Economic theorists have hailed the strategy as administratively simple, efficient, and fair, but the executive interviews describe the strategy in much different terms:

> I think it should be repealed. . . . It's one of the stupidest laws I've ever seen. It's like handing somebody the death penalty for possessing marijuana. . . . It even denies authority to the courts. . . . it's one of those . . . principles that are caused by the political concern of the moment.[12]

Individual companies and trade associations including Duquesne Light Company, Pennsylvania Power Company, the American Iron and Steel Institute, and the Chemical Manufacturers Association brought suit challenging the noncompliance penalty policy. Industry argued that the rules implementing the strategy are inflexible and do not allow the business sector to present its view of the noncompliance problem.[13] These assertions were rejected for the most part in the federal courts. Specifically the Court of Appeals for the District of Columbia Circuit found that judicial review of an NCP determination is available and exemptions exist which build in "flexibility" for sources which demonstrate that noncompliance is beyond their control or which meet other tests. The court concluded that it "is more than five years since Congress enacted this section (NCP); it is certainly time to put into operation the penalty assessment system Congress mandated."[14]

The regulated community vigorously opposes attempts to legislate greater use of the criminal sanction. The degree of opposition raises concern over efficient use of enforcement resources; employing criminal sanctions may raise a flag for industry and engender business responses to enforcement efforts based on principle rather than on considerations of cost-benefit analyses. What may be admitted and resolved quietly if classified as civil may become a cause célèbre if criminal, "like the acts of a mugger or rapist."[15]

Some enforcement personnel take a much different view of use of the criminal sanction. The Los Angeles district attorney described a case of deliberate dumping of toxic materials into the city sewers:

> There is only one way to deal with someone in a life threatening activity and this is jail. . . . If it is only a fine, it [the fine] would be considered part of the cost of doing business.[16]

Indeed, some commentators conclude that vigorously attacking the most flagrant violators, or what are called "the bad apples" (Kagan and Scholz, 1981), is essential to a meaningful deterrence posture:

The worst case deterrence threat is what really determines the level of "voluntary compliance" that firms and enforcement agency tacitly agree on. Firms are not concerned with just the initial probabilities of detection and punishment, but with the long-term probabilities that increase dramatically as the agency focuses its attention on the major violations.[17]

This assessment argues for at least some kind of draconian responses to noncompliance in appropriate situations. These include criminal sanctions.

Cost-Benefit Calculations of the Regulatee

The small defendant may perceive the criminal sanction, at least at first, as something it must fight—regardless of costs—because of the destructive negative publicity associated with an indictment. Cost-benefit calculations can also take a back seat when an influential executive treats an enforcement act as a personal insult. Idiosyncrasies of CEOs, including views of their own expertise, can lead to reactions to prosecution that purely on the criterion of efficiency the firm would do best to settle. For example, the CEO may be particularly knowledgeable about the health effects of a chemical emission or of the Congressional intent regarding balancing health effects with economic factors. He or she may conclude that the interpretation given to a law by a citizen litigant, an environmental public interest group, or a government agency fails to reflect this knowledge. What in another area of law enforcement would be ignored as too trivial to pursue may consume an inordinate amount of time and resources—to fight a matter on principle.

Just as individual idiosyncrasies of top management can lead to a company's "digging in" and fighting implementation of environmental law, the preferences of top managers are an important factor in responsive behavior (Roberts and Bluhm, 1981). Executives may exert influence in a number of different ways. The CEO may have a personal commitment to environmental protection which translates into his subordinates' undertaking cost-benefit calculations in unique ways: What seems costly down the street may be calculated as the cost of doing business here. Or, regardless of personal preferences, the managers may establish controls which discipline company units to comply as standard operating procedure. (As we will see in Chapter 7, both the preferences and the controls may have less than perfect influence in highly differentiated firms.)

Despite individual differences, business does at times respond to environmental law in classical cost-benefit terms (Brown and Stover, 1977; Downing and Watson, 1974). Studies have shown that the costs incurred by the firm for noncompliance are trivial when compared with profits that can be made through violations. Marlow (1982, p. 170) concluded for OSHA:

> If OSHA is to increase the injury control resources of firms above that generated in the private market, it must increase the costs of noncompliance to the point of equality with the rates of return on alternative investments.

Former Los Angeles City Attorney Ira Reiner described the analysis done by a company charged with unlawful storage and disposal of PCB:

> There is a rhetorical question that must be asked: Why would an otherwise
> responsible corporation engage in conduct that is life threatening to the pub-
> lic? . . . In this case the answer is money.[18]

The case allegedly involved disposal by two unqualified machine brokers. The firm
hired the men for much less than the bid of $43,915 it had received from General Elec-
tric Company to dispose of the material property.

Thus, whether a sanction can contribute to an effective enforcement policy depends
in part on government capacity to identify the point at which fines affect the competitive profile of a firm. No legal reasoning impedes setting fines in recognition of a firm's
size and wealth, at levels that probably will affect the organization's cost-benefit calculations.[19] Some monetary penalties, however, will simply be added to the costs of doing
business. Fisse (1980, p. 17) argues that a fine of even several million dollars to a company with annual sales of billions of dollars "would be tantamount to the payment of a
tax or license." But there are limits to the private sector's ability to pass on costs; all firms
have their "breaking points." Yet Stone (1981) concludes that, although "the law's money
threats" may be superior to other sanctions in influencing business behavior, firms vary
considerably in their sensitivity to threatened impacts on profit. Also, although fines at
an *in terrorem* level may be legislatively available, it is not at all certain "that judges, pros-
ecutors and juries will invoke them to the fullest" (p. 885).

Diver (1980, p. 266) has pointed out that in order to be effective "the regulator must
estimate not the actual probabilities (of violation detection) but the probabilities as perceived by the regulated population." Other commentators (Likens and Kohfield,
undated) note that the cost-benefit analysis is but a skeletal summary statement of the
firm's forecasts, decisions, and responses. Diver (1980) and Fisse (1978) identify potential tort liability, business losses following adverse publicity, future litigation costs, and
costs incurred in coming into compliance.

Stone (1978) suggests that corporate losses derived from enforcements of health and
safety laws are not of the same salience as other losses. Certain legal actions are seen as
acts of God and are not added to the ledger of analyzed and budgeted costs. Further,
stark cost-benefit thinking does not take into consideration the various ways in which
business approaches risk taking (Stigler, 1970). There exists no common monetary measuring rod for preferences in the politics of regulation. As Wilson (1980, p. 359) concludes, profit maximization is "an incomplete statement of corporate goals."

> Enforcement, happily, is not the sole means of assuring compliance with reg-
> ulatory directives. Business obeys regulations for a host of reasons—moral or
> intellectual commitment to underlying regulatory objectives, belief in the
> fairness of the procedures that produced the regulations, pressure from peers,
> competitors, customers, or employees, conformity with a law-abiding self
> image.

Business responses to the costs of coming into compliance vary. Had he known of the
expenses of defending himself in an environmental lawsuit, a small businessman
reported, he would have purchased the technology that could bring him into compliance:
"It would have been foolish for me not to."[20] Yet he decided against a plea bargain that

would have cost one-half of the legal fees needed to pursue the case: "We are innocent and we didn't want to compromise."[21] Another interviewee from a large corporation decided to enter a *nolo contendere* plea because it would result in a fine only one-seventeenth as large as the cost of pursuing a full criminal defense. "Certainly you sometimes will compromise some matter which you may think you're right on, simply because . . . protecting or preserving that position does not justify the costs."[22] Another company issued public statements that, because of its good compliance record, it would never plead guilty or "no contest" in an air pollution case. The suit involved alleged deterioration of neighboring residences and health effects linked to the firm's smokestack emissions. Nonetheless, the company later entered a *nolo contendere* plea after the court admitted dozens of citizen complaints as evidence. The firm's attorney stated that, despite continued belief in innocence, "it's not worth the cost involved to prove it."[23]

Perceptions of cost also vary with other factors in the compliance framework. Activity by enforcers and support groups can influence the "base line" of cost calculations that the firm employs. As Roberts and Bluhm (1981) found:

> What appeared to be cheap or expensive to each organization depended heavily on their expectations, which changed over time. Decision rules and standard operating procedures adjusted to new circumstances; what had once appeared to be an enormous and inappropriate burden could begin to seem normal and routine. Particulate controls are a good example. . . . Up to a point, they no longer seem unreasonable, unexpected, or impossible to bear, whereas twenty years ago they would clearly have been seen as all three (p. 337).

We find sufficient examples of cost-benefit calculations in the toxic dumping cases to support the conclusion that in some areas of environmental control the "rational man" model may be useful for devising control policies. Some executives compute profits from illegal dumping activities, analyze the probability of being apprehended, and assess their ability to avoid penalties or to dilute the negative publicity of a possible conviction. After a raid on the Los Angeles-based Aaro Company, when Aaro personnel were apprehended in the act of discharging toxics into the Los Angeles city sewers, the city attorney described the company motivation: An Aaro executive did not wish to spend $7,000 a month to dispose properly of wastes into a permitted facility "when he could do it, in effect, for free by pouring it down the sewer."[24]

In thinking in cost-benefit terms, the target may take the long run into consideration. A company may seek a precedent-setting victory which would remove any threat of future prosecution. One auto executive described a low-probability defense to an EPA action this way: "Quite frankly, what we were looking for in litigating that particular case was kind of no-harm no-fault decision. It might have been a longshot. . . . We didn't get it."[25]

From the government perspective, business targets can affect the cost-benefit calculation by strategically manipulating legal procedure. A routine enforcement activity can be very costly. In *Oxford Mushroom*,[26] the EPA was unable to quash a subpoena of the administrator to testify personally in a distant city courtroom on his involvement in rule promulgation; the court concluded that the administrative burden and inconvenience were "slight." But slight inconveniences aggregated over several cases can lead government officials to step back from prosecution in all but very strong cases.

Innovative criminal and civil sanctions offered to address white-collar and corporate crime suggest that the nature of the incentive or penalty, rather than the nature of the law, may most strongly determine the deterrence and compliance-promoting power of regulatory performance. A series of civil suits[27] may be costly to the company's image. A well-publicized administrative order may be timely in a given economic environment. Conference and conciliation with the new regime of a firm can also be influential if professionally undertaken by top agency administrators. Perhaps less important than whether a punishment or incentive derives from a civil or criminal cause of action are the costs which the firm associates with an enforcement approach, the behavior required of a businessman for noncompliance, and the attitude of the regulatee toward the overall regulatory policy. These are mediated by several characteristics of enforcement policy addressed below.

Fairness, Legitimacy, and Rationality of Enforcement Policy

Although strong enforcement efforts in certain situations can produce compliance (Boydstunm 1975; Kelling et al., 1974; Muir, 1967), perceived fairness of enforcement promotes business's willingness to comply and makes specific enforcement attempts more acceptable (Roberts and Bluhm, 1981; Rodgers, 1973; Stolnick, 1968; Stigler, 1970). Conversely, if sanctions are considered excessive, a businessman may assume that a law is not likely to be enforced or, if enforced, that it should be challenged (Argyris et al., 1978; Levin, 1972; Packer, 1968; Sabatier and Mazmanian, 1978). Industry may take a posture of defiance, testing an enforcement policy in practice, if not legally. This reaction explains why some companies respond differently to civil and criminal sanctions. The deterrent objective of civil sanctions is more understandable to businessmen: It seems more reasonable than punishment linked to criminal sanctions.

In a sense, any enforcement scheme that business accepts might be labeled "fair"; all others are "unfair." One corporate executive admitted: "I think equity is basically a debating point because if I want to go and resist your proposed regulation, I will always use the equity argument, will always seek one, will always find one."[28]

But some objective indicators of unfairness exist. Industry cites as inequitable approaches to the choosing of enforcement targets. The American automobile industry considers itself more vulnerable to suit than other pollution sources.[29] "Government attitude is the key. . . . We would like an even handed approach," one automobile company executive summarized.[30] The industry criticizes the EPA's implementation of the selective enforcement audit (SEA), used to monitor compliance with emission control requirements; American companies are reportedly subjected to SEA out of proportion to the numbers of vehicles they manufacture. The EPA personnel are said to travel to Japan for audits only when the weather is bad in the United States.[31]

Other automobile company executives complain that the control of pollution should be analyzed in terms of cost to society; from the focus on the automobile industry gross inequities result:

If there needs to be control of these pollutants, surely it should be done at the least cost to the customers, to the public. You don't do that by squeezing automobiles right down to the very last drop of blood if you could have done it cheaper, such as by controlling electrical generating plants which also release the same substances. That is in fact what has happened. The automobile has been squeezed almost to the breaking point.[32]

Business complains when it seeks enforcement linked to political ambitions—for example, a prosecutor trying to develop a national reputation by pursuing highly publicized environmental lawsuits. One automobile executive said:

You garner more votes by attacking industry and appearing to uphold the little man against big industry. You have more votes than by taking a more reasonable approach.[33]

Stationary sources also argue the equity issue. The debate over plans to achieve federal pollution control standards in the air quality regions is a case in point. For example, the revised SCAQMD plan, announced in late 1982, admits that the Los Angeles basin will not be able to meet the 1987 standards for ozone. Under one interpretation, the petroleum industry and the electric power generators would incur about 80 percent of the overall expense of clean up.[34] This allocation may seem reasonable because these industries do account for a large percentage of the air pollution problem. But while the plan was being developed elected officials in California were evading the federal requirement to impose automobile inspection and maintenance programs. The region has six million sources of pollution in the form of automobiles. Mobile sources account for 50 percent of reactive organic gases and much larger percentages of nitrogen oxide and carbon monoxide. In this context, business strongly questions the fairness of selecting individual industries for the most expensive controls.

Business may actively oppose an enforcement effort when it perceives sanctions as excessive. A Chrysler corporation spokesman called "outrageous"[35] a fine of $400,000 for what he judged to be a trivial violation. The company was also shocked to learn that another emission control violation could have resulted in penalties of $91 million.[36] Identical sanctions for grossly different violations also lead to criticism,[37] as do sanctions imposed after requirements that business considers infeasible or for which government does not provide technical assistance.[38]

The regulated industry bemoans lodging of both criminal and civil powers in the same agency:

So that when you get yourself into a bargaining situation with an attorney over what should be a simple matter, although he doesn't necessarily say it, you know he's got the brick in his hand that he can threaten you with and can use . . . bringing criminal sanctions if he doesn't like the way the civil case is going. There are only a very few areas in the Justice Department where they have combined civil and criminal [powers] as in the Land and Natural Resources division. And that can lead to . . . substantial abuse.[39]

In some circumstances the failure to clearly communicate the enforcement strategy might pose a hardship for a firm. Industry has come to expect some notice of violation before action is taken, and this reliance has become part of the business-government relationship. In *Frezzo*, the plaintiffs argued that the EPA "must either give them some notice of alleged violations of the Federal Water Pollution Control Act, or institute a civil action before pursuing criminal remedies under the Act."[40]

The court decided otherwise but noted the existence of conflicting legislative history on the issue:

> Senator Muskie expressed the view in the Senate's consideration of the Conference Committee Report that an abatement order or civil action was mandatory under the Act. . . . A similar view was espoused by Representative Harsha in the House during debate on the House bill.[41]

Nevertheless, the court relied on the final House Committee Report "which clearly indicated that written notice of the violation, administrative, civil, or criminal remedies under the Act were to be *alternative* remedies."[42]

What can be done to increase the sense of fairness of environmental law enforcement? Government-business contracts can foster a sense of equity. Some executives report that they are involved throughout the development of rules and of enforcement strategy, and they would consider it a corporate blunder if they learned of a regulation only after it was published in the *Federal Register*. Such persons appear to be more receptive to government activity. One vice-president described his corporation's intelligence work this way:

> So we would tend automatically to resist these [regulatory] ideas because of that inability [to know about them in advance]. . . . We want to keep track of what's going on, what ideas are surfacing, how they're being surfaced, where they're being surfaced which means you have to know a lot of people . . . in the intelligence sense. Now that's the extreme leading edge.[43]

Intelligence involves keeping informed of governmental activity at the federal, state, and local levels and monitoring corporate affiliate groups and union concerns and interests. Participation in the enforcement phase includes informal contacts during the period of development of agency strategies. Some regional EPA offices "would like to work with you to resolve what they perceive to be a problem. . . . Others tend to be much more like state troopers—you know, they've caught you in a violation and there's punishment."[44]

An expanding literature offers mediation of environmental disputes as one approach to fostering a sense of fairness in enforcement practices (Chapter 3). Although not all alleged violations are amenable to mediation (when, for example, noncompliance is egregious, deliberate, organized, and seriously health threatening, cooperative approaches may be inappropriate), mediation may effectively resolve many cases (Edelman and Walline, 1984; Patton, 1984). If properly orchestrated, mediation can avoid a firm's adversarial reaction to detection of (or speculation about) an environmental problem. Furthermore, mediation may conserve an agency's enforcement resources for more significant violations. Finally, interactive processes can promote communications between regulator and firm which generalize beyond the immediate problem.

Mediation can fit within an overall enforcement policy especially in situations in which possible disputes are recognized early. Parties to mediation can manage controversies in ways which avoid the formalization and rigidification of position required in litigation (Susskind et al., 1983). In dispute resolution (as opposed to the more amorphous process of rule negotiation), parties with an interest are likely to come forward, and therefore in the enforcement phase the challenge to cooperative approaches of interest group identification is less disturbing. Thus the same cooperative process which increases the firm's perception that government's environmental position is equitable may, in select cases, expedite dispute resolution.

Business also stresses rationality of the enforcement strategy. The dimension is subjective but regulatees consistently voice the theme. The firm criticizes some enforcement activity as irrational because the violation is *de minimis*. Government attempts to punish industry activity that has "zero public health consequences" are criticized as wasteful. Minor runoffs, temporary equipment failures, and small, inadvertent discharges of pollutants should be reported by the violator but not be subject to government action.

Government efforts are called irrational when enforcement activities are expensive, time-consuming and ultimately ineffective. One top executive described an air pollution action against his as "sheer lunacy." The case was resolved in the defendant's favor. The proceeding was counterproductive to the EPA's mission because it diverted scarce enforcement resources.

"Government conceives of industry as the fat cats."[45] Representatives of the automobile-manufacturing industry articulated this theme while questioning the rationality of certain enforcement activities. Regulators centered attention on the auto industry because historically car making has been quite profitable. The position has an ironic note. Industry respondents gleefully offered economic difficulties as proof that the effects of regulation had not been exaggerated by the corporate sector.[46]

Certainty and Imminence

Certainty and imminence of enforcement or reward foster organizational compliance (Chambliss, 1966; Ermann and Lundman, 1975; Gibbs, 1968; Horai and Tedeschi, 1969; Rodgers, 1973). These dimensions are not easily established; a variety of events can militate against a sanction affecting a target. Some inhibitors involve the agency's inability to secure sufficient evidence to make a case. Industry can be quite hostile to compliance monitoring. Opposition to OSHA inspection is legendary, but problems are not limited to the occupational sphere. Recently government employees have suggested that EPA enforcement agents carry weapons during inspections of alleged violations by organized crime of waste disposal laws.[47] In one year alone a dozen violent or close to violent incidents involving EPA inspection agents were reported, ranging from firing on agents to releasing attack dogs on an air quality inspector.[48] On the site, the inspector may be inhibited or intimidated. An employee of an air quality management district reported:

> So I checked by again in about a month and they were smoking again [describing the stacks in a firm he had been inspecting]. So I went in, and unfortunately when I went in the guy had just received a letter for the last

violation and a fine included, and he was already upset. He was fed up. So I was trying to be very careful with him. . . . It was a very sensitive issue. This time I was in . . . the small room where the guy was operating. I didn't want to stop him because the tires were spinning and it was very dangerous to get in there. So . . . before I could explain anything he just flew off the handle and threatened to kill me and he was going to knock me through the window, saying: "You can't tell me I'm not doing anything to stop the emission." He was doing it for his employees because he thought he was being belittled . . . and he started cussing. He said, "I don't have to sign that ticket" I said, "You don't have to," and I just laid the ticket down and said, "I'm not going to argue with you because you're obviously upset," and I left. But all the way out of the plant he's yelling and screaming at me and all the employees are looking, and he's calling me every name you can possibly imagine.[49]

Personnel movement within the company and diffusion of responsibility for the firm's actions can make threats of sanctions and promises of rewards meaningless. Prosecution can fall outside of the time frames according to which personnel operate, or enforcement efforts may not be directed to appropriate parties. Government often reduces the credibility of enforcement threats by extending compliance deadlines (Marcus, 1980), as was the case for electroplating operations which have consistently failed to meet standards under the Water Pollution Control Act regarding discharges of heavy metals.[50] *The Wall Street Journal* reported that many companies were watching to see if the EPA would actually impose the very large threatened fines on General Motors for violating these rules. In particular, smaller firms were monitoring the EPA-GM negotiations "before they go ahead with large investments to clean up discharges from electroplating plants and other industrial sources."[51]

Numerous organizational deficiencies counter imminence and certainty of enforcement. These range from inadequate resources for surveying likely noncomplying sites to agency inexperience in law enforcement and in use of sophisticated testing equipment.[52] Some attempts to make enforcement more efficient may actually be counterproductive. Commenting on the failure of the government in pollution control cases to decentralize enforcement, one former assistant United States attorney described some of the costs of so-called coordination:

The problem with criminal enforcement is that the [government] insists that the case bounce around for a couple of months [within the bureaucracy]. The right way to do it is to have the agent in the field work directly with the U.S. Attorney. This avoids the hassle of [a case] bouncing to [Washington] D.C. Centralization makes good sense in a tax case, but not here. . . . It discourages good cases from being brought. You need to turn the prosecutor loose with an enthusiastic agent who wishes to make a case.[53]

Agency failure to monitor consent agreements also produces skepticism about the imminence of enforcement activity. Even cases of obvious fault and guilt take considerable time and enormous judicial resources to process. It may be years before the midnight dumper, "caught in the act," has exhausted all options within the legal system and finally has to serve a sentence or pay a fine. Litigation can postpone the final articulation of an order. Budget and staff limitations, absence of data, lack of interagency coordination, and agency reputations of enforcement laxness all reduce the potency of regulatory threats (Clinard and Yeager, 1980).

The *Distler* case (Chapter 1) illustrates one message given by the criminal justice system. Recall that the defendant was a small businessman who was indicted on several counts of water pollution law violations for dumping of hazardous wastes. He received a record sentence in an environmental law case: two years in prison and a fine of $50,000. But it took over four and one-half years to end his legal appeals; by that time the defendant had developed a new reputation in the community. He had begun a successful business, one that required licensing by a state board that reviews the character of the applicant. Finally he did enter a minimum security prison and served part of the sentence.

Well-known aspects of criminal procedure partially explain the time period between violations and punishment. Whatever the merits of excuses, attributions of fault to the government, appeals, requests for rehearings, and other time-consuming legal maneuverings counter an image of effective government sanctions.

Surprise and "Compliant for a Day"

Publication of enforcement strategies that informs violators of the probabilities of being inspected, sued, or prosecuted also dilutes the perceived imminence of enforcement (Diver, 1980). Industrial targets can come into compliance for the period in which government inspects, or companies can otherwise alter behavior just enough to avoid prosecution and then return to noncompliant performance. The EPA decided in February 1982 that "no enforcement action would be undertaken" when a violation "does not evidence intentional or repeated disregard for the law."[54] At one point in the early months of the administration of President Reagan, the EPA simply announced that, rather than using the adversarial approach that had characterized the past four years, the agency would "sit down and discuss the pollution problem with" industry. The aim would be to come up with a mutually acceptable schedule for achieving compliance,[55] not to identify violators and prosecute them. And in October 1982 the agency publicized its even newer enforcement priorities for criminal cases: over half were to be aimed at hazardous waste violations under Superfund and the Resource Conservation and Recovery Act and at "willful contempt of . . . consent decrees."[56] The EPA did not guarantee companies not covered by these sets of environmental regulations that they would not be investigated; but the perceived probability of an enforcement action decreased with the agency announcements.

An earlier description of EPA enforcement priorities is another case in point. Overall enforcement efforts were to focus on: (1) conduct causing substantial harm or posing health hazards; (2) sustained and significant violations in circumstances in which compliance is clearly feasible; (3) falsification, concealment, and destruction of material records and information; and (4) willful contempt of civil consent orders. Polluting industries can reasonably conclude on the basis of these criteria that enforcement activity will center in the last two areas, where violations are egregious and government can identify targets through simple routines. A cynical interpretation is that such factor analyses are a way in which government can wink at industry while announcing its enforcement policy. A notorious example involved the regulation of lead in gasoline in 1982. Reportedly the EPA administrator, in response to a waiver request of the federal rules which would allow greater lead content in gasoline, "did not grant the waiver in writing. But . . . she gave her word that she would not enforce the existing standards, and she encouraged . . . [the petitioner] . . . to ignore them."[57] According to a document written by one of the participants at a meeting with the administrator:

> We all thanked her and then left to meet [the assistant administrator] for a social visit. [One of the petitioners] however, remained behind with [the administrator] momentarily. When he came out he told us that the administrator explained to him that she couldn't actually tell us to go out and break the law, but she hoped that we had gotten the message.[58]

An environmental agency communicates that enforcement is neither imminent nor certain when it awards variances to noncompliers and extends deadlines to meet once strictly articulated standards. Or government may simply drop, as it did in 1981, dozens of enforcement actions, some because of statute limitations problems.[59] These decisions do not go unnoticed. Subsequent to an extension deadline when manufacturers were to substitute water for oil in producing paint, the *Los Angeles Times* reported under the headline, "Smog Board Again Extends Deadline on Latex Enamels":

> Paint manufacturers have been given another two years to learn how to make good quality water-based interior enamels as a way to help reduce smog in South Coast Air Basin. Friday's action marked the seventh time since it first adopted air pollution controls on the contents of paint cans that the board of the South Coast Air Quality Management District changed the rule. Had the rule not been amended, oil-based enamels would have been barred from store shelves and manufacturing plants next month. . . . The Board left the way open to extend the deadline on enamels again in two years, if the industry shows that it still cannot produce suitable paints.[60]

Regulators often describe extensions as part of an innovative and flexible enforcement policy laid out in prescriptive terms, to make it appear as if no major change in enforcement approach is planned. Government will allow extensions only if a series of conditions are met, but the conditions may be no more than a rearticulation of industry's reasons in insisting it cannot comply. Consider the criteria imposed by the EPA for new compliance deadlines with air regulations by stationary sources:

> Both the Justice Department and EPA's Office of Legal and Enforcement Counsel have concluded that a district court has equity power to fashion relief that allows a source to continue in operation beyond 1982 while taking steps to come into compliance . . . if . . . at a minimum all of the following threshold criteria are met: 1) the source must be unable to comply by December 31, 1982, other than by shutdown; 2) the source must demonstrate that there is a public interest in continued operation of the source which outweighs the environmental costs of an additional period of noncompliance;

and 3) if there is any doubt about the source's financial condition, the source must demonstrate that it will have sufficient funds to be able to comply expeditiously.[61]

Although nonjudicious use of variances and extensions clearly counters industry's motivation to comply, it is not always clear under what conditions government should grant a petition for more time. In administrative hearings, often run like litigation, the complex trade-offs involved in implementation of environmental law are developed in great detail. Petitioner may argue that an extension now will buy greater compliance in the future. The company seeking the variance may assert that it is waiting for a new technology to enter the market and that a vendor promises new controls "within a short period of time." The petitioner will outline the effects of imposing controls immediately; these may include great monetary costs and layoffs that are linked to stricter controls. Agencies committed to maintaining original compliance deadlines will do so in the face of immense pressure for delays. These delays, considered individually, promise greater benefits with little cost.

Changes in enforcement policy militate against compliance. Industry dislikes uncertainties that derive from alterations in case settlement policy; yet inconsistency across administrations, coupled with knowledge of the time required for careful investigation and filing of charges, allows potential violators to estimate the probability and timing of a sanction's imposition.

Enforcement personnel changes with political administration, and these shifts weaken overall enforcement effectiveness. In 1980, the federal government was increasing use of criminal sanctions, but three months later the criminal strategy was set aside; the EPA now favored decentralization of enforcement and placed faith in approaches that rely on industry profit motivations. Substitution of conservative, business oriented heads of enforcement for liberal, environmental activists within the major federal agencies leads to the conclusion that the federal role in environmental protection will decline. Subsequently, subordinate activist lawyers leave government. They are replaced with people who are more sympathetic to explanations of noncompliance or who, because of inexperience, do not fare well against industry lawyers. In this regulatory environment, the polluting business may contest enforcement activities that previously would be considered certain losses.

Despite textbook presentations of effective compliance systems, the unexceptional performances of regulators, government and business lawyers, and spokespersons also affect information flow. Mediocre performance is not a surprise in light of the demands on both regulators and the regulated. Both industry and government face turbulent regulatory environments; there is much to be learned and much that is not known in the field of environmental protection. Proceedings aimed at improving controls are often long and laborious, not because of malicious motives of those involved, but because of their inability to comprehend or to fully process relevant information.

The absence of machinelike processing of information is not limited to the administration of policy. Policy making also suffers from institutional inexperience. What appear as good ideas for getting compliance when considered in the silence of a professor's office or in an administrator's diary are often difficult to communicate persuasively to groups which must be won over. Use of incentives techniques is one area plagued by complexity. A SCAQMD Board member candidly lectured its advisory board:

> Frankly, despite the number of times you have presented the idea of full cost emissions charges, I doubt if more than three people in the room (of a Board numbering a dozen) knew what the hell you were talking about.[62]

Enter the Courts

Judicial proceedings can also counter general compliance as they contribute to an impression that enforcement is uncertain and slow (Marcus, 1980). Part of the delay in environmental law has to do with normal judicial proceedings and may not be greater than in other areas. For example, the average period from time of filing a complaint to resolution of a case under the California Environmental Quality Act[63] is less than two years even when appeals are made; and cases are completed under the Michigan Environmental Protection Act[64] in well under a year.[65] But environmental law cases are not often expedited and the opportunity for getting continuances are great.

Use of innovative, ingenious, and time-consuming defenses is widespread. Consider again *Oxford Mushroom.*[66] The defendant argued that:

> The Government circumvented the letter and the spirit of the Act by failing to afford the Administrator the opportunity to become involved in a meaningful way in the case . . . and that only through questioning Schramm and Costle may the extent of their apparent and actual control over the enforcement of the Federal Water Pollution Control Act and the initiation of criminal prosecution be learned.[67]

The United States had moved for a motion to quash subpoenas of Jack J. Schramm, a regional EPA official, and of the EPA administrator, Douglas Costle. The government described the busy schedules of these men; but the court, not moved by the agency's response, denied its motion. Requiring attendance by high-level agency personnel at individual judicial proceedings could effectively halt enforcement activity. It is unlikely that *Oxford Mushroom* actually decided that the testimony of the EPA administrator was essential to a fair trial. Rather, the litigation strategy may have been to make prosecution personally costly to agency administrators with the aim of encouraging a favorable settlement. (To be fair, another interpretation is conceivable. The defendant may have concluded that he was subject to criminal action for practices that, at the very worst, were slight aberrations from standard farming practices in his locale. A jail sentence was a possibility and a fine almost a certainty. Adverse publicity had already occurred. To call the "boss of the agency" who was suing the boss of the defendant company may appear quite logical to a small businessman. Such logic, in fact, explains a good share of business conclusions about the effects of regulatory law.)

A more common example of manipulation of judicial proceedings sees business producing for the regulatory agency reams of irrelevant information, ostensibly in support of the defendant's assertions. The strategy is legal but adds to the time necessary to reach a judgment. Requesting a jury can also postpone a trial, although in environmental law cases the use of a jury may not favor the defendant.

Judicial attention to due process and property rights is an important part of the American legal system that compliance goals should not overwhelm. Nonetheless, application of traditional understandings of these rights is often strained to protect white-collar defendants.

Studies confirm that the courts view white-collar crimes (of which some environmental violations are examples) as a special category. Mann, Wheeler, and Sarat (1980), using interviews of federal court judges, conclude that in sentencing white-collar criminals judges are primarily interested in general deterrence. Judges consider the process of indictment to be punishment enough for the white-collar criminal, and they wish to limit the harm done to innocent parties, including the relatives of the convicted. Rather than addressing allegations on the basis of established facts and law, the judiciary often adds an element of compassion and understanding in environmental compliance suits— a factor which would be unusual if not bizarre in other criminal cases.

In *A-Z Decasing*,[68] a suit charging a battery company with polluting soils with toxic chemicals by improper production and disposal methods, the judge stated that he was "perfectly satisfied" that A-Z was "trying to comply" with the California Health and Safety Code. At a hearing on a permanent injunction, the defense succeeded in having the court delay for several months a decision on whether to compel a cleanup. The court hoped that the defendant could show that it had corrected the remaining violations. Similarly in *Capri*,[69] the judge, declaring that "the time for any danger to the community has long since passed,"[70] excused the defendant from probation and dropped a contempt of court citation. The court considered whether a general outcome, the clean up of hazardous acids and contaminated soils, had been achieved rather then whether deadlines established for that outcome had been met. Originally, the company's owner had been sentenced to thirty days in jail, and a $3,000 fine had been imposed. The court suspended the sentence to allow the owner of Capri to clean up the site. The lawyer for the defendant declared the judge's action a "complete vindication" of his client's behavior. Through such treatment, government passes a message to industry that, even in the 1980s, environmental violations are viewed differently from other crimes: the threat of sanctions, although forcefully made by a small group of environmentally oriented government officials, will not always result in true criminal punishment.

In certain situations the judiciary will also establish the burden of proof in ways that make it difficult for government lawyers to prevail. Moreover, judges are typically not familiar with evidentiary matters in environmental cases. Especially in the lower courts judges may lack the background to assess arguments on causation and proof in cases, for example, in which health effects of pollution are at issue; when experts differ strongly about the relevance or meaning of a scientific study or about the cumulative significance of many studies; or when the intricacies of risk assessment are being laid out. Special attention is required to educate the judiciary on issues relating to probabilities of one or another harmful outcome, on uncertainties inherent in predictions of harm and about the wide range of understandings within the scientific community as to what is a health effect of concern. Effects that may manifest themselves in twenty to thirty years and may lead to other types of health problems are different from the more clearly binary events reviewed by the judiciary in other areas of law.

Delays in decision making caused by the complexity of evidence are not unique to the courts. But the decision rules employed by the judiciary and the procedural protections it provides postpone the impact on business of a government enforcement action.

Continuity and Consistency

To promote compliance the enforcement or incentive policy must be perceived as continuous (Schwartz and Orleans, 1967; Skolnick, 1968), that is, not subject to change with shifts in the economy or in administrative personnel. Business may urge continuity by reference to enforcement of a particular mandate, or it may evaluate the total program of enforcement within an agency or within government generally (Ericson and Gibbs, 1975). Business knows whether the legislature has ceased its oversight function, leaving follow-up to an indifferent, understaffed agency or perhaps even to one that is hostile to the law. Industry monitors whether the judiciary has interfered with an agency's approach. Whether a priority item under one administration will remain so under another is important intelligence for a regulated firm. The private sector will comply with many regulations only if government cares whether it complies.

A former EPA employee expressed the need for consistency:

> It is unreasonable to expect the "assembly line" [investigating and analyzing cases, negotiating a settlement or bringing suit] to work if it is regularly dismantled or reorganized or if top management does not send consistent signals about its commitment to making the system operate.[71]

The ex-enforcement agent was complaining about interference with his attempts to negotiate a settlement in the *Inmont* case,[72] which involved a hazardous waste cleanup. After he found the company "suddenly" unwilling to respond to his settlement offer, he learned that another EPA administrator had approached Inmont with a different summary of the EPA's position: a $700,000 settlement package and not the $850,000 figure he was using.[73]

Shifts in enforcement policy in the early years of President Reagan's administration were numerous. Enforcement procedures were drafted and redrafted with changing emphasis on cooperation, civil penalties, and selective criminal enforcement. The government moved enforcement authority back and forth from Washington to the regional office.[74] In assuming the role of enforcement counsel at the EPA, a new unit director announced that his guidelines would "supersede the policies and procedures issued by the (former) enforcement counsel . . . which are revoked in their entirety."[75] The "old policies" had been announced just six weeks earlier. EPA observers predicted significant additional changes in policy once William Ruckleshaus assumed the office of administrator and again when he resigned.

Industry finds ludicrous and unconvincing regular statements of a new stringency or a new attitude toward enforcement. Just before President Carter was defeated in his bid for reelection, the Assistant Attorney General for Land and Natural Resources promised, "Now, however, I believe we stand on the threshold of significant change in the nature of environmental enforcement litigation."[76] When business people hear these grandiose statements about energetic approaches to promoting compliance they may be somewhat concerned, but they also know that effective enforcement policy requires a commitment of resources over time and more than the impassioned rhetoric of an individual in a lame-duck political administration. To be sure, the Carter administration had put much of industry on warning that enforcement of the environmental laws would be of high priority, but affected businesses also recognize the important function they themselves play in determining the longevity of any political regime.

Solomon and Nowak (1980) describe an impact of inconsistent enforcement policy in another regulatory arena. The initial success of the Federal Trade Commission's use of consent orders to control corporate behavior was threatened by modifications which greatly altered industry willingness to cooperate.

> The prospect of industrywide regulation has dampened the receptivity of the targeted companies to the potential benefits of compliance with the consent order provisions. Instead, the companies have retreated to an adversarial position, certain that no good can come out of administrative intervention. (p. 140)

To be effective, an enforcement approach, perhaps any approach, must be perceived as having some staying power.[77]

On the practical side, businesspeople conclude that an agency which demonstrates a long-standing commitment to achieving compliance will withstand industry attempts to erode the agency's influence. Nonetheless, the effects of continuity derive from dynamics other than the practical. Continuity in orientation to achieving the goals of a regulatory program leads to a kind of social contract that industry enters with the government. It is a contract that becomes background for business decisions and planning, although the private sector may seek changes at the margin through institutional means. In this sense, regulatory programs become another cost of doing business—the equivalent of complying with a well-known although thoroughly disliked tax law.

NOTES

1. Interview with James Frezzo, December 28, 1981.
2. Letter to the Editor, *Los Angeles Times*, July 29, 1983, Metro Section, at 4, col. 4.
3. Survey enforcers discussed in Chapter 2, p. 36.
4. See Chapter 2, pg. 36.
5. Interview F. (To maintain anonymity respondents are referred to here by letter only.)
6. Interview A.
7. Interview X.
8. Marc G. Kurzman and Judd Golden "Formaldehyde Litigation: A Beginning," *Trial 19* (January 1983), at 82–85; "Insurance Law and Asbestosis—When Is Coverage of a Progressive Disease Triggered?" *Washington Law Review* 58 (1982), at 63; Anderson, Warshauer, and Coffin, "Asbestos Health Hazards Compensation Act: A Legislative Solution to a Litigation Crisis," *Journal of Legislation* 10 (1983), at 25.
9. The appropriateness of civil law because of its aim of correction, rather than punishment, was also noted by a few respondents to the enforcers survey (as discussed in Chapter 2, p. 36).

10. Interview X.
11. *Duquesne Light Co. vs. EPA,* 698 F. 2d 456, at 463. For more on NCP, see Chapter 3.
12. Interview B.
13. *Inside EPA,* February 11, 1983, at 14.
14. *Duquesne Light Co. v. EPA,* 698 F. 2d 456, at 486.
15. Interview E.
16. Ira Reiner, *Los Angeles Times,* May 26, 1982.
17. Personal communication from John T. Scholz, June 19, 1984.
18. *The Register* (Santa Ana, California), December, 1983, at A1, col. 2.
19. *State ex rel. Brown v. Dayton Malleable, Inc.* 438 N.E. 2d 120 (Ohio).
20. Interview E.
21. Interview E.
22. Interview C.
23. Interview H.
24. Ira Reiner, *Los Angeles Times,* May 26, 1982.
25. Interview D.
26. *United States v. Oxford Royal Mushroom* (see Appendix for complete citation.)
27. One example involved a large chemical company after government had acted civilly against seven of its plants. A spokesman concluded: "There's a heightened awareness (of environmental matters) within the company." *The Wall Street Journal,* September 19, 1981 at 48, col. 1.
28. Interview B.
29. Interviews A, B. See also *The Wall Street Journal,* June 6, 1982, at 1, 25: " . . . domestic automakers complain that it is inequitable that the foreign car makers get off so lightly."
30. Interview X.
31. Interview Y.
32. Interview D.
33. Interview Z.
34. *Los Angeles Times,* August 31, 1982, Part II, at 1, cols. 5, 6.
35. Interview (interviewee not indicated to preserve confidentiality).
36. *United States v. Chrysler Corporation* No. 76-1800 (D.D.C. filed Sept. 27, 1976).
37. Interview C.
38. Interview E.
39. Interview C. 42% of the surveyed enforcers, discussed in Chapter 2, p. 36, who are authorized to employ both civil and criminal sanctions reported that they were most satisfied with resolution of cases when a combination of criminal and civil sanctions was pursued as compared to 8% when criminal sanctions only were pursued and 25% when civil sanctions only were pursued.
40. 602 F.2d 1123, 1126 (1979).
41. 602 F.2d 1123, 1126 (1979).
42. 602 F.2d 1123, 1126 (1979).
43. Interview B.
44. Interview C.
45. Interview D. See Frezzo's similar complaint in Chapter 1.
46. Interviews C and B.
47. In July, 1984, DOJ temporarily deputized EPA agents as U.S. marshals *The Wall Street Journal* January 7, 1985 at 14, col.1.
48. *The New York Times,* October 26, 1983, cols. 5, 6.

49. Interview H.
50. *The Wall Street Journal,* June 29, 1984.
51. *The Wall Street Journal,* June 29, 1984.
52. *The Wall Street Journal,* January 7, 1985.
53. Interview with Bruce Chasan January 8, 1985.
54. *Inside EPA,* February 26, 1982, at p. 8.
55. *Inside EPA,* November 13, 1981, at p. 12.
56. *Inside EPA,* October 29, 1982, at p.12.
57. Eliot Marshall, "The Politics of Lead," *Science* 216 (April 1982), 496.
58. Ibid.
59. "EPA, Citing State Deferrals, Asks Justice to Drop 49 Enforcement Cases." *Inside EPA,* November 13, 1981, at p. 14.
60. *Los Angeles Times,* August 8, 1983, Part II at 3, col.2.
61. Quoted in *Inside EPA,* September 24, 1982, at 3, 4. The EPA's reasonable efforts program is of interest here. The program, not authorized by legislation, addresses EPA treatment of nonattainment areas where compliance with the 1987 Clean Air Act standards is considered impossible. Under the program, rather than bringing enforcement actions, the agency will review the control measures proposed by nonattainment air quality districts. The agency will share information about innovative control strategies used in other districts, and it will assist the nonattainment district to adopt rules which will move toward attainment in the long term. EPA will then undertake cooperative audits to determine if control measures are being implemented. Among the program aims is the avoidance of sanctions where reasonable efforts are being made to achieve air quality results. The program is controversial. See Chapter 6, pp. 117, 118.
62. South Coast Air Quality Management District Advisory Council meeting, January 23, 1985.
63. Cal. Pub. Res. Code §§ 210001 et seq.
64. Mich. Comp. Law Ann §§ 691.1201–.1207 (Supp. 1973).
65. Precise statistics are not available. These estimates come from Sax and DiMento (1974); telephone conversation with attorney in enforcement division of Environmental Analysis Group, State of Michigan Department of Natural Resources, October 27, 1983; and with W. Dickson, Legal Clerk, California Resources Agency, October 27, 1983.
66. *United States v. Oxford Royal Mushroom.* (See Appendix for complete citation.)
67. *Oxford Royal Mushroom,* Defendants Response to Motion to Quash Subpoena, at 3.
68. *A-Z Decasing* (see Appendix for complete citation).
69. *Capri* (see Appendix for complete citation).
70. *Los Angeles Times,* August 21, 1982, Part II, at 7, col. 1.
71. *Los Angeles Times,* April 3, 1982.
72. *Inmont* (see Appendix for complete citation).
73. *Inside EPA,* April 9, 1982, at 8.
74. See "Sullivan: Civil Cases, Penalties Cut, State, Criminal Actions Stressed," *Inside EPA,* Nov. 13, 1981 at 13, 14; and "Perry Shifts Policy to Give EPA Regions Power to Issue Superfund Orders," *Inside EPA,* Oct. 22, 1982 at 1.
75. *Inside EPA,* April 30, 1982 at 11, 12.
76. Testimony by James Moorman before the Senate Subcommittee on Environmental Pollution, May 24, 1979, quoted in N. Tennille, Jr. Remarks to ABA Natural Resources Law Section "Criminal Liability Under Federal Environmental and Energy Laws: The House Counsel's Perspective," Denver, Colorado, March 24, 1982, at 2.
77. Gilbert Geis has offered an alternative view of the effects on compliance in policy under cer-

tain conditions. Absence of consistency prevents a firm from behaving in a rational and self-protective manner. In a sense, a target is forced to be on guard constantly, making compliance much more risky. This phenomenon may be more relevant for companies prone to avoid regulations in stable regulatory environments. Personal correspondence, May 20, 1985. And Sax has argued:

> We must put aside the dominating idea that the legal system is to be designed essentially to institutionalize stability and security. Probably nothing is more urgently required in environmental management than institutions for controlled instability. . . . The old idea of a stable and predictable regulatory agency, patiently negotiating solutions that will then be fixed and unquestionable for years, or even decades, is hopelessly outdated. A mixture of legal techniques—designed to destabilize arrangements that have become too secure—is precisely what is needed for a milieu in which rapid change is the central feature. (J.L. Sax, "A General Survey of the Problem," in *Science for Better Environment*, Ed. Science Council of Japan. 1976, pp. 753, 755, 756. Quoted in Anderson, Mandelker, and Tarlock, *Environmental Protection: Law and Policy* (Boston: Little, Brown, 1984.))

Reading 2

The Negotiator's Dilemma: Creating and Claiming Value*

David A. Lax and James K. Sebenius

This chapter investigates the essence of the negotiation process. We assume that each negotiator strives to advance his interests, whether they are narrowly conceived or include such concerns as improving the relationship, acting in accord with conceptions of equity, or furthering the welfare of others. Negotiators must learn, in part from each other, what is jointly possible and desirable. To do so requires some degree of cooperation. But, at the same time, they seek to advance their individual interests. This involves some degree of competition.

That negotiation includes cooperation and competition, common and conflicting interests, is nothing new. In fact, it is typically understood that these elements are both present and can be disentangled. Deep down, however, some people believe that the elements of conflict are illusory, that meaningful communication will erase any such unfortunate misperceptions. Others see mainly competition and take the cooperative pieces to be minimal. Some overtly acknowledge the reality of each aspect but direct all their attention to one of them and wish, pretend, or act as if the other does not exist. Still others hold to a more balanced view that accepts both elements as significant but seeks to treat them separately. In this chapter, we argue that *all* these approaches are flawed.

A deeper analysis shows that the competitive and cooperative elements are inextricably entwined. In practice, they cannot be separated. This bonding is fundamentally important to the analysis, structuring, and conduct of negotiation. There is a central, inescapable tension between cooperative moves to create value jointly and competitive moves to gain individual advantage. This tension affects virtually all tactical and strategic choice. Analysts must come to grips with it; negotiators must manage it. Neither denial nor discomfort will make it disappear.

* Reprinted with permission of The Free Press, a division of Simon & Schuster, Inc., from *The manager as negotiator: Bargaining for cooperative and competitive gain* (pp. 29–45) by David A. Lax and James K. Sebenius. Copyright © 1986 by David A. Lax and James K. Sebenius. Citations in endnotes of this reading refer to source book.

Warring Conceptions of Negotiation

Negotiators and analysts tend to fall into two groups that are guided by warring conceptions of the bargaining process. In the left-hand corner are the "value creators" and in the right-hand corner are the "value claimers."

Value Creators

Value creators tend to believe that, above all, successful negotiators must be inventive and cooperative enough to devise an agreement that yields considerable gain to each party, relative to no-agreement possibilities. Some speak about the need for replacing the "win-lose" image of negotiation with "win-win" negotiation, from which all parties presumably derive great value. For example, suppose that the mayor of a southern city learns when negotiating with the city's police union that, compared to the union, she places relatively greater weight on wage reductions than on the composition of a civilian review board. She may find that offering changes in the composition of the board for previously unattainable wage reduction may create benefit for both parties compared to the otherwise likely agreement with higher wages and with the current civilian review board composition.

Communication and sharing information can help negotiators to create value jointly. Consider the case of a singer negotiating with the owner of an auditorium over payment for a proposed concert. They reached impasse over the size of the fee with the performer's demands exceeding the owner's highest offer. In fact, when the amount of the fixed payment was the issue, no possibility of agreement may have existed at all. The singer, however, based his demand on the expectation that the house would certainly be filled with fans while the owner projected only a half-capacity crowd. Ironically, this difference in their beliefs about attendance provided a way out. They reached a mutually acceptable arrangement in which the performer received a modest fixed fee plus a set percentage of the ticket receipts. The singer, given his beliefs, thus expected an adequate to fairly large payment; the concert-hall owner was happy with the agreement because he only expected to pay a moderate fee. This "contingent" arrangement, of the sort discussed in Chapter Five, permitted the concert to occur, leaving both parties feeling better off and fully willing to live with the outcome.

In addition to information sharing and honest communication, the drive to create value by discovering joint gains can require ingenuity and may benefit from a variety of techniques and attitudes. The parties can treat the negotiation as solving a joint problem; they can organize brainstorming sessions to invent creative solutions to their problems. They may succeed by putting familiar pieces of the problem together in ways that people had not previously seen, as well as by wholesale reformulations of the problem.

Roger Fisher and Bill Ury give an example that concerns the difficult Egyptian-Israeli negotiations over where to draw a boundary in the Sinai.[1] This appeared to be an absolutely classic example of zero-sum bargaining, in which each square mile lost to one party was the other side's gain. For years the negotiations proceeded inconclusively with proposed boundary lines drawn and redrawn on innumerable maps. On probing the real interests of the two sides, however, Egypt was found to care a great deal about sovereignty over the Sinai while Israel was heavily concerned with its security. As such, a creative solution could be devised to "unbundle" these different interests and give to each what it valued most. In the Sinai, this involved creating a demilitarized zone under the Egyptian flag. This had the effect of giving Egypt "sovereignty" and Israel "security." This situation exemplifies extremely common tendencies to assume that negotiators' interests are in direct opposition, a conviction that can sometimes be corrected by communicating, sharing information, and inventing solutions.

Value creators advocate exploring and cultivating shared interests in substance, in maintaining a working relationship, in having a pleasant nonstrident negotiation process, in mutually held norms or principles, and even in reaching agreement at all. The Marshall Plan for economic rehabilitation of postwar Europe arose in part from the common interests in a revitalized Europe seen by Truman, Marshall, many in Congress, as well as numerous key Europeans. The Marshall Plan thus created great value for many.

We create value by finding *joint gains* for all negotiating parties. A joint gain represents an improvement from each party's point of view; one's gain need not be another's loss. An extremely simple example makes the point. Say that two young boys each have three pieces of fruit. Willy, who hates bananas and loves pears, has a banana and two oranges. Sam, who hates pears and loves bananas, has a pear and two apples. The first move is easy: they trade banana for pear and are both happier. But after making this deal, they realize that they can still do better. Though each has a taste both for apples and oranges, a second piece of the same fruit is less desirable than the first. So they also swap an apple for an orange. The banana-pear exchange represents an improvement over the no-trade alternative; the apple-orange transaction that leaves each with three different kinds of fruit improves the original agreement—is a joint gain—for both boys.

The economist's analogy is simple: creativity has expanded the size of the pie under negotiation. Value creators see the essence of negotiating as expanding the pie, as pursuing joint gains. This is aided by openness, clear communication, sharing information, creativity, an attitude of joint problem solving, and cultivating common interests.

Value Claimers

Value claimers, on the other hand, tend to see this drive for joint gain as naive and weak-minded. For them, negotiation is hard, tough bargaining. The object of negotiation is to convince the other guy that he wants what you have to offer much more than you want what he has; moreover, you have all the time in the world while he is up against pressing deadlines. To "win" at negotiating—and thus make the other fellow "lose"—one must start high, concede slowly, exaggerate the value of concessions, minimize the benefits of the other's concessions, conceal information, argue forcefully on behalf of principles that imply favorable settlements, make commitments to accept only highly favorable agreements, and be willing to outwait the other fellow.

The hardest of bargainers will threaten to walk away or to retaliate harshly if their one-sided demands are not met; they may ridicule, attack, and intimidate their *adversaries*. For example, Lewis Glucksman, once the volatile head of trading activities at Lehman Brothers, the large investment banking firm, employed the hardest sort of bargaining tactics in his bid to wrest control of Lehman from then-Chairman Peter G. Peterson after being elevated to co-CEO status with Peterson. As co-CEO, Glucksman abruptly demanded full control of the firm, making a thinly veiled threat that unless his demands were met, he would provoke a civil war at Lehman and take the entire profitable trading department elsewhere. When Peterson and others desperately sought less damaging accommodation, Glucksman conveyed the impression that "his feet were set in cement," even if that meant the destruction of the firm. (Ultimately, Peterson left with a substantial money settlement and Glucksman presided briefly over a shaken Lehman that was soon sold at a bargain price to American Express.)

At the heart of this adversarial approach is an image of a negotiation with a winner and loser: "We are dividing a pie of fixed size and every slice I give to you is a slice I do not get; thus, I need to *claim* as much of the value as possible by giving you as little as possible."

A Fundamental Tension of Negotiation

Both of these images of negotiation are incomplete and inadequate. Value creating and value claiming are linked parts of negotiation. Both processes are present. No matter how much creative problem solving enlarges the pie, it must still be divided; value that has been created must be claimed. And, if the pie is not enlarged, there will be less to divide; there is more value to be claimed if one has helped create it first. An essential tension in negotiation exists between cooperative moves to create value and competitive moves to claim it.

While creating value by exchanging civilian review board provisions for wage reductions, the southern city mayor may be able to squeeze out large wage reductions for minor changes in the composition of the civilian review board. Or, the concert hall owner may offer the singer a percentage of the gate combined with a fixed fee that is just barely high enough to induce the singer to sign the contract. Even when parties to a potential agreement share strong common interests, one side may claim the lion's share of the value the agreement creates. To achieve agreement on plans to rebuild Europe, Truman was forced to forego much of its value to him by not incorporating it into his election campaign and by explicitly giving credit to others—the *Marshall* Plan sounds quite different from what he would have preferred to call the *Truman* Plan.

The Tension at the Tactical Level

The tension between cooperative moves to create value and competitive moves to claim it is greatly exacerbated by the interaction of the tactics used either to create or claim value. First, tactics for claiming value (which we will call "claiming tactics") can impede its creation. Exaggerating the value of concessions and minimizing the benefit of others' concessions presents a distorted picture of one's relative preferences; thus, mutually beneficial trades may not be discovered. Making threats or commitments to highly favorable outcomes surely impedes hearing and understanding others' interests. Concealing information may also cause one to leave joint gains on the table. In fact, excessive use of tactics for claiming value may well sour the parties' relationship and reduce the trust between them. Such tactics may also evoke a variety of unhelpful interests. Conflict may escalate and make joint prospects less appealing and settlements less likely.

Second, approaches to creating value are vulnerable to tactics for claiming value. Revealing information about one's relative preferences is risky. If the mayor states that she gives relatively greater weight to wage reductions than to civilian review board composition, the union representative may respond by saying that the union members also feel more strongly about wage reductions, but would be willing to give in a little on wage reductions if the mayor will compensate them handsomely by completely changing the board. The information that a negotiator would accept position A in return for a favorable resolution on a second issue can be exploited: "So, you'll accept A. Good, Now let's move on to discuss the merits of the second issue." The willingness to make a new, creative offer can often be taken as a sign that its proposer is able and willing to make even further concessions. Thus, such offers sometimes remain undisclosed. Even purely shared interests can be held hostage in exchange for concessions. Though a divorcing husband and wife may both prefer giving the wife custody of the child, the husband may "suddenly" develop strong parental instincts to extract concessions on alimony in return for giving the wife custody.

In tactical choices, each negotiator thus has reasons not to be open and cooperative. Each also has apparent incentives to try to claim value. Moves to claim value thus tend to drive out moves to create it. Yet, if both choose to claim value, by being dishonest or less than forthcoming about preferences, beliefs, or minimum requirements, they may miss mutually beneficial terms for agreement.

Indeed, the structure of many bargaining situations suggests that negotiators will tend to leave joint gains on the table or even reach impasses when mutually acceptable agreements are available. We will use an extended, simplified example of a cable television operator negotiating with a town over the terms of the cable franchise to explore the tactical dilemmas that often lead to suboptimal outcomes.

Stone versus Ward

Mr. Stone, representing MicroCable, Inc., and Mayor Ward, representing the town council of a town we will call Clayton, are negotiating three issues: the price the town residents would have to pay for their subscriptions, the date by which the system would be fully operational (the completion date), and the number of cable channels to be offered.

The Mayor places the greatest weight on a speedy completion date, in part because of his upcoming reelection campaign. Within the range of feasible prices and numbers of channels, he cares approximately the same about the price, which he would like to minimize, and the number of channels, which he would like to maximize. The cable company gives the greatest weight to price and the least weight to the number of channels. MicroCable would of course like the highest price and the slowest completion; but perhaps surprisingly, Stone estimates that, though providing more channels involves additional costs, it would ultimately pay off handsomely because he will be able to sell more pay TV subscriptions. Neither party is certain about the other's beliefs and preferences. If both were to reveal their preferences to a third party and to ask her to construct a jointly desirable agreement, the agreement might well specify the maximum number of channels, a high price, and relatively fast completion.

In preparing for the negotiation, Mayor Ward recalls the experience of a colleague who had negotiated with a different cable firm. His colleague had publicly expressed a strong interest in a quick completion time—which he ultimately obtained but only after being unmercifully squeezed on price. Mayor Ward fears that Stone would respond opportunistically to a similar announcement, insisting that fast completion would be very costly for him but that perhaps he could arrange it only in return for very high prices and few channels. Such an agreement would be barely acceptable to the Mayor and the town, but would, the Mayor guesses, be quite desirable for Stone. In other words, Mayor Ward fears that if he attempts to jointly create value by sharing information about his preferences, Stone will attempt to claim the value by being misleading about his preferences. Thus, the Mayor elects to be a bit cagey and plans to downplay his interests in completion and the number of channels. He also plans to exaggerate his interest in a low price, with the hope of ultimately making a seemingly big concession on that issue in return for a big gain on completion and channels.

Stone has similar inclinations. If he lets the Mayor know that he is much more concerned with price than with speed of completion and that he actually wants more channels, he reasons, he will have given up all his bargaining chips. Mayor Ward would, he guesses, initially offer a moderately high price but only in return for an unbearably early completion date. And, he fears that the Mayor would use the town's political process to make it difficult to be dislodged from his offer. Thus, Stone is also afraid that if he attempts to create value by sharing information about his preferences, the Mayor will attempt to claim that value by being opportunistic about his and may also try to make a binding commitment to his preferred position. So, Stone also chooses to be cagey, but plans to let the Mayor and the town know, early on, that a moderate completion time and a moderate number of channels are barely possible and are very costly to him. He has an assistant prepare slides detailing the costs, but not the revenue forecasts, of additional channels. The assistant also prepares financial analyses that are intended to show that he will need high prices to recoup the cost of even such moderate concessions. Ultimately, he hopes to concede a little on the completion date for a modest price increase, and to appear magnanimous in making a final concession of the maximum number of channels for a last major price increase.

The negotiation begins in the conference room at Clayton City Hall. The Mayor welcomes Stone and his associates. He talks at some length about the value that his town's citizens place on cable television and about the fine reputation of Stone's firm. He then expresses his strong hope and belief that Clayton and MicroCable will come to a mutually beneficial agreement as the first step in a working relationship. Stone thanks the Mayor for his warm welcome. He feels that it is important to draw attention to their common ground: both the town and MicroCable want to see a fine cable system in Clayton. In this negotiation, they are thus looking out for each other's interests.

As the formal negotiation starts, Mayor Ward and Stone begin to thrust and parry. The Mayor stresses the importance the city places on keeping the price down. He also mentions that speedy completion and a large number of channels would be preferred by Clayton's residents. Stone responds sympathetically but explains the high cost of even normal completion times and of the number of channels in a basic system. Adding channels to the system and accelerating construction of the system faster than its "normal rate" are sufficiently costly that a cable franchise would be virtually unprofitable. He presents financial analyses showing the costs both of more channels and of "accelerated" completion dates.

Unable to counter directly, Mayor Ward alludes to (not yet formally received) strong offers by other cable operators. Stone parries by mentioning another town that eagerly seeks the superior MicroCable system, but says that he of course would rather do business in Clayton. They move beyond this minor impasse by concentrating on the price, in which both sides have expressed strong interest. They bargain hard. The Mayor claims that neither the town council nor the citizenry could approve a franchise with anything more than a moderate price, unless the services were extraordinary. Stone then cites still more of his financial analyses. Each searches for a favorable wedge. After arguing about difference definitions of "fair and reasonable profit" and "fair return on investment," they compromise by agreeing on the price reached in a negotiation between a neighboring town and one of MicroCable's competitors. The Mayor never realizes that Stone could be more flexible on completion dates and does not arrange as early a date as he might have gotten for the price. And, ironically, Stone's careful financial presentation about the costs of adding channels makes it difficult for him to offer the town the maximum number of channels without losing face. The bargaining is tense, but they ultimately settle at a compromise on each issue: a moderate price, a moderate completion date, and about half the maximum number of channels.

Both men leave feeling good about the outcome. As Stone says to his assistant, "We didn't get everything we wanted but we gave as good as we got." Before the town council's vote on the franchise agreement, the Mayor describes the negotiation as a success: "If both sides complain a bit about the agreement, then you know it must be a good deal." The town council approves the proposal unanimously.

In the negotiations, each of the parties was afraid that his attempt to create value by sharing information would be exploited by the other's claiming tactics. Each chose to attempt to mislead or claim a bit, in self-protection. And, relative to what was possible, they ended up with an inferior solution. They left joint gains on the table. Both would have preferred the maximum number of channels and both would have preferred a higher price in return for earlier completion. A pity, but not uncommon.

The Negotiator's Dilemma

Let us abstract from this example. Consider two negotiators (for continuity named Ward and Stone), each of whom can choose between two negotiating styles: creating value (being open, sharing information about preferences and beliefs, not being misleading about minimum requirements, and so forth) and claiming value (being cagey and misleading about preferences, beliefs, and minimum requirements; making commitments and threats, and so forth). Each has the same two options for any tactical choice. If both choose to create value, they each receive a good outcome, which we will call GOOD for each. If Ward chooses to create value and Stone chooses to claim value, then Stone does even better than if he had chosen to create value—rank this outcome GREAT for Stone—but Ward does much worse—rank this outcome TERRIBLE for him. Similarly, if Stone is the creative one and Ward is the claimer, then Ward does well—rank this outcome as GREAT—while Stone's outcome is TERRIBLE. If both claim, they fail to find

Stone's Choice

	Create	Claim
	GOOD	GREAT
Create		
	GOOD	TERRIBLE
	TERRIBLE	MEDIOCRE
Claim		
	GREAT	MEDIOCRE

Ward's
Choice

Figure 4.1

The Negotiator's Dilemma. The lower left entry in each cell is Ward's outcome; the upper right is Stone's.

joint gains and come up with a mediocre outcome, which we call MEDIOCRE for both. [Figure 4.1] summarizes the outcomes for each choice. In each box, Ward's payoff is in the lower left corner and Stone's is in the upper right. Thus, when Ward claims and Stone creates, Ward's outcome is GREAT while Stone's is TERRIBLE.

Now, if Ward were going to create, Stone would prefer the GREAT outcome obtained by claiming to the GOOD outcome he could have obtained by creating; so, Stone should claim. If, on the other hand, Ward were going to claim, Stone would prefer the MEDIOCRE outcome from claiming to the TERRIBLE outcome he would receive from creating. In fact, no matter what Ward does, it seems that Stone would be better off trying to claim value!

Similarly, Ward should also prefer to claim. By symmetric reasoning, if Stone chooses to create, Ward prefers the GREAT outcome he gets by claiming to the GOOD outcome he gets from creating. If Stone claims, Ward prefers the MEDIOCRE outcome he gets from claiming to the TERRIBLE outcome he gets from creating.

Both negotiators choose to claim. They land in the lower-right-hand box and receive MEDIOCRE outcomes. They leave joint gains on the table, since both would prefer the GOOD outcomes they could have received had they both chosen to create value and ended up in the upper-left-hand box.

This is the crux of the Negotiator's Dilemma.[2] Individually rational decisions to emphasize claiming tactics by being cagey and misleading lead to a mutually undesirable outcome. As described, this situation has the structure of the famous "Prisoner's Dilemma."[3] In such situations, the motivation to protect oneself and employ tactics for claiming value is compelling. Because tactics for claiming value impede creation, we expect negotiators in many settings to leave joint gains on the table. And, over time, the inexorable pull toward claiming tactics is insidious: Negotiators will "learn" to become value claimers. A negotiator inclined toward sharing information and constructive creative, mutually desirable agreements, after being skewered in several encounters with experienced value-claimers, may bitterly come to alter his strategy to a more self-protective, value-claiming stance. Williams' description of new attorneys learning to negotiate out-of-court settlements is consistent with this analysis:

> During the first few months of practice, they encounter some attorneys who hammer them into the ground, exploiting and taking advantage of them at every turn, and others who are trying to teach them to be good lawyers. The experience is not calculated to engender trust in fellow officers of the court. Rather, the tendency in young lawyers is to develop a mild paranoia and to distrust everyone. This is unfortunate, because some opponents are providing valuable information, albeit in subtle ways.[4]

Because both sides in our negotiation would prefer to end up with a GOOD-GOOD (create-create) outcome rather than a MEDIOCRE-MEDIOCRE (claim-claim) one, experience may "teach" negotiation lessons that both sides, like Williams's young attorneys, would be better off not having "learned."

Taking the Negotiator's Dilemma Metaphor Seriously But Not Literally

The Negotiator's Dilemma characterizes the whole of a negotiation. Yet the dilemma is a simplification, a metaphor. As presented, it appears to condemn each negotiator to a once-and-for-all choice as a creator or claimer; clearly there are many choices along the way.

The dilemma is also meant to apply to each tactical choice. Even here, the line between "creating" and "claiming" need not be clear-cut. A negotiator can reveal information early, late, throughout, or not at all; she can mislead by omission, commission, or be straight. She may discover a new option for mutual benefit, a joint gain, but present it in such a way that it emphasizes only agreements highly favorable to her. She may offer a creative proposal or hold back because it conveys sensitive information about trade-offs or minimal requirements. Yet at a basic enough level, tactical choices embody the creating-claiming tension, even if they contain elements of both.

Thus, we take the Negotiator's Dilemma seriously, even though we do not take the matrix representation literally. The tension it reflects between cooperative impulses to create value and competitive impulses to claim it is inherent in the large and in the small. The essence of effective negotiation involves managing this tension, creating while claiming value.

This chapter presents a broad-brush portrait. To understand what is involved in managing this central tension, we must return with finer brushes to several parts of the canvas:

1. What precisely does it mean to create value? Where do joint gains really come from? What tactics are required to realize them?
2. What do we really mean by claiming value? What tactics are appropriate?
3. If negotiation involves an inescapable tension between competitive and cooperative impulses, how can one manage it effectively?

4. Can't we manage this tension by separating the creating from the claiming? Why not do all the creating first and then just divide the cleverly created joint gains? Or, why not get the hard claiming out of the way and then try to find all the available joint gains? What other choices do we have?

A Roadmap in Pictures

The quest for answers to these and related questions animates Part I of this book. The remainder of this chapter lays out the elements of negotiation we will examine and explains the relations among them. As we go along, we also introduce a graphical metaphor that will help organize the ideas we develop.

The point of negotiation is for each negotiator to do better by jointly decided action than he could do otherwise, better than his "no-agreement alternatives." For example, recall the humble example of Willy and Sam whose trade of bananas, pears, and apples we discussed earlier. If they had been unable to reach agreement, there would be no trade at all. The no-agreement alternative for each boy was to keep whatever fruit he had. Chapter Three somewhat ironically begins our tour through negotiation analysis by looking outside the negotiation itself and focusing attention on the crucial and often neglected role of no-agreement alternatives.

Once a negotiator establishes his no-agreement alternative, he seeks to improve on it by jointly decided action. Thus, he needs a deep understanding of his interests. Chapter Four discusses interests and provides a logic and method for making the sometimes painful trade-offs among them.

Negotiators jointly create value by harmonizing their interests, much as Willy and Sam did in finding mutually beneficial trades. In Chapter Five, we ask where joint gains really come from and set forth the different ways that interests can be converted into joint gains.

[Figure 4.2] graphically illustrates one such joint gain. The horizontal axis shows the value of an agreement to Willy. Thus, points farther to the right represent agreements that better serve Willy's interests. Similarly, the vertical axis shows the value of an agreement to Sam. The more Sam values an agreement, the higher it is on the graph. The point labeled 0, at the origin, represents Sam and Willy's no-agreement alternative, no trade at all. Their first trade, where Willy gives Sam a pear in exchange for a banana, makes both happier because each prefers what he received to what he gave up. This new agreement is represented by point A; the fact that it is northeast of the no-agreement point reflects the fact that both Sam and Willy prefer the trade. This trade "created value" and thus represents a joint gain with respect to no agreement. Similarly, their next trade of an apple for an orange, represented by point B, makes each of them still happier. Because point B represents a joint gain compared to point A, B is to the northeast of A. Chapter Five goes well beyond such simple trades in showing ways of joint action to create value.

But value is both created and claimed. [Figure 4.3] shows a third agreement, point C, that is also a joint gain compared to Willy and Sam's original agreement, point A. Willy prefers point C to point B and Sam prefers the reverse. By clever tactics to claim value, Willy may induce Sam to accept point C. Thus, Willy would have claimed most of the

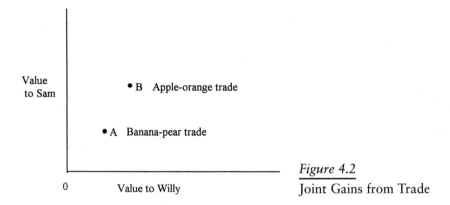

Figure 4.2

Joint Gains from Trade

jointly created value. Of course, Sam may be employing similar tactics to reach point B so *he* can claim the lion's share of the jointly created value. Chapter Six explores how value is claimed.

Willy and Sam prefer agreements B and C to agreement A. Willy prefers C to B and Sam prefers B to C. Indeed, if Sam had discovered agreement C, he might never mention it to Willy. Instead, he might seek to make agreement B salient, emphasize its desirability, and then push for early closure hoping that Willy never discovers agreement C exists. Or, Sam might vigorously assert that C is not acceptable to him, that it is simply worse for him than agreement A. In either case, the way that the value is created affects the way it is divided; the process of creating value is *entwined* with the process of claiming it. Effective negotiation requires managing the tension between the need to create value and the need to claim it. How this is and can be done is the subject of Chapter Seven.

By being clever, Willy and Sam may find agreements that both prefer to point B and others that both prefer to point C. But the effects of their cleverness are necessarily limited. Eventually, they will find that they cannot improve on certain agreements for one boy except at the other's expense. In more complex bargains, there are a large number of such agreements, as illustrated in [Figure 4.4]. The set of such agreements is known as the "possibilities frontier" or the "Pareto frontier." From any point of the frontier, Willy

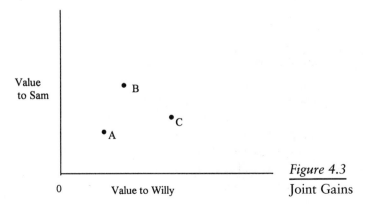

Figure 4.3

Joint Gains

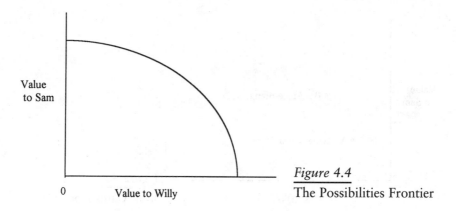

Figure 4.4
The Possibilities Frontier

cannot find another agreement that makes him better off without making Sam worse off. This frontier is an abstraction, an heuristic, that is usually not known to the negotiators. It represents what is ultimately possible by joint action after the negotiators have shared all information about themselves and exhausted all creativity and ingenuity. Because the parties know different things, each will have his own perceptions of what is jointly possible (where the possibilities frontier lies). Throughout this book, we will again and again refer to this image of a possibilities frontier as perceived by the parties.

So far, we have assumed that a fixed set of negotiators with well-defined interests and fixed no-agreement alternatives meets to discuss a given set of issues. But a negotiator can also create and claim value by adding a new issue or excluding one, bringing in a new party or leaving one out, improving her no-agreement alternatives or making another's alternatives worse, and so on. Every element of the negotiation can itself be subject to tactical manipulation. In Chapter Nine, we enumerate many ways to change the game and provide means to decide whether such changes are likely to help. Thus, we complete our framework by incorporating ways that a negotiation's structure evolves over time.

In short, this logic of negotiation guides the logic of the chapters that follow and the approach we espouse. Any feasible joint action must do better for the parties than their alternatives to agreement; Chapter Three studies this minimum requirement. But "doing better" is only measured by one's interests, which are the subject of Chapter Four. Fashioning the means of doing better—jointly creating value—follows in Chapter Five. Chapter Six explores how individuals claim value and some of the ethical issues raised in the process. The ways that negotiators and third parties can or might manage the tension between the conflicting needs to create and claim value are examined in Chapter Seven. Chapter Eight explores the themes developed thus far by dissecting the case of a complex budget determination. Proceeding further with the basic argument, Chapter Nine adds an "evolutionary" dimension, analyzing how negotiators also create and claim value by bringing in a new issue, excluding a party, and more generally, by changing the game itself. Chapter Ten summarizes our approach as a whole and takes a look at the often misunderstood concept of negotiating "power."

The subjects we have chosen to examine bear on each part of a model of possible joint action. In this sense, our analysis and prescriptions form a whole to which a myriad of richer contextual aspects may be related.

Notes

1. Fisher and Ury (1981).

2. Several authors have discussed versions of similar negotiation dilemmas. See for example Zartmen (1976) and Pruitt (1981). In our judgment, the best such discussion, usefully developed in a different direction, can be found in Walton and McKersie (1965, 1966). An abstract version of a similar dilemma is currently being investigated by game theorists studying bargaining with incomplete information. One major result, due to Myerson (1979), is that in highly simplified situations that are analogous to the ones we discuss, fully honest revelation of private information by individual bargainers and Pareto efficiency cannot simultaneously be achieved. This is a starkly abstracted analogue of the result we described that tends to result from the tension between cooperative moves to create value and competitive moves to claim it individually.

3. In addition to the payoff structure, the classic Prisoner's Dilemma involves rules of interaction: no communication and the inability of the parties to make prior, communicated, binding commitments to one choice or the other. Under these rules, the equilibrium in a single play of the Prisoner's Dilemma is for both players to defect (claim). (For a perceptive discussion of the Prisoner's Dilemma, see Luce and Raiffa, 1957.) In negotiations, of course, communication is possible, and credible irreversible commitments to cooperate are difficult but not always impossible to make. Thus, we suggest that the structure of the Negotiator's Dilemma implies a tendency for both parties to choose to claim value, but not that this is an irrevocable equilibrium. Moreover, we shall argue below that a negotiation in fact contains a sequence of choices with much the same structure, though again the rules of interaction differ. The economic equilibrium for playing a finite number of repetitions of the Prisoner's Dilemma is to defect (claim) in every play. But experimental results suggest that people playing the finitely repeated Prisoner's Dilemma often do better than the "rational" players of game theory and are sometimes able to cooperate for substantial mutual gain. Thus, we do not take the analogy to the repeated Prisoner's Dilemma to imply that people will use game-theoretic equilibrium strategies, but to suggest a powerful tendency toward such behavior.

4. Williams (1983:29).

Reading 3

*Squaring Off at the Table, Not in the Courts**

Lawrence Susskind and Laura van Dam

In late 1978, the U.S. Congress ordered the Environmental Protection Agency to develop standards governing the cleanup and disposal of uranium mill-tailings. Almost five years later, the agency finished issuing its rules. Despite its technical research, public hearings, and attempts to heed the comments made during the six-month public review and comment period, it was sued. Not until late 1985, seven years after the process began, did the court uphold the rules, excepting one provision.

Such a time-consuming process would be unfortunate even if this were an isolated case. But consider that about four of every five rules that the EPA promulgates are challenged in court. Not only is time wasted, but the courts often prove to be inappropriate arbiters of technical regulatory disputes. It's no wonder that many people think the rule-making process no longer works.

Today, an alternative called "negotiated rulemaking" offers great promise. The process involves gathering all interested parties together to hammer out a rule they can agree on. Informally known as "regneg," for "regulatory negotiation," this alternative could reduce court caseloads and increase agencies' speed in issuing rules. It also could produce wiser rules by eliminating the growing use of "advocacy science," in which concerned parties pay experts to undercut opponents' scientific claims. Advocacy science gradually is eroding the credibility of all scientific testimony in public disputes.

To test negotiated rulemaking, the EPA has conducted several demonstrations of the process in the 1980s. For starters, it concentrated on a regulation that concerned truck emission standards. Once this was completed in 1984, the agency chose a rule focusing on the criteria for issuing emergency exemptions from pesticide-licensing regulations. Such exemptions allow farmers to use pesticides that are still undergoing tests for health risks. The Public Disputes Program, which is part of the Program on Negotiation at

Harvard Law School, monitored the two demonstrations for the EPA. Both have been successful: no one challenged the negotiated rules in court. Plus, the rules took less than the standard two years to promulgate.

Of course, two demonstrations are not a complete proof. Earlier this year, during a third EPA demonstration of negotiated rulemaking, which concerned pesticide protection for farmworkers, several farmworkers' representatives stopped attending meetings. They alleged that the proceedings had not been conducted fairly. The EPA continued to meet with the scaled-down negotiating group, leaving the door open for the farmworkers to return or at least comment on the draft regulations before the formal review and comment stage.

The EPA's demonstrations of negotiated rulemaking and similar tests by other federal agencies have shed light on how and when negotiation can—and cannot—be used to develop regulations. Usually, regulations can be negotiated if they involve several issues that negotiators value differently. Then the participants can make trades. A regulation typically cannot be negotiated when it centers on a single emotionally charged issue. People are unlikely to resolve disputes if they have to compromise deeply held beliefs.

From Neighborhoods to Federal Agencies

Mediated negotiation was tested for the first time as an alternative to litigation in the late 1960s, when experimental neighborhood justice centers tried to help residents informally handle such problems as landlord-tenant clashes. The idea caught on, and by the mid-1970s, what had become known as "alternative dispute resolution" was being used to settle all kinds of complex disagreements. For example, governmental bodies began using mediated negotiation successfully to decide where to locate highways, landfills, and airports.

By 1985, more than 25 dispute-resolution organizations had formed to help mediate a range of public disputes, from electricity-rate squabbles to controversies about the licensing of waste-treatment plants. Also, several federal agencies had recognized that they could apply negotiation techniques to potential regulatory conflicts. Now, the EPA, the Federal Aviation Administration, and the Occupational Safety and Health Administration have actually experimented with that process.

At the EPA, the idea of developing rules through negotiation emerged during the Carter Administration. Momentum slowed with the 1981 change in administration—but only for a short time. Then Republicans bent on regulatory relief recognized that the process might be more efficient than the traditional rule-making method. In 1983, the EPA announced that it was ready to develop several regulations using negotiation.

This meant altering a little of the standard rule-making procedure. Conventionally, a federal agency relies on its in-house expertise and consults with advisory committees made up of independent experts when it drafts a proposed rule. Then it publishes the draft in the *Federal Register*. That sets the stage for individuals, organizations, and even other government agencies to respond during a formal review and comment period. The agency must justify its final version of the rule in light of all the comments it receives.

For its demonstrations of negotiated rule-making, the EPA kept most aspects of the standard procedure intact. But it convened all interested parties to help draft, by consensus, the proposed rule.

In 1983, the agency came close to negotiating a rule that would set the minimum volume of low-level radioactive waste that had to accumulate before federal hazardous-waste regulations would come into play. Very quickly, the agency learned it had made a mistake, for environmentalists said they would refuse to negotiate this topic. They said they believed that *any* amount of waste should be treated as dangerous. From this experience, the EPA realized that negotiation cannot work when the focus is on a single issue that parties will not break down into components they can trade off.

The EPA settled on two less gut-wrenching topics from a list proposed by some environmental groups initially skeptical about negotiated rulemaking. First, it organized a negotiation to develop a set of financial penalties for truck-engine manufacturers who fail to meet the Clean Air Act's emission requirements. The resulting regulation, negotiated by manufacturers as well as environmentalists, allowed noncomplying companies time to catch up. But it forced them to pay significant fees until they complied.

The agency also announced its intention to negotiate a rule concerning emergency exemptions from pesticide-licensing regulations. About a year earlier, a number of critics had expressed concern that the EPA was granting too many emergency exemptions.

The rulemaking on emergency exemptions illustrates how consensus building can work. The EPA began by setting a strict deadline, which was intended to keep negotiators from debating indefinitely. Further, the agency recognized that the parties—including farmers, chemical manufacturers, environmentalists, and state and federal officials concerned with health, pesticides, and agriculture—had different priorities about the issue. For example, they disagreed on what should constitute an emergency. Thus, the parties could make trade-offs. In the lingo of negotiation theory, there was room for a "win-win" settlement.

After choosing the emergency-exemption rule for a demonstration, the EPA hired ERM-McGlennon Associates, a Boston environmental consulting firm with extensive negotiation experience, to organize this negotiation. ERM-McGlennon contacted more than 100 groups to learn who might want to participate. Some 16 organizations besides the EPA expressed interest in participating. These included four environmental groups, four state agencies, four farmers' associations, two manufacturing associations, and the U.S. Department of Agriculture. Six more parties were added later, after they learned of the pending negotiations through a notice in the *Federal Register* and asked to be included.

The negotiations probably could not have produced credible results without the involvement of such a diverse group of interested parties. But why were the organizations willing to participate? The reason is that they knew that a rule would be promulgated, no matter what. The offer to negotiate a draft of the proposed rule was too attractive to pass up. Presumably, they would have a chance to influence the rulemaking without having to pay for a court challenge. And the participants didn't want to miss out on a process their opponents wanted in on.

The negotiating team met for an orientation session several weeks after the *Federal Register* announcement and adopted a set of ground rules. They agreed to operate by consensus rather than majority vote. They agreed that members could call time-out to caucus in small groups whenever necessary. And they agreed to a provision that represented both a safeguard and a threat: any party could withdraw from the process at any time.

During negotiations, the participants would have ample opportunities to review drafts with their organizations. And they were assured that any regulation resulting from the negotiations would be subject to the normal public review and comment procedure.

In the introductory session, the negotiators established an agenda and organized smaller working groups. The purpose of these group was to examine specific topics of concern. In keeping with the open character of the negotiations, anyone could choose to be a member of any working group.

One working group was set up to develop guidelines on the use of up to $50,000 that the EPA made available to the negotiators. Half of this money had been put up by the agency, and the remainder of it had been donated by private foundations. Upon agreement from everyone, it could be used to fund fact-finding studies or to reimburse needy participants for travel and similar costs.

As it turned out, $20,000 from the resource pool paid the travel costs of some participants who convinced the group that they needed this support to attend. No money went to research.

In some negotiations, however, groups must commission technical research together. This is what the negotiators did in the first EPA demonstration of negotiated rulemaking: they selected a single researcher to design a fair method of sampling engines that would be tested for emissions. In joint fact-finding studies, the negotiators can specify the research protocols they deem reasonable. This prevents arguments about the validity of technical claims. Plus, joint research keeps some negotiators from wielding more influence because their organizations have more money for the studies. Finally, joint fact-finding means that the agency responsible for a rule does not have to choose between inconsistent facts that otherwise might be presented by different parties. Having to choose between data usually leads to opposition after a rule is developed.

During the first meeting, the EPA's Office of Pesticide Programs unexpectedly submitted an early draft it had drawn up for the emergency-exemption rule. The negotiators could have ignored that draft, since it was up to everybody to help with one. But they decided to use the document as a point of departure for their work. This not only gave them a head start but allowed the EPA to indicate what a rule promulgated under the traditional procedure might look like.

The first session also gave the negotiators a chance to become acquainted with the facilitator, the person the EPA had chosen to manage arrangements, keep the minutes, and orchestrate the consensus-building process. In any regneg, the facilitator has to make sure that everyone has a chance to talk and that the group stays on track. The facilitator must be nonpartisan and acceptable to all the negotiators.

The next time the group met, on September 28, 1984, it began to negotiate in earnest. The work continued through six formal meetings, including three that lasted two working days each. Negotiations ended four months after they began. The smaller working groups met throughout this period.

At the start of negotiations participants usually wonder which parties have the most power to achieve their goals. Generally, people presume that parties with fewer financial resources or less political influence will be overwhelmed or co-opted. But negotiators who are effective in expressing their views or in inventing suggestions that others can accept are likely to come out ahead. So are participants who back their claims with solid evidence or who build working relationships by listening well. And less politically powerful participants can increase their influence by forming coalitions.

That is what the environmentalists did in the rulemaking on emergency exemptions. Instead of attending a casual dinner the facilitator hosted before the second meeting of the negotiators, the environmental representatives met to develop a coalition strategy and work out their differences. This separate meeting initially upset some other negotiators, but everyone soon realized that coalition building was key to the negotiation process. In fact, behind-the-scenes caucusing became common throughout the negotiations, as the facilitator used shuttle diplomacy to get various groups to make trades.

The Nitty-Gritty

In the emergency-exemption demonstration, the definition of the word "emergency" was critical, since the resulting rule would concern emergency situations when certain pesticides could be used. The negotiators' give-and-take as they argued about the meaning of "emergency" reveal as much about the nitty-gritty aspects of a negotiated rulemaking.

The problem in defining the word concerned how widespread a pest outbreak has to be to justify using pesticides that have not yet been fully tested for health effects. Can a single farm experience an emergency? Or does an entire region have to be damaged?

The negotiators set up a working group to answer these questions, and almost everyone in the negotiations—16 people—joined. The first time the group met, there were numerous false starts and disagreements. The representatives from the farmers' associations wanted individual farms to qualify for emergency exemptions, while the environmentalists thought exemptions should be available only when whole regions were affected. Some participants were noticeably unwilling to be persuaded by others' arguments. Nothing was settled, but the participants did hear each other's views.

Later, the working group members agreed that the definition of "emergency" should hinge on the definition of "significant economic loss," since the extent of the loss would determine how dire a situation was. But a subsequent meeting was inconclusive.

While it would appear that little progress was being made, the members of the group were actually working hard, acquiring a better understanding of each other's concerns. Peter Schneider, the ERM-McGlennon principal at the meetings, suspects that the participants were checking back with their organizations to see what they had to stay firm on and what opposing arguments they could accept.

Finally, the full negotiating team decided that five key participants should tackle the matter. That task force reached what appeared to be a breakthrough in its first session. At this meeting the two environmental representatives indicated that they would not accept any rule in which the phrase "significant economic loss" applied to a situation with less than a regional impact. David Kronenberg, who monitored the sessions for the Public Disputes Program, believes the environmentalists thought that the regulations should allow only for those exemptions that would benefit a relatively broad sector of the public. After all, public health might be at risk if certain pesticides were used. Recognizing that the environmentalists would not waver, the rest of the group agreed to bring this proposal to the full negotiating team for discussion.

But the group concluded that the definition of the extent of an impact should be flexible. It reasoned that applications for exemptions should be considered on a case-by-case basis. So the language in the rule was left ambiguous.

The negotiators also had to decide whether a significant economic loss should be measured in terms of crop yield or profitability. Several environmentalists pushed to define economic loss in terms of decreased crop yield. They suggested that farmers should not worry about apples with harmless spots caused by infestation, for example. The farmers' representatives argued that such spots could lower profits enough to result in a "significant economic loss." After extensive give and take, the full group finally agreed on a definition based on profitability.

The negotiators worked for several months with only minimal progress—not an unusual situation in a negotiation. Typically, at the outset negotiators busy themselves with fact-finding and sounding out each other's views. Focusing on issues happens later, often after participants have developed alliances.

A collaborative style marked the later full negotiating sessions. According to a summary of the fifth meeting of the entire group, the participants "showed a clear willingness to listen to, discuss, and negotiate solutions that would be mutually beneficial, or at least mutually acceptable. The regulatory-negotiation process led to temporary partnerships that were, looking back at the beginning of the negotiations, nearly inexplicable. Who would have predicted that Earl Spurrier of the National Agricultural Chemicals Association, a representative and advocate of pesticide manufacturers, and Jay Feldman of the National Committee Against the Misuse of Pesticides, would find themselves working together . . . [to] meet the needs of both their organizations?"

By the end of the last scheduled meeting, the negotiators had drafted the entire rule, partly in working groups and partly en masse. This was quite different from the first EPA negotiated rulemaking, when participants decided to reach consensus on the principles of the regulation rather than on the actual language of the rule. The emergency-exemption negotiators signed the proposed regulation, signifying that as individuals they would support it during the review and comment stage.

Three months later, on April 8, 1985, the proposed emergency-exemption rule was published in the *Federal Register*. In the meantime, the negotiators had explained the basis for the draft to their organizations, trying to ensure their support. Like anyone, members of these groups could have spoken against the draft rule during the several-month public review and comment stage. But none did.

The EPA received 16 comments from parties that had not been in the negotiations. The points were so minor, however, that none of the participants felt it was worthwhile to reconvene to discuss them. On January 15, 1986, the final rule was published. No lawsuits followed.

"Not the Ogres You Thought"

It was a noticeable mark of success that the rule passed the close scrutiny of people who had not been directly involved in the negotiations. But there were other measures of success, too.

Generally, the participants were pleased with the result. By the end of the process all but one group indicated that the negotiations had produced a rule more representative of their interests than the standard process probably would have, and with less conflict. The participants were inclined to feel good about the outcome, since they had had a hand in shaping it. The process had given them more control than the traditional method of developing rules.

Several participants said they had benefited from the chance to communicate directly with each other and iron out long-standing disagreements in person. About half the representatives for the agricultural industry said they had gained a clearer appreciation of the environmentalists' motives. One negotiator commented, "In working with the opposition you find they're not quite the ogres you thought they were, and they don't hate you as much as you thought."

The EPA's technical staff also cheered the results. Staff scientists familiar with the details of pesticide regulation are convinced that the agency's statutory mandate to ensure technical soundness was upheld. These scientists believe that an extremely wise rule emerged.

Answering the Worrywarts

Regardless of such success, some observers still fear that informal negotiation may be a dangerous way to develop regulations.

For example, when people first learn about negotiated rulemaking they often question whether certain interests that ought to be represented might not make it to the table because they are not well organized, don't have the resources to participate, or fail to find out about the negotiations in time. These criticisms would be more accurately leveled at the traditional rule-making process. At least the EPA's negotiated rulemaking has included an outreach effort by an independent party—one of ERM-McGlennon's jobs in the second regneg demonstration. And funds can be used to reimburse participants' costs. Moreover, a negotiated rule is subject to a full review and comment procedure. Finally, once the regulation is published, anyone can challenge it in court. Of course, the point of regulatory negotiation is to avoid courtroom battles, but the possibility of a challenge must remain as a safeguard.

David Doniger, senior staff attorney of the Natural Resources Defense Council, has urged that money from the resource pool be available for more than research and travel costs. He thinks the money should also be used for per diem compensation for those who need it. He has argued that negotiators representing relatively small, nonprofit organizations must be compensated, because their groups' resources can be stretched quite thin when a staff member participates in extended negotiations. He has pointed out that negotiated rulemaking requires more staff time than merely preparing comments on proposed rules. While negotiators have not decided to use any funds for compensation so far, they always could if they wanted to.

Some administrative law experts distrust negotiation because they believe it can lead one side to coopt the other. They worry that individual participants might cozy up together and reach agreements that would not satisfy their organizations' memberships. If this happened, however, distraught members could criticize the drafted rules during the public review and comment stage. And groups are always free to set up their own review and comment periods before allowing their negotiators to agree to drafts. Moreover, every organization retains a direct veto over what its representatives have negotiated. Also, a group can replace its negotiators at any time if they fail to protect its interests.

Harvard Law Professor Richard Stewart and other administrative law experts believe that a government agency may compromise its authority if it agrees beforehand to be bound by a negotiated rule. But this criticism is beside the point. While delegating too much power to the negotiators could cause trouble, the participating agency can veto proposals in a regulatory negotiation.

Walkouts do pose a problem. The agency is left with a tough choice: should it continue the negotiations with the remaining participants, in the hope it will produce something close to consensus, or should it revert to the traditional approach? In either case, at least officials understand the interested parties' concerns better than if negotiations had not been attempted. Consider what has happened in the EPA's third negotiated rule-making demonstration. The negotiating group, focusing on pesticide protection for farmworkers, lost seven of its eighteen participants earlier this year when the farmworkers' representatives announced after attending several meetings that they would not return to the talks. In their withdrawal statement, they said they were not given "the same respect and consideration" as agribusiness and agricultural chemical representatives, and the proceedings were not conducted "in a fair, neutral and impartial manner." The EPA and the remaining negotiators offered to change facilitators, but the farmworkers' representatives declined. Actually, the farmworkers may have left for more reasons than they stated. They may have decided that they would lose an important organizing tool if they reached an agreement with their opposition.

The EPA and the other participants in this negotiation decided to proceed, hoping that the farmworkers' representatives would return. Hoping to make the final draft as acceptable as possible to everyone, the remaining negotiators also asked the farmworkers to comment on any drafts before the public review and comment stage.

Beside walkouts, there is one other danger with negotiated rulemaking. The process should not be seen as a panacea for all the problems with the rule-making process. There will always be emotionally laden rules that present win-lose situations. The rule on low-level radioactive waste is one of those.

The Idea Spreads

While many more agencies are likely to find it fruitful to develop some regulations by negotiation, they should be careful about which rules they choose to develop using this approach. They should steer clear not only of single-issue, win-lose rules but also of regulations that are not controversial and are not likely to be litigated. Such lessons from the regneg tests are now being disseminated to all federal agencies by the Administrative Conference of the United States, an organization that includes senior administrative staff from all the federal agencies.

The conference's backing for negotiated rulemaking may explain why more agencies are showing interest now. In February, the Department of the Interior requested a facilitator for a regneg concerning air pollution that may result from oil drilling off the California coast. In May, the Federal Trade Commission announced it was considering negotiating a rule on the use of alternatives to lawsuits for resolving consumer complaints about warrantied products.

For its part, the EPA has continued examining negotiated rulemaking. Since March, the agency has been involved in a negotiated rulemaking concerning performance standards to control air pollution from wood-burning stoves. It is also exploring the possibility of taking on at least two additional regulatory negotiations.

Interest in negotiated rulemaking will undoubtedly spread. In less than five years, negotiated approaches could be used to develop as much as 10 percent of all rules.

Such an increase will require that interested agencies designate at least one senior staff member to oversee their negotiation work. These staff members will have to keep up to date with the latest breakthroughs in negotiation. Also, agencies will need additional appropriations to fund the collaborative technical studies that negotiators may call for. Extra money may be necessary to help some negotiators attend meetings as well. Typically, an agency that hopes to negotiate five rules a year might need to budget $250,000 or more annually for them.

Regulatory negotiation doesn't have to stop with negotiated rulemaking. Permitting, licensing, and rate-setting disputes can be resolved through negotiation, too; and this work can be done at the local, state, and federal levels. Consider how negotiation has entered the regulatory arena in New Mexico. That state's Public Utility Commission recently invited a broad range of interested parties to help draft a plan to soften the impact a new nuclear plant will have on utility rates. Without a plan, consumers would be hit with significantly higher bills to pay for the plant's construction costs. In Massachusetts, Wisconsin, and Rhode Island, the state legislatures have enacted facility-siting laws requiring that builders of waste-treatment plants negotiate with potential host communities before receiving state licenses.

The key obstacle to more widespread use of negotiation in the regulatory process is doubt as to whether the method can really work. But doubt should not stop lawmakers from testing the technique. There is little to lose, even if negotiation doesn't succeed. Information will have been shared, and differences will have been narrowed. And if negotiation works, the courts' burden will be lessened, costs will be reduced, and the government's legitimacy as a regulator will be improved.

Reading 4

Mediation and Other Forms of Assisted Negotiation*

Lawrence Susskind and Jeffrey Cruikshank

In an ideal world distributional disputes would be settled by the parties themselves, as in the *Jordan Lane* case. But, because the participants in multiparty, many-issue disputes are usually unable to deal with their differences on their own, assisted negotiation is often necessary.

Assisted negotiation is the complement to unassisted negotiation. Many public disputes—in fact, the great majority of the distributional disputes to which we have alluded—do not meet the preconditions outlined in the last chapter for successful unassisted negotiation. Most public disputes are highly complex, for example, and the affected groups are hard to identify and difficult to represent. Disputing parties often have great difficulty initiating and pursuing discussions. Emotional, psychological, or financial stakes may be so high that the disputants are unable to sustain the collaborative aspects of unassisted negotiation. Finally, power imbalances may preclude direct and unassisted dealings among disputants.

Consider, for example, the problems posed by relatively the simple task of initiating a dialogue—or, as we have labeled the first step in the prenegotiation phase, "getting started." We have already discussed some of the psychological traps that come into play as disputing parties consider whether or not to pursue negotiations. Like some couples involved in marital squabbles, each partner refuses to make the first conciliatory gesture. "You started this," each says, "so you solve it." In other words, public postures alone may preclude unassisted negotiation. If that is the case, then the disputing parties have only two choices: they can resort to the conventional legislative, administrative, or judicial means of resolving distributional disputes, or they can seek the help of a nonpartisan intermediary—a facilitator, mediator, or arbitrator—and engage in assisted negotiation.

"Getting started" is relatively easy, when compared with some of the subsequent phases of negotiation. Suffice it to say that when complexities arise, a neutral intermediary is often the only solution.

Entry

There are numerous ways that intermediaries can arrive on the scene. As suggested earlier, an unassisted negotiation can easily get bogged down; and as the frustration level rises, one of the disputing parties may suggest the need for a "neutral." Alternatively, a neutral may present himself or herself to the various stakeholders and indicate a willingness to provide assistance. Finally, a disinterested observer may advise the disputing parties seek outside assistance.

This last approach is particularly fruitful when the various parties are "frozen" into uncompromising public postures. In such cases, all parties may in fact want to initiate negotiations, but fear the consequences of appearing weak. ("If I seem eager to negotiate, the others will attempt to gain more by hardening their positions.") This may be partially true, but the overriding reality is that these parties are unlikely to resolve their dispute without help. Therefore, the neutral may have to be introduced into the dispute by a nonparticipant.

A second problem of entry has to do with perceptions of control. In many cases, one or more disputants is convinced that employing an intermediary will amount to surrendering control over the outcome. This is a common misperception, which arises out of the publicity that often accompanies binding arbitration, a process in which an arbitrator listens to each side's arguments and arrives at a judgment by which the parties have agreed to be bound. In contrast, there are several types of assisted negotiation which are not binding, and which proceed only with the continuing assent of the negotiating parties. In other words, all parties must be satisfied with the settlement reached through such a consensual process, or there is no settlement. Because the stakeholders retain veto power over the final outcome, they retain a vital measure of control.

Government agencies and officials are particularly sensitive to issues of control. "I have a legal mandate," such officials frequently tell us. "It would be inappropriate and perhaps illegal for me to accept terms dictated by someone else." The answer, of course, is that in the types of consensual negotiations described in this book, no one dictates terms, or has terms dictated to them. Government agencies are constantly entering into negotiations that produce legally binding agreements—for example, labor contracts. Given that fact, nothing prevents government officials from engaging in nonbinding negotiations, assuming, of course, that they are attentive to "sunshine" laws and other due process considerations.

Two other issues of entry—the neutrality and competence of the proposed helper— often present themselves early in the negotiating process. How can all sides be certain that the go-between is unbiased, and will be equally helpful to all the parties? Wouldn't it be easy for a seemingly disinterested helper to favor one side over the others while disguising his or her stance as neutral? Even if all sides can be sure that the intermediary is impartial, can they be sure of his or her competence? What if the neutral botches the job, causing everything to take far longer and cost far more than would otherwise have been the case?

The question of neutrality is actually not difficult to resolve. Once again, "veto power" is the key. Any party to a dispute can disqualify a proposed helper who seems biased. Obviously, the background and affiliation of the intermediary are fundamental considerations. It is much easier for a helper to be accepted by all the parties, for example, if he or she has had no direct affiliation with any of the stakeholders. Also, the record and reputation of the proposed helper should be reviewed and approved by all the participants. If the helper begins work before all anticipated participants have joined the negotiations, it should be with a clear understanding that the helper may still be disqualified by a late participant with a complaint about bias.

These same four criteria—background, affiliation, record, and reputation—are equally useful in assessing a potential intermediary's competence. For specific advice about finding and hiring a helper, please consult the next chapter, in which we discuss these and other practical issues (who is going to pay?) in greater detail.

Different helpers have distinct styles. Some define their role very narrowly; others are willing to take on a broader set of roles. Some expect the disputants to handle many of the details of the negotiation; others are willing to carry more of the burden.[1] It makes sense to ask a potential helper to submit a proposed contract enumerating his or her concerns and commitments. It is not uncommon for disputants to collect written information about and interview half a dozen potential helpers before settling on one. A written agreement spelling out the disputants' expectations regarding the helper's role and obligations can avoid misunderstandings later.

Roles and Functions of an Intermediary

The easiest way to think about the functions that a helper plays in a public dispute is to refer again to the three phases of the consensus-building process described in chapter 4. There are several tasks that the helper can complete at each step. [See Table 4.1.]

Getting started, as we have already emphasized, may well depend on the assistance of a nonpartisan convenor. The helper, however he or she entered the process, will probably have to spend a substantial amount of time meeting with potential stakeholders to convince them that a negotiated approach can work. Because the notion of joint problem solving is alien to most parties in public disputes, helpers often find it necessary to describe situations in which consensual approaches produced better outcomes than conventional approaches. This means that the intermediary needs to be well versed in the actual practice, and not just the theory, of dispute resolution.

The neutral can allow all parties to maintain the appearance of "toughness" while still supporting the search for integrative outcomes. This is accomplished by allowing the parties to communicate cooperative messages through the helper while maintaining a less cooperative "public" stance in meetings of the full group. To the extent that the helper can alert the parties ahead of time to the fact that an uncompromising statement is about to be made, but that the statement does not really represent that stakeholder's "bottom line," the helper can head off confrontations. In addition, by suggesting neutral turf for the first meeting, handling all the logistical arrangements, and proposing a provisional set of protocols to guide the initial discussions, the helper can assist the parties in overcoming many of the initial obstacles to successful negotiation.

Table 4.1. Tasks of the Mediator

Phases	Tasks
PRE-NEGOTIATION	
Getting started	Meeting with potential stakeholders to assess their interests and describe the consensus building process; handling logistics and convening initial meetings; assisting groups in initial calculation of BATNAs
Representation	Caucusing with stakeholders to help choose spokespeople or team leaders; working with initial stakeholders to identify missing groups or strategies for representing diffuse interests
Drafting protocols and agenda setting	Preparing draft protocols based on past experience and the concerns of the parties; managing the process of agenda setting
Joint fact-finding	Helping to draft fact-finding protocols; identifying technical consultants or advisors to the group; raising and administering the funds in a resource pool; serving as a repository for confidential or proprietary information
NEGOTIATION	
Inventing options	Managing the brainstorming process; suggesting potential options for the group to consider; coordinating subcommittees to draft options
Packaging	Caucusing privately with each group to identify and test possible trades; suggesting possible packages for the group to consider
Written agreement	Working with a subcommittee to produce a draft agreement; managing a single-text procedure; preparing a preliminary draft of a single text
Binding the parties	Serving as the holder of the bond; approaching outsiders on behalf of the group; helping to invent new ways to bind the parties to their commitments
Ratification	Helping the participants "sell" the agreement to their constituents; ensuring that all representatives have been in touch with their constituents
IMPLEMENTATION OR POST-NEGOTIATION	
Linking informal agreements and decision making	Working with the parties to invent linkages; approaching elected or appointed officials on formal behalf of the group; identifying the legal constraints on implementation
Monitoring	Serving as the monitor of implementation; convening a monitoring group
Renegotiation	Reassembling the participants if subsequent disagreements emerge; helping to remind the group of its earlier intentions

It may appear that we are describing a "chicken-and-egg" problem: The parties must meet in order to identify a helper who will help them arrange a meeting. This is rarely the case in practice. Typically, a potential helper is contacted by one side (without the concurrence of the others) or by a noninvolved observer. The helper then calls the other parties and (assuming conditions are right) proposes either an initial get-together, at which everyone can talk, or a round of private caucuses between the helper and each stakeholding group. The helper has no guarantee that he or she will be paid, or that negotiations are even likely to happen. This is an "up-front" investment of time that potential helpers must make, comparable to the investment builders make when they prepare a bid for a possible project.

Representation is another prenegotiation task that helpers are often called upon to handle. Before a professional mediator or facilitator will invest the time needed to complete a conflict assessment or to help with representation, however, he or she will probably require a contract. Such a contract might cover only the first few steps in the proposed negotiation process. It might be written initially with just the key stakeholders, and amended later as more groups are added, and as the stakeholders decide to commit to a full-fledged negotiation. The preliminary contract gives the helper an indication of the seriousness of the group's commitment to the process.

Intermediaries can advise potential stakeholders about strategies for selecting spokespersons. They can also assist all the participants in undertaking a preliminary analysis of their alternatives to negotiation. They can make it clear to groups anxious about perceived imbalances of power that everyone will have a chance to be heard, and that available information will be shared.

As a spokesperson for and manager of the process, the helper is the only one in a position to promise the parties that the rules of the game will be enforced. The helper can also serve as a link to the media. In fact, it is often advisable for the helper to be the only person who talks to the press during an ongoing negotiation. This minimizes the temptation some groups may feel to negotiate through the press.

The neutral can play a critical role in bringing recalcitrant parties to the bargaining table. For example, by offering assurances that the rules of the game will be strictly enforced, the helper may be able to sign on less powerful groups. Conversely, the neutral may bring subtle pressure to bear on more powerful parties, by convincing them that sitting on the sidelines could entail a high price. If used heavy-handedly, of course, such tactics usually backfire. But if used skillfully, they may overcome what would otherwise be insurmountable barriers to consensus building.

Development of protocols and agenda setting are tasks that are best managed by a neutral—first through private discussions with each party, and then in group discussion. The listing of potential agenda topics may seem a simple mechanical task, but in fact there is an art to compressing numerous items into a manageable set of priorities that all parties can accept.

Experienced intermediaries can also save disputants a great deal of time by drafting preliminary protocols. Blending elements from past dispute situations, the helper can provide a draft that the group can use as a starting point. At the very least, illustrations of the ways in which other groups have handled similar problems are reassuring. The helper can also include the draft agenda and the agreed-upon protocols as conditions of his or her contract. This not only commits the neutral to procedures the participants want, but it also reassures mistrustful parties that the protocols will not be ignored.

Joint fact-finding may require various kinds of assistance from a neutral. For example, the group may rely on a helper to come up with names of potential expert advisors that all stakeholders can accept. The intermediary may serve as the "banker" for studies that are jointly commissioned—holding and allocating funds contributed by each of the stakeholders. In situations involving confidential or proprietary information, the helper may be asked to summarize data in ways that protect one party's legitimate need for privacy, without concealing useful data. A variation on this role arises when negotiators must share business information, but such sharing may constitute a violation of antitrust laws. The neutral, in such a circumstance, can serve as a repository for information, using summaries of findings without mentioning particular companies.

A neutral may also be asked to assist in raising money to establish a resource pool—that is, a "kitty" of money which the group as a whole can draw upon. At one point, for example, the EPA created a resource pool to ensure the availability of funds to the participants in that agency's "negotiated rulemakings."[2] The participants were meeting, at EPA's request, to help draft regulations to implement a portion of the Clean Air Act. The funds in the resource pool were available to any of the twenty-five participating groups who needed reimbursement for travel or other expenses incurred during the negotiations. Resources were also available to the group as a whole to commission joint fact-finding studies. The convenor—not an EPA official—held the funds for the group and allocated them in accordance with decisions made by the group as a whole.

Sometimes a *team* of intermediaries is needed. This is particularly useful in complex disputes hinging on scientific questions. In such a case, an expert in process management may want to team up with a neutral who has relevant technical background. Again, the second member of the team would also have to be acceptable to all the stakeholders, even though he or she would advise the process manager rather than the participants.

Even more elaborate teams are sometimes appropriate. In the Harmon County sewage cleanup case described in chapter 3, the out-of-state mediator appointed by the court teamed up with a local mediator—who had a thorough knowledge of the state's political and legal systems—as well as with several engineering professionals, who developed a computer model the mediators could use to forecast the costs of various settlement proposals.

Inventing options, as we indicated in the previous chapter, requires a process of brainstorming and intensive subcommittee work. The neutral can be the one to declare a period of "inventing without committing." He or she can also be the compiler of good ideas. The helper may even put forward options that participants want considered but feel uneasy about suggesting themselves. So, for example, one or another group might approach the helper privately and ask that he or she mention an option without revealing its source.

Inventing options has its perils, though. Intermediaries have to be careful not to become too closely identified with particular options or proposals, for if a participant feels that the helper has become too supportive of a specific proposal, that stakeholder may feel that the helper can no longer be trusted to remain neutral. This does not mean, of course, that intermediaries cannot offer suggestions. Skilled neutrals should know how to present ideas in a dispassionate fashion, thereby reassuring the participants that the intermediary is nonpartisan.

Packaging is the step that generally involves the greatest skill and insight. It is here that helpers can play their most important role. By meeting privately with each participant, an intermediary should be able to discover which items are tradeable. Typically, the helper says to each party in a private caucus, "What's most important to you?" Or, "What can you most readily give up?" Through confidential questioning, an effective intermediary should be able to figure out a set of trades that will bring the participants as close to agreement as they can possibly get. (Of course, this can only occur if the neutral has already demonstrated competence and earned the trust of the parties.)

An intermediary can offer the parties a chance to suggest possible trades without making commitments. In a private conversation, the helper might say, "I know what you've said in the full meetings, but tell me: Would you will be willing to trade X if the others offered you Y and Z?" At this point, the disputant might say, "I won't say it out loud at the meeting, but if I were offered Y and Z, yes, I would trade X." This is crucial information which the helper must find a way of testing with the other parties—without violating a confidence, of course.

A skilled intermediary can, in private meetings with the other participants, explore whether they would be willing to give up Y and Z in exchange for X. This might be phrased, "What if I could get them to give up X? Would you trade Y and Z?" Of course, the neutral already knows that such a trade is possible. He or she must phrase the question, though, in what-if format to protect the confidentiality of the information secured earlier. If the answer is "yes," the helper might call everyone together and offer the following observation: "I have a hunch that if the folks on this side of the room were willing to offer X the others would promise to give Y and Z. Am I correct?"

By proceeding in this fashion, the intermediary has made no promises, and has attributed no commitments to anyone. The end result, if all goes well, is a package that everyone can accept.

Written agreements need to be drafted by someone, and in most cases the neutral is the obvious person to play this role. To the extent that an intermediary can produce a single text and carry it from party to party, he or she can ensure that everyone agrees to the same thing. This is a great advantage in negotiations. Long-time international treaty negotiators use the "single-text" procedure described earlier, which is much more likely to produce agreement than a process in which each party drafts its own version of the final agreement and those versions are later integrated.

In the single text procedure, the helper asks each party to suggest "improvements" in a draft attributed to the intermediary. Because the draft is not "extreme" and refrains from arguing only for what one side or the other wants most, progress is likely to ensue.

Binding the parties involves the invention of enforcement mechanisms. We have already described the device of setting aside funds. In some instances, the intermediary may be the person favored by all sides to "hold the bet." In other instances, the helper may be asked to approach someone who has not been involved in the negotiations, to see whether that individual might play a role in binding the parties. It is usually the case that skilled helpers can assist disputing parties in inventing new ways to bind each other to an agreement.

Ratification requires each participant to go back to his or her constituents and seek approval of the draft agreement. For some participants, this may present difficulties, particularly if their group began the negotiations with utterly unrealistic expectations. The helper may be able to aid such participants in "selling" the agreement to their members, perhaps by pointing out how far all the other stakeholders have come in accepting the draft agreement. The helper may also be able to emphasize truthfully how effective the group's negotiator was. ("You should have seen how far along your spokesperson was able to pull the rest of the group. She was an incredibly effective advocate of your interests.") The group's spokesperson, of course, could not make such claims without seeming to brag. If true, though, the fact of effectiveness is significant, and needs to be pointed out.

The process of *linking the informal agreement and formal decision making* requires interaction with elected or appointed officials, who may not have participated directly in the negotiations (although they should have been apprised of the progress of the negotiations by their staff or appointed observers). Because the neutral is an advocate of the process and not of any particular outcome, it is usually easier for officials to accept a helper's claim regarding the legitimacy of the process than the claims of a stakeholder.

The participants may want the helper to play a role in *monitoring* implementation of the agreement. Although this is not often the case (it is better to have monitoring performed by people on the scene), it is sometimes a possibility. The helper may be asked by the participants to approach outsiders who have not been involved in the negotiations to ask them to play the monitoring role. In many cases, it is easier for the helper to make these contacts, and to be convincing about the legitimacy of the process, than it is for any one of the disputants.

It is likely that the participants will want to specify in the agreement what the helper's role will be if *renegotiation* (or "remediation") is necessary. Who better to reassemble the parties, or to remind them of their previous commitments? Also, the parties are likely to feel that the helper will be a fair referee of what was originally intended, should subsequent disagreements arise. It should be noted, though, that very few helpers will accept a renegotiation role if they have assisted in drafting the original agreement; they prefer to move on to new disputes.

When we describe the roles and functions of intermediaries in distributional disputes, some people mistakenly conclude that helpers in public disputes do roughly what intermediaries in labor disputes or international disputes do. But those familiar with the roles of such intermediaries (or "third parties," as they are often called, as there are usually only two disputing sides in labor negotiations) will recognize immediately from the preceding descriptions that there are very substantial differences between assisted negotiation in distributional disputes and other kinds of assisted negotiation.

In short, neutrals in distributional disputes need to be more activist. They have a much broader array of responsibilities, because the context in which they work is much less structured. They need a different kind of background, different skills, and perhaps a different temperament from their counterparts in labor relations and international relations. Intermediaries in distributional disputes usually need to be quite conversant with the ways in which the public sector operates, because they may spend as much time creating the context in which negotiations take place as they do managing the consensus-building process. They also need more sharply honed communication skills, since they may have to spend significant amounts of time "selling the process" to potential participants and the community at large.

Given the scope of the intermediaries' involvement in most distributional disputes, it is important that they be willing to accept some responsibility for the fairness, efficiency, wisdom, and stability of the outcomes. This is not inconsistent with the concept of neutrality. While those who participate directly must "own" the agreement, the neutral must also assure himself or herself that everything possible has been done to meet the concerns of those who chose not to participate directly as well as the concerns of those who did. Long-term voluntary compliance requires that this test be met. Unless it is, the credibility of the consensus-building effort is likely to erode. In addition, to the extent that consensual dispute resolution processes are likely to be judged against the conventional judicial, administrative, and legislative mechanisms, assisted negotiation must meet the same tests of performance they do.

Three Forms of Assisted Negotiation

Within the realm of assisted negotiation, various approaches can be taken. We will consider three: *facilitation, mediation, and nonbinding arbitration.* These techniques, though distinguishable, are not mutually exclusive. In fact, a helper may find it advantageous to move back and forth among them as a negotiation progresses. These approaches are presented separately in the following pages primarily to make clear what each entails.

In general, the stakeholders must make a preliminary decision about the form of assistance they want—if only to help them choose an appropriately skilled neutral. The question they must first answer is, "How much help will we need in order to work together effectively?" Conceived differently, the same question may be phrased, "How much assistance in managing the negotiation process are we likely to require in order to reach a satisfactory conclusion?" Process is the key word here. Facilitation, mediation, and nonbinding arbitration assign different degrees of procedural responsibility to the helper. In all negotiations, the issues of managerial responsibility is paramount. Ideally, the disputing parties should retain as much control as possible over the dispute resolution process. If they do, they are much more likely to produce an agreement they will support.

Indeed, this was our rationale for focusing first on unassisted negotiation. We maintain that it is best when disputing parties retain full control over both the process and substance of a dispute resolution effort. But when unassisted negotiations fail, or when the problem is obviously too complex for resolution without help, the disputing parties must consider the various forms of assistance available.

As noted, we have chosen to limit our discussion and recommendations to facilitation, mediation, and nonbinding arbitration. We have not included a fourth technique: binding arbitration. One compelling argument against employing binding arbitration in distributional disputes is a legal one. In most cases, public officials are not permitted to delegate their authority to an arbitrator. Therefore, the application of binding arbitration is severely limited. More important, in the context of this book, is our conviction that disputing parties can and should deal with their differences themselves. They are more likely to confront the sources of difficulty and improve long-term relationships if they do. Turning over responsibility for decision making to an outsider rarely resolves underlying conflicts.

Facilitation

Facilitation is the simplest form of assisted negotiation. The facilitator focuses almost entirely on process, makes sure meeting places and times are agreed upon, sees that meeting space is arranged appropriately, and ensures that notes and minutes of the meetings are kept. He or she sometimes acts as a moderator, usually when many parties are involved.

Even in the moderator's role, however, facilitators rarely volunteer their own ideas. Instead, they monitor the quality of the dialogue and intervene with questions designed to enhance understanding. "Are you really listening to each other?" the facilitator might ask. "I've jotted down what each person has said. Are you sure you've identified what's most important to you? Why don't you say again what you are really concerned about, so that the others can focus on that?"

Comments of this type certainly touch on the substance of the issues being discussed, but the facilitator's emphasis is on communication. He or she uses whatever tools are available to create and foster an environment conducive to joint problem solving. Without pretending to be a therapist, the facilitator also tries to make it easier for the participants to express their emotions.

A facilitator must improvise from meeting to meeting, taking cues from the negotiations themselves. Perhaps the best way to illustrate this improvisational activity—as well as the more general and constant activities of the facilitator—is to return to two of our original cases: RiverEnd and the dioxin dispute.

Facilitating the RiverEnd Dispute Resolution Effort

The RiverEnd negotiations took place over fourteen months, with the participants meeting one evening every two weeks. Meetings were held in a state agency field office in the RiverEnd area. Attendance rarely dropped below twenty-five, and there were almost always observers and reporters present, in part because all meetings were listed in the local newspapers. Participants agreed at the onset that no formal votes would be taken, and that informal procedures would be used in preference to Robert's *Rules of Order*. Facilitator Elliott Lawrence was asked to chair all the meetings, to regulate the pace and topics of conversation, and to assume whatever other responsibilities for managing the process he deemed necessary.

Included in the group of active participants were engineers, landscape architects, and environmental scientists. All had backgrounds and professional credentials equal to or greater than those of the agency personnel or the consultants selected by the state government to assist the group. Neighborhood representatives had extensive firsthand information about such significant factors as flooding patterns, water flow, noise levels, and wildlife habitats. The citizen participants, to their credit, were not intimidated by claims that certain evidence or analytical techniques might be too complex for them to understand. They plowed through the reports, references, and documents produced by the consultants, and spent hours debating the merits of baseline estimates, forecasts, and impact assessments.

The negotiations generally confirmed the adage that the best ideas occur to prepared minds. A consensus could not have emerged before the individuals stakeholders understood the details of the proposed project, and were unfamiliar with each interest group's priorities. Preparation, therefore, was essential, and the facilitator Lawrence used five techniques to enhance the group's understanding: (1) "charettes," (2) opinion surveys and straw polls, (3) brainstorming sessions, (4) role playing, and (5) collective image building.

Charettes, or intensive problem-solving workshops, were used to explore specifics such as possible alignments of the transit tracks through residential areas. Participants sketched the most desirable alignments and station locations on a large map. Each participant or coalition presented its map and argued for its proposals. The rest of the participants then indicated their concerns and raised questions about possible engineering constraints.

Between meetings, participants were asked by Lawrence to mail back questionnaires designed to clarify underlying conflicts. For instance, a poll with multiple-choice answers detailing the probable advantages and disadvantages of different parking garage sizes narrowed the scope of the debate, and suggested that a broader basis of agreement existed than was indicated by the participants' public positions. Presentation of these survey results eliminated the need for extended debate and sharpened the agenda to everyone's satisfaction.

Brainstorming sessions were used to generate additional design options, and also to identify issues about which the participants were confused. For instance, early attempts to generate new roadway and ramp designs indicated that many of the participants were unclear about the constraints posed by grade, slope, and soil characteristics, even though they had already heard general presentations on these subjects. As a result, the facilitator scheduled additional presentations by outside experts acceptable to the entire group.

Role-playing exercises, which encouraged disputants to switch positions, helped to build respect and understanding for opposing points of view. The most ardent developers, for example, were teamed up with the environmentalists to examine the probable environmental impacts of suggested roadway designs. Similarly, environmentalists were asked to look at the same roadway proposals with an eye toward maximizing the return on private investment and increasing tax revenues for Capital City.

Finally, in an effort to focus the participants' thinking about possible open-space improvements, the group examined color slides of parks and parklike elements—such as landscaping along highways, lighting, and pedestrian walkways—from other places in the country. These explorations helped the group crystallize its concerns about esthetics. One of the most interesting outcomes of the collective imaging process was that after viewing slides of other garages (including some superimposed on the proposed RiverEnd site), almost everyone agreed that a 10,000-car garage, the size proposed initially by the state, was utterly inappropriate.

As meeting after meeting clarified concerns and sharpened differences, facilitator Lawrence searched for ways to help the parties put together a package that would be acceptable to everyone. He encouraged the formation of a subcommittee to think about the opportunities created by the regional mass transit facility, rather than just the problems or adverse impacts it was likely to cause. At his suggestion, the group was headed by the most ardent environmentalist, Horst Seybolt, and dubbed itself the "Linear Park group." It envisioned parklike landscaping along the transportation corridor that would connect open space areas, soften the impact of the automobile, and create a pleasant atmosphere for pedestrians. Other environmentalists supported this idea because they thought it would reinforce the hoped-for "human scale" of the new transit facilities, and enhance the visual appearance of the area. It also had some potential to channel federal and state transportation money into a "kitty" that could be used to add recreational and open spaces, improve pedestrian and bicycle paths, and restore the long-vanished parklike atmosphere along the roadway.

The Linear Park group, with consulting assistance arranged by Lawrence, prepared and presented detailed proposals to the full group. The development-oriented members of the group agreed that the linear park concept would provide a competitive edge in attracting commercial investment and new customers. Landscaping and land acquisition would complement, rather than impede, construction of the new subway station and garage.

The linear park concept emerged in large part because the environmentalists were unhappy with most of the options put forward by the state and regional agencies. The proposals generated by the state presumed that the primary objective of the project was to create a regional transit stop that would spur economic development; it was clear that effecting environmental improvements was not an important agency objective.

The environmentalists originally felt they had no choice but to argue for the no-build option, which they did. They were immediately accused of impeding progress, of sabotaging the planning effort, and of frustrating the legitimate economic interests of the neighborhoods. This was an uncomfortable position. Moreover, they soon realized that a constructive alternative would give them additional bargaining leverage. Although they threatened more than once to block the entire project in the courts, they ultimately decided instead to use the proposed subway extension to seek environmental improvements. Why? Because they had reached a crucial realization: No outcome resulting from a lengthy court battle was likely to reverse RiverEnd's decline, which after all had resulted from decades of neglect and unplanned development.

RiverEnd, then, can serve as a useful model of facilitation. Through the activities designed and managed by the facilitator, the stakeholders began to see items that could be traded. The emergence of the linear park proposal, through which almost every group could gain at least partially, helped to persuade skeptics that a consensual approach was both possible and promising. By managing meetings to ensure effective communication and by assisting the participants in programming their time, Lawrence created a climate in which joint problem solving was possible. Significantly, he did not offer proposals. He did not meet privately with the parties between meetings. He did not carry confidential messages back and forth among the factions at the bargaining table. He did not help the parties produce a written agreement, or design mechanisms for binding each other to their commitments. Lawrence basically "managed" the group discussions—and, by the time those discussions concluded, all parties felt they had achieved a fairer, more stable, more efficient, and wiser agreement than would otherwise have emerged.

Facilitating the Dioxin Negotiation

You will recall that Dr. Gene McGerny, the facilitator in the dioxin case, was asked by the Academy of Sciences to bring together the scientists and engineers who disagreed about the risks associated with the proposed resource recovery plant at the Federal Navy Yard. Most of the members of the city council (or representatives from their staff) were in the audience; they faced the assembled experts seated at the front of the room. Approximately thirty neighborhood and environmental groups, including many residents of the Brownstone neighborhood, were also in attendance.

Dr. McGerny had worked hard before the meeting to get the city council members to list in writing the issues that most concerned them. The questions he received in response were easily grouped under three headings: the nature of the dioxin risk, the possibility of reducing or eliminating the risk, and the health impacts of dioxin emissions. The first set of questions was most usefully put to environmental scientists; the second to engineers; and the third to medical or public health specialists. Dr. McGerny had taken special care to assemble balanced panels: None of the participants had as yet taken a public stand on the question posed by the city council.

As Dr. McGerny put the first set of questions, one at a time, to the panel of scientists, he tried to avoid any indication that he was taking sides. Each panelist was given all the time he or she needed to answer each question. Panelists had the chance to pose questions to each other, as well as to comment on what the others had said. City council members had the opportunity to ask follow-up questions through Dr. McGerny. Whenever the interaction among the scientists drifted into highly technical exchanges, McGerny interrupted, seeking clarification in "plain English."

By the end of the first panel on the nature and sources of dioxin, it had become clear that there were two very different schools of thought. One side believed strongly that dioxin was the natural and inevitable by-product of incinerating plastic and paper at the same time (a theory popularized by the ubiquitous ecologist, Professor Lassiter, who attended the session). The other side disputed this view, arguing that dioxin and its dangers could be eliminated entirely by proper burning.

By the end of the second panel—which examined the prospects of controlling the dioxin risk, if it indeed arose—conflicting views had again emerged. One group of engineers believed that burning municipal trash at a high enough temperature, and by simultaneously controlling the amount of oxygen present, dioxin emissions could be all but eliminated. Whatever tiny amounts remained could be captured by flue filters or removed by precipitators. But another group of engineers argued that based on the data they had obtained from resource recovery plants operating elsewhere, high temperatures, controlled oxygen flow, and filters and precipitators would still permit the escape of a significant amount of dioxin.

A split also developed among the health experts regarding the nature of the risk to humans posed by dioxin in the air. They disagreed on whether it was reasonable to infer from tests on laboratory rats what the effects of dioxin would be on people. Each side posited different models of events that might lead to unsafe dioxin emissions from the resource recovery plant. One model, for example, depicted a chain of events in which the plant broke down during the summer. Emissions then drifted into homes through open windows, dust settled on the floors and windowsills, and dioxin was ultimately ingested through hand contact.

As the panelists talked, the facilitator highlighted their arguments on large pads of paper displayed at the front of the room. As each page was filled, the facilitator taped it to the wall. Soon paper covered practically every available inch of wall space. Dr. McGerny repeatedly checked with the panelists to be certain that he had recorded the points they thought were most important. This somewhat exhausting process lasted almost eight hours, but as certain patterns began to emerge, it proved to be time well spent.

For example, some of the conflicts arose from reliance on different sets of data, with one side claiming that precedents cited by the other were irrelevant. The engineers could not even agree on whether existing resource recovery plants were similar enough in design to the plant proposed for the Navy Yard to permit comparisons.

A second source of conflict could be traced to the different ways in which the experts framed their questions. For instance, one health-effects expert attempted to answer the question, "Is there any chance that a dangerous amount of dioxin could escape into the environment?" His answer was yes. His scientific adversary, however, was trying to answer a different question, "Is it likely that a dangerous amount of dioxin will escape?" His answer was no. When pressed by the facilitator, the first expert agreed that the chances of getting cancer from a dioxin leak were less that a nonsmoker's chances of getting cancer from living with a smoker. Both experts agreed, on the other hand, that if a large amount of dioxin did manage to escape into the air, the cancer rate in Metropolis might well increase significantly.

The most important source of controversy, however, did not result from these sorts of scientific, engineering, and epidemiological differences. The disagreement hinged, as it turned out, on one side's use of a "worst case" scenario and the other's reliance on a "most likely case." It soon became clear that what had been thought of as a fundamental disagreement regarding the facts—in other words, the basic science of the dispute—was in reality a disagreement over the choice of a method of analysis. (Everyone had agreed, we should note, that the state's proposed dioxin emission standard was reasonable.)

Although the sessions were somewhat heated, the debate proceeded in an orderly fashion. After hearing the presentations, the council had to consider its options. First, however, after some prodding from Dr. McGerny, Professor Lassiter made what appeared to be a significant concession. He agreed to support construction of a pilot resource recovery plant if the city would promise that (1) a careful and regular dioxin monitoring procedure would be adopted; (2) the commercial builder of the plant would sign a contract indicating a willingness to have the plant closed down permanently if it emitted more dioxin than permitted under the state standard; and (3) all liability for accidents or injuries caused by the plant would be covered by either the city or the commercial builder of the plant.

Professor Lassiter, it seems, was assuming that no commercial vendor would agree to build the plant under such unattractive conditions. He was evidently surprised when the Department of Sanitation immediately indicated its readiness to accept these terms. Perhaps that readiness should not have come as such a surprise. After all, from the city's standpoint, a plant ought not to be licensed unless it could meet the agreed-upon state standard. On this point, then, agreement was possible because the contending interests continued to operate with totally different assessments of probable risks. Lassiter, for his part, thought the risk of significant dioxin emissions was high and that no vendor would be willing to live with a double-edged sword of shutdown and liability dangling over its head. The city, on the other hand, was convinced that the technology had been proven effective, and that finding a vendor willing to build a plant that would meet the state standards would be no problem. Therefore, the financial risk was, in their view, small. Although the disputing parties continued to disagree on the nature of the risk, they were—by exploiting their differences—able to agree on how to proceed.

In this case, the facilitator spent little or no time meeting privately with the parties. Instead, McGerny devoted most of his energies to making the meeting work. He was able to clarify the sources and nature of the disagreements, and to make sure everyone understood what was being said. Finally, the facilitator played almost no role in devising the actual terms of an agreement. Instead, Dr. McGerny focused on achieving an agreement in principle.

Facilitation: A Summary

Because facilitation is the simplest form of assisted negotiation, and because the facilitator restricts himself or herself to procedural questions, it might seem that the facilitator's role is insignificant. This is not the case. The facilitator makes possible a negotiating process that would otherwise be impossible. Consider a situation in which each of the disputing parties is unwilling to make the first phone call. ("We don't want to look too anxious; let's wait for them to call us.") Clearly, unassisted negotiation is unlikely to begin in such a situation, let alone succeed. In other cases, one or more of the parties may make it clear that they will not even consider coming to the table, if by so doing they must give up any control over the substance of the negotiation. Again, the facilitator makes otherwise impossible negotiations possible.

Even after negotiations have begun and seem to be proceeding well, the facilitator can play a vital role. What happens, for example, if one of the disputing parties stalks out of the proceedings as a result of a real or imagined slight? Without a facilitator, the negotiations simply stop. With a facilitator, there is a chance that they can resume, perhaps on an improved footing. "Let me talk with the others privately," the facilitator can say to the aggrieved party. "Let me see if I can get them to recognize that from your standpoint they are being unreasonable."

In summary, facilitation is called for when the disputing parties need some assistance, but want that help limited to focusing or moderating their discussions. The facilitator serves at the pleasure of all the negotiating parties. All parties must jointly choose the facilitator, but each group has the right to "fire" that person if they conclude that he or she is biased, incompetent, or otherwise unsatisfactory. The facilitator, a skilled process manager, takes whatever procedural steps are necessary to keep the discussion on a useful course.

Mediation

Mediation intensifies the substantive involvement of the neutral without removing control over the outcome from the parties. It also involves the helper in a great deal more confidential interaction with the parties. Just as some disputes are too complex for unassisted negotiation, others are too formidable for facilitation. In such cases, the disputing parties should decide ahead of time that they need more help from an outside neutral.

The parties may begin with facilitation and discover that they are not making much progress, or that the progress they are making is too slow. Or—simply put—the parties may not be good at sitting in a room together. The "hardness" of their public postures may preclude real give and take. If this is the case, they may need someone to relieve them of responsibility for devising and presenting options. "We know we need help," they may conclude, "and that means more than someone to facilitate communication and arrange meetings. We need someone who can meet with each side privately and give us a sense of how far apart we really are."

For those private meetings to succeed, the neutral must be knowledgeable about the issues of concern to the parties. This is one important function of the mediator: carrying private messages among parties. In essence, the mediator plays a transforming role—helping the parties out of a zero-sum mind-set into an integrative bargaining framework. Early in the negotiating process, private caucuses are crucial to understanding the real interests of the parties and the ways they have calculated their BATNAs. To ensure candid exchanges, the mediator must be able to promise confidentiality.

With the inside knowledge that comes from these meetings, the mediator is not in the position to understand what is tradeable and what is not. Moving back and forth among the parties, the mediator is in a position to launch trial balloons. As we mentioned earlier, the mediator may begin meetings with statements like this: "I have a hunch that if Group A offers this and Group B offers that, you will find yourselves much closer together than you imagined."

While taking a large measure of responsibility for the substance of the agreement that emerges, the mediator must remain neutral. In other words, the mediator must submerge his or her sense of what is "best," and focus instead on the disputing parties' own measures of success. For many professional mediators, this is a very difficult role to play. Many of them have extensive knowledge about the substance of the dispute; this means they are likely to have personal feelings about what will work and what will not. Their previous mediation experience, furthermore, may tempt them to "steer" the negotiations toward solutions that have proven successful in the past.

Both of these temptations must be resisted. As for the mediator's own conclusions regarding the substance of the negotiated agreement, they can be destructive if expressed in a way that implies partiality. A mediator with a commitment to a particular outcome is akin to a real estate agent—who seems to act as a neutral intermediary, but is in fact an advocate for one side, with a direct financial interest in the sale price. At the same time, the mediator must generate enthusiasm and support for a proposed settlement. If the mediator steers a negotiation in a direction that the parties only halfheartedly support, subsequent implementation of the agreement will be difficult.

There are qualities of a negotiated agreement for which a mediator must be willing to be held accountable. The perceived fairness of the outcome, for example, is as much the mediator's responsibility as it is the parties'. If the mediator permits a process that is viewed as unfair at its conclusion, and does not urge the parties to consider other, more appropriate ways of proceeding, he or she will not have done a creditable job. This is very much an interventionist posture, because raising such concerns does not necessarily guarantee that the parties will make adjustments. (If they fail to do so, of course, the mediator must ultimately decide whether or not to remain a part of the negotiations.) The long-term credibility of a mediator depends on ensuring that every possible effort was made to meet the interests of all the parties involved. If a proposed settlement appears exploitative or unworkable, the mediator is obligated to question the validity of such a settlement. He or she should seek to "raise doubts," either by invoking concerns about subsequent implementability or fairness.

Sharing responsibility means that the mediator will raise these concerns. It is not the mediator's role, however, to dictate terms, or to represent specific interests who may be having trouble representing themselves effectively. When conflicts arise—whether between the disputing parties or between the parties and "outside-world" interests—the mediator rarely says, "I'll tell you what you ought to do." Instead, the mediator tends to ask, "Can't we review the procedures we have followed, and come up with something that will get everyone closer to their individual objectives? I'll tell you how I think the outside world will respond to what we have come up with so far; but my job is to help you reach an agreement that is yours."

Three of the cases introduced in chapter 3—the fishing rights dispute, the Harmon County sewage dispute, and the conflict over social service block grant priorities—were resolved with the help of mediators. The circumstances were different and therefore different approaches to mediation were required. Nevertheless, they illustrate clearly the advantages of mediation.

Mediating the Fishing Rights Dispute

Judge Eastman encouraged the disputants to select a mediator from the list of twelve candidates he had identified. (His assumption was that the parties would be more inclined to work with someone they had selected.) The disputants settled on mediator Leslie Burmaster, who was hired with funds provided by the federal and state governments. Each level of government put $100,000 into a "kitty," from which the mediator could be paid by the court (at a specified hourly rate), and through which technical studies could be purchased.

Burmaster spent three months getting to know the parties. The key participants included the director of the state's Department of Natural resources, a lawyer for the state, the deputy undersecretary of the U.S. Department of Interior, and the negotiators for the tribes. Burmaster also spent the first few months assembling a team of technical consultants, whose responsibility it would be to advise the parties about the impact of alternative management policies on the total fish catch. The consultants, including specialists from a range of disciplines, put together detailed models of the lake's ecology.

Before beginning the full negotiations, Burmaster decided to bring the tribes together to negotiate an intertribal allocation plan. She encouraged them to negotiate an agreement that would go into effect whether or not the tribes and the state reached an agreement. From Burmaster's perspective, whether the tribes collectively ended up with 20 percent or 80 percent of the overall catch, they would still have to agree on how to divide their share. Burmaster saw a successful intertribal negotiation as an inducement to the state to bargain seriously. Finally, she knew that the intertribal negotiations could only help the relatively inexperienced tribal negotiators sharpen their bargaining skills.

The tribes met for five days under Burmaster's watchful eye. Burmaster spent most of the time helping the parties understand each other's positions. She talked to them in a way that they could not, or would not, talk to each other. Burmaster made no effort to develop specific proposals; these, she felt, should come from them. In a relatively short period, the tribes were able to reach agreement, allocating certain sections of the lake to each tribe, and indicating specific times of the year when each tribe would be allowed to fish in given areas.

Having settled their internal differences, the tribes then collectively demanded 70 percent of the whitefish catch, leaving the remainder of the whitefish and the blue trout to commercial and sports fisherman. State officials resisted this demand for an overall allocation of the catch; they preferred instead to allocate the right to fish in certain zones of the lake. This might have been a difficult point, except for the fact that the federal government offered substantially more money than expected to cover the costs of managing the fisheries. The state, by prior agreement, was forced to match this increased federal allocation. The combined sums available for fish management assured the tribes that the total catch would increase, and that a rigid allocation of the catch was unnecessary.

In brief, the agreement divided the lake into zones for tribal fishing, nontribal commercial fishing, and game fishing. Several blue trout refuges were established and made off limits to all parties. Federal and state funds were assigned to a biological monitoring system, as well as the new fisheries management program. Mechanisms for implementing the agreement (which was to remain operative for fifteen years, until 2000) were also negotiated. Three joint committees were established: one to monitor the fish, one to decide how to manage the resources, and one to resolve disputes.

Although the drafting of a written agreement took a great deal of time, the final version was completed in a two-day session. Working through the night, the parties had nearly completed a final draft when the process stalled in the predawn hours. Everyone at the table was exhausted and short-tempered. Nevertheless, Burmaster feared that if she allowed the parties to break for even a few hours, the fragile understandings arrived at to that point might well unravel. She took a calculated risk: leading the key parties into a private room, she closed the door and staged a mock tantrum. Burmaster told them curtly that the agreement would almost certainly fall apart if they did not finish quickly. In fact, she said, they had to decide then and there whether they really wanted an agreement; then she stalked out of the room. The ploy worked: The parties quickly agreed on a final draft of the document.

Burmaster made several strategic choices that paid off. She decided to play a less intrusive role in shaping the agenda and formulating specific proposals than she might have. She encouraged the parties to think in terms of a fifteen-year agreement, rather than one that would last "in perpetuity." This took some of the pressure off the parties: If they made a mistake, there would be an opportunity to renegotiate. She also realized that "zoning" the lake was the key to transforming a win-lose situation into an all-gain opportunity.

As noted, she worked first with the tribes to produce an intertribal agreement, which in turn could be used to bring the state to the table. Burmaster decided to work directly with the parties, rather than their lawyers. (The lawyers were later assigned the task of drafting a document consistent with the commitments the parties had made to each other.) In short, she concentrated on enhancing the parties' ability to understand each other. Through her active interventions, the parties were able to reframe issues, share and generate new information, and develop procedures that allowed them to work together in spite of a lack of trust.

Above all, Burmaster focused on getting agreement in principle, assuming that the design of an implementation strategy could be handled afterward. This assumption turned out to be correct—largely because Burmaster was functioning as a special master under the aegis of the court. When one of the tribes unexpectedly reneged at the last minute on the terms of the final agreement, Judge Eastman ruled that the negotiated agreement was the agreement that the court would enforce. All the parties eventually concurred.

Mediating the Regional Sewage Dispute

Ron Jones and his local assistants, the mediation team, did as Judge Rollenkamp suggested: They searched for a cost allocation formula that all sides could accept. For the first few months, Jones did nothing but meet privately with the stakeholders—thirty-nine municipalities, the Harmon County Regional Sewage Authority, the Randall Company, the state agencies, and various other interests such as the County Homebuilders Association. At each meeting, he asked the same two questions, "What do you think a fair formula would be, and why?"

Jones also consulted with a variety of experts in the area of utility cost allocation. He needed a computer program that the parties could use to forecast the cost implications of alternative formulas.

As the private meeting progressed, the mediation team clarified and added to the list of concerns previously expressed by the parties. From the standpoint of the city of Harmon, the dominant issue was affordability, while the suburban communities and smaller towns were much more concerned about fair cost allocation. The communities in the northern part of the county wanted the sewage system in their district to be designed differently and to operate independently of the main plant in Harmon. This, they argued, would save everyone money. Finally, many of the communities expressed strong distrust of the regional Sewage Authority.

The mediators called in experts to review the detailed design of the sewage system proposed by the Sewage Authority. They sought advice on alternative strategies for financing the system. The more they explored the technical complexity of the dispute, however, the more mired in detail they became. Small but worrisome questions arose by the hundreds. Who, for example, would do a quarterly billing? Who would be responsible for unpaid sewer bills?

The development community, for its part, was worried that the overall capacity of the new regional system might not be sufficient to sustain future growth. Local officials were determined to receive compensation for past investments in local collection systems and treatment plants. Moreover, almost all the local officials wanted some additional role in the management of the new regional system, arguing that the Sewage Authority was not adequately accountable to local concerns.

At a large meeting to which all interested parties were invited, Jones asked for responses to a preliminary "package" of ideas the mediation team had drafted. The proposal had been sent to more than one hundred stakeholders before the meeting. The all-day session produced a number of suggested refinements that were blended into a revised proposal, which Jones submitted to Judge Rollenkamp for review. The judge distributed it for formal comment.

Jones was surprised when negative reactions began pouring into the Judge's office. He thought the proposed agreement had responded to all the issues raised by the parties. As it turned out though, the city of Harmon had decided to press for an even more favorable cost allocation. From Jones' point of view, the adverse reaction arose at least in part because the judge had asked the wrong question. Judge Rollenkamp had asked, "Are you completely happy with this agreement?" Jones would have preferred the judge to ask, "Can you live with this agreement?"

While agreeing that the mediator's package was reasonable, some of the smaller communities argued that they still preferred not to be included in the regional system at all. Indeed, almost every stakeholding group indicated some change it wanted in the proposed agreement.

The judge thanked Jones, and indicated his satisfaction that the issues in the dispute had been narrowed. He also found all the background material and forecasts Jones and his staff had assembled to be quite useful. Jones was not satisfied, however; he asked for a six-week extension, and one more chance to develop an agreement that all the parties would accept. Judge Rollenkamp agreed.

The mediators began another round of private meetings, hoping to find out what it would take to bring the dissenters on board. They soon realized that there were three possible ways to reach closure: first, reduce the overall cost of the system through redesign; second, reduce the cost to the dissenters by bringing in new state or federal funds; or third, redefine the scope of the sewage clean-up problem so that the funds already in hand would be sufficient. Not wanting to limit his options prematurely, Jones decided to push on all three fronts. First, he pressed the regional authority to consider the merits of smaller treatment plants, instead of one large one. He and his staff met with federal and state officials to see if they would increase their financial contributions, in exchange for the parties dropping all pending litigation, and taking prompt action to clean up the rivers and streams. Finally, he pressed the EPA and the state Department of Environmental Protection to consider reducing the scope of the effort—or at least dividing the project into phases, which would have the effect of spreading the project's cost over a much longer time.

After five weeks of intensive negotiations, Jones proposed another package. This time, the city and the Randall Company promised in advance to support the package. The reason for their switch lay in a revised basis for calculating annual sewage charges. Previously, those charges were to be municipally defined "shares" based on each community's percentage of the total flow into the regional system. Under the new plan, there would be a consistent average household charge for everyone in the entire region. (This reduced Harmon's overall charge.) Other towns found tempting amendments in the new package as well. For example, the revised package included a promise of a long-term, no-interest loan from the state, a shift in responsibility for billing and collection from the local to the regional level, compensation to municipalities for abandoned treatment facilities, an option for smaller decentralized treatment plants (if they could be built at lower cost to the region), and the creation of a local advisory board that would ensure greater regional accountability to local concerns.

This time the package won practically unanimous approval. In response to his second "poll" of disputing groups, Judge Rollenkamp heard again from several municipalities that they would still prefer to stay out of the system altogether. This time, though, they indicated a new willingness to live with the proposal if the judge decided to impose it. All the other participants agreed to drop their lawsuits and work together to implement the plan.

Jones and his staff, obviously, played a very active role at every stage of the negotiations, generating proposals and working hard to "sell" those proposals to the parties. The mediators assembled a team of consultants across a broad range of disciplines to back up their efforts. They also worked out a sequence of hoped-for agreements. For example, although they focused first on generating an agreement on the basic components of a cost allocation formula, they also knew that each local official would require a precise forecast of what that formula would mean to his or her constituents before any commitments could be made.

Jones spent a great deal of time meeting behind the scenes with senior state officials. The state's promise of a no-interest, long-term loan to assist in the financing of the second stage of the regional sewage system proved to be the key to lowering each community's total cost. Indeed, when some municipal officials heard that the average annual sewerage charge for the new system would be less than $300 per household per year, they simply lost interest in the entire issue. They had been led to believe that such changes might exceed $1,000 a year. The mediators' success resulted in part from their ability to put together a package that was less onerous financially than what the parties had come to expect and dread.

Social Service Block Grant Allocations

When over one hundred participants met to discuss priorities for the allocation of the "public/private partnership" social service funds, they filled a large hall in one of the universities located in the central part of the state. The mediator, Denise Donovan, had met privately with each of the teams and with the team leaders prior to the first full negotiation session.

Donovan had been chosen by a mediator-selection committee that included five of the initial organizers from each of the four teams. She had been one of the three finalists the committee interviewed. Her contract was officially with the state government (for a total of $35,000), but the terms of the contract had been approved by each of the teams.

It took six hours to reach agreement on the major agenda items and on the protocols that would structure the negotiations. Throughout these initial steps, a great deal of skepticism was expressed by some team members, who felt that there was no chance of reaching a consensus.

The state agency team, headed by the assistant commissioner of the Department of Social Services, included staff from the department's various regional offices. This group pressed for new state guidelines that would give funding priority to underserved groups.

The private donors team was headed by one of the directors of the United Way; this group made it clear that they wanted more flexible matching requirements for donors. The citizen/consumer team was headed by a professor of public administration who had been active on behalf of minority groups in the state, and whose particular interests she intended to serve. The Association of Social Service Providers team was headed by the elected chair of that statewide organization; on behalf of his constituents, he planned to press hard on the issue of wage parity between privately supported and publicly supported social service workers.

Donovan assembled a staff of assistant mediators, who began to meet regularly with each of the teams. They also served as support staff for subcommittees (consisting of two people from each team) assigned to generate possible responses to each of the agenda items: matching provisions, needs assessment, minority and underserved client groups, monitoring and evaluation of contracts, timing and duration of requests for proposals from new grantees, and overall service priorities.

The teams met monthly for almost a year. There were two points at which the process almost fell apart. First, the social service providers team refused to discuss any changes in priority setting procedures until the other three teams endorsed their position on wage parity. The others were put off by this "take-it-or-leave-it" attitude. At a team leader's meeting organized by Donovan, the four groups managed to work out an understanding. Formally, it was agreed that no one would be asked to commit anything until the full draft of a package was complete. Informally, everyone agreed that the wages for providers in nonprofit agencies were much too low.

The second stumbling block arose when the state team presented its proposed changes in overall spending priorities—that is, naming specific client populations that ought to be the focus for further spending. The providers team insisted that no change in priorities should be permitted if it eliminated grantees who had been eligible in the past. The solution, suggested by Donovan, was to find the best way of spending any *increment* in block grant money that the group as a whole could get from the governor and the legislature. By concentrating on the allocation of an increment, the group was able to avoid a zero-sum situation. Indeed, by presenting a united front on the need for more money they were able to advance their individual as well as their common interests.

Eventually a draft agreement was worked out. Copies were distributed to more than 2,500 groups and individuals throughout the state prior to the final signing. The mediator prepared and distributed more than 10,000 copies of a quarterly newsletter describing the progress of the negotiations.

Almost eighteen months from the time they began, a consensus was reached. In their agreement, the groups spelled out monitoring and implementation procedures designed to ensure appropriate follow-up evaluation. A number of the procedural suggestions that emerged during the course of the negotiations were implemented immediately by Commissioner Dorada. Other reforms, everyone agreed, would take more time. Some real shifts in spending priorities were approved when it became clear that the public/private partnership program would receive a substantial overall increase in state funding. In the commissioner's view, these shifts were important: but more important, she had the consensus she wanted. She considered the negotiations extremely useful.

Mediator Donovan's success illustrates two facts that we feel are significant in an era of diminishing governmental resources. First, despite the apparent zero-sum aspect of fund allocations, it is possible to establish spending priorities through a consensus-building process. Second, such consensus building can take place even among a very large group of participants, none of whom have negotiated before.

Nonbinding Arbitration

As we have already explained, binding arbitration has only limited application in public disputes because most public officials cannot legally delegate their authority to an arbitrator. Public officials appear to be equally wary of nonbinding arbitration—a process whereby a private judge or panel listens to the arguments of all sides, and then suggests an appropriate solution that the parties can either accept or reject.

Because nonbinding arbitration is a relatively new and untried approach in distributional disputes, we will introduce it in hypothetical terms. The approach has been tested in complex private disputes, but these are only partially relevant. Based on these applications, it seems clear to us that nonbinding arbitration may well be an acceptable and desirable means of resolving the types of distributional disputes that do not give way to facilitation or mediation.

Imagine that the parties in a public dispute have reached an impasse even after working with the mediator. Perhaps their estimations of their BATNAs, constantly undergoing revision, have led them to question, once again, whether they could do better away from the table. They can agree only on one thing: They need a solution. A great deal of time, money, and energy had been invested in the negotiations to date, and deadlines of one sort or another are looming. What are their alternatives? One alternative, of course, is to admit failure and go to court. Let us assume, however, that the outcome of adjudication is unclear, that the case is likely to be resolved on a winner-takes-all basis, and that neither side wants to risk losing everything.

Instead, the disputants decide to submit to nonbinding arbitration. In so doing, they may adopt any one of a number of strategies. For example, they may jointly choose a private "judge"—perhaps a retired jurist, or someone else with a background the disputants think appropriate—to whom they present their respective arguments, and from whom they seek a judgment. "After you have heard our arguments, tell us how you think the case will come out if we go to court," the disputing parties might say. "We are not necessarily bound by your judgment, but we want to hear it." Alternatively, the disputing parties might assemble a jointly chosen panel of private arbitrators and ask for a majority ruling (again, not binding). Finally, with appropriate assistance, the parties may stage a mock trial, and invite the heads of all the participating groups or organizations (not just their negotiators) to watch. This last technique may be helpful when one or more of the constituent groups insists on demands that its own negotiators know to be unrealistic.

In many cases, stalled negotiations reflect the simple fact that the expectations of one or more parties are unrealistic. Learning what would probably happen in court, and why, can change those expectations. (In other words, nonbinding arbitration can make a BATNA seem less attractive.) Lowered expectations, in turn, allow the disputing parties to go back to the bargaining table—either unassisted, or with facilitation or mediation—and reach a mutually satisfactory accord.

As noted earlier, few distributional disputes have been resolved through nonbinding arbitration thus far. There have been a significant number of nonbinding arbitrations in the private sector, however, and it seems likely that some version of the technique will cross over into the public sector. We will therefore summarize the ways in which the private sector currently employs nonbinding arbitration, particularly through "minitrials."[3]

Since about 1980, minitrials have proven to be a quick, low-cost mechanism for settling disputes between corporations. Because minitrials are voluntary, confidential, and nonbinding, many corporations embrace them with enthusiasm. In general, corporate minitrials have had four objectives:

- Narrowing the dispute to each party's summary of the critical issues
- Promoting a face-to-face dialogue between the heads of the companies involved
- Encouraging more realistic BATNA calculations
- Preventing business disputes from turning into lawyers' disputes by avoiding many of the legalistic distractions of courtroom procedure

The elements of a minitrial generally include (1) a short period of pretrial preparation; (2) a meeting or meetings in which top management representatives—who are authorized to settle on behalf of their companies—meet to hear informal summaries of each party's "best case"; (3) a meeting or meetings for questioning and rebutting the best-case summaries; and (4) an opportunity to negotiate a settlement. In most cases, if the parties fail at this last stage to reach such a settlement, the judge or panel will present an analysis of the strengths and weaknesses of the positions heard.

All procedural aspects of a minitrial are negotiable, as the parties must feel comfortable with the process if settlement is to be reached. In general, there are only two essential aspects of a minitrial process: first, an opportunity for each side to state its case with an assurance of confidentiality; and second, the participation of leaders with the authority to enter into an agreement. (A neutral advisor, expert either in the subject matter of the dispute or in the processes of dispute or in the processes of dispute resolution, is also typically involved.) Negotiation by top corporate officials—preferably without their lawyers—can be a chief ingredient for success.

Corporate minitrials held so far have proven relevant in cases involving product liability, patent infringement, and employee grievances. They also have been successful in antitrust cases, in instances when competitive practices were in question, and in circumstances requiring an expert analysis of highly technical issues. These private sector applications suggest a number of potential public sector applications especially in disputes over standards (that is, cases in which scientific authorities disagree on such subjects as acceptable health risks). Scientific and technical portions of distributional disputes could then offer their views in an effort to encourage the disputants to settle.

To summarize: In nonbinding arbitration, the disputing parties still control the design of the process and must still approve the ultimate outcome, but the intermediaries take more responsibility for devising possible solutions. The disputing parties are no longer saying, "Help us help ourselves." Instead, they are saying, "Give us an answer." Obviously, then, the intermediaries in nonbinding arbitration must be substantively knowledgeable—even more so than mediators. Ideally, they understand not only the complexities of the issues in dispute, but also the legal processes that may come to bear if all else fails.

From Zero-Sum to Integrative Bargaining

Neutrals in any kind of dispute should seek to assist the parties in reaching satisfactory, as opposed to ideal, agreements. This process usually begins with an effort to ascertain that the parties understand their own interests, as well as what the others want and need. Once all the parties understand each other's interests, and they still find themselves in conflict, the neutral's next step is to assist the parties in exploring ways of reframing the dispute so that hidden common interests can be uncovered.

If it becomes clear that basic interests are in conflict (and more than just communication or personality problems are involved) and that there is little common ground, the neutral switches gears. That is, when it becomes clear that disputants are in a zero-sum situation (in which it appears that the only way for one to gain is for the others to lose), the intermediary seeks to "change the game" by introducing the possibility of trading things, especially things that the parties value differently.

There are obviously limits on what can be traded, including constraints on what the parties in their real-life situations can offer. Finally, if a package of trades that would satisfy all sides cannot be found, the helper must work privately with the disputants to be sure that they have calculated their BATNAs realistically. If they have, and their away-from-the-table options are likely to produce better results for some or all of them, the neutral should probably exit.

The search for satisfactory agreements, then, involves clarification of interests; the search for common ground; the creation of a setting in which the parties can work together to discover differences, which can then be exploited to produce joint gains; and the constant reassessment of alternatives to negotiation. If the parties have overlapping interests, a clarification of those interests and the search for common ground should produce a satisfactory agreement. If the parties have conflicting interests, the task of the neutral is to transform the dispute from a zero-sum situation to an integrative problem-solving activity. There is, of course, no magic wand that the helper can wave, and neutrals are not in the business of cajoling disputants into making concessions in the name of harmony or peaceful coexistence. The transformation involves exploiting the multidimensionality of most conflict situations.

When there are lots of issues on the agenda and the parties rank them differently, this creates the possibility of trades. If the parties place a different value on certainty (or respond differently to risk), a small-but-certain victory sometimes can be traded for a larger-but-uncertain victory. If the parties calculate the time-value of money differently, this can open up trading possibilities. For example, one side may, for tax reasons, suggest a settlement that involves small payments, from the other side to them, each year for a number of years rather than a larger lump-sum payment. The other side may agree, finding this solution less of a strain in terms of cash flow. Even individual issues can be fragmented into smaller parts, permitting trades across elements of an issue. Symbolic commitments are a good example: They cost one side very little, and can often be exchanged for money or other tangible returns.

The transformation from zero-sum to integrative bargaining requires the invention and packaging of items to trade. A clear danger is that such trading may encourage extortionate behavior. If one side says to itself, "I get the idea; I'll gain by making my list of demands longer and longer," the game is then akin to blackmail. In such a case, the problem for the neutral is how to pursue the search for joint gains without encouraging excessive claiming.

Negotiation researchers have documented the inevitable tension between "creating and claiming value" in any dispute resolution situation.[4] This follows earlier studies of "mixed-motive bargaining." Every negotiation, whether zero-sum or integrative, recreates this tension.

In a zero-sum situation, the tension is obvious. Every proposal that one offers in an effort to discover possible joint gains—that is, to create value—will not be accepted by the others without promises in return. This is to be expected if the disputants are thinking solely in zero-sum terms. But even in an integrative bargaining situation, in which the parties have indicated a desire to find an all-gain outcome, the possibility exists that an honest statement of what one side might give up in exchange for something will be exploited by one of the other participants.

Even assuming that disputing parties have been successful in creating joint gains by exploiting differences, this fact alone is no guarantee that the gains they have created can or will be divided equally. So, for example, the parties may find things to trade that they value differently. One side may come out a little bit ahead and the other may come out way ahead. Nobody is worse off, but they are not equally better off.

Intermediaries in public disputes must be honest about this problem. When they say to the parties that they can help find all-gain outcomes, they should clarify that they are not promising that everyone will "beat their BATNA" (or satisfy their interests) to the same extent. We might imagine that everyone would be happy as long as assisted negotiation allowed them to satisfy their underlying interests; nevertheless, we are all aware of situations in which one side would rather not accept a gain if it means that another side gains even more. Thus, neutrals have to keep an eye on the overall "score card" as the parties search for joint gains. They should remind the parties that real costs are associated with not finding mutually beneficial trades. In addition, they should indicate that excessive or extortionate claiming will undermine the very process of inventing joint gains which leads to satisfactory agreements.

The transformation from a zero-sum perception of a conflict to a willingness to search for joint gains does not depend on the parties adopting "soft" (as opposed to "hard") negotiating styles. Based on extensive studies, negotiation researchers have established that cooperative negotiators are not necessarily more successful than competitive negotiators in reaching satisfactory agreement. Negotiators of either style can be effective or ineffective, and this is true regardless of the style of the negotiators they are matched against.[5] Thus, the search for joint gains does not require everyone to be "nice" or to make concessions; nor does it require one side to mimic the attitudes of the other. Effective but tough negotiators know their own interests, and they know that by participating in a collaborative process of creating joint gains they may be more likely to serve their own interests. They also know that there will be very little to claim if differences cannot be exploited through packaging and trading.

Creating and claiming, as noted earlier, are distinct activities. "Competitive-style negotiators are likely to stress the claiming part of the process, and may require tangible "victories" at each step along the way. By contrast, "cooperative-style" negotiators are less inhibited about throwing themselves into the creating part of the creating and claiming process. They are also more willing to wait until the end to tote up the score.

But claiming can preempt creating, and it is important for the participants to realize this. Some negotiators attempt to solve this problem by constantly switching their negotiating posture from claiming to creating and back again. It may be impossible to move back and forth between the two attitudes, however, if claiming creates tension or hostility. It may in fact be necessary in some disputes to go through a period of claiming, or zero-sum bargaining, so that the parties see what they might be able to achieve this way. Once the process of creating begins, though, and an integrative problem-solving mode is established, it is best to stay on this track.

Facilitators and mediators rarely try to convince the disputants to change their styles of negotiation. They do, however, take advantage of the emergence of the "group mentality" that develops as negotiations proceed.

As the parties "go at it" over an extended period of time, relationships develop, just as they do when a jury is sequestered. The group may begin as total strangers, but constant interaction at close quarters can lead to accommodation, if not friendship. Though the negotiators are there to advance the interests of the groups they represent, they cannot help but get caught up in the new "group" of which they are a part.

This new group may pressure an individual who has not been very forthcoming into changing his or her attitude. As it approaches closure, the group may also bring pressure to bear on a party that is holding out. Momentum in such situations is almost tangible. While the intermediary may encourage all the parties to check back with their constituents before concluding a draft agreement, the group may prefer to push toward a conclusion. There is almost a "team spirit" that emerges as the disputants reach the end of their joint task.[6]

An effective intermediary may use the emergence of group pressure to move the transformation along, saying to one party, for example, "I don't know how much longer the rest of the group will stick with this, if you don't give some sign of your willingness to accept the trades that have been proposed." This is not to say that the neutral will encourage a party to ignore or sell short its own interests; rather, the neutral may use the pressure of the group to encourage a party to change its behavior, make a more realistic calculation of its BATNA, or offer a counterproposal that the others are likely to be able to accept.

We generally hold the view that any distributional dispute in the public sector that appears to be a zero-sum conflict can be transformed into an occasion for integrative bargaining assuming the parties have adequate assistance. These sorts of conflicts are uniformly complex, but creative negotiators in any dispute usually will be able to find some possible trades—whether they be across issues, over time, relative to risk, or whatever.

This is not to say, though, that every distributional dispute will yield to resolution through assisted negotiation. The parties may have utterly unrealistic BATNAs, and they may refuse to reassess them regardless of what happens in the negotiations. Even though legitimate interests could be met through the creation of joint gains, the parties may hold out for more gains than can possibly be created.

Even with the assistance of a skilled intermediary, the parties may not be willing to move from inflated demands to ways of satisfying their true interests—either because they do not want to be seen as having backed down from their stated positions, because they are caught in psychological traps that work against their own best interests, or because internal pressures within their organizations lead them to attach a higher value to sustaining the conflict than to resolving it.

Assisted Negotiation: Concluding Comments

At present, three techniques are available for assisted negotiation in the resolution of public disputes: facilitation, mediation, and nonbinding arbitration. By any rational accounting, these tools are underutilized. These techniques are not mutually exclusive. They can be used sequentially in the same dispute; in some situations, the line between facilitation and mediation may be blurred as the neutral moves into a more active behind-the-scenes role. They are highly mutable and can be applied in different ways by individual dispute resolution practitioners. In all cases, though, they involve the search for all-gain outcomes through a move from zero-sum to integrative bargaining.

We have already alluded to the biggest obstacle to their acceptance: fear on the part of public officials that facilitation, mediation, and nonbinding arbitration will infringe on their authority. We contend that this fear is misplaced, given that the outcomes of all three processes remain entirely under the control of the parties, including these same public officials.

In the next chapter we will describe in practical terms the ways in which public officials, citizens, and business interests can use consensual approaches to resolve distributional disputes.

Notes

1. The debate on the role of the mediator is presented in Joseph B. Stulberg, *Taking Charge/Managing Conflict.* (Lexington, Mass.: Lexington, 1987).
2. The details of how the EPA's resource pool worked are reviewed in Lawrence Susskind and Gerard McMahon, "The Theory and Practice of Negotiated Rulemaking," *Yale Journal of Regulation* 3, 1 (1985):133–165.
3. For more on minitrials, see Eric Green, "The CPR Mini-Trial Handbook," in *Corporate Dispute Management* (New York: Matthew Bender, 1982).
4. David Lax and Jim Sebenius, *The Manager as Negotiator* (New York: Free Press, 1986).
5. Gerald Williams, *Legal Negotiation and Settlement* (St. Paul, Minn.: West, 1983).
6. This point is further explained by Jacob Bercovitch, *Social Conflicts and Third Parties: Strategies of Conflict Resolution* (Boulder, Colo.: Westview, 1984).

Reading 5

The Risks and the Advantages of Agency Discretion: Evidence from EPA's Project XL*

Lawrence E. Susskind and Joshua Secunda*

I. Introduction

Academic criticism of the administrative state has increased exponentially over the past several years, particularly with regard to environmental regulation. Many commentators insist that the command and control approach to enforcement is no longer useful. Further, they content that this approach likely will discourage innovation and create a disincentive to continuous environmental improvement. They also assert that many prevailing environmental regulations are economically inefficient, violate free market principles, and are undemocratic.[1] Most commentators urge some form of "regulatory reinvention." Agreement ends, however, when it comes to which reforms to adopt.

Since 1995, the U.S. Environmental Protection Agency ("EPA" or the "Agency") has tried to implement some reforms of its own, including Project XL (which stands for "Excellence in Leadership"). Through Project XL, the EPA is exploring more flexible approaches to encourage collaborative performance-oriented compliance with federal and state standards. Much of what the EPA has attempted is based on "adaptive management" theory. However, this theory is very much at odds with the enforcement philosophy upon which the EPA was founded.[2]

In implementing Project XL, the EPA has faced intellectual, legal and cultural obstacles of many kinds. This paper analyzes a number of ways these obstacles have impeded

*Reprinted from Susskind, L.E., and Secunda, J., *UCLA Journal of Environmental Law and Policy*, vol. 17, no. 1 (1998–1999). Copyright © 1999 by the Regents of the University of California.

EPA efforts to adopt a more flexible approach to regulation that relies more on "market mechanics."

Part I reviews the strategic considerations behind the founding of the EPA, as well as its institutional structure and operation. The EPA's history and structure make it a problematic setting in which to apply adaptive management techniques. The EPA was designed to carry out a quasi-military mission, featuring vertical review of all decisions taken at lower levels. In addition, a more flexible and decentralized approach to decision making would require the Agency to alter its mission. Since the Agency's focus remains result-oriented and its management style almost entirely reactive, a clash between philosophies of adaptive management and command and control is inevitable.

Part II reviews the doctrine of administrative discretion, noting that the dominant perspective in administrative law has been "to fear discretion, reluctantly accept its presence, and attempt to control it."[3] According to this view, Congress chronically delegates broad authority to administrative agencies. Thus, agencies are relatively unsupervised in their exercise of regulatory discretion. Part II concludes by arguing that this view is incorrect; Congress does not habitually abdicate its lawmaking responsibilities to agencies. In fact, Congress retains more oversight of agencies like the EPA than most commentators presume.[4] There is a surprising amount of discretion built into the administrative system. Unfortunately, most of it is not the kind that will encourage the EPA or the private sector to pursue innovation.

Part III outlines several related attempts to move the EPA toward more collaborative and "performance-based" approaches to achieving compliance under the Bush and Clinton administrations. These initiatives were actually the precursors to Project XL. Significantly, building on adaptive management principles, XL sought to incorporate the results of these experiments into the EPA's existing institutional framework. Part III also describes the first group of proposed XL projects.

Part IV analyzes the political reactions to Project XL and reviews intra-agency disagreements over the appropriate exercise of discretion in specific XL projects. In addition, Part IV considers the strong reactions of the public and regulated community to this move toward more flexible and performance-based regulation.

Part V suggests ways in which the Agency and the regulated community might work together to overcome obstacles to an increased reliance on administrative discretion, which is critical to the success of Project XL and similar reform efforts.

II. The EPA's Organizational Structure and History

Throughout its history, EPA has failed to articulate a mission that has survived beyond a single administration. This failure explains, in large part, EPA's enormous political vulnerability and institutionally reactive posture. Indeed, this is an unpromising context into which to introduce a new philosophy of environmental regulation. A brief review of the EPA's history explains why.

Major EPA programs include air and water quality, drinking water, hazardous waste, Superfund, pesticides, radiation, toxic substances, enforcement and compliance assurance, pollution prevention, oil spills, and leaking underground storage tanks. In addition, the EPA provides assistance in the design and construction of wastewater treatment, drinking water, and other water infrastructure projects. The Agency is responsible for conducting research; establishing environmental standards; monitoring levels of pollution; enforcing compliance; managing audits and investigations; and, providing technical assistance and financial support to states and tribes to which the Agency has delegated authority for program implementation. Finally, the Agency participates in a narrow range of international activities.

The EPA's regulatory operations are, with the exception of Superfund, centered around issuing permits. The Agency can allow facilities to discharge specific levels of certain pollutants within prescribed limits. Permits sometimes (but not always) mandate specific technologies that must be used to achieve specified limits. Permit holders are required to file regular reports indicating their emission levels. These reports are screened for compliance with permit conditions, and periodic site visits are made to confirm the accuracy of self-reporting. Violations are referred to an enforcement division, which files suit against entities that exceed their permit conditions.

The EPA's approach to duties other than enforcement tends to be passive. For example, in issuing permits, the applicant must prepare and file the necessary studies and forms. The EPA processes these forms, comments on the material provided, returns the application for further study, when necessary, and requests appropriate revisions. EPA personnel understand that it is not their job to work with an applicant to ensure a mutually acceptable set of permit conditions.

Practically all environmental statutes provide for delegation of certain powers to the states or tribes so that they can issue permits, screen for violations and enforce compliance. For this to happen, a state must apply to the EPA for permission to operate a program and the EPA must certify the adequacy of the state's proposed efforts. If the program is delegated, the EPA remains involved in an oversight capacity. If a state presents no program for authorization, the EPA remains the permitter of last resort.

The Agency's oversight function is meant to ensure that the permitting activities it has delegated to the states are being carried out as the EPA expects. In some cases, the EPA has rescinded state programs and resumed enforcement and permitting functions itself.[5]

The EPA's regional structure follows the ten region model created during the Nixon administration. This was designed to encourage devolution of responsibility, although a great deal of decision making is not decentralized. The broad division of labor between the EPA headquarters and regions is as follows: headquarters writes regulations, standards and policy, funds research and development, and oversees the regions to assure national consistency in the enforcement of statutory mandates; regions implement enforcement, authorization and oversight programs.

Congress did not create the EPA, nor did it ever give the Agency a clear mandate or efficient long-term priorities.[6] Further, Congress provided the EPA no means to allocate resources among different environmental statutes in a balanced way. For this reason alone, it is difficult for the Agency to set priorities. Finally, in reaction to Reagan-era environmental policies, Congress compounded the Agency's problems by including in key pieces of environmental legislation deadlines for the promulgation of regulations, detailed instructions, and "hammer" clauses threatening penalties for missed deadlines.[7]

The scope of scientific information that the EPA, industry and the public must integrate from medical, economic, engineering, legal, and other sources before reaching decisions is enormous. At the same time, laws and regulations governing how certain decisions should be made are often internally inconsistent with regard to the kinds of information that should be taken into account.

There is also a significant and growing discrepancy between the responsibilities assigned to the EPA via statute and the resources Congress provides the Agency to carry them out. Congress has charged the EPA with the implementation of a complex set of functions. To carry these out, the Agency must administer a collection of laws specifying how pollution is to be managed within specific "media" or programs. The Agency's task is to design, implement and enforce an enormous number of regulations. This requires substantial institutional capacity. Yet, the EPA's institutional capacity is actually shrinking. The EPA had 7000 employees and a budget of $3.3 billion in 1971; at the time, 12 percent ($512 million) of this money was spent on program administration. The remainder was used to fund state and local grants. By 1980, the Agency's employee base had increased to 12,000 and its budget to $5 billion, $1.5 billion was spent on program administration. The 1989 budget totaled only $4.8 billion, with $1.6 billion set aside for program administration—a drop in real terms of 15 percent over the decade. Congress has never restored the resources it cut.[8]

The EPA's organizational structure has created an imposing barrier to technological innovation. Despite recent attempts at cross-media re-organization, the EPA remains oriented towards a traditional medium-by-medium or law-by-law enforcement strategy. Enforcement consumes a majority of the Agency's resources. Indeed, the EPA's budget is largely determined by Congress' assessment of the number of enforcement actions the Agency took (and penalty dollars it collected) in each prior fiscal year.

The EPA views enforcement as an outcome, not as a means to an end. This has been the Agency's position since 1970, when its first administrator, William Ruckleshaus, adopted this view. In order to ensure Congressional and public support, Ruckleshaus believed it was vital to establish the new Agency's credibility by demonstrating its commitment to achieving environmental goals. Thus, his strategy was to "hit the ground running" by giving enforcement top priority. Alternate organizational strategies were considered—strategies that concentrated on research and development, or on regional assessment and planning. However, these would have been considerably more difficult to implement, and would not have produced measurable results nearly as quickly. Making enforcement a priority required only that Ruckleshaus order a corps of attorneys to file suit, under statutes already in place, against polluters known to be out of compliance.[9]

His strategy may well have been correct for its time. It established the EPA in the public eye and encouraged the private sector to internalize costs associated with environmental compliance. However, over the decades, Congress and the EPA have come to rely on enforcement as an end in itself. They stress enforcement numbers ("beans," in Agency parlance) when measuring the Agency's success.

This emphasis on enforcement helps to explain the EPA's difficulty in recognizing that the initial phase of America's environmental policy has ended.[10] Indeed, the EPA's continued reliance on traditional enforcement strategies is inappropriate given environmental problems the Agency and the country now face. In the words of Malcolm K. Sparrow, "[l]ining up industrial polluters for prosecution has limited tangible effect on the quality of the environment. There are too many violators, too many laws to be enforced and not enough resources to get the job done."[11]

New challenges must be approached in a different way. Ideally, it would be best if the Agency could find a way to encourage all private actors to adopt more environmentally sustainable development behaviors *voluntarily*. Since the costs of each additional unit of environmental improvement are going up steadily, it also makes sense to carefully tailor pollution control and prevention strategies to each situation. Those strategies that take account of the unique problems facing each regulated actor are likely to be most effective. Collaboration, not confrontation, and a flexible approach to regulation that emphasizes environmental performance rather than penalties and expensive litigation should be the goal.

III. The Doctrine of Administrative Discretion

In every administrative system, regulators have some degree of freedom. Although it may seem counterintuitive, such discretion offers insulation from reversal or revision by outside reviewers or administrators higher up the ladder because an agency has a right to be wrong.[12] Nevertheless, for a variety of reasons, the dominant perspective in administrative law has been "to fear discretion, reluctantly accept its presence, and attempt to control it."[13]

Commentators generally agree that untrammeled agency discretion can lead to unfairness and inefficiency.[14] Nevertheless, Congress chronically delegates broad authority to administrative agencies.[15] The alternative would be for Congress to micromanage each agency's activities by writing all statute-implementing regulations itself. Congress does not have the resources to do this for one agency, let alone the entire administrative bureaucracy.

Further, Congress' delegation of discretion to the federal bureaucracy has deep historical roots. When the "spoils system" was replaced by Civil Service in the 1880s, the goal was eminently practical: hire qualified people to administer the program and let them do their best under general guidelines without attempting to spell out the minutiae for them. Giving professional civil servants "large discretion as to the management of the fires and ovens," wrote Woodrow Wilson soon after the creation of the Civil Service, would liberate government from the procedural quagmire of the courts. No procedural protection from the bureaucrats was needed; neutral professionals were themselves the protection from the unabashed partisan politics that had flourished under the spoils system. The vision of neutral experts, liberated from procedure, remained the bureaucratic ideal.[16]

Critics argue that this concept of bureaucracy never worked as intended. As one put it, "The age-old tendency of institutions to build up layers of process, like sediment on a harbor bottom, soon also bogged down the budding regulatory state. . . . The temptation to compromise by promising one more layer of review and oversight is apparently irresistible."[17] In the words of another critic, "Reliance on the expectation that principles of rational administration will be self-limiting is risky business. It requires stepped-up legislative vigilance to keep administrative power within bounds."[18]

According to this view, excessive and unchecked agency discretion in the formulation of policy undermines the legitimacy of the administrative state. The remedy, presumably, is to encourage the involvement of interest groups in agency decision making and to protect that involvement through judicial intervention. This would cause agencies to assume the role of "honest brokers" among competing interest groups that bargain over policy. Judges then ensure that all relevant parties are represented by requiring agencies to take these parties' views into account in reasoned decision making. Through the threat of legal challenge, parties derive indirect bargaining power.

Advocates for tight constraints on discretion reason that:

- Congress delegates a subset of its legislative powers to administrative agencies by statute.
- Congress outlines regulatory directives via statute.
- The statutes instruct the agencies to promulgate rules and regulations implementing Congress' intentions.
- Agencies translate these statutory outlines into specific rules controlling private behavior.

Thus, regulations are, in effect, administratively-derived statutes completing the initial legislative design. Critics pinpoint this last step as the weak link in controlling discretion within the administrative system. In allowing agencies to formulate specific rules, Congress gives away "great swaths of lawmaking power" to the executive and other agencies.[19] Agencies are therefore relatively uncontrolled in their exercise of regulatory discretion; these same critics believe that judicial review no longer provides adequate oversight of agency decision making.

The authors do not agree with the view set out above that Congress habitually abdicates its lawmaking responsibilities to agencies, resulting in their untrammeled power to make administrative law. Experience and study show that Congress retains more oversight of agencies like the EPA than most commentators presume.[20] However, Congress concentrates its control on limiting an agency's procedures to specific regulatory methods; at the same time, Congress often fails to protect against discretionary abuse.[21] The key to improving the regulatory process thus lies in identifying precisely what categories of agency discretion Congress should retain, and which to delegate. Close examination of the structure underlying major environmental statutes demonstrates that Congress places tight controls on the agency's choice of regulatory methods, rather than focusing on mandating environmental outcomes and allowing agencies to develop processes to efficiently achieve them.[22]

There is a surprising amount of discretion built into the existing administrative system. Unfortunately, most of it is not the kind that will encourage the EPA or the private sector to pursue innovation.[23] It is not discretion per se, but Congress' means of *defining and controlling* what categories of discretion an agency can utilize, that inhibits innovation and creates inefficiency.

It is a mistake to define "discretion" unidimensionally. Indeed, there are several kinds of discretion that Congress confers upon EPA.[24] Some, such as the power to set standards, should probably be used sparingly. They provide no motive to innovate, nor do they encourage corporate attempts to reduce emission levels below regulatory benchmarks. Other kinds of discretion, typically those allowing latitude in how performance is achieved, should be increased.

A. From Theory to Practice: The EPA's Use of Discretion

The primary constraint on agency behavior is the Administrative Procedure Act (APA).[25] The APA requires that agency rule-making must be preceded by a Notice of Proposed Rule Making in the *Federal Register* and by consideration of and response to the public comments received. More formal, on the record, agency adjudication must be accompanied by trial-like procedures.[26] The APA further bounds agency discretion by calling for judicial review of various agency actions, including rule-making.

By specifying the procedural requirements that must accompany various types of agency action, Congress seeks to bound agency discretion. However, there is a growing consensus that the procedural burdens imposed by the APA have made rulemaking "excessively costly, rigid and cumbersome . . . impos[ing] perverse incentives that conspire to undermine sound public policy."[27]

EPA reaction to the constraints imposed by the APA was to resort to new forms of policy creating immunity from judicial review: for example, interpretive rules, policy statements and "guidances" are exempt from APA requirements.[28] The EPA increasingly issues unreviewable nonlegislative guidances to advance its policy agenda. Courts have generally sidestepped the Agency's challenge on this issue, refusing to mandate additional procedural requirements unless a judge perceives them to already exist in the Constitution, the APA or an enabling statute.[29]

Thus, the EPA relies as much as possible on informal regulatory instruments (interpretive rules and policy guidances) to avoid the procedural constraints imposed by formal and informal rule-making. The Agency deals with specific questions of interpretation through the release of interpretive guidance letters. It resolves more general ambiguities at the headquarters level, through the issuance of nonlegislative interpretive rules. Issuance of interpretive material helps to ensure consistency in day-to-day administration by Agency staff. However, it leaves the EPA open to charges that it can exercise too much administrative discretion.

Of course, agency guidance on correct legal interpretation is not legally binding; courts and members of the public are free to ignore it. In practice, however, an agency's view of the correct resolution of specific legal questions usually prevails. Few informal agency guidance interpretations are challenged in court; the ones that are, are almost always upheld.[30]

The fact is, the EPA enforcement and regulatory personnel exercise discretion on a daily basis at all levels of responsibility. For example, EPA staff exercises almost complete discretion over its enforcement activities. All the following decisions are within the Agency's discretion: whether to initiate a hazardous waste inspection of a particular facility; whether to audit a company's monthly Clean Water Act compliance reports; against which companies to initiate enforcement actions; what laws to enforce against them; whether to do so criminally or civilly (in consultation with the U.S. Department of Justice); whether to bring an enforcement action administratively or in federal court;

whether to impose a high monetary penalty or to accept a defendant's performance of an environmentally beneficial project. Additionally, EPA personnel have broad discretion to issue operating permits under the Clean Water Act, Clean Air Act, hazardous waste statutes and other statutes.[31] Finally, the EPA can grant statutorily-sanctioned variances or exemptions from certain regulatory requirements, a form of discretion upon which Project XL proposals largely depend. Sometimes headquarters drafts guidance documents to advise staff on the proper exercise of these discretionary functions. When such guidance is not issued, regional staff members develop "regional guidances" to ensure consistency of action within the region and to build some protective administrative "common law" precedents.

In sum, federal agencies have developed or been granted more discretion than they admit. The constraints on the use and abuse of this discretion are imposed by the APA, Congressional oversight and judicial review. These undoubtedly limit what agencies might otherwise do; however, they also create rigidity, time delays and inefficiencies of their own. This article explores how encouraging greater agency discretion can ensure that the intent of federal legislation is achieved in the least burdensome and most creative ways, while guarding against abuse.

IV. The Development of Alternate Regulatory Models

Traditionally, Congress carefully specifies a methodological framework in each regulatory regime it delegates to the EPA. Command and control instruments are extremely attractive to bureaucrats and lawmakers alike. In one analyst's view, they "represent the shortest distance between two points: if Congress decided it wanted the price of natural gas reduced, the most direct and obvious thing to do would be to legislate a cap on its price." The analyst continues: [h]owever . . . the wisdom of policy design is almost wholly independent of directness. Command and control is frequently an inappropriate approach despite its directness, apparent administrability and enforceability because it precludes or at least problematizes adaptation to divergent and changing circumstances."[32]

The criticism leveled against the inherent rigidity of command and control approaches to enforcement has resulted in pressure to try alternate regulatory techniques. One alternative involves an incentive-based option. This method emphasizes the importance of cost-effectiveness analysis to determine what regulatory strategy will produce optimum social and economic benefits. It seeks to take account of all direct and indirect social costs prevented by and/or caused by a proposed regulation.[33] It presumes that the costs and benefits caused and avoided by a given action can be measured. The new discipline of environmental economics tracks this effort to reorient regulatory thinking. It argues that command and control might be the most direct route to accomplishing a regulatory objective, but it is likely to produce substantial inefficiency that could be avoided by a case-by-case release on cost-effectiveness analyses.

Incentive theory seeks less socially costly methods to achieve the same regulatory ends. It claims to do this by "harnessing the power of markets," assuming the best way to accomplish a regulatory objective is to offer the regulated community "a direct and daily self-interest" in attaining it.[34] "Sin taxes" illustrate this idea. Proponents argue that increasing taxes on tobacco and alcohol not only generates revenue that can be used for other beneficial purposes, but increases prices in such a way as to discourage consumers from purchasing and using harmful substances. By making undesirable behavior more costly, market-based approaches presumably give members of the regulated community an economic stake in conforming to government-specified social goals. Moreover, incentives of this sort, at least in theory, should lead to the achievement of regulatory goals at "the least" cost to society. Wilkins and Hunt explain why:

> [I]f . . . EPA [were] to promulgate a pollution tax on the emission of particular contaminants into the air, every firm would have a direct monetary incentive to find the best and cheapest technology or other method of reducing its output of such pollutants. The more pollution a company prevents, the less tax it would pay. Under a command and control regime, a firm might be required to reduce pollution emissions by installing a filtering device at a cost of two thousand dollars. . . . [F]aced with a choice under an incentives approach between reducing one unit of pollution by installing a filtering device at a cost of two thousand dollars [or] reducing a unit by purchasing cleaner raw materials at a cost of one thousand dollars . . . a profit motivated firm will select the cheaper option.[35]

The EPA has implemented a number of incentive-based regulatory measures that build on these ideas, including the "bubble" concept under the Clean Air Act and the tradable emissions permit program under the 1990 amendments to the Clean Air Act.[36] In both cases, once clean air objectives were set, the regulated community was allowed greater flexibility in choosing the means it preferred to use to achieve these goals. In the case of the bubble concept, industry could make cross-media comparisons and choose to meet some regulations by exceeding others. In the case of tradable permits, regulated companies could "buy" the right to pollute (within strict limits) from others who had already exceeded the required standards.

These two trial programs are interesting. However, they do not represent a new compliance philosophy or standard (other than a reliance on basic market principles). Along with the voluntary and "compliance-plus" approaches described below, they represent an inconsistent, experimental approach to innovation. A plethora of environmental issues remain unaddressed by either scheme: Which, if any, pollutants can be "traded" given cost-benefit and health concerns? How should the public, the Agency and the private sector come to agreement on this question? Is a market (or incentive-based) scheme capable of incorporating a community's collective assessment of a clean environment into the prices that it sets? Market realities might encourage larger companies to buy the pollution rights of smaller entities, rendering them non-competitive; it is not clear that this would be a good outcome. While the stockpiling of pollution credits might create satisfaction with the status quo—in the same way that command and control already does—this could discourage technological innovation that might lead to an even cleaner environment at lower cost.

It should make sense to monitor the results of the "bubble" concept and the tradable emissions permit program. Even if they generate unintended negative consequences, it will be difficult for the EPA to withdraw them; their promulgation created constituencies that now have a vested interest in their continuation.

A. Voluntary and Compliance-Plus Approaches

The Bush Administration pursued a non-legislative strategy to push for government-sponsored environmental improvement. It engaged corporate voluntarism, enticing companies with the lure of being named a "corporate environmental leader" by the President of the United States. Voluntary strategies encouraged business to focus on preventing pollution at its source, instead of focusing on "end of the pipe" solutions. At the same time, the Agency hoped voluntary partnerships would institutionalize cooperation and trust between government and the regulated community. Examples of this approach included the 1991 "Green Lights" program, which encouraged businesses to install energy-efficient light fixtures and bulbs, and the "33/50" program, designed to voluntarily reduce the use and release into the environment of 17 especially toxic chemicals by 50 percent by the end of 1995.[37]

These programs produced modest gains, leading to calls for their adoption as techniques for creating more efficient and environmentally protective strategies.[38] By one account, "[a]dministrative costs in voluntary programs are certainly lower than those in mandatory programs. . . . As to social costs, although some industries doubtless bore some expense in attaining these reductions . . . some likely even experienced savings."[39] Other observers noted, "[i]ndeed, if these volunteer efforts were to have drastically increased industry's net costs, profit-motivated companies responsible to their investors would not and could not continue to sign up."[40]

However, the EPA's enthusiasm for voluntary compliance worried environmentalists and certain members of Congress. "They suspected industry of cooking the books, of changing measurement systems and definitions and switching . . . [statutorily] listed chemicals to unlisted ones; all to make themselves look good without any real benefit to the environment." Others thought the EPA could not set important new directions for environmental protection relying on voluntarism and targeting issues like energy-efficient light fixtures.[41]

Neither the EPA nor its serious critics want the Agency to rely entirely on voluntary appeals for pollution reduction. Voluntary cooperation is not an alternative to enforcement in many situations. The ultimate goal is to push for innovations through a novel mix of tactics.

B. Adaptive Management and Project XL

Project XL represented a natural outgrowth of earlier efforts to experiment with incentive-based and voluntary approaches to achieving compliance. It also built on the theory of adaptive management. Proponents argue that feedback through experimentation provides opportunities to examine and inform the ways in which producer and consumer practices in the economy may be altered to create environmentally compatible industrial ecosystems.[42] Collectively, these are known as adaptive management techniques. Philosophically, adaptive management treats economic uses of nature as experiments, assuming that humankind will continue to learn what works and what does not. The adaptive management process presumes ongoing institutional transformation; entities should develop their philosophies and strategies in an evolutionary way through continuous adaptation and assessment. These changes should be driven by a constant flow of information, gathered from purposeful experiments. Adaptive management may be thought of as a research strategy designed to generate feedback. Thus, governing institutions using adaptive management techniques should evolve towards increased efficiency in meeting environmental policy goals based on continuous learning.

This approach to natural resource policy embodies a simple imperative: policies are experiments; learn from them. In order to live, man must use the resources of the world; yet our species does not understand nature well enough to know how to live harmoniously within environmental limits. Adaptive management takes that uncertainty seriously, treating human interventions in natural systems as experimental probes. Its practitioners take special care with information. First, they are explicit about what they expect, so that they can design methods to make reliable measurements. Second, they collect and analyze information so that expectations can be compared with reality. Finally, they translate comparisons into learning: they seek to correct errors, improve their imperfect understanding, and change action and plans. In theory, Project XL hopes to implement an adaptive management approach by jointly planning experiments and monitoring their results for possible integration into the existing regulatory system. Its proponents want encourage the private sector to collaborate with the EPA to plan, run, and monitor experimental efforts to achieve compliance, rethink regulation, and test new technologies.[43] Unfortunately, these outcomes have not occurred to the extent XL's designers had aspired.

C. Project XL

The EPA envisions Project XL as a national pilot program to test innovative ways of achieving better and more cost-effective public health and environmental protection. Through site-specific agreements with project sponsors, the EPA gathers data and project experience that the Agency can use to redesign existing approaches to public health and environmental protection. Under Project XL, sponsors (private facilities, industry sectors, federal facilities and communities) can implement innovative strategies that produce superior environmental performance, escaping some regulatory mandates, and promoting greater accountability.

Proposals that have become XL pilot projects were intended to be real-world tests of innovative strategies that might achieve cleaner and cheaper results than conventional regulatory approaches. Indeed, the EPA proposes to grant regulatory flexibility (i.e., greater choice in *how* standards were to be met) in exchange for commitments to achieve better environmental performance than might be attained through full compliance with regulations. The EPA's initial goal was the implementation of 50 pilot XL projects in four categories: specific facilities, industrial sectors, government agencies, and communities.

Criteria for individual project selection are *superior environmental performance, regulatory flexibility* and *stakeholder involvement*. Development of XL projects is divided into three phases. First, the project sponsors (usually the regulated company and any co-sponsoring organizations) propose a project to the EPA, which reviews the proposal in collaboration with the appropriate state(s). The EPA uses a competitive process for initial selection of such proposals. Proposals spell out: 1) the environmental benefits the project seeks to generate; 2) what regulatory flexibility the applicant is requesting; and, 3) how the applicant intends to involve those who may be affected by the proposed effort. Thus, under XL, a corporation can propose an alternate compliance strategy that would require the Agency to authorize a revision or reinterpretation of an existing regulatory requirement. The suggested compliance strategy must result in *environmental performance superior to that which would have been achieved under normal circumstances;* that is, performance superior to that which would have been achieved if the applicant had merely complied with the existing regulatory scheme.

A development phase then follows during which project conditions are analyzed and negotiated. This culminates in the negotiation of a non-enforceable, non-binding memorandum of understanding known as a Final Project Agreement (FPA).[44] FPAs have been negotiated between applicants, the EPA and, where applicable, state environmental protection agencies and project stakeholders. FPAs, when complete, contain a detailed blueprint of the steps the company will follow to run the experiment and improve its environmental performance.[45]

The EPA and the applicable state agencies then generally issue the company a new, enforceable permit intended to last the life of the experiment. XL contemplates that the Agency will issue permits granting businesses the flexibility to make process changes and increase emissions (up to specified levels) without having to secure the approvals normally required. Thus, the "XL" permit breaks regulatory barriers by exempting corporations from precise regulatory requirements that would otherwise have barred such experiments. Alternatively, the Agency may resort to discretionary rationales involving reinterpretation of a rule's presumed intent, or may grant a variance from existing regulations.

Finally, XL projects enter an implementation and evaluation phase. Experiments are implemented at participating facilities and then evaluated for effectiveness, transferability to other industry sectors, and their potential effect on the existing regulatory structure. This evaluation is conducted by project sponsors, stakeholders, regulatory agencies and other parties.

The EPA was particularly concerned that all relevant points of view be taken into account in developing and evaluating these experiments. Thus, the EPA views projects proposed by "stakeholder groups" most favorably. The input and ultimate support of environmental groups, elected officials, other industries, and affected communities have been essential to Agency approval.

Proponents in the White House and the EPA viewed (and still view) XL as a long overdue opportunity for the private sector and EPA to cooperate in permit design. However, critics were and remain skeptical that firms would always use XL to improve environmental performance or test transferable technologies. "XL could be a recipe for undermining existing environmental standards under the guise of regulatory reinvention."[46] They suspected that XL participants would offer the EPA multimedia trades that might pose new and worse hazards to workers and the environment. They argued that community groups were neither sufficiently funded nor well enough informed to be either meaningful participants in, or credible watchdogs over, FPA negotiations and permit implementation.

D. Information on Specific XL Projects

As of mid-1997, projects had been implemented by Berry Corporation, Intel Corporation and Weyerhaeuser.[47] Three other projects were determined to be worthy of development, although not sufficiently innovative to satisfy XL criteria at the time they were reviewed by the EPA. These are going forward under a separate process.[48] Twelve projects are in various stages of development and five others are under consideration. Twenty-five proposed XL projects have been rejected by the EPA or withdrawn by their sponsors.[49]

E. Projects Under Development

Below are brief descriptions of 12 projects currently under development in order to demonstrate the types of proposals that XL has received thus far.[50]

1. PCS Nitrogen, L.P.

PCS Nitrogen, L.P., of Baton Rouge, Louisiana, is a major manufacturer of food-grade phosphoric acid. The phosphoric acid production process generates large amounts of phosphogypsum as a byproduct. This phosphogypsum is stored in inactive "gyp stacks" at the facility. Significant runoff is generated from the inactive stacks. PCS discharges 190 million gallons of this runoff annually directly into the Mississippi River under a Clean Water Act (CWA) National Pollution Discharge Elimination System permit. This runoff contains up to fourteen million pounds of phosphoric acid, which must be reported to the EPA's Toxic Release Inventory (TRI).

PCS wants to reduce its TRI reporting burden and curb the expanding gyp stacks. Specifically, the company plans to make a product for enhancing agricultural soils by composting the gyp from their facility, runoff waters from their inactive stacks, and organic waste from outside sources such as sugar cane processing. The composting would occur at the stack itself in a patented biological process that combines fifty percent gyp with fifty percent organic waste to manufacture the soil enhancer.

PCS believes that the resulting soil enhancer—referred to as "Gyp-Post"—has multiple agricultural and horticultural applications. Through the incorporation of gyp, the product is high in calcium and sulfur. The presence of the organic waste serves as a further supply of nutrients and increases the bindability of soils.

However, existing Clean Air Act (CAA) regulations prohibit PCS from utilizing gyp in this manner. Thus, to proceed with its plan, PCS needs an exemption under CAA regulations. Existing CAA regulations are aimed at preventing radiation risk from land application of gyp in the event the agricultural lands are subsequently converted to residential use. Under these CAA rules, waste gyp with radioactive content higher than ten picocuries per gram cannot be used for agricultural purposes. PCS's gyp, by and large, has higher radiation content—up to thirty seven picocuries per gram. However, the company proposes to use only gyp with radiation content no higher than fourteen picocuries per gram to make "Gyp-Post." Since this gyp would be combined with fifty percent non-radioactive materials, the company claims that the net radiation for the soil enhancer would be no greater than seven picocuries per gram. Consequently, the EPA's concerns about radiation risk would be adequately addressed.

2. Hadco Corporation

Hadco Corporation manufactures printed wiring boards for the computer industry. Hadco proposes to enhance the direct recycling of metal bearing streams from its printed wiring board (PWB) manufacturing facilities. Because of their toxicity, etching solvents in wastewater treatment (WWT) sludge from PWB manufacturing were listed as hazardous wastes in the 1970s under the Resource, Conservation and Recovery Act's (RCRA) Subtitle C. Hadco proposes that the EPA delist its sludge because the industry has since switched to less toxic etching solvents; delisting would reclassify the sludge as nonhazardous. The sludge generated by electroplating operations is regulated as hazardous waste because of its assumed cadmium, chromium cyanide and nickel levels. Hadco intends to show that its modern sludges contain substantially lesser amounts of these constituents presumed by the EPA when it defined PWB sludge as a listed hazardous waste over twenty years ago.[51] Hadco proposes that a delisting will allow it to transport WWT sludges directly to recycling facilities rather than having to trans-ship the wastes through specially permitted hazardous waste treatment facilities. Currently, Hadco must transport its WWT sludge to Pennsylvania, where it is treated and then sent to Canada or overseas for recycling.

Based upon the cost savings of delisting, the second phase of this proposal would allow Hadco to purchase on-site sludge dryers so it can recycle other non-RCRA process wastes. In addition, the company proposes to create a market for PWB WWT sludge, whereby Hadco could accept nonhazardous wastes from smaller PWB manufacturers for recycling.

3. Imation

Imation's Camarillo, California, facility manufactures magnetic data storage cartridges for the computer industry. (The facility was established by Minnesota Mining and Manufacturing Company ["3M"] in 1963 and was transferred to a newly created spin-off company, Imation, in 1996.)

Magnetic tape manufacturing requires regular changes to plant operations, requiring frequent amendments to Imation's multiple air permits. Imation proposes to simultaneously simplify its operations and improve its environmental performance by obtaining a performance-based "Beyond Compliance" permit. A single, simplified multimedia permit would establish emission caps below existing regulatory limits and implement a simplified reporting system and Environmental Management System verification process. This proposal would allow Imation to operate with more flexibility, reduce costs and paperwork, explore innovative approaches to environmental management and provide environmental benefits. Imation will accomplish this by working with various communities to develop plans for the generation and use of emission reduction credits.

In exchange for enhanced environmental performance, Imation would be given flexibility to make changes in operations without undergoing Agency review. Imation will obtain a new multimedia permit that will affect numerous federal, state, and local regulations focusing mainly on air emissions, but also include wastewater and waste generation. The air regulations affecting the facility include New Source Review in both nonattainment and attainment areas, Reasonably Available Control Technologies, Maximum Achievable Control Technologies, Title V Clean Air Act operating permit programs and others. Reporting requirements will also be included in the permit as Imation will develop public reporting procedures.

4. Lucent Technologies

Lucent Technologies, in fulfillment of the ISO 14001 standard for environmental management systems (EMS), seeks to certify an EMS through Project XL.[52] It proposes using its EMS as a framework to develop specific proposals simplifying permitting, record keeping and reporting requirements. The proposal would first establish an EMS for the entire microelectronics unit of Lucent Technologies and then develop specific proposals for regulatory flexibility at other Lucent facilities. Lucent intends to use this proposal to test the broad applicability of ISO 14001 as a standard to determine regulatory flexibility and enhanced environmental performance.

The proposal does not yet address any specific regulations, but discusses permitting, permit modification, compliance monitoring and record keeping requirements under the Clean Air Act, the Clean Water Act, RCRA and the Toxic Substances Control Act.

5. The Massachusetts Department of Environmental Protection (DEP)

The DEP proposes to streamline its permitting and reporting processes. The DEP developed the Environmental Results Program to reduce the number of permits applied for, renewed and issued through a program of facility-wide, performance-based self-certification. The project will begin with a demonstration project; the first two industry sectors are dry cleaners and photo processors. Without developing permits for each facility, industry representatives will cooperate with the DEP to establish criteria for reporting compliance with state performance and operating standards.

The project is intended to reduce resources expended by both the DEP and industry in the permitting process, as well as to improve compliance by offering companies flexibility in the ways they move toward pollution prevention. The majority of federal and state environmental regulatory programs are based on the issuance of permits. Therefore, the DEP believes this program should be transferable to other industry sectors.

6. Merck & Company, Inc.

Merck is a large manufacturer of pharmaceuticals. Its XL project involves the negotiation of an innovative draft air permit with the Virginia Department of Environmental Quality and the EPA that would result in environmental benefit to the surrounding area while providing operational flexibility at the Merck site.[53]

The draft permit would provide a sitewide cap on total criteria air pollutants (ozone, sulfur dioxide, particulates, carbon monoxide and oxides of nitrogen) emitted from the site. The cap should result in an initial emission reduction of 950 tons of criteria pollutants; the initial reduction would be achieved by converting the facility's main powerhouse from coal to natural gas. As long as emissions remain below the cap, Merck will be allowed change existing manufacturing operations or add new processes and equipment without seeking prior approval from regulators. Should new regulations be promulgated, the facility will have the option of either complying with the rule as written, or lowering the emission cap by the amount that the rule would have reduced the site's emissions.

Merck's XL proposal also features an innovative three-tiered approach to monitoring, record keeping and reporting. Each tier has specific monitoring, record keeping, and reporting requirements that come into effect once that tier is reached. This approach is designed to give Merck added incentive to minimize emissions in order not to trigger higher tiers, which would result in more frequent and comprehensive requirements.[54]

7. Minnesota Pollution Control Agency (MPCA)

MPCA is seeking approval to implement three to five proposals from specific facilities. The Minnesota proposal aims to allow greater operating flexibility in exchange for meeting emission caps beyond current levels required by existing regulations. Permitting requirements under the major media statutes (RCRA, CAA and CWA) would be affected. Current stakeholders are the state of Minnesota and a committee comprised of industry, academic, government and citizen group representatives.

Minnesota's most fully developed project was proposed by U.S. Filter Corporation; it would allow the company to implement new recycling operations that would otherwise require major modifications of its RCRA Subtitle C permit. Specifically, U.S. Filter will recover and reuse spent hydrochloric acid contaminated with metals and cyanides used in its manufacturing operations. The used hydrochloric acid would otherwise be defined as hazardous waste (under existing regulations) and be difficult or impossible to recycle. The company also proposes to recover and reuse its contaminated process wastewater.

Anderson Windows has submitted a similar project proposal to recycle its spent vinyl, sawdust and window components for use in new products. These actions would otherwise violate portions of RCRA.

8. Molex, Incorporated

Molex proposes to segregate the wastewater stream at its new electroplating facility in Lincoln, Nebraska. Molex suggests that recognizing that its waste contains valuable by-products and reclassifying them as hazardous materials (not hazardous waste) would result in significant financial savings and environmental benefit. It claims that the treatment of segregated wastewater streams could result in at least a fifty percent reduction in mass loadings of its treatment plant and lower sludge disposal costs because pure metal sludges can be sold directly to processors. Since pure sludge does not require disposal, the proposal eliminates disposal fees. Reclassifying valuable by-products under RCRA from hazardous wastes to hazardous materials would shift the method of shipping to common carriers, no longer requiring shipping by licensed hazardous waste haulers.

9. New York State Department of Environmental Conservation (NYSDEC)

RCRA requires producers of hazardous wastes at remote locations, such as manholes and trenches, to transport any quantity of waste directly to a treatment, storage and disposal facility and to obtain a separate the EPA identification number for each location. The producer must also file a Hazardous Waste Report for each instance of hazardous waste spillage.

NYSDEC's project will allow public utilities to consolidate essentially identical hazardous wastes and store them for up to ninety days (the regulatory maximum) before transport and disposal. This should result in fewer vehicle trips, with larger loads. The project is expected to minimize unnecessary paperwork and facilitate more efficient use of time and labor. NYSDEC also claims that allowing public utilities to consolidate essentially identical hazardous wastes and store them for up to ninety days will increase public safety and significantly reduce costs to public utilities and the EPA.

Supporting stakeholders include NYNEX for the telephone industry, Con Edison for the electric power industry, and Brooklyn Union Gas for the oil and gas pipeline industry.

10. OSi Specialties, Inc.

OSi is a specialty chemical manufacturer. It proposes a project for its Sisterville, West Virginia, plant that would result in overall lower emission levels at the facility than would be expected from simple compliance with new RCRA air emission standards for its surface impoundments and tanks. In exchange for the EPA's deferral of certain RCRA regulations controlling air emissions, OSi will add controls to its existing polyether production process unit to drop facility emissions substantially below current levels. OSi estimates that it will be able to reduce overall air emissions by about 309,000 pounds per year at a much lower cost. In addition, 500,000 pounds per year of methanol will be removed from the wastewater system, thus avoiding about 800,000 pounds per year of sludge generation.

11. Union Carbide (UCC)

UCC, in consultation with Louisiana, the EPA and other parties, has proposed two demonstration projects at its Taft, Louisiana, facility. The first would use alternative technologies or containers for the satellite accumulation of hazardous wastes for periods of three days or less. The second would eliminate redundant waste analysis requirements for materials treated at a permitted/interim treatment, storage and disposal or recycling facility, and would establish a general waste classification. UCC proposed four projects that generally fit these two categories. The projects affect air and water emissions, and hazardous waste. All fall under RCRA.

12. Vandenburg Air Force Base (VAFB)

VAFB proposed to take money it now spends on permitting, record keeping, monitoring, training and other administrative requirements of the Clean Air Act and to use those funds to upgrade and retrofit boilers, space heaters and other equipment. Through this phased retrofitting program, VAFB expects to reduce the facility's emissions from approximately sixty tons per year to twenty five tons per year. In the short term, the focus will reducing emissions from boilers, furnaces and process heaters. In the long term, the focus will be on opportunities to prevent pollution by reducing emissions from internal combustion engines, solvent, and surface coating applications, as well as other sources of ozone precursors.

F. First Impressions

What is most interesting about these projects is their generally prosaic nature. Despite statements from industry, scholars, and commentators on the need for alternatives to command and control, these proposals suggest only modest relief from discrete environmental regulations. They would permit new recycling activities under RCRA, allow more relaxed temporary hazardous waste storage under RCRA, establish more flexible Clean Air Act permit limits in exchange for an overall reduction in air emissions, and permit experimentation with ISO 14001 standards for environmental management systems. Possible reasons for the collective lack of ambition suggested by these proposals are discussed below.

V. From Theory to Realpolitik: The Agency's Experience Implementing Project XL

Interviews were conducted with eighteen EPA staff members, academics, members of the business community, nongovernmental organizations (NGOs) and other stakeholders involved in XL. By agreement, quotations are not attributed to specific interviewees.[55] The interviewees concluded nearly unanimously that the EPA's institutionalized "enforcement culture" was a critical barrier to operating in the new ways called for by Project XL. According to one XL administrator, "Philosophically, the greatest resistance to flexibility is within the agency itself. . . . A 'command and control' agency cannot run an initiative stressing innovative approaches; it seems evident to everyone but . . . EPA. But then again, these institutional values run so deep in us. They are hard to step far enough away from for us to see." Overall, they believe that Project XL has not yet achieved its broader mission, despite modest successes in a number of instances.

A. The EPA's Cultural Values and Institutional Goals

The EPA has invested in enforcement-oriented activities for decades. A significant number of Agency personnel at all levels reacted to XL specifically (and adaptive management notions generally) as a threat to a system that has worked reasonably well to protect the environment and to advance their careers. As an XL regional team member described it,

> [The XL regional teams] keep going through the same experience: first, political appointees on the headquarters level tell us to 'throw away the rule book' in formulating XL projects. We then negotiate agreements with participating companies and environmental group stakeholders. We submit our agreement by consensus to various Agency headquarters offices. They either disagree with each other, or individual offices disagree on separate points. In the end, we are told that our innovative agreement conflicts with headquarters' understanding of the pertinent regulation. We thought the point of the initiative was to propose innovative solutions to persistent regulatory problems! Schizophrenia rules.

A regional XL coordinator observed that:

> [O]ur headquarters-oriented approval structure has always been 'top-down.' It didn't change for Project XL. As the initiative progressed [in 1996 and 1997], headquarters exerted more and more command and control over the regional personnel involved, particularly with regard to our exercise of discretion over what might constitute a supportable regulatory interpretation. It was as though, faced with an initiative demanding flexible and creative analy-

sis, they reacted by retreating to the safety of the tried and true. This dampened our regional desire to keep proposing innovative approaches to them; they [headquarters offices] simply could not cede control of any XL issue to us. They would not use their discretion to ratify FPAs cooperatively crafted by the regions, the stakeholders and the company. In the end, we stopped advocating for innovative experimental approaches because we were consistently shot down by headquarters. The only way to get by our own people was to shoehorn all projects into conformity with some notion of the existing regulatory structure, using discretion as a justification for doing so. To some degree, this undermined the legitimacy of the mechanisms governing the Agency's exercise of discretion. I think that this defeated a purpose of XL: the collaborative exploration for regulatory improvement lying 'outside the box' of our existing structure.

"EPA hasn't cultivated or rewarded the skills necessary to successful innovation since Reagan was elected," remarked a regional XL team member. "It doesn't know how to experiment. Nor did it attempt to attract the expertise to evaluate research and development proposals floated by the regulated community, and our lack of entrepreneurial skills hurt us on Project XL. Instead of . . . participating as a partner in project development, we treated each project as a permit application to be passively processed." A fellow team member replied, "Why should we have done anything else? We are not a research and development corporation; we are a public sector enforcement agency. The skills to do XL are not at EPA; the very concept was deeply distrusted. It's a fact that, in our region, those who participated in Project XL were considered turncoats by certain important middle-level managers." Another XL regional coordinator echoed this perception. "In the end, these managers reminded us that our success is measured simply by how many actions we take and how many penalty dollars we collect. Nothing else counts."

Strategic moves to protect the status quo were not confined to the EPA headquarters. As one the EPA regional enforcement manager described it, "Many of us put the blame solely on the headquarters divisions, but our regional inability to view compliance as a flexible concept, achievable through collaborative experimentation, was equally at fault." A regional XL coordinator stated,

> In my region, certain senior attorneys lobbied to be appointed to specific XL projects because they wanted them killed. They were old-line enforcers and saw them [XL projects] as yet another plot to weaken our enforcement capability and erode their [own] status. With that agenda coming in, how could any innovative project requiring collaboration succeed?

Career concerns, in combination with institutional enforcement biases, generated managerial hostility to XL. A regional coordinator who acted as an XL liaison between his region's enforcement team and the regional administrator's office stated that

> [On the regional level], middle level managers and their directors were generally opposed to Project XL. Most of them didn't have a philosophical bias one way or the other. But they were certain that the Agency's enforcement

mission as its primary activity wasn't going to change. They knew that head-quarters wasn't going to award the region's extra resources to staff the project. Where were those XL resources going to come from? You got it out of the existing enforcement personnel pool. So, if staff goes to XL, where were the enforcement 'beans' going to come from?

An XL regional attorney perceived the problem as a battle between the political demands behind Project XL and the status quo:

> Headquarters wanted it both ways; they wanted to say that nationwide, enforcement numbers were up and that we were administering loads of XL projects. This was impossible. . . . In the end, EPA veterans knew the enforcement demand would win out, particularly when the presidential election was over. So they fought XL staffing whenever it threatened to affect the stability of their day-to-day operations.

Interviewees spoke of the EPA's institutionalized fear of failure, combined with internal confusion over what the Agency defined as "success." For an enforcement agency, "success" might be defined as good settlements and favorable court decisions. For those favoring adaptive management, however, "success" is the generation of useful data. Data can be generated by experiments that produce "good results" (i.e., a transferable technology) or that "fail" (i.e., prove that a proposed regulatory innovation does not achieve a predicted reduction in emissions at a certain cost). These competing definitions were never reconciled by those in charge.

An XL regional coordinator who is also an attorney reflected that: "[E]nforcement agencies are justifiably afraid to fail. If you bring a case to court and lose, you might set a negative legal precedent that could haunt you for decades. From a litigator's point of view, it's better for EPA to bring only cases it is sure of winning and let the rest go. Unfortunately, this kind of thinking carried over into these XL projects, where it is fatal to a spirit of experimentation. Regional and headquarters managers demanded 'success.' But how can you run an experiment and demand a guarantee of success from your team? If we are assured of a successful result, why run the experiment?"

An EPA program and XL engineer agreed:

> I never understood the rhetoric about 'bold experimentation.' I'm a scientist by training. I experiment to 'find out.' To get answers, I have to carefully design an experiment, monitor it, chart the results and deduce why it came out that way. I then adjust the experiment in accordance with my deductions and go on testing. But the EPA has insufficient will to pursue this kind of long-range, low profile quest. And, on the political level, [EPA] has neither the courage nor the patience. Also, we have no system in place to record institutional memory and that's fatal to our growth—fatal no matter how you decide to 'grow' EPA—toward pure enforcement, pure experimentation, whatever. And since there is no real method developed to gather the data generated from experiments and no institutional memory, EPA 'lifers' see no value to an adaptive management approach. Even if all this were not true,

there is certainly no method by which we are forced to consider how such results should affect the way we operate. No feed-back loop at all.

An EPA enforcement manager tracking XL in his region bemoaned XL's failure to transfer relevant data into the Agency's day-to-day activities:

> There was no attempt at double-loop learning—[no attempt] to consistently feed back the results of XL experiments into our existing way of doing business. So, without that, what's the point of all the blood letting? XL did some good things. But we've made no attempt to look at a project's success and transfer it. And transferability was both a major goal of adaptive management and one of the major attractions of the XL project. It ended up being project approval for short-term political gain. We needed to consider transferability of these projects, both from the Agency's point of view in upgrading operations and to meet industry's interest in creating collaborative new technologies it could actually use. We never did.

Project XL sought to employ administrative flexibility so that unique solutions to the problems of certain industries, even simple facilities, could be found. It also sought to stimulate experimentation that would lead to "new ideas" and "reforms" that could and would be copied widely. The logic of adaptive management (and its emphasis on regulatory flexibility and experimentation) is not antithetical to the desire for systematic reform—as long as good information is collected about each "experiment" and shared widely.

Interviewees also cited impediments posed by the traditional adversarial relationship between the EPA and state regulatory agencies, corporations and non-governmental organizations. An EPA enforcement attorney serving on an XL team remarked that,

> [T]raditionally, the EPA and those whom we regulate don't talk to each other. When we do talk, we automatically distrust what the other side is saying. Along comes XL asking us to brainstorm to create new ways of achieving new relationships with each other and to agree on new ways to comply with environmental regulations. But with that as a starting point, how quickly could we learn to collaborate with these folks? They have no idea how to do it either. We don't even know how to listen to each other, much less collaborate.

Interviewees had little hope XL would have any serious influence on the Agency's culture and modus operandi. Another EPA enforcement attorney serving on several XL teams believed XL was being undermined by its exploitation for headline value:

> XL uses adaptive management theory in a fascinating, constructively subversive attempt to incrementally change EPA's perception of how to create efficient environmental compliance from the bottom up, starting at the regional level. I wonder if anyone at the White House level realized the implications? In any case, someone at the EPA recognized it, because XL quickly became election year window dressing. There was and is no commitment to adaptive

management concepts at the headquarters level. That will not change until new and creative thinking is institutionalized and rewarded. . . .

An XL regional attorney perceived the failure as largely attributable to the EPA's internal problems:

> My frustration was that, despite problems, XL actually explored some creative regulatory options—one-stop shopping for permits, exploring alternative methods of delisting hazardous wastes, operating flexibility under air permits, and setting performance-based emissions goals to name a few. But none of these results are being rerouted into our existing system. Why? We've become a bloated bureaucracy obsessed with dealing with ourselves—not looking outward. So turf issues are always most important to those who run the Agency. In fact, my XL experience shows me the Agency reacted to XL by becoming less flexible, not more.

B. Internal Policy Conflicts

EPA headquarters failed to organize an open, consensus-building process to define XL's mission and to coordinate efforts to achieve the initiative's goals. The Agency's limited resources made it likely that enforcement numbers would remain stable or fall if personnel were reassigned to XL projects. Given the EPA's enforcement bias, it was vital that headquarters confront this issue and inform the regions whether this might be permissible. This did not happen. Nor did the leadership at headquarters create a strategic mechanism to resolve this macrocosmic impasse nor any discrete barriers impeding individual projects. "No one office or person at headquarters seemed willing, let alone authorized, to cross lines of authority and resolve project roadblocks," said a regional enforcement manager and XL coordinator. The coordinator continued:

> Headquarters and the regions never talked to each other to work out a memorandum of agreement (MOA). An MOA would have allowed us to clarify among ourselves what XL was designed to do, how much of that design we would try to accomplish, and how we were going to work together to marshal the resources to do it. As time went on, it seemed to me that the various headquarters groups never even coordinated with each other, except in reaction to problems and pressure; never proactively.

It was clear to most interviewees that Project XL was a priority to high-level headquarters managers and to Administrator Carol Browner. However, when conflicts arose between headquarters divisions concerning competing institutional goals, no one in an authoritative position decisively intervened to facilitate, mediate or clarify. An XL coordinator remarked, "below the political appointee level, it seemed that headquarters was bitterly divided in its feelings toward innovation and adaptive management; so much so that it was difficult for them to give us a straight answer on basic questions."

Nor did headquarters effectively intervene when disputes flared up on interregional projects. An XL attorney-coordinator observed that,

[O]ur regions differed in interpretation of policy and on the relative priority of environmental protection issues. For instance, our region is very concerned with groundwater protection and our companion region was not. However, the success of our joint project depended on the resolution of groundwater protection issues. Headquarters left our two regions to 'duke it out'; they basically stood back and waited to see which region would win or whether the project would simply collapse as a result of our inability to reach agreement. They were ultimately interested in the politics of it—the appearance of either crediting themselves with a success or disassociating from a failure—and not the merits of the project.

A major headquarters function is to unite all ten regions around an interpretation of a significant policy issue; national legal interpretation is generally the responsibility of EPA's Office of General Counsel (OGC). This did not happen. There were serious and unaddressed splits between various headquarters and regional divisions. At headquarters, XL program proponents were often in conflict with positions taken by the attorneys in OGC. Many EPA interviewees at the regional and national levels echoed this comment by a regional XL coordinator: "OGC disliked XL. It was sensitive to the possibility that successful XL projects might create the perception that OGC's pronouncements were neither the most correct nor the most beneficial to foster environmental improvement and efficiency."

Another XL regional coordinator stated that "several headquarters offices were involved in our projects. In our negotiations with them, it became clear that they understood these projects primarily as threats to their status and [to their] established functions. Headquarters divisions had their own turf concerns and became a veritable ball and chain in approving any projects." At EPA headquarters, some personnel admitted as much. "Headquarters never developed a coherent statement on what XL meant in terms of signaling permissible parameters for projects the regions were reviewing. The short-term political agenda behind its creation didn't give us the time to do so," said one interview subject.

An EPA regional XL coordinator agreed:

> Consensus on XL's mission and operational strategy had to be built throughout the Agency. But it wasn't. So we ended up modeling the very behavior we were trying to surmount: conflicts, wasted time and energy, achievement of policy goals sacrificed on the altar of career agendas. We expected conflict with the proposing corporations and with environmental groups. But what happened internally was terrible.

The defensive strategic proclivities of regional administrators affected the fate of XL. A regional XL coordinator observed,

> Our regional administrator [RA] saw nothing to gain. He is a career government type, administratively driven. He demanded high enforcement and permit-processing numbers. So he refrained from encouraging XL in any useful way. In other regions, you had RAs who were intensely political, literally run-

ning for office. In those regions, innovative projects were aggressively pursued for headline value. When staffing became an issue, those regional administrators simply ordered their managers to reassign people to XL.

A high-ranking EPA director analyzed this dysfunction in leadership as follows:

> A failure to clearly enunciate a mission is typical of Browner's leadership style, which is designed to survive short-term political fire-drills, not to advance policy. But it didn't start with her and won't end when she leaves. We are not culturally encouraged to be a proactive force; instead, we react to short-term political fire drills. Generally, EPA culture dictates that those who act are left behind. Those who confine themselves to reaction are promoted. It's no accident that Browner never brings her assistant administrators into the same room to align them on important, cross-cutting issues. She believes that she will survive only by being all things to all people. If Congress holds hearings premised on the notion that the EPA is soft on enforcement and too strong on collaboration with the 'enemy,' Browner sends her pit bull assistant administrator to testify about how punitive the Agency really is. When Congress investigates why EPA is so needlessly aggressive, rigid and punitive toward a generally well-meaning private sector, she sends the assistant administrator who preaches the joys of innovation, reinvention and cooperation. This is the reality of the EPA; it is a political football for Congress.

C. The Private Sector: Interests and Disincentives

In the words of a corporate director of environmental affairs,

> Don't forget that cultural problems exist here as well. Environmental managers are people whose jobs are defined as *compliance*. They do not like or trust the XL 'leap.' Their definition of success is how far you keep EPA away. XL [projects] only bring [EPA] closer. Our culture discourages and distrusts the idea of partnership with outsiders, too, particularly with an enforcement agency. And despite the XL rhetoric, our company didn't believe EPA knew how to collaborate. For instance, few of us thought EPA would actually forego an enforcement action if it came across something negative while visiting the plant or reviewing an audit we ourselves had prepared. . . . And what if an XL project of ours failed? We suspected that EPA would then be looking for private sector victims to blame at that point. So, what was really in it for us?

For their part, Agency personnel were puzzled by the modest nature of the projects industry suggested for XL's first round. As someone at the EPA headquarters level stated,

> We were surprised at the inferiority of the XL proposals themselves. It was the corporations, after all, which kept claiming that they could exceed current environmental standards cheaper, faster and so on. All they needed was

relief from inflexible rules or, alternately, they argued that all they needed was relief from our inflexible interpretation of what were, in fact, flexible rules. So, we expected proposals that reconfigured basic command and control tenets: alternative permitting instruments, paradigm-shifts to performance-based standards with no specified technologies, and so on. Instead, industry chose only to nibble at the margins. It was as if they were resigned to the system as is.

Another EPA national XL coordinator remarked,

A lot of the disappointment in XL was generated by industry, not EPA or the NGOs. Industry pressured us into XL through the Clinton administration's Reinvention Campaign. But many of the projects that they promised would deliver improved environmental results at lower cost simply didn't. In the end, a generator of pollution must achieve some objective number measuring its emissions. But most XL proposals said something like, 'If you give us the regulatory flexibility allowing us to substitute *our* number for yours, we can always come pretty close to our number and occasionally even hit your number. And we will save a lot of money!' A lot of XL proposals were rejected by us for that reason. I think Project XL called the private sector's 'cheaper/better' bluff.

Another headquarters coordinator concluded his interview by remarking that,

[P]art of what I learned on the national level was that perhaps command and control should not be viewed so negatively. Environmental results are quite difficult to measure, let alone define. When you attempt to do so, EPA and the industries get involved in battles between experts, and this is always a zero-sum battle. Command and control may no longer be politically correct, but it may be the only regulatory method that business and politicians can agree on.

Not surprisingly, those we spoke to in the regulated community did not agree entirely. A corporate attorney retorted,

First, EPA assured us that our experiments would be litigation-proof through its employment of 'enforcement discretion' but we knew that enforcement discretion was not enough to protect us from NGOs. Environmental statutes contain citizen suit provisions; any member of the affected public could bring an action against us without EPA's blessing or involvement. Despite White House assurances, needed legislation was never passed. Clinton and Browner were too scared to support it in an election year. EPA didn't have the will to step up to the plate on the issue. They provided little leadership on the day-to-day XL review process. It was our problem to identify and convene all stakeholders and get their agreement. This eventually stood XL on its head. We spent more time and money drumming up interest in the project than on the project itself. And in our case, there simply was no stakeholder interest. EPA's obsession with the welfare of the stakeholder process was misplaced. If

EPA wanted it, it should have coordinated it. Instead of it being an innovative technology initiative, it made the projects captive to the opinions of the NGOs. For me the way EPA handled the stakeholder issue was its worst failure.

An EPA national coordinator confirmed problems with the stakeholder process:

Stakeholder participation is vital, but it needs to be bounded. Industry is understandably loath to make significant proposals in cases where it can be held hostage by any member of the public with any agenda. Stakeholders should be involved, but the success of the entire process cannot depend on whether a particular NGO is happy. That's not what consensus is.

Several corporate XL participants and EPA regional team members agreed with the following statement, made by an XL regional engineer team member:

In the end, it's EPA's responsibility to make decisions on the efficacy of environmental compliance proposals. Yet the Agency's obsession with stakeholder involvement turned XL into something not entirely relevant to the collaborative development of technology: a stakeholder-designed, from the ground up exercise in process development. That was not XL's stated purpose.

A law professor was surprised EPA expected to see industry propose paradigm-shifting projects during round one.

EPA cannot throw away the rule book as it originally claimed. If you want to change paradigms, you need to change the underlying statutes and change the definition of the kind of discretion EPA can use in carrying out a statutory mandate. EPA cannot unilaterally do this, nor can it approve projects that propose to do so. Also, the Clinton administration didn't pursue legislation that would have clarified the application and approval process to protect its participants from a certain degree of legal exposure. The degree to which these two parties fundamentally misunderstand each other's interests is incredible. There are too many institutional impediments to propose groundbreaking regulatory ideas at this time. This is only the first round of XL. The parties don't trust each other. Neither has a clear idea of how the other side defines the goals of XL or evaluates the incentives to participate. They can't easily come to agreement on the subject, either, since they never developed a process within which to interact. EPA didn't pursue a statutory endorsement of XL. Thus, EPA has no way legally to define such projects as experiments and permissible, within specific limits, outside the current regulatory structure. Lastly, it is economically naive to expect industry to begin by challenging old regulatory paradigms. Industry has long since sunk the funds to buy technology allowing it to comply with the last twenty years of environmental regulation. Those battles are past history. The technology they bought still has useful life in it. Industry is now interested in what is about to come over the horizon. When safeguards to possible legal and financial exposure are addressed by EPA, the initiative paradigms will expand—not before.

By fall 1996, industry's disenchantment with the XL approval process became apparent. First, state environmental officials issued negative public statements echoing business' frustration with the gap between the EPA's promises of regulatory flexibility and their actual experience in trying to get it.[56] The Massachusetts Environmental Commissioner stated that there was a disconnect between Agency officials touting the program's promise and program staff who thwarted projects with bureaucratic delays, ratcheting down the flexibility of XL as they went. The Deputy Director of Michigan's Department of Natural Resources believed that EPA officials constantly changed the rules for approval, thereby making an XL project "a continual moving target" and "extremely poorly managed at every level. There's so much suspicion on the part of the regulated community that it's not worth spending much time on it anymore."

However, certain business leaders involved with specific XL projects were supportive despite their many frustrations. An Intel spokesperson attributed most difficulties to companies' general reluctance to invest enough effort up front, when only 'uncertain benefits' were possible, and to an accompanying certainty of criticism from environmentalists down the road. "But just because [Project XL] needs refinement doesn't mean it's bankrupt,"[57] a Hadco Corporation representative stated, noting that, while the XL process had been complicated and frustrating, the potential gains were worth it. "We recognize it's a new program. However, the benefits for companies like [ours] could be substantial."[58]

D. Environmental NGOs

NGOs supported the EPA's move toward an adaptive management approach, at least in theory. However, they were generally concerned about environmental impacts that might result. They believed business would subvert XL by offering the EPA multimedia emissions trade-offs that could pose new and more serious hazards to workers and the environment. Thus, industry could use XL as a cover to achieve lower operating costs by increasing emissions. NGOs otherwise attracted to the adaptive management possibilities inherent in the initiative perceived additional dangers. A representative of the Natural Resources Defense Council saw XL as posing a serious strategic problem. "Adaptive management demands policy making from the bottom up, which is not necessarily bad. But if the EPA authorizes ten different policy experiments that simultaneously bubble up from ten different EPA regions, NGOs don't have sufficient resources to cover them, at least not before the first *Federal Register* notice, and that's too late." Without sufficient resources to participate meaningfully in project formulation and review, "the concept of transferability becomes our ultimate enemy," the representative concluded.

These suspicions were exacerbated by the experiences of certain stakeholder groups. The XL public participation process was not clearly defined by the EPA and often took up many more meeting days per project than anyone expected. Thus, the costs to NGOs of participating in these meetings and meaningfully analyzing the data supporting proposed projects rose alarmingly. NGOs worried that this state of affairs would become

XL's normal operating mode; a mode that would effectively (if not intentionally) insulate projects from meaningful public scrutiny. The combination of time pressures and shrinking resources turned many stakeholder meetings into distributive negotiation sessions, in which all parties strategized to protect or achieve their own interests. Integrative interaction between stakeholders eroded. According to one participant:

> I know what an adaptive management approach should entail, and we weren't engaging in it on our project. We were not defining and solving problems. We became, instead, a group of negotiators, each with different interests for which we were advocating. Those stakeholders that had the funds to stay in the process, obtain expert analysis and file briefs did better than those who didn't have such resources.

Some NGO representatives suspected (and still believe) that this experience proved one of their initial presumptions: that NGOs' only legitimate source of leverage is through litigation or through the media. Certain NGOs believed that only by resorting to their traditional weapons could they persuade business to even consider engaging in an open process. Indeed, in informal communications with other EPA XL regional coordinators, the authors learned that by fall 1996, a number of NGOs were already hinting at lawsuits against XL project approvals based on abuse of discretion.

Finally, NGO concerns emanated less from strategic, and more from philosophical points of view. They wondered whether a chronic lack of resources would prevent agencies from being held accountable if a new regime were created collaboratively. "Indeed," wrote one observer, "critics fear that . . . Project XL [is a vehicle] through which the Agency, industry and powerful public interest groups can collude to undermine the public interest. Rather than an alternative to interest representation, these processes threaten to achieve its perfection. Agencies will be reduced to brokering deals between powerful interest groups."[59]

E. The Agency Retreat

The EPA reacted to the above described criticisms by moving away from its initial reliance on a discretionary "re-writing of the rulebook." Regions were urged to find flexibility within existing regulations. If a project could not be defined within regulatory parameters, but was statutorily permissible, the Agency resorted to site-specific permits, or permits containing special conditions.

This is reflected in changes in headquarters' instructions to the regions regarding the proper uses of discretion in authorizing proposed projects. At the beginning of the initiative, headquarters hoped to use discretion expansively. As stakeholder positions hardened, headquarters retreated.

An EPA regional XL coordinator reflected,

> EPA saluted the administration's XL concept and ran it up the flagpole too quickly. And they did so without taking a hard look at the 'carrots and sticks' offered to the players. Industry's corporate attorneys did not consider the doctrine of administrative discretion as adequate protection of their interests. They wanted and expected legislation, which they didn't get and NGOs dis-

trusted EPA's public participation mechanisms. They did not trust the existing APA [Administrative Procedure Act] protections to effectively rein in
improper exercises of EPA discretion. So the NGOs resorted to business as
usual: the threat of a high profile lawsuit. They contacted the companies
and—most importantly—Clinton's reelection people. NGOs know that the
threat of litigation and bad publicity is their ultimate trump card; it gives
them the power to get to the bargaining table on a project like XL, or to scare
everyone away from sitting down at the table in the first place.

Another EPA XL coordinator agreed:

There were plenty of sticks to go around. But where were the carrots? NGOs
were suspicious of XL as both a potential evasion of agency accountability
and a potential sell-out [to business interests]. Business was worried that
EPA couldn't steer the initiative coherently, which would open them to legal
action by NGOs or the Agency itself, depending on the policy mood and
political needs at headquarters or a region on a given day. And we at EPA
were, in fact, hopelessly divided with no XL czar to resolve differences and
use those resolutions to make clear policy for all the players. Those . . . interested in implementing XL were given no institutional incentives to persevere.
And on the regional level, at least, it became clear that our continued participation might not be the best of career moves.

An XL regional team member recalled, "Headquarters started by telling us to throw
away the rule book. Of course, no one took that too literally. But, still, we were taken
aback by how quickly headquarters backed away from this position as business found discretion inadequate and NGOs considered our proposed use of it as potentially abusive."
His regional XL coordinator agreed:

Headquarters' various guidances on discretion were never more than plati-
tudes. This was one of XL's most significant weaknesses. Enforcement discretion as an approval mechanism was quickly de-emphasized after NGOs
and business weighed in. We ended up using discretion as a concept to mar-
ginally rethink what a permissible regulatory reinterpretation might be.

A national XL coordinator came to the same conclusion. "In retrospect, I now believe
that certain regulations are flexible enough to allow collaborative experimentation without change. . . . Many regulations are flexible enough for XL purposes. It's our guidance
documents interpreting them that are fossilized." An XL regional coordinator sees no
improvement:

The original headquarters guidance on the relationship between discretion
and XL was a brave response to Congressional challenges to be innovative
and [to] welcome collaborative problem-solving methods. But after hearing
initial reactions from NGOs and industry, headquarters became entirely reactive; their instructions increasingly seemed to come from a position of fear.
Headquarters' guidance on discretion became increasingly shaky, ill-defined
and oral instead of written. As on XL's general mission, headquarters could

come to no consensus upon which to build a workable definition of discretion or flexibility in using it. Throughout the life of XL so far, definitions continue to fluctuate from department to department.

Headquarters' XL staff was beleaguered by complaints from the regions, businesses and NGOs. "We heard the criticisms. But we simply weren't ready to issue good affirmative guidance. Who knew what issues were going to hit us from the regions? Each project presented a different challenge for us to interpret 'superior environmental benefit,' craft permissible borders for specific regulatory meanings, and so on."

Informed of this comment, a regional attorney retorted:

> They still don't get it. We didn't need their opinion on each definition of discretion or degree of flexibility on specific projects. It was our job to make that initial determination on the regional level, a determination that should have gotten a high degree of deference from headquarters. What we needed from Washington was general guidance on policy goals and parameters. Just another example of the headquarters' uncontrollable instinct to control at the 'tree' level, when what we needed was their assistance in defining the parameters of the 'forest.'

F. Specific Successes

Despite the institutional toll taken by the conflicts described above, Project XL has achieved some potentially significant successes.

The Berry Corporation project provides one example. This project, now in operation, produced a truly adaptive permitting system for its plant. The Berry permit replaced seven individual permits with one comprehensive operating permit, known as a "COP." Critical to the XL regime is measuring the degree to which a plan achieves its predictions. The Berry COP measures the plant's compliance with mandated outcomes and loops the data back into a dynamic compliance system. Significantly, the project envisions a creative, provisional regulatory scheme to run the plant, setting up a scheme capable of compliance measurement and continuous revision. It also conceives of the permit as an ongoing problem-solving tool through which the original agreement will be reviewed and revised in light of new information. One analyst summarized the process,

> In light of the data produced, the Agency, the company and other stakeholders will determine [whether] environmental benefits exceed what would have been achieved under a traditional permitting regime. For each area of environmental performance in the COP, the company has predicted improvement over a baseline, identified the means of achieving it and agreed to a monitoring and disclosure mechanism.[60]

Another example is the Intel Corporation's FPA, also in operation. It proposes that multimedia emission trades be implemented within the framework of a traditional permit.[61] The entire Intel plant is treated as operating under a single emissions cap. Within that cap, Intel may make process changes without applying for the usual permit modifications from state agencies. However, Intel must always maintain air emissions below the levels required by the cap, as set out in the FPA. Such a strategy requires taking some risk. As with the Berry FPA, the Intel agreement has the potential to produce more adaptive approaches to implementation and enforcement than traditional permitting. While Intel succeeds in obtaining pre-approval of process modification, the company committed to tie its emissions levels to production without knowing the details of how those processes will work in the future. All sides agree that this approach would not have surfaced in the context of traditional, adversarial permitting.[62]

The Weyerhaeuser Company's pulp manufacturing facility in Oglethorpe, Georgia proposes to minimize the environmental impact of its manufacturing processes on the Flint River and surrounding environment. The Weyerhaeuser FPA implements a long-term plan to create a minimum (environmental) impact mill. The EPA and the State of Georgia have agreed to propose changes in relevant RCRA and Clean Water Act rules to support this experiment in minimum impact manufacturing.

Through a combination of enforceable requirements and voluntary goals, Weyerhaeuser is cutting its bleach plant effluent by fifty percent over ten years; reducing water use by about one million gallons a day; cutting its solid waste generation in half over the same ten-year period; improving forest management practices on 300,000 acres of land; and adopting ISO 14001 as its plant-wide environmental management system. The EPA is offering Weyerhaeuser the flexibility to consolidate routine monthly compliance reports into two reports per year. Further, Weyerhaeuser will be allowed to use alternative means that would not otherwise have been approved without close examination and permit revisions, to meet the requirements of any new regulations that prescribe maximum, achievable control technology. The EPA is also waiving government review prior to certain physical plant modifications, provided that emissions do not exceed stipulated levels.

Finally, these projects envision continued contact among stakeholders *after* the conclusion of the FPA negotiation and provide some degree of shared responsibility for review and modification of the final project agreement. Thus, an ongoing consensus-building process is incorporated into the structure of all these agreements.

V. Conclusions and Recommendations

A. Conclusions

Many critics charge that while the administrative state is economically inefficient and discourages experimentation and innovation, agencies exercise too much discretionary power without adequate accountability. These same critics believe these deficiencies undermine environmental enforcement.

However, our analysis of Project XL suggests that the critics of command and control cannot have it both ways. If agencies are to become more efficient in market terms, they need *more* discretion in different categories, not less discretion overall. Discretion to experiment with regulatory techniques—to learn what works and what does not—is crucial to tailored solutions that balance governmental objectives with the needs of the regulatory community. At the same time, care must be taken that agency exercise of discretion is constrained in order to minimize the risks of abuse and ensure fairness; concerns about abuse of discretion justifiably increase as bureaucracies stretch to encompass goals outside the borders of their enabling statutes. XL provides some insight into these dynamics, shedding light on both the "upside" and the dangers. To date, XL results are basically disappointing. There have been few breakthroughs, fewer real experiments and little lasting reform. This can be attributed to several things. First, inertia and resistance to change within the EPA are problematic. Indeed, the most serious impediments to increasing agency discretion at EPA are internal. Second, the EPA management never supplied an adequate mandate or resources for the EPA personnel working on the XL initiative. Third, industry was overly cautious, failing to propose projects sufficiently innovative to test the potential of the initiative.

The lesson to learn from Project XL is that the best way to encourage technological and regulatory innovation and promote efficiency is to *expand* the use of certain types of administrative discretion. Agencies should be granted increased discretion to experiment with regulatory systems designed to achieve congressionally mandated goals. In that context, XL-like initiatives have the potential to serve as policy laboratories in which such experiments, and safeguards against their abuse, can be tested.

B. Recommendations

XL participants consistently expressed frustration when attempting to move outside the "regulatory box." A number of causes were cited: statutory mandates; long-standing, inflexible interpretations of existing regulations; and business, Agency or NGO culture. These barriers comprise significant limits to innovation. Further, most stakeholders still believe their respective interests will not be well served by a collaborative, rather than adversarial, approach to regulation. For those who participated in the XL initiative, it is clear that unless Congress provides a new legislative mandate that gives the EPA the freedom to experiment, innovative projects like XL are crippled before they even begin. In the words of one EPA participant, "Just one abusive or environmentally harmful XL experiment will obviate a dozen individual successes." Even worse, political interests will react to such an outcome by firmly returning the EPA to the comfort of its command and control past.

The EPA uncertainty regarding the appropriate exercise of discretion limited XL from the start. The EPA stated that it would "use a variety of administrative and compliance mechanisms to provide regulatory flexibility for final project agreements."[63] However, for projects involving multimedia trades, the EPA never determined whether such projects were, indeed, within the Agency's enforcement discretion and thus immune from judicial reversal.[64]

XL and similar reforms would have a better chance if Congress specifically passed legislation authorizing such activities. In this way, Congress could authorize the exercise of regulatory flexibility for specific projects, even in cases where there is a conflict with promulgated rules and statutory limits. As a safeguard against abuse, a new statute could require the EPA to certify that for any given project: 1) there was a significant promise of superior environmental performance (i.e., a result superior to that mandated by statute or regulation that would have to be documented on a regular basis); 2) the proposed experiment posed no potential threat to human health or the environment; 3) the actual management of the experimental project would be as transparent as possible—open to the direct scrutiny of all potentially affected stakeholders; 4) impartial monitoring by independent parties would be provided; and 5) the EPA or any other affected party would be empowered to have a project stopped immediately in federal court should these conditions not be met.[65] This strategy would obviate the need for Agency staff to squeeze XL experiments into tortured regulatory reinterpretations. It would also decrease the temptation to stretch the concept of discretion beyond appropriate limits, thus buttressing accountability. Most importantly, such a statute would insulate XL-like efforts from bureaucratic resistance from inside the EPA through the pressure of Congressional oversight.

According to Browner, it is unwise to ask Congress to "spell out every detail of not only what the EPA must do but also what business must do."[66] Thus, Congress and the EPA should form the same performance-based relationship that others advocate for the EPA and the regulated community. Congress should push the Agency to achieve certain outcomes while granting it the discretion to choose the most appropriate method of achieving them. This is unlikely to happen in the short term, so greater explicitness in Congressional mandates is still appropriate.

Timothy Wilkins and Terrell Hunt recognize the dangers inherent in a performance-based relationship. They point out that an agency, "[M]ay defy Congress' will, either deliberately or as a result of simple bureaucratic inertia, and occasionally ignore direct mandates, pursue their own agendas or both. . . . Moving toward an outcome focus and away from methodological controls could exacerbate this problem, particularly because failures to comply with outcome controls, unlike controls on regulatory method, might simply be blamed upon well-meaning but failed experiments."[67] Therefore, they suggest that Congress adopt explicit administrative objectives when it proposes administrative reforms.

In consultation with the Agency and the Office of Management and Budget (OMB), Congress should develop and publish measurable performance standards to evaluate success relative to the EPA's mission, as well as assess cost-effectiveness in pursuit of those ends.

The introduction of new concepts of flexibility may require incentives to prevent abuse, including merit-based pay to agency personnel calculated not on individual performance, but on overall agency achievement of statutory goals. The pay of all civil servants could be pegged to the same objectively measurable standards by which Congress evaluates the agency's success. Thus, agency employees would be motivated by their stake in the success of the organization as a whole. Institutionally-based incentives could be provided for high-level administrators as well. If the EPA performed well over time, Congress might grant it a reduction in oversight, and/or increasing freedom to explore performance-based controls. Abuses of discretion would result in a reinstitution of tighter congressional oversight.

Another safeguard under this model could be instituted by engaging NGOs or other independent technical entities to monitor results. This could lend legitimacy to XL-like projects, where industry has ample motivation to exaggerate the expected "superior environmental results" to be achieved. These independent entities might ultimately evolve into an analog of the Government Accounting Office (GAO), making it a dependable and independent source of data, tracking actual Agency and private sector performance. The delegation of monitoring and compliance duties to independent parties should rotate, ensuring independence.

On an institutional level, the short history of Project XL confirms that conflicting incentives among stakeholders discourage innovation. However, it also seems evident that important constituencies within all these groups understand that adaptive management holds great promise for the improvement of environmental compliance regimes. Project XL still has the potential to move all stakeholders (including the EPA) towards the institutionalization of collaborative processes for formulating improved environmental compliance goals. The steps required to do so can be achieved within the confines of the existing XL initiative. They include: a focus on problem solving; information sharing and open deliberation among all stakeholders, including the EPA; meaningful participation by all interested and affected parties at all stages of the process; and a new perception of rulemaking as an ongoing formulation of provisional solutions to emerging problems.

Under such a collaborative approach, all rules should come to be viewed as temporary and subject to revision. "To this end, continuous monitoring and evaluation are crucial. . . . New arrangements, networks, institutions, or allocations of authority may replace or supplement the traditional regulatory regime. EPA becomes a convener/facilitator of multi-stakeholder negotiations. It provides incentives for reluctant or untrained parties to participate. It acts as a capacity builder of parties and institutions."

The transformation of relationships among the EPA, business, and NGOs will take time. However, XL is a signal that the process of transformation has begun. If adaptive management is allowed to take hold, the Agency could cast off the shackles of command and control without jeopardizing (indeed, enhancing the changes of attaining) the environmental performance goals it was created to achieve.

NOTES

The views expressed do not necessarily represent the positions or policies of the U.S. Environmental Protection Agency. Report Prepared for the Environmental Technology and Public Policy Program, Department of Urban Studies and Planning, Massachusetts Institute of Technology, Cambridge, MA. The authors thank Gabriela Martha Krockmalnic for her assistance.

1. The examples are legion. They include: Harter, Philip J. 1992. "Regulatory Negotiation: A Cure for Malaise," *Georgetown Law Journal* 71; Gore, Al. 1993. *Report of the National Performance Review: From Red Tape to Results: Creating a Government That Works Better & Costs Less.* U.S. Government Printing Office; Orts, Eric W. 1995. "Reflexive Environmental Law," *Northwestern University Law Review* 89:1227; Drucker, Peter F. 1995. "Really Reinventing Government," *Atlantic Monthly Magazine* February.

2. Lee, Kai N. 1993. *Compass and Gyroscope: Integrating Science and Politics for the Environment.* Washington, D.C.: Island Press; Sparrow, Malcolm K. 1994. *Imposing Duties: Government's Changing Approach to Compliance.* Westport, Conn.: Praeger Publishers.

3. Edley, Christopher F. 1994. *Adminsitrative Law: Rethinking Judicial Control of Bureaucracy* 6; Greene, Abner S. 1994. "Checks and Balances in an Era of Presidential Lawmaking," *University of Chicago Law Review* 123, 125.

4. The authors acknowledge the work of Timothy A. Wilkins and Terrell E. Hunt on this point. See Timothy A. Wilkins and Terrell E. Hunt, 1995. "Agency Discretion and Advances in

Regulatory Theory: Flexible Agency Approaches Toward the Regulated Community as a Model for the Congress–Agency Relationship," *George Washington Law Review* 63:479.

5. Details of the EPA's revocation of the Connecticut Resource, Conservation and Recovery Act (RCRA) program are set out in the *Federal Register*, Vol., 55, p. 51707 (December 17, 1990). The details of an attempted RCRA state program revocation in North Carolina are set out at *Federal Register*, Vol. 52, p. 49303 (November 17, 1987).

6. The EPA was created through an executive order issued by President Richard Nixon, Reorganization Plan No. 3 of 1970. The order consolidated nine programs from five different federal agencies and departments into the new EPA. Unlike most federal agencies and departments, the EPA was not created by legislative action. Thus, the Agency lacks the benefit of a congressional charter defining its mission and priorities.

7. This is particularly significant, given EPA's shrinking personnel base. The process EPA must administer under its authorizing statutes is extremely complex. For example, 10,000 pages of regulations had to be drafted, revised after public comment and promulgated to implement the 1990 Clean Air Act Amendments alone.

8. Philip B. Heyman, 1987. *The Politics of Public Management.* New Haven, Conn.: Yale University Press; Rosenbaum, Walter A. 1995. *Environmental Politics and Policy.* 3rd ed. Washington, D.C.: CQ Press. The budget figures are transcribed from data on file with the U.S. EPA.

9. Rosenbaum, Walter A. 1971. *Environmental Politics and Policy.* 3rd ed. Washington, D.C.: CQ Press; Landy Marc K., Marc J. Roberts and Stephan R. Thomas. 1990. *The Environmental Protection Agency: Asking the Wrong Questions.* New York: Oxford University Press.

10. *The Eagle Agenda: An Agenda for the Future of Environmental Protection.* (Unpublished essay by George S. Hawkins, Esq., on file with the authors.)

11. Sparrow, Malcom K. 1994. *Imposing Duties: Government's Changing Approach to Compliance.* Westport, Conn.: Praeger.

12. Rosenberg, Maurice. 1967. "Judicial Discretion of the Trial Court, Viewed from Above." *Syracuse Law Review* 22: 635, 637.

13. Edley, *supra* note 3, at 217.

14. A frequently cited example occurred in 1993, when the state of Washington submitted its Clean Air Act (CAA) operating permit program to the EPA for approval. Washington's application proposed exempting a number of sources as "insignificant emitters" of air pollution. The EPA had approved a number of state programs exempting "insignificant activities and emissions levels" from certain requirements. This was done to reduce the regulatory burden on the state and the emitter. Although Washington's proposed plan was analogous to other state proposals already approved, the EPA refused to approve the state plan in 1994, making full approval conditional on the deletion of these exemptions. In 1995, a lawsuit was filed against the EPA for abuse of discretion. In 1996, three full years after Washington's initial submission, the EPA's refusal to approve the program was found by the U.S. Court of Appeals for the Ninth Circuit to be an abuse of discretion. See *Western States Petroleum Association et al. v. Environmental Protection Agency,* 87 F.3d 280; 1996 U.S. App. LEXIS 14612.

15. An impressive scholarly treatment in support of this view is Kenneth C. Davis & Richard J. Pierce, Jr. *Administrative Law Treatise* §2.6, at 74; see also Greene, Abner S. 1994. "Checks and Balances in an Era of Presidential Lawmaking." *University of Chicago Law Review* 61: 123. For popular "broadsides" along similar lines, see Rauch, Jonathan. 1995. *Demosclerosis: The Silent Killer of American Government.* New York: Times Books.

16. Howard, Philip K. 1994. *The Death of Common Sense.*

17. Id., at 77.

18. Krauss, E.P. 1992. "Unchecked Powers: The Supreme Court and Administrative Law." *Marquette Law Review* 75: 797, 812.

19. Edley, *supra* note 3, at 6; Greene, Abner S. 1994. "Checks and Balances in an Era of Presidential Lawmaking," *University of Chicago Law Review* 61: 123, 125.
20. The authors wish to acknowledge the work of Timothy A. Wilkins and Terrell E. Hunt on this point. See Wilkins, *supra* note 4, at 479.
21. Part III argues that sections of the EPA's command and control system should be replaced by noncommand approaches, focusing on outcomes and driven largely by economic self-interest. Statutes and regulations should be retooled to monitor and control outcomes or performance, leaving the EPA free to experiment, collaborate and implement more optimal methods of regulation.
22. "Regulatory method" refers to the specification of policy details or regulatory methods. For example, the choice between controlling air pollution through mandatory pollution control technologies and levying emissions taxes is an example of competing regulatory methods.
23. See 42 U.S.C. §7470 (1988). The chronic dysfunction that exists between EPA and Congress on this issue is illustrated by The Prevention of Significant Deterioration (PSD) program (Title I, Part C) of the Clean Air Act. There, Congress explicitly detailed the mechanisms to be employed by EPA to achieve its performance goals: preserving levels of clean air wherever it exists. In fact, ratcheting up the statutory specificity of the PSD program increased the complexity and difficulty of its implementation and compliance, while sacrificing legitimate policy options and barring consideration of important case-by-case situational concerns. See Meiberg, Stanley A. 1991. *Protect and Enhance: "Juridical Democracy" and the Prevention of Significant Deterioration Of Air Quality.*.
24. Rosenberg, *supra* note 13, at 635; Dworkin, Ronald. 1967. "The Model of Rules," *University of Chicago Law Review* 35: 14.
25. 5 U.S.C. §§551-559, 701-706 (1994).
26. But see §303 of the Negotiated Rulemaking Act of 1990 (Pub.L. 101-648, Nov. 29, 1990, 104 Stat. 4969) (codified at 5 U.S.C.A. T. 5 Pt. I, Ch. 5, Subch. III (1998)) (allowing a negotiated option that is somewhat less formal).
27. Freeman, Jody. 1997. "Collaborative Governance in the Administrative State," *UCLA Law Review* 45: 1, 5. In the late 1980s, up to 80 percent of the rules promulgated by EPA were challenged in federal court. See William Ruckleshaus, "Environmental Protection: A Brief History of the Environmental Movement in America and Its Implications Abroad." *Environmental Law* 15: 455, 463.
28. See 5 U.S.C. § 553(b)(A), (d)(2) (1994).
29. See *Vermont Yankee Nuclear Power Corp. v. NRDC,* 435 U.S. 519 (1978).
30. See *Chevron U.S.A. Inc. v. NRDC,* 467 U.S. 519 (1978). See also Asimow, Michael. 1985. "Nonlegislative Rulemaking and Regulatory Reform," *Duke Law Journal* 381, 385.
31. Denial of such permits generally means closure of the facility in question.
32. Asimow, *supra* note 30, at 383.
33. Rose-Ackerman, Susan. 1992. *Rethinking the Progressive Agenda: The Reform of the American Regulatory State.* This theory has been widely criticized for its failure to account for environmental values due to the difficulty in assigning them a "non-input" monetary value.
34. Stavins, Robert and Thomas Grumbly. 1993. "The Greening of the Market: Making the Polluter Pay." In Will Marshall and Martin Schram, eds., *Mandate for Change.*
35. Wilkins, *supra* note 4, at 479–489.
36. See Clean Air Act Amendments, Pub. L. No. 101-549 section 401, 104 Stat. 2399, 2584 (1990). The Clean Air Act's "bubble concept" treats an entire plant as a single emissions source instead of attempting to monitor each of the (possibly) hundreds of individual sources existing within the plant's boundaries. Title IV of the act established an innovative emissions trading program: each major coal-fired plant is allocated a set amount of permis-

sible sulfur dioxide emissions that it may trade, buy or sell. The first government sponsored auction of the rights took place in March 1993.

37. Clinton, William J. 1992. *U.S. Actions for a Better Environment: A Sustained Commitment.* U.S. Public Information Office.

38. In a 1992 speech, EPA Administrator William Reilly stated that voluntary programs had produced reductions "faster and more cost effectively than under any regulatory program I administer." See Sparrow, *supra* note 11, at 96.

39. See "Over 280 Companies Commit to Reduce, Reuse, Recycle Waste, EPA Announces." *Bureau of National Affairs Chemical Regulation Daily* July 21, 1994 (Noting multimillion dollar savings experienced by firms under WasteWise, a comparable voluntary source reduction program for solid waste).

40. Wilkins, *supra* note 4, at 479, 495.

41. Sparrow, *supra* note 11, at 96.

42. See Richards, Deanna J. Braden R. Allenby and Robert A. Frosch, eds. 1994 "The Greening of Industrial Ecosystems: Overview and Perspective." In *The Greening of Industrial Ecosystems.* Washington, D.C.: National Academy Press, p. 1–19.

43. See Regulatory Reinvention (XL) Pilot Projects, 60 Fed. Reg. 27282. Project XL is one of several initiatives undertaken by EPA, pursuant to the Clinton Administration's Regulatory Reinvention agenda. Project XL also solicited project proposals from entire industry sectors and from various government agencies, including states, cities and towns.

44. The FPAs are unenforceable. However, their terms and conditions are ultimately subsumed within a permit or other legal instrument, which is enforceable.

45. See Regulatory Reinvention (XL) Pilot Projects, 60 Fed. Reg. 27282. See also EPA Project XL homepage at http://www.epa.gov/ProjectXL.

46. Freeman, *supra* note 27, at 38.

47. The Berry Corporation and Intel Corporation projects are discussed in Section V.

48. The companies involved are IBM, Akzo Chemical and South Coast Air Quality Management District. Such projects are "facilitated" to the implementation stage by EPA personnel. This is done through informal meetings and data exchange between EPA, the project proposer and stakeholders.

49.

IMPLEMENTED AND EVALUATED
1. Berry Corporation
2. Intel Corporation
3. Weyerhaeuser

UNDER DEVELOPMENT

1. PCS Nitrogen, L.P. (formerly Arcadian Fertilizer)
2. Hadco Corporation
3. Imation
4. Lucent Technologies
5. Massachusetts Dept. of Environmental Protection
6. Merck & Co., Inc.
7. Minnesota Pollution Control Agency
8. Molex Incorporated
9. New York State Dept. of Environmental Conservation
10. OSi Specialties, Inc.
11. Union Carbide
12. DoD: Vandenberg Air Force Base

PROPOSED

1. CITGO
2. Dow-Texas
3. Eastman Chemical
4. DoD: Elmendorf Air Force Base
5. DoD: Air Force Plant #4

SUCCESSFULLY FACILITATED WITH THE HELP OF XL, BUT NOT XL PROJECTS
1. IBM
2. Akzo Chemical
3. South Coast Air Quality Management District

Note: For the most up-to-date information on EPA's Project XL, see Website http://www.epa.gov/ProjectXL/XL_home.nsf.

50. The EPA lists twelve projects as being under development. All project descriptions are taken from EPA's Project XL website: http://www.epa.gov/ProjectXL.

51. WWT sludge from PWB manufacturers is subject to a blanket F006 listing as a hazardous waste under Subtitle C of RCRA 40 C.F.R. Section 261.31.

52. ISO is a set of environmental management systems designed by the Geneva-based International Standards Organization.

53. The negotiators include the National Park Service, EPA, the Virginia Department of Environmental Quality and the communities of Elkton and Rockingham County. Regional environmental organizations were sought out for comment on the evolving draft permit.

54. Tier I: Whenever the actual total criteria pollutant emissions for the last 12 months are determined to be greater than 0 percent and less than 75 percent of the total emissions cap, compliance with this tier is required; Tier II: whenever the actual total criteria pollutant emissions for the last 12 months are determined to be equal to or greater than 75 percent and less than 90 percent of the total emissions cap, compliance with requirements in this tier is required; Tier III: whenever the total actual criteria pollutant emissions for the last 12 months are determined to be equal to or greater than 90 percent of the total emissions cap, compliance with requirements of this tier is required.

55. The interviews were designed to encourage subjects to explore the strategic and political tensions generated by stakeholders in the XL process inside and outside the Agency, tensions that profoundly affect project implementation. The interviews also explored the XL participants' perception of the factors that influenced the negotiation of their individual projects. Interviews were conducted in person and by telephone from March 1995 through May 1997. Interviewees included Christopher Knopes, the EPA's national XL coordinator; George Wyeth, of the EPA's Office of General Counsel; Brian Grant, of the EPA's Office of General Counsel; George Hawkins, who is with Vice President Al Gore's National Performance Review and was formerly XL coordinator of the EPA's Region I; Anne Kelly, XL coordinator, EPA Region I; Kenneth Rota, RCRA Enforcement Specialist and Hadco XL team member, EPA Region I; Ira Leighton, chief of the Enforcement Office, EPA Region I; William Patton, program manager, EPA Region IV; Jeffrey Rosenbloom, attorney, EPA Region IX; and Jody Freeman, acting professor of law, University of California at Los Angeles. Other interviewees requested anonymity.

56. Meeting between thirteen state environmental officials and Carol Browner, EPA Administrator, in Washington, D.C. (Oct. 31, 1996). See "Project XL: US EPA, Intel Sign Landmark Agreement, *Greenwire* November 20, 1996, available in LEXIS, News Library, Grnwre File.

57. Meeting between thirteen state environmental officials and Carol Browner, EPA Administrator, in Washington, D.C. (Oct. 31, 1996).

58. Id.

59. Freeman, *supra* note 27, at 83.

60. Freeman, *supra* note 27, at 57–8.

61. Intel Corporation is a manufacturer of computer chips. See Final Project Agreement for the Intel Corporation Ocotillo Site Project XL 8-9 (October 9, 1996) (on file with author).

62. Id. at 45

63. See Regulatory Reinvention (XL) Pilot Projects, 60 Fed. Reg. 27282, 27287 (1995).

64. The problem centers around that fact that FPAs, once published in the *Federal Register,* become rules. Once this happens, FPAs are susceptible to all procedures for informal rulemaking set out at §553 of the APA.

65. Many of these same ideas are also endorsed by Jody Freeman. See *supra* note 27 at 87–91.

66. Browner, Carol M. 1994. "The Common Sense Initiative: A New Generation of Environmental Protection." Address before the Center for National Policy, July 20.

67. Wilkins, *supra* note 4, at 531.

Bibliography

The following books and articles provide in-depth information on various aspects of negotiation, mediation, and consensus building in the environmental arena. Many, but not all, of these titles are referenced in this volume.

Amy, D.J. (1987). *The politics of environmental mediation.* New York: Columbia University Press.

Bacow, L.S., and M.Wheeler (1984). *Environmental dispute resolution.* New York: Plenum Press.

Bingham, G. (1985). *Resolving environmental disputes: A decade of experience.* Washington, D.C.: Conservation Foundation.

"Broken trust: The regulators" (1997, January 7). *The Cape Cod Times.*

Cairncross, F. (1995). *Green, Inc.: A guide to business and the environment.* Washington, D.C.: Island Press.

Carpenter, S.L., and W.J.D. Kennedy (1988). *Managing public disputes.* San Francisco, Calif.: Jossey-Bass.

DiMento, J.F. (1986). *Environmental law and American business: Dilemmas of compliance.* New York: Plenum Press.

Dukes, E.F. (1996). *Resolving public conflict: Transforming community and governance.* New York: St. Martins.

Federal Facilities Environmental Restoration Dialogue Committee (1996, April). *Consensus principles and recommendations for improving federal facilities cleanup.* Keystone, Colo.: The Keystone Center.

Fisher, R., W. Ury, and B. Patton (1998) *Getting to yes: Negotiating agreement without giving in.* New York: Penguin Books.

Forester, J., and D. Stitzel (1989). "Beyond neutrality: The possibilities of activist mediation in public sector conflicts." *Negotiation Journal* 5 (3), 251–264.

Harter, P. (1982). "Negotiating regulations: A cure for malaise." *Georgetown Law Journal* 71, 1–118.

Harter, P.J. (1997). "Fear of commitment: An affliction of adolescents." *Duke Law Journal* 46, 1389–1428.

Kunde, J. (1999). "Dealing with the press." In L. Susskind, S. McKearnan, and J. Thomas-Larmer, eds. *The consensus building handbook: A comprehensive guide to reaching agreement.* Thousand Oaks, Calif.: Sage Publications.

Landy, M., and M. Levin (1995). *The new politics of public policy.* Baltimore: Johns Hopkins University Press.

Lax, D.A., and J.K. Sebenius (1986) *The manager as negotiator: Bargaining for cooperative and competitive gain.* New York: Free Press.

Martindale-Hubbell dispute resolution directory (1997). New Providence, N.J.: Martindale-Hubbell.

Massachusetts Military Reservation Installation Restoration Plan, final draft (1995, July 15).

Mazmanian, D., and D. Morell (1992). *Beyond superfailure: America's toxics policy for the 1990s.* Boulder, Colo.: Westview Press.

Menkel-Meadow, C. (1985). "For and against settlement: Uses and abuses of the mandatory settlement conference." *UCLA Law Review* 33, 485–514.

Mercury Products Work Group (December 1997). *Facilities Loading Subcommittee Report, Phase II.* Boston: Author.

Mnookin, R., and L.E. Susskind (in press). *Negotiating on behalf of others.* Thousand Oaks, Calif.: Sage Publications.

Moore, M.H. (1995). *Creating public value: Strategic management in government.* Cambridge, Mass.: Harvard University Press.

Napier, C., ed. (1998). *Environmental conflict resolution.* London: Cameron May.

O'Hare, M., L.S. Bacow, and D. Sanderson (1983). *Facility siting and public opposition.* New York: Van Nostrand Reinhold.

Oakley, E., and D. Krug (1993). *Enlightened leadership: Getting to the heart of change.* New York: Simon and Schuster.

Paley, E. (1997, October). "Partnering helps you end-run costly disputes." *Consensus* 12.

Powell, D., and W. Leiss (1997). *Mad cows and mother's milk: The perils of poor risk communication.* Montreal, Quebec: McGill-Queens University Press.

Plume response plan (1994, June). Prepared by the Plume Management Process Action Team.

Raab, J. (1994). *Using consensus building to improve utility regulation.* Washington, D.C.: American Council for an Energy-Efficient Economy.

Rubin, J.Z., D.G. Pruitt, and S.H. Kim (1994). *Social conflict: Escalation, stalemate, and settlement* (2nd edition). New York: McGraw Hill.

Save the Harbor/Save the Bay (undated booklet). *Boston Harbor and Massachusetts Bay: Ten Years of Change (A Citizen's Report).* Boston: Author.

Schwarz, R.M. (1994). *The skilled facilitator: Practical wisdom for developing effective groups.* San Francisco: Jossey-Bass.

Sessler, A. (March 22, 1998). "A toxic waste issue: Do physicians violate their oath?" *The Boston Globe,* p. 9, South Weekly section.

Sipe, N. (1998, Summer). "An empirical analysis of environmental mediation." *Journal of the American Planning Association* 275–285.

Stulberg, J. (1981). "The theory and practice of mediation: A reply to Professor Susskind." *Vermont Law Review* 6, 85–117.

Sullivan, T.F.P., ed. (1992). *The greening of American business: Making bottom-line sense of environmental responsibility.* Rockville, Md.: Government Institutes, Inc.

Susskind, L. (1981). "Environmental mediation and the accountability problem." *Vermont Law Review* 6 (1), 1–47.

Susskind, L., and The Consensus Building Institute (1999). *Using assisted negotiation to settle land use disputes: A guidebook for public officials.* Cambridge, Mass.: Lincoln Institute of Land Policy.

Susskind, L., and J. Thomas-Larmer (1999). "Conducting a conflict assessment." In L. Susskind, S. McKearnan, and J. Thomas-Larmer, eds. *The consensus building handbook: A comprehensive guide to reaching agreement.* Thousand Oaks, Calif.: Sage Publications.

Susskind, L., and P. Field (1996). *Dealing with an angry public.* New York: Free Press.

Susskind, L., and J. Cruikshank (1987). *Breaking the impasse: Consensual approaches to resolving public disputes.* New York: Basic Books.

Susskind, L., and L. van Dam (1986, July). "Squaring off at the table, not in the courts." *Technology Review* 36–44, 72.

Susskind, L., and G. McMahon (1985). "The theory and practice of negotiated rulemaking." *Yale Journal on Regulation* 3, 133–165.

Susskind, L., and A. Weinstein (1980/81). "Towards a theory of environmental dispute resolution." *Boston College Law Review* 9, 311–357.

Susskind, L., S. McKearnan, and J. Thomas-Larmer, eds. (1999). *The consensus building handbook: A comprehensive guide to reaching agreement.* Thousand Oaks, Calif.: Sage Publications.

Susskind, L.E., and J. Secunda (1997). "The Risks and the advantages of agency discretion: Evidence from EPA's Project XL." *UCLA Journal of Environmental Law and Policy* 17 (1), pp. 67–116.

Susskind, L., E. Babbitt, and P.N. Segal (1993). "When ADR becomes the law: A review of federal practice." *Negotiation Journal* 9 (1).

Susskind, L., L.S. Bacow, and M. Wheeler (1983). *Resolving environmental regulatory disputes.* Cambridge, Mass.: Schenkman Publishing.

Toward a balanced strategy to address contaminated groundwater plumes at the Massachusetts Military Reservation (1996, May). Final report of the Technical Review and Evaluation Team.

Mediation/Facilitation Resources

The following listing of mediation and facilitation organizations was reprinted from *Consensus,* a quarterly newsletter published by the MIT-Harvard Public Disputes Project.

New England

Center for Policy Negotiation/Common Ground, 20 Park Plaza, #520, Boston, MA 02116—(617) 482-8660. Contact: *Thomas J. Scott.*

Conflict Management Group, 9 Waterhouse Street, Cambridge, MA 02138—(617) 354-5444; fax: (617) 354-8467. Contact: *Lee Doucette.*

Consensus Building Institute (CBI), 131 Mt. Auburn St., Cambridge, MA 02138—(617) 492-1414; fax: 492-1919. e-mail: consensus@igc.org. Contact: *Mieke van der Wansem.*

Gosline, Reitman & Ainsworth Dispute Resolution Services, 47 Ocean Dr., Brunswick, ME 04011. Contacts: *Jonathan Reitman* (207) 729-1900 (jreitman@blazenetme.net), *Ann Gosline* (207) 737-2775 (gosline@igc.org), or *Kathryn Monahan Ainsworth* (207) 772-0259 (kma207@aol.com).

Interaction Associates, Inc., 20 University Road, Cambridge, MA 02138—(617) 234-2700; fax: 234-2727. Contact: *David Straus.*

JAMS/Endispute, Inc., 73 Tremont Street, Boston, MA 02108—(617) 228-0200; fax: (617) 228-0222. Contact: *Eric Van Loon.*

Massachusetts Office of Dispute Resolution (MODR), 100 Cambridge St., Room 1005, Boston, MA 02202—(617) 727-2224. Contact: *Fredie D. Kay,* Executive Director.

The Mediation Group, 3 Harvard Ave., 2d Floor, Brookline, MA 02446—(617) 277-9232; fax: (617) 277-1699. Contacts: *David Matz, Brad* and *Jane Honoroff.*

Raab Associates, Ltd., 280 Summer St., Boston, MA 02210—(617) 261-7111; fax: (617) 261-7887; e-mail: raabj@aol.com. Contact: *Dr. Jonathan Raab.*

Roberta Miller & Associates, 14 Centre St., Watertown, MA 02172—(617) 923-8896. Contact: *Roberta Miller.*

Susan Podziba & Associates, 21 Orchard Rd., Brookline, MA 02445—(617) 738-5320; fax: (617) 738-6911; e-mail: podziba@mit.edu. Contact: *Susan Podziba.*

John G. Wofford, 47 Winter St., Boston, MA 02108—(617) 426-4455; fax: (617) 426-1466. Contact: *Jack Wofford.*

East

Accord Associates, 117 South 17th St., Suite 402, Philadelphia, PA 19103—(215) 563-8564. Contact: *John Good.*

American Arbitration Association, 140 W. 51st St., New York, NY 10020—(212) 484-4000; fax: (212) 765-4874. Contact: *Toni Griffin.*

Conflict Resolution Education Network (CREnet), 1527 New Hampshire Avenue, NW, Washington, D.C. 20036—(202) 667-9700; fax: (202) 667-8629. Contact: *Doug Harbit.*

CPR Institute for Dispute Resolution, 366 Madison Avenue, New York, NY 10017—(212) 949-6490; e-mail: jkelly@cpradr.org. Contact: *Panel Management Group.*

Executive Decision Services, LLC., P.O. Box 9102, Albany, NY 12209-0102—(518) 465-8872; e-mail: sschuman@albany.net. Contact: *Sandor P. Schuman.*

F.A.B.E. Inc., 68 Fletcher St., Winchester, MA 01890—(781) 729-3656; fax: (781) 729-8531; e-mail: bares@fabe.ultranet.com. Contact: *Fioravante "Van" Bares.*

JAMS/Endispute, Inc., 461 Park Ave. South, 6th Floor, New York, NY 10016—(212) 725-6160; fax: (212) 779-3095. Contact: *Michael Young.*

JAMS/Endispute, Inc., Suite 501, 1201 Connecticut Ave., N.W., Washington, D.C. 20036—(202) 429-8782; fax: (202) 728-2920. Contact: *Jonathan Marks.*

The Keystone Center, 1020 15th Street, NW, Suite 300 West, Washington, D.C., 20005—(202) 783-0248; fax: (202) 783-0328; Web site: www.keystone.org. Contact: *Judy O'Brien.*

McCammon Mediation Group, Ltd., 1111 E. Main St., #1700, Richmond, VA, 23219—(888) 343-0922; fax: (804) 343-0923. Members throughout Virginia. Contact: *John McCammon.*

Mediate-Tech, Inc., P.O. Box 607, Front Royal, VA 22630—(540) 636-8900 or (800) 967-4555; fax: (540) 636-3033; e-mail: clickson@mediatetech.com. Website: www.mediatetech.com. Contact: *Charles P. Lickson J.D., Ph.D.*

Office of Dispute Settlement, Dept. of the Sec. of State Advocate, CN 850, 25 Market St., Trenton, NJ 08625—(609) 292-1773; fax: (609) 292-6292. Contact: *Eric Max,* Director.

Office of Hearings & Mediation Services, NYSDEC, 50 Wolf Rd., Albany, NY 12233-1550—(518) 457-3468; fax: (518) 485-7714. Contact: *Daniel E. Louis.*

PennACCORD Training and Dispute Resolution Services, P.O. Box 194, Swarthmore, PA 19081—(610) 328-1339. Contact: *Wendy Emrich.*

Section of Dispute Resolution, American Bar Association, 740 15th St., N.W., Washington, D.C. 20005—(202) 662-1680; fax: (202) 662-1683. Contact: *Jack Hanna.*

Winsor Associates, P.O. Box 432, Ardmore, PA 19003—(610) 896-9909. Contact: *Eleanor W. Winsor* or *Phoebe Sheftel.*

South

A.A. White Dispute Resolution Institute, University of Houston, 325 Melcher Hall, College of Business Administration, Houston, TX 77204-6283—(713) 743-4933; fax: (713) 743-4934. Contact: *E. Wendy Trachte,* Executive Director.

American Arbitration Association, Washington, D.C.—(202) 296-8510; Charlotte—(704) 347-0200; Atlanta—(404) 325-0101; Orlando—(407) 648-1185; Miami—(305) 358-7777; New Orleans—(504) 522-8781; Nashville—(615) 256-5857; Dallas—(214) 702-8222; Houston—(713) 739-1302; Richmond—(804) 649-4838.

Center for Public Policy Dispute Resolution at The University of Texas School of Law, 727 E. 26th St., Austin, TX 78705—(512) 471-3507; fax: (512) 471-6988. Contact: *Jan Summer,* Executive Director.

Chorda Conflict Management, Inc., 1717 West 6th St., Suite 215, Austin, TX 78703—(800) 856-5570; fax: (512) 474-4645; e-mail: chorda@chorda.com. Contact: *Karl A. Slaikeu, Ph.D.*

Consensus Solutions, Inc., 400 Perimeter Center Terrace, NE, Suite 900, Atlanta, GA 30346—(770) 392-4265; e-mail: asaslow@c-solutions.org. Contact: *Adam R. Saslow.*

Florida Growth Management Conflict Resolution Consortium, Building G, Suite 100, 325 John Knox Rd., Tallahassee, FL 32303-4161—(904) 921-9069. Contact: *Bob Jones.*

The Management Edge, Inc., 12600 Seminole Blvd., Suite B2, Largo, FL 33778—(813) 588-9481; fax: (813) 588-9541; e-mail: mgtedge@aol.com. Contacts: *Gayle Waldron, Kelly Hollinger,* or *Sheila Divoll.*

Southeast Negotiation Network, P.O. Box 52527, Atlanta, GA 30355—(404) 875-1983. Contacts: *Michael Elliott* or *Gregory Bourne.*

Central

American Arbitration Association, Pittsburgh—(412) 261-3617; Minneapolis—(612) 332-6545; Detroit—(313) 352-5500; Chicago—(312) 616-6560; Cincinnati—(513) 241-8434; Cleveland—(216) 891-4741; St. Louis—(314) 621-7175; Kansas City—(816) 221-6401.

JAMS/Endispute, Inc., 303 W. Madison, 17th Floor, Chicago, IL 60606—(312) 419-4650. Contact: *William E. Hartgering.*

Mediation and Conflict Management Services, 8000 Bonhomme, Suite 201, St. Louis, MO 63105—(314) 721-4333. Contact: *Robert D. Benjamin.*

Minnesota Office of Dispute Resolution, 340 Centennial Building, St. Paul, MN 55155—(612) 296-2633; fax: (612) 297-7200. Contact: *Roger Williams.*

Nebraska Office of Dispute Resolution, Supreme Court of Nebraska, Adm. Off. of the Courts/Probation, P.O. Box 98910, Lincoln, NE 68509-8910—(402) 471-3730; fax: (402) 471-2197. Contact: *Kathleen Severens,* Director.

North Dakota Consensus Council, Inc., 1003 Interstate Ave., Suite 7, Bismarck, No. Dak. 58501-0500—(701) 224-0588; fax: (701) 224-0787. Contact: *Larry Spears.*

Ohio Commission on Dispute Resolution and Conflict Management, 77 South High St., 24th Floor, Columbus, Ohio 43266-0124—(614) 752-9595. Contact: *Maria L. Mone.*

Popovich Lynch Associates, 18365 W. Sioux Vista Drive, Jordan, MN 55352-9206—(612) 492-7722. Contact: *Diane Lynch.*

Program for International Dispute Resolution and Global Development, Political Science Dept., University of Illinois, Urbana, Illinois 61801—(217) 352-7700. Contact: *Stuart S. Nagel,* Coordinator.

Rocky Mountains

American Arbitration Association, Denver—(810) 352-5500.

Assent Ascent, 2039 11th St., Suite 3, Boulder, CO 80302—(303) 440-8190. Contact: *Todd A. Bryan,* President.

CDR Associates, 100 Arapahoe Ave., Suite 12, Boulder, CO 80302—(303) 442-7367 or 1-800-MEDIATE. Contacts: *Mary Margaret Golten, Christopher Moore, Susan Wildau,* or *Bernard Mayer.*

Colorado Center for Environmental Management (CCEM), 999 18th St., Suite 2750, Denver, CO 80202—(303) 297-0180; fax: (303) 297-0188. Contact: *David C. Shelton,* Executive Director.

The Keystone Center, 1628 Saints John Road, Keystone, CO 80435—(970) 513-5800; fax: (970) 262-0152; Web site: www.keystone.org. Contacts: *Dennis Donald* or *Sue Wilcox.*

Montana Consensus Council, Office of the Governor, State Capital Bldg., Helena, MT 59620—(406) 444-2075; fax: (406) 444-5529. Contact: *Matthew McKinney,* Director.

West

American Arbitration Association, Honolulu—(808) 531-0541; Las Vegas—(702) 252-4071; Salt Lake City—(801) 531-9748; Seattle—(206) 622-6435; San Francisco—(415) 981-3901; Los Angeles—(213) 383-6516; San Diego—(619) 239-3051; Orange County—(714) 474-5090; Phoenix—(602) 234-0950.

Barber & Gonzales Consulting Group, 6963 Douglas Blvd., Granite Bay, CA 95746—(916) 786-4368. Contact: *Deidre Rose.*

Barrett & Associates, P.O. Box 7510, Menlo Park, CA 94026-75100—(415) 854-2505; fax: (415) 854-2495. Contact: *Robert Barrett.*

California Center for Public Dispute Resolution; Contacts: *Susan Sherry,* Cal. State Univ., Sacramento, 1303 J Street, Suite 250, Sacramento, CA 95814—(916) 445-2079; *Ed Villmoare,* McGeorge School of Law, 3200 5th Ave., Sacramento, CA 95817—(916) 739-7049.

CONCUR, Inc., Contacts: *John Gamman,* 333 Church St., Ste. C, Santa Cruz, CA 95060—(831) 457-1397; fax: -8610; *Scott McCreary,* 1832 2nd St., Berkeley, CA 94710—(510) 649-8008; fax: -1980. Website: www.concurinc.com

Dispute Resolution Services, S.W. Fifth Ave., Suite #2121, Portland, OR 97204—(503) 241-0570; fax: (503) 241-0914; e-mail: forester@mediate.com. Website: mediate.com/forester. Contact: *J. Richard Forester.*

First Mediation Corp., 16501 Ventura Blvd., #606, Encino, CA 91436—(818) 784-4544; fax: (818) 784-1836; e-mail: jkrivis@mediate.com. Contact: *Jeffrey Krivis.*

Geoff Ball & Associates, 164 Main Street, Rm. 210, Los Altos, CA 94022—(415) 941-1497. Contact: *Geoff Ball.*

Hallmark Pacific Group, LLC, 1220 SW Morrison, 10th Floor, Portland, OR 97205—(503) 243-2493; fax: (503) 243-3683; e-mail: hpg@pacifier.com. Website: www.mediate.com/hallmark. Contacts: *R. Elaine Hallmark, Karen Hannan.*

Hawaii State Judiciary's Center for Alternative Dispute Resolution, P.O. Box 2560, Honolulu, HI 96804—(808) 522-6464; fax: (808) 522-6440; e-mail: ekent@hawaii.edu. Website: www.state.hi.us/jud/cadr.htm. Contact: *Elizabeth Kent.*

Institute for Conflict Management, Inc., 208 SW 1st Ave., Ste. 360, Portland, OR 97204—(503) (503) 224-9014; fax: (503) 224-0789. Contact: *Sam Imperati,* Exec. Director.

ISADR Institute for Study of ADR, Humboldt State University, Arcata, CA 95521-8299—(707) 826-4750. Website: www.humboldt.edu/~isadr. Contact: *Christine Taylor.*

Interaction Associates, Inc., 600 Townsend St., Suite 550, San Francisco, CA 94103—(415) 241-8000. Contact: *Peter Gibb.* (See listing under New England.)

JAMS/Endispute, Inc., One Market Place, Spear St. Tower, 8th Floor, Suite 890, San Francisco, CA 94105—(415) 546-6746. Contact: *Joyce Richardson.*

The Mediation Center, Inc. P.O. Box 51119, Eugene, OR 97405—(541) 345-1456; e-mail: jmelamed@mediate.com. Website: www.to-agree.com. Contact: *James C. Melamed, J.D.,* Director.

Northern California Mediation Center, 100 Tamal Plaza, Ste 175, Corte Madera, CA 94925—(415) 927-1422. Website: www.ncmcmediate.org. Contact: *Nancy J. Foster, J.D.*

Northwest Renewable Resources Center, 1411 4th Avenue, Suite 1510, Seattle, WA 98101-2216—(206) 269-2357. Contact: *Elizabeth Reynolds.*

Public Affairs Management, 101 The Embarcadero, Suite 210, San Francisco, CA 94105—(415) 989-1446; fax: (415) 291-8943. Contacts: *Kay Wilson* and *Bonnie A. Nixon.*

Public Policy Program, Oregon Dispute Resolution Commission, 1201 Court St. NE, Suite 305, Salem, OR, 97310—(503) 378-2877; fax: (503) 373-0794. e-mail: rebecca.sweetland@state.or.us. Website: www.odrc.state.or.us. Contact: *Rebecca A. Sweetland.*

Triangle Associates, Suite 255, 811 First Ave., Seattle, WA 98104—(206) 583-0655; fax: (206) 382-0669; e-mail: info@triangleassociates.com. Website: www.triangleassociates.com. Contacts: *Alice J. Shorett, Lois Schwennesen, Alinda Page,* or *Dennis Clark.*

Canada

IBI Group, 230 Richmond St. West, Toronto, Ontario M5V 1V6—(416) 596-1930. Contact: *Larry Sherman.*

SOLVE-IT, 621 Healy Avenue, Radville, Saskatchewan, SOC 2GO—(306) 869-2230; fax: (306) 869-2552. Contact: *Rod MacDonald.*

About the Authors

Lawrence Susskind is one of America's most experienced mediators and negotiation trainers. For more than 20 years he has provided consensus building, dispute resolution, and conflict management assistance, training, and advice to public and private clients throughout the world.

Susskind is Ford Professor of Urban and Environmental Planning at the Massachusetts Institute of Technology. He was the first executive director of the Program on Negotiation at Harvard Law School, where he still serves as the director of the MIT-Harvard Public Disputes Program. Professor Susskind is also founder and president of the Consensus Building Institute. He is the author of 14 books, including *Breaking the Impasse* (with Jeffrey Cruikshank, 1987, Basic Books), *Dealing With an Angry Public* (with Patrick Field, 1996, Free Press), and *Negotiating on Behalf of Others* (with Robert Mnookin, in press, Sage). He is the editor of the *Consensus Building Handbook* (with Sarah McKearnan and Jennifer Thomas-Larmer, 1999, Sage).

Professor Susskind has offered tailored training programs for more than 50 major companies in North America and Europe including CBS, Time-Life, Pfizer, American Cyanamid, Guinness PLC, Digital, NYNEX, Credit Suisse, Gemini, Winnipeg Hydro, Edison Electric Institute, Amoco, Rich Sea-pak, and Nabisco. All told, he has given workshops and seminars to more than 35,000 corporate executives, public-sector managers, and citizen activists.

Professor Susskind is also an experienced public dispute mediator, having assisted in the resolution of more than 50 complex disputes. He has helped to resolve regulatory disputes for the World Trade Organization, United Nations Development Programme, and the Climate Change Secretariat, as well as national environmental agencies in more than 15 countries. Susskind holds a B.A. in sociology and english literature from Columbia University, a master in city planning from MIT, and a Ph.D. in urban planning from MIT.

Paul F. Levy is executive dean for administration of Harvard Medical School. Previously, he was adjunct professor of environmental policy at the Massachusetts Institute of Technology, where he taught environmental policy and infrastructure planning and development. He has also served as executive director of the Massachusetts Water Resources

Authority (MWRA), a public authority providing water and wastewater service to 2.5 million people in the Boston metropolitan area. In that capacity, he directed the Boston Harbor Cleanup project, one of the largest environmental protection efforts in the world. In carrying out this and other projects, he negotiated numerous environmental agreements with federal and state regulators, and with industries subject to the MWRA's regulatory authority. Mr. Levy has also served as chairman of the Massachusetts Department of Public Utilities and director of the Arkansas Department of Energy.

Mr. Levy is currently the arbitrator for a number of interconnection agreements in Massachusetts under the Telecommunications Act of 1996. He has resolved disputed interconnection provisions in a consolidated arbitration proceeding between Bell Atlantic and AT&T, MCI WorldCom, Sprint, Teleport Communications Group, and Brooks WorldCom. He has also been the arbitrator for a case between Bell Atlantic and COVAD.

Mr. Levy has conducted numerous training programs in negotiation. With professor Susskind, he conducts the Negotiating Environmental Agreements workshop on which this book is based. With Dr. David Lax, he has conducted programs entitled Breakthrough Negotiation, sponsored by the Electricity Journal for electricity, telecommunications, and natural gas utility managers. He was an instructor in a 1997 World Bank international training program entitled "Utility Regulation and Strategy" for utility regulators from around the world. He has also conducted specialized negotiation training sessions for corporate managers at Boston Gas Company, Kennametal, Inc. (Pennsylvania), Ontario Hydro (Toronto), and the New England Gas Association.

Mr. Levy is a graduate of MIT, having received an S.B. in economics, an S.B. in urban studies and planning, and a master in city planning.

Jennifer Thomas-Larmer is a self-employed writer and editor specializing in dispute resolution-related topics. She is co-editor of the *Consensus Building Handbook* (with Lawrence Susskind and Sarah McKearnan, 1999, Sage) and is the editor of "Practitioner's Notebook" in *Consensus,* a newspaper published by the MIT-Harvard Public Disputes Program.

Ms. Thomas-Larmer has served as the editor of numerous negotiated agreements and consensus reports developed by multistakeholder dialogue groups, including those sponsored by the U.S. Environmental Protection Agency, U.S. Department of Health and Human Services, and the Center for Strategic and International Studies. Other clients have included the President's Council on Sustainable Development, the National Recycling Coalition, the Meridian Institute, MIT, and Interaction Associates.

Ms. Thomas-Larmer previously worked as a facilitator/mediator with The Keystone Center, a nonprofit dispute resolution organization, where she mediated policy dialogues on endangered species protection, nutrition labeling, agriculture, industrial eco-efficiency, and other topics. She holds an M.S. in environmental policy from the University of Michigan's School of Natural Resources and Environment and a B.A. in biology from Principia College.

Index

Aaro Company, 211
Academy of Sciences, 260
Adaptive management theory, 286–87
  Project XL and, 277, 286–87
Administrative Dispute Resolution Act of 1990,
  13
Administrative Procedure Act (APA), 282–83
Air National Guard, 167, 169
Alternative dispute resolution, 13, 241
  see also Assisted negotiation
American Iron and Steel Institute, 208
Anderson Windows, 292
Arbitration:
  binding, 257, 271
  nonbinding, 257, 271–72
Army Corps of Engineers, Beach Road erosion
  problem and, 129, 131, 134
Ashumet Valley well, 167
Assisted negotiation, 249–76
  binding arbitration, 257, 271
  as complement to unassisted negotiation, 249
  facilitators, *see* Facilitation and facilitators
  forms of, 257
  mediators, *see* Mediation and mediators
  need for, 249–50
  nonbinding arbitration, 257, 271–72
  summary, 276
  from zero-sum to integrative bargaining,
    273–76
  see also Neutrals, professional
Attorneys:
  as obstacle to mutual gains approach, 9–10
  in traditional negotiated settlements, 2
Automobile industry as enforcement target,
    212–13, 215
A-Z Decasing, 221

Babbitt, E., 13

BATNA ("best alternative to a negotiated
    agreement"), 3, 22–23
  defined, 22
  in Delaware coastal zone regulation case, 144
  as dynamic, 36
  evaluating other parties', 7, 23, 35
  evaluation of your organization's, in
    preparation stage, 7, 23, 35
  helping all sides exceed their, 10
  measuring success of negotiation by
    comparing results with, 6
  mercury permit case, 110–12, 116
  nonbinding arbitration and, 271, 272
  in Superfund cleanup case, 175
  "zone of possible agreement," 36
Beach Road, Martha's Vineyard, *see* Shoreline
    restoration on Martha's Vineyard, case
    of
Benson, Eugene, 112, 113, 115, 116, 118, 120
Berry Corporation, 288, 305
Best alternative to a negotiated agreement, *see*
    BATNA ("best alternative to a
    negotiated agreement")
Beth Israel Hospital, Boston:
  fined for Clean Water Act violation, 109
  warnings about mercury violations, 109
Binding arbitration, 257, 271
Binding the parties, role of neutral in, 252, 255
Bog Berries versus Federal Environmental
    Agency simulation, 89–91
  general instructions, 89–91
  issues to be resolved, 49, 89
  objectives, 89
  overview, 48–49
  parties to, 48
Boston Harbor, cleanup of, 109–10
Brainstorming, 24, 145, 254, 258
Brigham and Women's Hospital, 111

Browner, Carol, 298, 299, 301, 307
"Bubble" concept under the Clean Air Act, 285
Burden of proof in environmental cases, 221
Bush administration, 285

California Environmental Quality Act, 220
Cape Cod Times, 172
Capri, 221
Carper, Thomas, 144, 150
Carson Extension simulation, 99–101
    general instructions, 99–101
    issues to be resolved, 50, 99
    lessons, 101
    objective, 99
    overview, 50
    parties to, 50
    purpose of, 50
Carter administration, 222–23, 241
Case examples of negotiated agreements:
coastal zone regulations in Delaware, *see* Coastal
        zone regulations in Delaware, case of
    lessons from, 106–107
    mercury discharge permits, *see* Mercury
        discharge permits case
    overview, 105–107
    shoreline restoration on Martha's Vineyard,
        see Shoreline restoration on Martha's
        Vineyard, case of
    Superfund cleanup at the Massachusetts
        Military Reservation (MMR), *see*
        Superfund cleanup at the Massachusetts
        Military Reservation (MMR), case of
Case studies, simulations distinguished from, 41
ChemCo, Inc. simulation, 86–88
    general instructions, 86–88
    issues to be resolved, 48, 86, 87–88
    objectives of, 86
    overview, 48
    parties to, 48
    purpose of, 48
Chemical Industry Council, 145
Chemical Manufacturers Association, 208
Chrysler Corporation, 213
CIBA Specialty Chemicals, 145
Claiming of value, *see* Distribution of value
Clarifying interests:
    distinguishing positions from interests, 10, 24,
        36–37
    explanation of concept of, 24
Clean Air Act, 283, 290, 291, 292, 294
    "bubble" concept, 285
    noncompliance penalty (NCP), 207–208
    permitting requirements under, 1
    SCAQMD plan, 213, 220
    tradable emissions permit program, 285

Clean Water Act, 283, 291, 292, 305
    mercury discharges by Boston-area hospital,
        case example of, 109–27
    National Pollution Discharge Elimination
        System permits, 289
    permitting requirements under, 1
Clinton administration, 301
Coastal Zone Industrial Control Board
        (CZICB), 143, 150
Coastal zone regulations in Delaware, case of,
        106, 143–66
    conflict assessment, 144–45
    memorandum of understanding, 147–48, 150,
        151–66
    drafting of, 147
    the negotiations, 147–50
    ensuring implementation, 150
    the process, 147–48
    trading on differences to reach agreement,
        148–50
    negotiators' views and interests, 145–47
    on history of the conflict, 145–46
    key interests, 146–47
    offset provisions, 148–49, 150
    the outcome, 150
    overview, 106, 143–44
Command and control approach to
        enforcement, 277, 284, 294, 295, 300,
        306
Community groups:
    benefits of mutual gains approach for, 17, 18
    forming coalitions, 12
    perspective of the, 2
    tapping sources of power, 12
    understanding flexibility means a lack of
        uniformity, 18
    see also names of individual groups
Comprehensive Environmental Response
        Compensation and Liability Act
        (CERCLA) (Superfund), 168, 217
"Confidence-building measures," 40
Conflict assessments, 144
    for coastal zone regulations in Delaware,
        144–45
CONSENSUS, 10
Consensus Building Institute, 12, 143
Conventional wisdom in environmental
        negotiation, 3–4, 21–22
    improving of, *see* Mutual gains approach
Corporations, *see* Regulatees; *individual
        corporations*
Cost-benefit analysis of regulatee for sanctions,
        209–10
Cost-effectiveness analysis, 284
Costle, Douglas, 220

Creation of value, *see* Value creation
Criminal sanctions, 201, 203–12
  business perspective on, 205–209
  changes during Reagan administration, 217–18
  cost-benefit calculations of the regulatee, 209–12
  deterrent effect of, 204–205, 208–209, 212, 221
  failure to clearly communicate enforcement measures, 214
  media's reporting on, 207
  negative effects of, 206–207
  opposition to agency having both criminal and civil sanction powers, 213
  personnel movement within the company and, 215
  self-policing as alternative to, 207
  for unauthorized employee behavior, 207
Cruikshank, Jeffrey, 201, 249–78
Culligan Deionized Water Services, Inc., 203

Dana-Farber Cancer Institute, 111
Debriefing questions for simulations, 101–103
Delaware, coastal zone regulations in, *see* Coastal zone regulations in Delaware, case of
Delaware Coastal Zone Act (CZA), 143, 145, 148
Delaware Coastal Zone Regulatory Advisory Committee, 145, 147, 148, 149, 150
Delaware Department of Natural Resources and Environmental Control (DNREC), 143–66
  Environmental Indicator Technical Advisory Committee (EITAC), 148
  informal regulation system, 143, 145
  unsuccessful attempts to adopt formal regulations, 143
Delaware Nature Society, 145
Delaware State Planning Office, 145
Department of Agriculture, 242
Department of Defense, Installation Restoration Program (IRP), 167, 168, 169, 170, 171, 180
Department of the Interior, 247
DeVillars, John, 172
Diamond State Port Corporation, 145
DiMento, Joseph, 201, 203–23
Dioxin negotiations, 260–63
Discretion to negotiate, regulators', *see* Regulators, discretion to negotiate
Dispute handling mechanisms, 8
Dispute resolution centers, 13
Distler case, 217

Distribution of value, 25, 274–75
  Gadgets, Inc. simulation, 45, 47
  help of a neutral in, 8
  maintaining good relationships and, 25, 39
  mercury permit case, 113–14, 118
  the negotiator's Dilemma, *see* Negotiator's Dilemma
  objective criteria for, using, 8, 39
  overview of, 8
Doniger, David, 246
Drafting of agreements, role of neutral in, 252, 255
Dryden, L. M., 203–204
Dukes County Commission (DCC), 128, 131
Dupont Corporation, 145
Duquesne Light Company, 208

Edgartown, Massachusetts, 131
Efficiency of negotiation process, 6
  mercury discharge permits case, 119
Egyptian-Israeli Sinai negotiation, 229–30
Endangered species, 129, 131
Enforcement measures:
  certainty and imminence of, 215–22
  judicial proceedings and, 220–22
  surprise and "compliant for a day," 217–20
  command and control approach to, 277, 284, 294, 295, 300, 306
  continuity and consistency of, 222–23
  criminal sanctions, *see* Criminal sanctions
  failure to clearly communicate, 214
  fairness and legitimacy of, 212–15
  linked to political ambitions, 212
  monitoring, *see* Monitoring
  rationality of, 215
  sanctions, *see* Sanctions
  statute of limitations problems, 218
Environmental negotiations, 1–2
  assisted negotiation, *see* Assisted negotiation
  case examples of negotiated agreements, *see* Case examples of negotiated agreements
  licensing requirements and, *see* Licensing requirements
  mutual gains approach to, *see* Mutual gains approach
  negotiated rulemaking, *see* Negotiated rulemaking
  negotiating a settlement, *see* Carson Extension simulation
  negotiating compliance before the fact, *see* ChemCo, Inc. simulation
  negotiating your way back into compliance, *see* Bog Berries versus Federal Environmental Agency simulation; MC Metals simulation

Environmental negotiations (*continued*)
  the Negotiator's Dilemma, *see* Negotiator's
    Dilemma
  permitting requirements and, *see* Permits
  perspectives of parties on, 2
  simulations, *see* Simulations
  testing your skills at mutual gains approach,
    see Testing your skills
  traditional scenario, 3–4, 21–22
  improving on, *see* Mutual gains approach
  traditional settings for, 1–2
Environmental NGOs, Project XL and,
    300–301, 302–304
Environmental Policy Group, Massachusetts
    Institute of Technology, 2
Environmental Protection Agency (EPA), 10,
    211–12, 283
  budget, determination of, 280
  certainty and imminence of enforcement by,
    217–19, 222
  command and control approach to
    enforcement, 277, 284, 294, 295, 300, 306
  compliance monitoring by, 215–16
  Congress and, 279–80, 307
  delegation of authority to states, 279
  discrepancy between responsibilities and
    resources of, 280
  exercise of discretion by, 282–83
  Project XL and, 287–308
  extension of compliance deadlines, 216
  "Green Lights" program, 285
  guidances, 283
  history of, 278–79
  inconsistency among regional offices in
    enforcement policies, 214
  interpretive rules, 283
  Massachusetts Water Resources Authority
    (MWRA) and, 110–11, 120
  negotiated rulemaking and, *see* Negotiated
    rulemaking
  Office of General Counsel (OGC), 298–99
  Office of Pesticide Programs, 243
  organizational structure, 279–80
  oversight functions, 279
  permit process and, 279
  permit requests and, 1
  policy statements, 283
  Project XL, *see* Project XL, EPA's
  regional structure, 279
  selective enforcement audit (SEA), 212
  Superfund and, 168, 169, 170, 171, 173, 175,
    176, 177, 179, 180
  "33/50" program, 285–86
  Toxic Release Inventory (TRI), 289
Eppstein, David, 109, 111–17, 119

ERM-McGlennon Associates, 242, 244
"Expanding the pie," 135, 229
Expectations of the future, trading across
    differences with, 38

Facilitation and facilitators, 257–63
  in dioxin negotiation, 260–63
  negotiated rulemaking and, 243
  overview of functions of, 257–58, 263
  in RiverEnd negotiations, 258–60
  sources of, 10
  tasks of, 10–11
  see also Neutrals, professional
Facilitative leadership, 9
Falmouth, Massachusetts, 167
Federal Aviation Administration, 241
Federal Facilities Environmental Restoration
    Dialogue Committee, 173
Federal Navy Yard, resource recovery plant at,
    260
Federal Register, 214, 241, 245, 282
Federal Trade Commission, 247–48
Federal Water Pollution Control Act, 214
Feldman, Jay, 245
Field, Patrick, 145
Fisher, Roger, 3, 7, 8, 24, 36, 229
Fishing rights dispute, mediation of, 265–67
Fitzgerald, John, 112
Follow through:
  achievable results, agreeing to, 26
  aligning organization incentives and controls,
    8, 26
  monitoring agreements, *see* Monitoring
  overview of, 8, 25–26
  providing for use of professional neutrals to
    resolve future disagreements, 26–27
  working to improve relationships, 26
Frezzo, 214
Friends of Sengekontacket (FOS), 131, 134

Gadgets, Inc. simulation, 53–85
  confidential instructions:
    for Deep Green director, 82–85
    for Department of Environmental
      Protection Secretary's special assistant,
      64–69
    for EPA representative, 61–64
    for Gadget Workers Union president,
      75–78
    for Newberg Bay Society chief scientist,
      79–82
    for vice president of Gadgets, Inc.,
      69–75
  conflict assessment matrix, 44, 46
  context, 55–59

CLEEN system, 57–59
environmental organizations, 59
Gadgets, Inc. and Gadgets Workers
Union, 57
SCRUB system, 57
distribution of value in, 45, 47
general instructions, 53–61
issues to be resolved, 43
options for each issue, 44
overview, 43–48, 53–55
parties to, 43
sample agreements, or packages for, 45
participants' ranking of, 45, 47
today's meeting, 59–61
"zone of possible agreement," 44, 45
Gascoigne, James, 145
General Motors, 216
Georgia, 305
Getting negotiations started, role of neutral in,
249–50, 251–52
Getting to Yes (Fisher et al.), 7
Gingras, Bob, 112, 116
Gluckman, Lewis, 229–30
Goals of mutual gains approach:
for regulatees, 19–20
for regulators, 20
Goods and services, trading across differences
with, 38
"Green Lights" program, 285
Ground rules, 12
"Gyp-Post," 290

Hadco Corporation, 290, 302
Ham, Rudman, 112
Harmon County regional sewage dispute,
mediation of, 267–69
Harvard Medical School, 111
Hunt, Terrell A., 284–85, 307–308

Imation, 290–91
Incentive-based regulatory measures, 284, 285
Industry, *see* Regulatees; *individual corporations*
Inmont case, 222
Intel Corporation, 288, 302, 305
Interested outside parties, perspective of the, 2
see also Community groups; Nongovernmental
organizations (NGOs)
Interests:
clarifying, *see* Clarifying interests
distinguishing positions from, 10, 24, 36–37
mercury permit case, 110–12, 116
Intermediaries, *see* Assisted negotiation;
Neutrals, professional
Inventing options, 24
in case examples, 147

neutral's role in, 252, 254
purpose of, 24
through brainstorming, *see* Brainstorming
trading across differences to create value, *see*
Trading across differences to create value
ISO 14001 standard, 294, 306
Israeli-Egyptian Sinai negotiations, 229–30

Johns-Mannville case, 207
Joint fact finding, role of neutral in, 252, 253–54
Judicial proceedings:
to challenge agency rules, 240
alternatives to avoid, *see* Negotiated
rulemaking
compliance with enforcement measures by,
220–22
requiring high-level agency personnel at,
220
time-delaying defenses in, 220
Judicial review of agency decisions, 283

Kennedy, Edward, 172
Kerry, John, 172
Krockmalnic, Gabriela Martha, 201, 277–308
Kronenberg, David, 244
Kuh, Willa, 145
Kunde, J., 9

Lassiter, Professor, 261, 262
Lawrence, Elliott, 258–60
Lax, David A., 201, 227–39
Leadership:
equating willingness to negotiate as sign of
weakness, 8–9
facilitative, 9
redefining, 12
Lehman Brothers, 229–30
Licensing requirements:
environmental negotiations relating to, 1
negotiating of, 248
Linking of informal agreement and formal
decision making, role of neutral in, 252,
256
Litigation:
negotiated settlements of pending, 1
Carson Extension simulation, *see* Carson
Extension simulation
reasons for resorting to, 10
Los Angeles Times, 218
Lucent Technologies, 291

McGerny, Dr. Gene, 260–63
McKearnan, Sarah, 145
McManus, Kevin, 111, 112, 113, 116, 118–19
Marshall Plan, 229

Martha's Vineyard, shoreline restoration on, *see* Shoreline restoration on Martha's Vineyard, case of
Martha's Vineyard Commission (MVC), 131, 134
Martindale-Hubbell, 10
Mashpee, Massachusetts, 168
Massachusetts, licensing of waste-treatment plants in, 248
Massachusetts Chapter 91, 130
Massachusetts Coastal Zone Management Office (CZM), 130, 134
Massachusetts Department of Environmental Management (DEM), 130, 134, 135–42
Massachusetts Department of Environmental Protection (DEP), 129, 130, 134, 169, 170–77, 179, 180
    Project XL and, 291–92
Massachusetts Division of Fisheries and Wildlife (DFW), 131, 134
Massachusetts Endangered Species Act, 131
Massachusetts Environmental Commissioner, 302
Massachusetts Highway Department (MHD), 129, 130, 134
Massachusetts Institute of Technology, Environmental Policy Group, 2
Massachusetts Military Reservation Installation Restoration Plan, final draft of, 170
Massachusetts Military Reservation (MMR), Superfund cleanup at, 167–202
Massachusetts Office of Dispute Resolution (MODR), 129–30
Massachusetts Water Resources Authority (MWRA):
    BATNAs of, 111, 116
    cleanup of Boston Harbor, 109–10
    discharge permits, 109, 120
    EPA's oversight of, 110–11, 120
    fining of hospitals for mercury in their waste steams, 109, 110
    implementation of first agreement with hospitals, 114–15
    implementation of second agreement with hospitals, 118–19
    interests of, 110–11
    memorandum embodying agreement with the hospitals:
        1994, 114, 120–22
        1997, 118, 122–27
    negotiation of first agreement with hospitals, 112–14
    negotiation of second agreement with hospitals, 116–18

    Sewerage Division of, 112
    Toxic Reduction and Control Department (TRAC), 111, 112, 115
Massachusetts Wetlands Protection Act, 128, 129, 130
MC Metals simulation, 92–98
    general instructions, 92–98
        background, 93–95
        lessons, 98
        present situation, 95–96
        upcoming informal conference and settlement, 96–97
    issues to be resolved, 49
    overview, 49–50
    parties to, 49
Media:
    criminal sanctions and, 207
    as obstacle to mutual gains approach, 9
Mediation and mediators, 214–15, 241, 263–71
    entry of, scenarios for, 263–64
    fairness of outcome and, 264–65
    in fishing rights dispute, 265–67
    fundamental role of, 264, 265
    in Harmon County regional sewage dispute, 267–69
    neutrality of, 264, 265
    in social service block grant allocation, 269–71
    sources of, 10
    tasks of, 10–11
    see also Neutrals, professional
"Mediation and Other Forms of Assisted Negotiation," 249–76
Medical Academic and Scientific Community Organization (MASCO), 109, 110, 111
    implementation of first agreement, 114–15
    implementation of second agreement, 112–14
    interests and BATNAs, 111–12, 116
    memoranda embodying agreements with MWRA, 114, 118, 120–27
    negotiation of first agreement with MWRA, 112–14
    negotiation of second agreement with MWRA, 116–18
Merck & Company, Inc., 292
Mercury discharge permits case, 109–27
    agreement of hospital to work with MWRA in resolving the problem, 112
    implementation of first agreement, 114–15
    implementation of second agreement, 118–19
    interests and BATNAs of parties:
        the hospitals, 111–12, 116
        MWRA, 110–11, 116
    memorandum embodying agreement between parties:

first agreement of 1994, 114, 120–22
second agreement of 1997, 118, 122–27
Mercury Products Work Group, 112, 114–20
negotiation of first agreement, 112–14
elements important to MWRA, 113–14
elements important to the hospitals, 112–13
negotiation of second agreement, 116–18
overview of, 105, 109–10
phase one, 110–15
the results, 119–20
Metropolitan District Commission, 110
Michigan Department of Natural Resources, 302
Michigan Environmental Protection Act, 220
Minitrials, 272
Minnesota Mining and Manufacturing, 290–91
Minnesota Pollution Control Agency (MPCA), 292
Molex, Incorporated, 292–93
Monitoring:
agreements, 8, 25–26
shoreline restoration case, 133
industry's hostility toward compliance monitoring, 215–16
role of neutral in, 252, 256
Muskie, Edmund, 214
Mutual gains approach:
BATNA ("best alternative to a negotiated agreement"), see BATNA ("best alternative to a negotiated agreement")
case examples of negotiated agreements, see Case examples of negotiated agreements
clarifying interests, see Clarifying interests
distribution of value stage, see Distribution of value
essential ingredient of, 18–19
failure to reach agreement, reasons for, 50–51
follow through stage of, see Follow through
goals of:
for regulatees, 19–20
for regulators, 20
as improvement on traditional negotiating scenario, 4–5
inventing options, see Inventing options
key elements of negotiation theory, 34–40
measuring success of, 5–6
negotiating permits with, contrasting conventional approach to, 28–34
examples of, 31–34
keys issues, 30
obstacles to using, 8–10
philosophy of, 17–18
preparation stage, see Preparation stage

putting your skills to the test, see Testing your skills
relationships and, see Relationships among the parties
simulations, see Simulations
stages of, 6–7, 25–26
testing your skills at, see Testing your skills
value creation stage, see Value creation
ways to overcome obstacles to, 10–13
adoption of new norms, 13
agreement about ground rules, 12
help of professional neutrals, 10–11
redefinition of functions of leadership, 12
tapping new sources of power, 12–13
training, 11–12

National Agricultural Chemicals Association, 245
National Committee Against the Misuse of Pesticides, 245
National Guard Bureau, 167
Natural Resources Defense Council, 246, 302
Negotiated rulemaking, 240–48
addressing distrust of, 246–47
compromise of agency authority, fears of, 247
contrasted with conventional rulemaking, 241
demonstrations of, 240–46
reaction of participants to, 245–46
for emergency exemptions from pesticide-licensing regulations, 242–45
inappropriate situations for, 241, 247
origins and trials of, 240, 241
resource pool for, 254
spread of, 247–48
walkouts problem, 247
Negotiating Environmental Agreements workshop, 2
Negotiation of environmental agreements, see Environmental negotiations
Negotiator's Dilemma, 227–39, 274
avoiding literal interpretation of, 235–36
crux of, 234
diagramming of, 233–35
fundamental tension of negotiation, 230–33
illustration of, 236–38
as metaphor, 235–36
overview, 227
tactical level, tension at the, 230–31
Stone v. Ward, case example of, 231–33
value claimers, 229–30
value creators, 228–29
"Negotiator's Dilemma: Creating and Claiming Value, The," 227–39

Neutrals, professional, 8, 10–11
  for binding arbitration, 257
  in coastal zone regulations case, 147
  competence of, 250, 251
  entry into negotiation process, scenarios for,
    250, 252, 263–64
  facilitators, *see* Facilitation and facilitators
  future disagreements, providing for use in,
    26–27
  mediators, *see* Mediation and mediators
  neutrality of, 250–51
  for nonbinding arbitration, 257, 271–72
  perceptions of control and, 250
  roles and functions of, 10–11, 251–57
    chart, 252
    negotiation stage, 252, 254–56
    post-negotiation or implementation
      stage, 252, 256–57
    pre-negotiation stage, 251–54
  in shoreline restoration case, 120–21
  sources of, 10
  in Superfund cleanup case, 178–79
  teams of, 254
  see also Assisted negotiation
New Mexico Public Utility Commission,
  248
New York State Department of Environmental
  Conservation (NYSDEC), 293
New York Times, 203
Nonbinding arbitration, 257, 271–72
Noncompliance penalty (NCP) under Clean Air
  Act, 207–208
Nongovernmental organizations (NGOs):
  Project XL and, 300–301, 302–303, 308
  see also specific organizations

Oak Bluffs, Massachusetts, 131
Oak Bluffs Conservation Commission, 129
Occupational Safety and Health Administration
  (OSHA), 241
  monitoring of compliance by, 215
Office of Management and Budget (OMB),
  308
Offset provisions in Delaware coastal zone
  regulatory scheme, 148–49, 150
OSi Specialties, Inc., 293
Oxford Mushroom, 211–12, 220

Packaging, role of neutral in, 252, 254–55, 259,
  267–69, 273
Partnering, 171–73, 179
Patton, Bruce, 3, 7, 8, 36
PCS Nitrogen, L.P., 289–90
Pennsylvania Power Company, 208
Permits, 292

  in Delaware coastal zone regulatory scheme,
    148
  delegation of authority by EPA to the states
    for issuing, 279
  environmental negotiations relating to, 1
  EPA's processing of, 279
  mercury discharge, *see* Mercury discharge
    permits case
  mutual gains approach to negotiate,
    contrasted with conventional approach,
    28–34
    examples, 31–34
    key issues, 30
  negotiating of, 248
  Project XL, 288
  for shoreline restoration on Martha's
    Vineyard, 128, 129, 134
Peterson, Peter G., 229–30
Philosophy of mutual gains approach, 17–18
Piping plover, 129, 131
Plume Response Plan, 167
Pollution prevention, 285
Positions distinguished from interests, 10, 24,
  36–37
Powerlessness, party's feeling of, 8, 12
Preparation stage, 6–7
  overview of, 6–7
Press, *see* Media
Prisoner's Dilemma, 234
Project XL, EPA's, 277–78, 286–308
  adaptive management theory and, 277,
    286–87
  conclusions, 306
  consensus-building process, failure to
    organize a, 298
  critics of, 288
  cultural values and institutional goals of EPA
    and, 294–98
  feedback from projects, 297
  Final Project Agreements (FPA), 287–88
  goals of, 287
  industry's evaluation of, 300–302
  internal policy conflicts and, 298–99
  NGOs and, 300–301, 302–304, 308
  project development phase, 287–88
  project implementation and evaluation phase,
    288
  project proposal phase, 287
    modesty of proposals, 300
  project selection criteria, 287
  projects under development, 288–94
    first impressions of, 294
    Hadco Corporation, 290
    Imation, 290–91
    Lucent Technologies, 291

Massachusetts Department of
    Environmental Protection (DEP),
    291–92
Merck & Company, Inc., 292
Minnesota Pollution Control Agency
    (MPCA), 292
Molex, Incorporated, 292–93
New York State Department of
    Environmental Conservation
    (NYSDEC), 293
OSi Specialties, Inc., 293
PCS Nitrogen, L.P., 289–90
Union Carbide, 293–94
Vandenburg Air Force Base, 294
proponents of, 288
purpose of, 287
recommendations, 307–308
retreat of EPA from initial reliance on
    discretion, 303–305
specific XL projects, information on, 288–94
successes, specific, 305–306
Protocols and agenda setting for negotiations,
    role of neutral in, 252, 253
Public Disputes Program, Harvard Law School,
    240–41
Publicity, trading across differences with, 38

Rate-setting disputes, negotiating of, 248
Ratification of negotiation package, role of
    neutral in securing, 252, 255–56
Reagan administration, 217, 222
Regneg, see Negotiated rulemaking
Regulatees:
    benefits of mutual gains approach for, 17, 18
    goals of mutual gains approach for, 19–20
    perspective of, 2
    understanding flexibility means a lack of
        uniformity, 18
    see also names of specific companies
Regulators:
    alternative regulatory models, development of,
        284–94
        incentive-based measures, 284, 285
        voluntary strategies, 285–86
    benefits of mutual gains approach for, 17, 18
    command and control approach of, 277, 284,
        294, 295, 300, 306
    discretion to negotiate, 281–84, 307–308
        EPA's Project XL and, 287–308
        as essential ingredient of mutual gains
            approach, 18–19
        hesitancy to admit, 2, 281
    goals of mutual gains approach for, 20
    perspective of, 2
    see also names of specific agencies

Reiner, Ira, 209–10
Relationships among the parties, 275
    "confidence-building measures," 40
    distribution of value and, 25, 29
    in follow through stage, 26
    measuring success of negotiations by, 6
    mercury discharge permits case, 120
    negotiating as if relationships mattered,
        27–28, 39–40
    Project XL and difficulty in changing, 297,
        300
    Superfund cleanup at Massachusetts military
        reservation, 170–73
    trust, see Trust
    voluntary compliance and, 285–86
Renegotiation, role of neutral in, 252, 256
Representation, role of neutral in establishing,
    252, 253
Resource Conservation and Recovery Act
    (RCRA), 217, 290, 291, 292, 293, 294,
    305
Resource pool, role of neutral is establishing a,
    254
Rhode Island, licensing of waste-treatment
    plants in, 248
"Risks and Advantages of Agency Discretion:
    Evidence from EPA's Project XL, The,"
    287–308
RiverEnd negotiations, 258–60
Role plays, 259
    distinguished from simulations, 41
    Rondeau, Karen, 115, 120
    Rubin, Jeffrey, 27
    Ruckleshaus, William, 222, 280
Rulemaking:
    negotiated, see Negotiated rulemaking
    by regulating agencies, 282–83

Sanctions:
    cost-benefit analysis by regulatee,
        209–10
    criminal, see Criminal sanctions
    excessive, perceived as, 213
    fairness and legitimacy of, 212–15
    opposition to agency having both criminal
        and civil sanction powers, 213
    personnel movement within the company
        and, 215
    rationality of, 215
Save the Harbor/Save the Bay, 109, 110
SCAQMD plan, 213, 220
Schneider, Peter, 244
Schramm, Jack J., 220
Schwarz, R. M., 9, 12
Sebenius, James K., 201, 227–39

Secunda, Joshua, 201, 277–308
Segal, P. N., 13
Segel, Jim, 112, 113, 116
Sengekontacket Pond, 128–29, 133, 134–35
Services and goods, trading across differences
    with, 37–38
Sessler, A., 109
Settlement agreements, *see* Litigation, negotiated
    settlements of pending
Seybolt, Horst, 259
Shoreline restoration on Martha's Vineyard, case
    of, 128–42
  history of the conflict, 128–30
  interests of the parties, 130–31
  memorandum of agreement, 133, 135–42
  the negotiations, 132–35
  overview, 105–106, 128
  permits involved in, 128, 129, 134
Sierra Club, 145
Simulations:
  Bog Berries, *see* Bog Berries versus Federal
    Environmental Agency simulation
  Carson Extension, *see* Carson Extension
    simulation
  case studies distinguished from, 41
  ChemCo, Inc., *see* ChemCo, Inc. simulation
  confidential instructions, 41, 42–43
  debriefing questions, 101–103
  described, 41–42
  failure to reach agreement, reasons for,
    50–51
  Gadgets, Inc., *see* Gadgets, Inc. simulation
  general instructions, 41–42
  MC Metals, *see* MC Metals simulation
  role plays distinguished from, 41
  rules for, 42
  as scorable, 42
"Single-text" procedure for written agreements,
    255
Sin taxes, 284
Skills, negotiating, 8
Sobel, Gregory, 128–35, 143–51
Social conflict: Escalation, stalemate, and settlement
    (Rubin), 27
Social service block grant allocation, mediation
    of, 269–71
Sparrow, Malcolm K., 280
Spurrier, Earl, 245
"Squaring Off at the Table, Not in the Courts,"
    240–48
State environmental agencies, 1, 279
  see also names of individual agencies
Statute of limitations and enforcement measures,
    218
Stewart, Richard, 247

Superfund cleanup at the Massachusetts
    Military Reservation (MMR), case of,
    167–202
  building a decision-making process, 177–78
  Executive Review Group (ERG), 171
  Joint Process Action Team (JPAT), 172, 177,
    179
  Management Review Group (MRG),
    171–76, 178, 179
  negotiating goals and criteria, 174–77
  overview, 106, 167–68
  partnering, 171–73, 179
  Plume Containment Team (PCT), 172
  Plume Response Decision Criteria and
    Schedule, 181–99
  project crisis of 1996, 168–69
  relationships among the parties, 170–73
  Remedial Program Managers (RPMs),
    171–80
  the results, 179–80
  role of the facilitation team, 178–79
  setting up an enforceable schedule, 173
  "60 percent design," 169, 180
  strategic partnering, 170–73
  Technical Review and Evaluation Team
    (TRET), 171, 172, 176, 177, 178
    formation of, 169–70
    report of, 169, 179, 180
Susskind, Lawrence, 12, 13, 201, 240–308
Sylvia State Beach, *see* Shoreline restoration on
    Martha's Vineyard, case of

Testing your skills, 41–103
  simulations for, *see* Simulations
"They Treated Me Like a Criminal": Sanctions,
    Enforcement Characteristics, and
    Compliance," 203–23
"33/50" program, 285–86
Thomas-Larmer, Jennifer, 12, 109–27
Time value of money, 37–38, 273
Tolou, Christophe, 144–45
Toward a balanced strategy to address contaminated
    groundwater plumes at Massachusetts
    Military Reservation, 169
Toxic Substances Control Act, 291
Tradable emissions permit program, 285
Trading across differences to create value, 37–38,
    273
  in case examples, 147, 148–50, 174
Trading concessions for concessions, 8
Training in mutual gains approach, 10–11
Truman, Harry S., 230
Trust, 25, 39, 40
  building and maintaining, 27
  undermining, 8

Union Carbide, 293–94
U.S. Air Force, 170–77, 179
   Defense Environmental Restoration Account
     (DERA), 172
U.S. Army, 167
U.S. Coast Guard, 167
U.S. Congress:
   delegation of broad authority to
     administrative agencies, 281–82,
     307–308
   EPA and, 279–80, 307
U.S. Department of Agriculture, 242
U.S. Department of Defense, Installation
     Restoration Program (IRP), 167, 168,
     169, 170, 171, 180
U.S. Department of the Interior, 247
U.S. Navy, 171
Ury, William, 3, 7, 8, 36, 229

Value claiming, *see* Distribution of value
Value creation:
   mercury permit case, 113–14, 117, 118,
     274–75

the negotiator's Dilemma, *see* Negotiator's
   Dilemma
   overview of, 7–8, 24–25
   trading across differences for, *see* Trading
     across differences to create value
Value distribution, *see* Distribution of value
Van Dam, Laura, 201, 240–48
Vandenburg Air Force Base, 294
Voluntary compliance, 285–86

Walkouts from negotiated rulemaking, 247
Wall Street Journal, 216
Water Pollution Control Act, 216
Weld, William, 172
Weyerhaeuser Company, 288, 305–306
Wheatley, Nancy, 111, 112
Wilkins, Timothy A., 284–85, 307–308
Wilson, Woodrow, 281
Wisconsin, licensing of waste-treatment plants
   in, 248

"Zone of possible agreement," 36
   Gadgets, Inc. simulation, 44, 45